From Autocracy to Communism: Russia 1894–1941

Michael Lynch

HODDER
EDUCATION
PART OF HACHETTE LIVRE UK

In memory of Philip James Lynch, 1934–2007

Study guides updated, 2008, by Geoff Woodward (OCR).

The Publishers would like to thank the following for permission to reproduce copyright material:

Photo credits

pp.72, 204 © Bettman/Corbis; **p.37** British Film Institute © Eureka Video; **pp.6, 75, 148, 233, 237** David King Collection; **pp.35, 48, 89, 97, 98, 101, 149** Getty Images; **pp.130, 133, 183** © Hulton-Deutsch collection/Corbis; **p.263** Poster Collection, RU/SU 650, Hoover Institution Archives; **pp.49, 63, 138** © Punch Ltd; **p.24** Time Life Pictures/Getty Images; **pp.105, 153, 156** Russian State Archives of Film and Photo Documents (Krasnogorsk)

Acknowledgements

p.83 Penguin for an extract from *The Eastern Front* by N. Stone; **p.83** extract from *Three Whys of the Russian Revolution* by R. Pipes, published by Harvill. Reprinted by permission of The Random House Group Ltd; **p.154** Routledge for a map from *Routledge Atlas of Russian History – 3rd edn* by Martin Gilbert © Martin Gilbert

Every effort has been made to trace all copyright holders, but if any have been inadvertently overlooked the Publishers will be pleased to make the necessary arrangements at the first opportunity.

Hachette Livre UK's policy is to use papers that are natural, renewable and recyclable products and made from wood grown in sustainable forests. The logging and manufacturing processes are expected to conform to the environmental regulations of the country of origin.

Orders: please contact Bookpoint Ltd, 130 Milton Park, Abingdon, Oxon OX14 4SB. Telephone: (44) 01235 827720. Fax: (44) 01235 400454. Lines are open 9.00–5.00, Monday to Saturday, with a 24-hour message answering service. Visit our website at www.hoddereducation.co.uk

© Michael Lynch 2008
First published in 2008 by
Hodder Education,
Part of Hachette Livre UK
338 Euston Road
London NW1 3BH

Impression number	5 4 3 2
Year	2012 2011 2010 2009 2008

Cover photo shows a painting, *Bolshevik*, by Boris Kustodiev (1920), courtesy of the Bridgeman Art Library
Illustrations by GreenGate Publishing Services and Derek Griffin
Typeset in New Baskerville 10/12pt by GreenGate Publishing Services, Tonbridge, Kent
Printed in Malta

A catalogue record for this title is available from the British Library

ISBN: 978 0340 965 900

Contents

Dedication

Keith Randell (1943–2002)

The *Access to History* series was conceived and developed by Keith, who created a series to 'cater for students as they are, not as we might wish them to be'. He leaves a living legacy of a series that for over 20 years has provided a trusted, stimulating and well-loved accompaniment to the post-16 study. Our aim with these new editions is to continue to offer students the best possible support for their studies.

1 Late Imperial Russia, 1894–1905

POINTS TO CONSIDER

Tsar Nicholas II came to the throne of the Russian Empire in 1894. His was to be a tragic reign and he was to be the last tsar. By the time he was murdered in 1918, Nicholas had abdicated, the Russian Empire had collapsed, and a new revolutionary force, the Bolsheviks, had seized power. This book describes these dramatic events and explains why they occurred. Particular attention is paid to the events of 1917 – the year of the Russian Revolution.

This first chapter sets the scene by examining:

- the main features of imperial Russia: the land and the people, the character of the tsarist system which Nicholas operated
- the political and economic problems that Russia faced as it tried to come to terms with the modern world
- economic reforms
- the opponents of tsardom
- the Russo-Japanese War.

Key dates

1854–6	Crimean War
1861	Emancipation of the serfs
1881	Assassination of Alexander II
1881–94	Reign of Alexander III
1894	Start of Nicholas II's reign
1894–1906	Sergei Witte's economic reforms
1897	Jewish Bund formed
1898	Social Democratic Party (SDs) formed
1901	Formation of the Socialist Revolutionary Party (SRs)
1903	SD Party splits into Bolsheviks and Mensheviks
1904–5	Russo-Japanese War
1905	Russo-Japanese peace treaty
	Formation of the Octobrists
	Creation of the duma
	Formation of the Kadets
	All-Russian Union of Peasants set up

1 | Character of the Tsarist State

To understand the problems that were to dominate the reign of Nicholas II, we need to grasp the character of the Russia that he inherited.

Russia's geography and peoples

In 1894, imperial Russia covered over 8 million square miles, an area equivalent to two and a half times the size of the USA today (see Figure 1.1). At its widest, from west to east, it stretched for 5000 miles; at its longest, north to south, it measured 2000 miles. It covered a large part of two continents. European Russia extended eastward from the borders of Poland to the Urals mountain range. Asiatic Russia extended eastward from the Urals to the Pacific Ocean.

The greater part of the population, which between 1815 and 1914 had quadrupled from 40 million to 165 million, was concentrated in European Russia. It was in that part of the empire that the major historical developments had occurred and it was there that Russia's principal cities, Moscow and St Petersburg, the capital, were situated.

The sheer size of the Russian Empire tended to give an impression of great strength. This was misleading. The population contained a wide variety of peoples of different race, language, religion and culture (see Table 1.1). Controlling such a variety of peoples over such a vast territory had long been a major problem for Russian governments.

Table 1.1: The major nationalities of the Russian Empire according to the census of 1897 (in millions, defined according to mother tongue)

Great Russian	55.6	Lithuanian	1.2
Ukrainian	22.4	Armenian	1.2
Polish	7.9	Romanian/Moldavian	1.1
White Russian	5.8	Estonian	1.0
Jewish (defined by faith)	5.0	Mordvinian	1.0
Kirgiz/Kaisats	4.0	Georgian	0.8
Tartar	3.4	Tadzhik	0.3
Finnish	3.1	Turkmenian	0.3
German	1.8	Greek	0.2
Latvian	1.4	Bulgarian	0.2
Bashkir	1.3	Uzbek	0.1

The tsar (emperor)

The peoples of the Russian Empire were governed by one person, the tsar (emperor). Since 1613 the Russian tsars had been members of the **Romanov dynasty**. By law and tradition, the tsar was the absolute ruler. Article I of the 'Fundamental Laws of the Empire', issued by Nicholas I in 1832, declared: 'The Emperor of all the Russias is an autocratic and unlimited monarch. God himself ordains that all must bow to his supreme power, not only out of fear but also out of conscience.'

Key question
Why had imperial Russia not modernised its governmental, political and economic systems?

Key question
What powers did the tsar wield?

Romanov dynasty
The royal house that ruled Russia from 1613 to 1917.

Key term

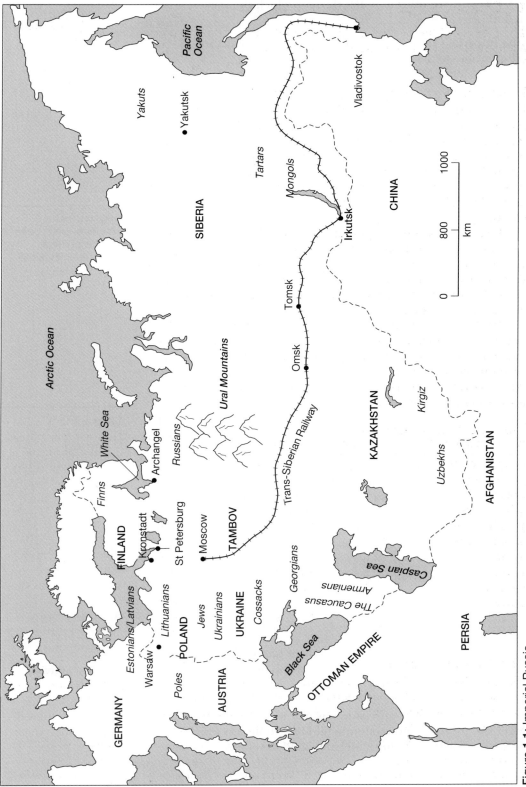

Figure 1.1: Imperial Russia.

There were three official bodies through which the tsar exercised his authority:

- the Imperial Council, a group of honorary advisers directly responsible to the tsar
- the Cabinet of Ministers, which ran the various government departments
- the Senate, concerned with supervising the operation of the law.

These bodies were much less powerful than their titles suggest. They were appointed, not elected, and they did not govern; their role was merely to give advice. They had no authority over the tsar, whose word was final in all governmental and legal matters.

Russia's political backwardness

What the tsar's power showed was how little Russia had advanced politically when compared with other European nations. By the beginning of the twentieth century all the major western European countries had some form of democratic or representative government. Not so Russia; although it had been frequently involved in European diplomatic and military affairs, it had remained outside the mainstream of European political thought.

Key question
Why had there been so little political progress in Russia?

Limited attempts at reform

There had been reforming tsars, such as Peter I (1683–1725), Catherine II (1762–96) and Alexander II (1855–81), who had taken steps to modernise the country. But their achievements had not included the extension of political rights. In Russia in 1894 it was still a criminal offence to oppose the tsar or his government. There was no parliament, and, although political parties had been formed, they had no legal right to exist. There had never been a free press in imperial Russia. Government censorship was imposed on published books and journals.

Such restriction had not prevented **liberal ideas** from seeping into Russia, but it did mean that they could not be openly expressed. The result was that supporters of reform or change had to go underground. In the nineteenth century there had grown up a wide variety of secret societies dedicated to political reform or revolution. These groups were frequently infiltrated by agents of the *Okhrana*. As a result, raids, arrests, imprisonment and general harassment were regular occurrences.

Extremism

The denial of free speech tended to drive **political activists** towards extremism. The outstanding example of this occurred in 1881, when Tsar Alexander II was blown to bits by a bomb thrown by a terrorist group known as 'The People's Will' (see page 20). In a society in which state oppression was met with revolutionary terrorism, there was no moderate middle ground on which a tradition of ordered political debate could develop.

Liberal ideas
Notions that called for limitations on the power of rulers and greater freedom for the people.

Okhrana
The tsarist secret police, whose special task was to hunt down subversives who challenged the tsarist regime.

Political activists
Those who believed necessary change could be achieved only through direct action.

Key terms

Key question
What role did the
Church play in
imperial Russia?

Key terms

Reactionary
Resistant to any form
of progressive
change.

God's anointed
At their coronation,
tsars were anointed
with holy oil to
symbolise that they
governed by divine
will.

Catechism
The primer used for
instructing the
people in the
essential points of
the Christian faith.

Key question
How unbalanced was
the distribution of the
classes in Russian
society?

The Russian Orthodox Church

The tsars were fully supported in their claims to absolute authority by one of the great pillars of the Russian system, the Orthodox Church. This was a branch of Christianity which, since the fifteenth century, had been entirely independent of any outside authority, such as the papacy. Its detachment from foreign influence had given it an essentially Russian character. The great beauty of its liturgy and music had long been an outstanding expression of Russian culture. However, by the late nineteenth century it had become a deeply conservative body, opposed to political change and determined to preserve the tsarist system in its **reactionary** form. How detached the Orthodox Church was from Russia's growing urban population is illustrated by the statistic that in 1900 a Moscow suburb with 40,000 people had only one church and one priest.

The Church did contain some priests who strongly sympathised with the political revolutionaries, but as an institution it used its spiritual authority to teach the Russian people that it was their duty to be totally obedient to the tsar as **God's anointed**. The **catechism** of the Church included the statement that 'God commands us to love and obey from the inmost recesses of our heart every authority, and particularly the tsar'.

The social structure of tsarist Russia
The social classes

The striking features of the social structure were the comparatively small commercial, professional and working classes and the great preponderance of peasants in the population. This is illustrated in Figure 1.2, which shows the class distribution of the population as measured by Russia's 1897 census.

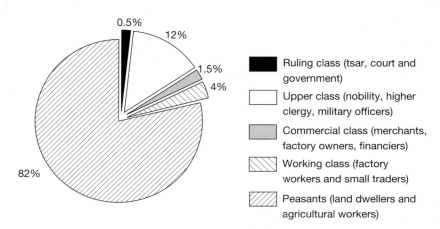

Figure 1.2: The class distribution of the Russian population, 1897.

УПРАВЛЯЮТЪ НАШИМИ ДЕНЬГАМИ

МОЛЯТСЯ ЗА НАСЪ

ѢДЯТЪ ЗА НАСЪ

СТРѢЛЯЮТЪ ВЪ НАСЪ

МЫ РАБОТАЕМЪ НА НИХЪ, А ОНИ —

A mocking socialist cartoon of 1900 showing the social pyramid in imperial Russia. The Russian caption for each layer reads (in ascending order): 'We work for them while they ...' '... shoot at us.' '... eat on our behalf.' '... pray on our behalf.' '... dispose of our money.'

The Russian economy

The remarkable difference in size between the urban professional and working classes and the rural peasants revealed a critical feature of imperial Russia – its slow economic development. The low number of urban workers was a sign that Russia had not achieved the major industrial growth that had taken place in the nineteenth century in such countries as Germany, Britain and the USA.

This is not to say that Russia was entirely without industry. The Urals region produced considerable amounts of iron, and the chief western cities, Moscow and St Petersburg, had extensive textile factories. Most villages had a smelting-works, and most peasant homes engaged in some form of cottage industry, producing wooden, flaxen or woollen goods to supplement their income from farming. However, these activities were all relatively small scale. The sheer size of Russia and its undeveloped transport system had limited the chances for industrial expansion.

A further restriction had been the absence of an effective banking system. Russia found it hard to raise **capital** on a large scale. It had not yet mastered the art of successful borrowing and investment, techniques that help to explain why expansion had been so rapid in western countries. Russia's financial sluggishness had discouraged the rise of **entrepreneurialism**.

Key question
Why was the Russian economy so undeveloped?

Key terms

Capital
The essential financial resource that provides the means for investment and expansion. No economy can grow without it.

Entrepreneurialism
The dynamic, expansionist attitude associated with western commercial and industrial activity.

Agriculture in tsarist Russia

Russia's unenterprising industrial system was matched by its inefficient pattern of agriculture. Even though four-fifths of the population were peasants, a thriving **agrarian economy** had failed to develop. Indeed, the land in Russia was a source of national weakness rather than strength. The empire's vast acres were not all good farming country. Much of Russia lay too far north to enjoy a climate or a soil suitable for crop growing or cattle rearing. Arable farming was restricted mainly to the Black Earth region, the area of European Russia stretching from **Ukraine** to Kazakhstan.

The great number of peasants in the population added to the problem. There was simply not enough fertile land to go round. Under the terms of the **Emancipation Decree of 1861**, the ex-serfs were entitled to buy land, but they invariably found the price too high. This was caused both by a shortage of suitable farming territory and by the government's taxation of land sales, imposed in order to raise the revenue needed to compensate the landowners for the losses caused by emancipation. The only way the peasants could raise the money to buy land was by borrowing from a special fund provided by the government. Consequently, those peasants who did manage to purchase property found themselves burdened with large mortgage repayments that would take them and their families generations to repay.

The peasant problem

Among Russia's governing class, which was drawn from less than one per cent of the population, there was a deeply ingrained prejudice against granting rights to the mass of the people. Over 80 per cent of the population were peasants. They were predominantly illiterate and uneducated. Their sheer size as a social class and their coarse ways led to their being regarded with a mixture of fear and contempt by the governing elite, who believed that these dangerous **'dark masses'** could be held in check only by severe repression. This was what Nicholas II's wife, the Empress Alexandra, meant when she said that Russia needed always to be 'under the whip'.

The existence in the second half of the nineteenth century of an uneducated peasantry, suspicious of change, and living with large debts and in great poverty, pointed to the social, political and economic backwardness of imperial Russia. Various attempts to educate the peasants had been made in the past, but such efforts had been undermined by the fear among the ruling class that any improvement in the conditions of 'the dark masses' might threaten its own privileges. It was commonplace for officials in Russia to speak of the 'safe ignorance' of the population, implying that any attempt to raise the educational standards of the masses would prove highly dangerous, socially and politically.

The Russian army

One common method of keeping the peasants in check was to conscript them into the Russian armed services. The lower ranks of the army and navy were largely filled by enforced enlistment.

Key question
Why was Russian agriculture so backward?

Key terms

Agrarian economy
The system in which food is produced on the land by arable and dairy farming and then traded.

Ukraine
The region in southern Russia containing the largest number of non-Russian people (23 million) in the empire. It was also the nation's largest food-producing region, hence its great importance.

Key question
What was meant by the term 'the peasant problem' in Russia?

Key term

Emancipation Decree of 1861
The reform that abolished serfdom – a Russian form of slavery in which the landowner had total control over the peasants who lived or worked on his land.

Key question
What function did the army serve in tsarist Russia?

Conscription was regularly used as a form of punishment for lawbreakers. Ordinary Russians dreaded this sentence; they knew that life in the armed forces was a brutalising experience for the common soldier. The Russian army was notorious in Europe for the severity of its discipline and the grimness of the conditions in which its soldiers lived. Special military camps had been set up in the remoter regions of the empire which operated as penal colonies rather than as training establishments. The rigours of service life had accounted for the deaths of over 1 million soldiers in peacetime during the reign of Nicholas I (1825–55).

It was a persistent belief in Russia that, as a large empire, it needed a large army. Throughout the nineteenth century the imperial forces were kept at a strength of around one and a half million men. The cost of maintaining the army and the navy accounted on average for 45 per cent of the government's annual expenditure. This was by far the largest single item of state spending, and, when compared with the four per cent devoted to education, shows how unbalanced government priorities were.

Weaknesses within the army

The higher ranks of the army were the preserve of the aristocracy. **Commissions** were bought and sold, and there was little room for promotion on merit. This weakened the army as a fighting force, but the truth of this tended to remain hidden because, with the exception of the Crimean War (1854–6), Russia was not engaged in a major conflict with a western European power for a whole century after 1815. The army's active service was essentially a matter of putting down national risings or serious disturbances within the empire or on its frontiers. There were frequent border clashes with Turkey throughout the nineteenth century, and at various times Russian forces saw action in Poland, Armenia and Persia.

The bureaucracy (civil service)

Ironically, it was in the area where there had been the largest attempted reform that the greatest corruption had developed. At the beginning of the eighteenth century, Peter I had attempted to modernise Russia by establishing a full-scale civil service with the aim of maintaining central government control throughout the empire.

However, by the middle of the nineteenth century many Russian critics had begun to condemn this civil service as a corrupt bureaucracy whose **nepotism** and incompetence were the principal reasons for Russia's backwardness. Writing in 1868, **Alexander Herzen** claimed that the bureaucracy had become 'a kind of civilian priesthood' – privileged, grasping and self-seeking. He accused the officials who ran Russia of 'sucking the blood of the people with thousands of greedy, unclean mouths'.

Tsarist Russia in the middle of the century, Herzen asserted, was run by a bureaucratic class that, for all its incompetence, still possessed the power to control the lives of the Russian masses. At local and national levels, the law, the government, the police and

Key terms

'Dark masses'
The term used in court and government circles to signify the fear and contempt they felt towards the peasants who made up four-fifths of the population.

Conscription
The forcing of large numbers of peasants into the army or navy.

Commission
The awarding of officer rank.

Nepotism
A system in which positions are gained through family connections rather than on merit.

Key date

The Crimean War, in which Russia was defeated by Britain and France: 1854–6

Key question
What was the fundamental weakness of the tsarist bureaucracy?

Key figure

Alexander Herzen (1812–70)
A leading revolutionary thinker and critic of the Russian government.

Key term

Militia
Local citizens called together and granted arms to deal with a crisis requiring force.

the **militia** were in the hands of a set of men whose first thought was their own convenience and advantage. Against this injustice, the ordinary citizen had no redress, since any challenge to the system was lost in bureaucratic procedures.

Herzen's savage attack provided powerful ammunition for those in Russia who wished to ridicule and undermine the tsarist system itself. However, it is important to remember that Herzen was a revolutionary propagandist intent on painting the blackest picture he could of tsardom. Efforts were made in the nineteenth century to reform the administration and limit its abuses.

Summary diagram: Characteristics of the tsarist state	
The land Russia's geography Its great size	**The people** The social structure Tiny dominant elite The 'dark masses' 80 per cent peasant population
The economy Undeveloped industry Backward agriculture	**The tsarist system** Autocratic government Reactionary Church Corrupt bureaucracy Oppressive army

Key question
Why was it so difficult to achieve reform in Russia?

2 | The Problem of Reform in Imperial Russia

Many members of the ruling class accepted that major reforms were needed if Russia was to overcome its social and economic backwardness. However, a major barrier to reform was a basic disagreement within the governing elite over Russia's true character as a nation. Since the days of Peter the Great, there had been serious differences between **'Westerners'** and **'Slavophiles'**. Their dispute made it difficult to achieve reform in an ordered and acceptable way.

Another barrier to planned reform was the autocratic structure of Russia itself. Change could only come from the top. There were no representative institutions, such as a parliament, with the power to alter things. The only possible source of change was the tsar. From time to time, there were progressive tsars who accepted the need for reform. Yet it was hardly to be expected that any tsar, no matter how enlightened, would go so far as to introduce measures that might weaken his authority.

The result was that reform in Russia had been piecemeal, depending on the inclinations of the individual tsar, rather than a systematic programme of change. It is notable that the significant periods of reform in Russia were invariably a response to some form of national crisis or humiliation. This was certainly true of

Key terms

'Westerners'
Russians who believed that their nation had to model itself on the advanced countries of western Europe.

'Slavophiles'
Russians who urged that the nation should preserve itself as 'holy Russia', glorying in its Slavonic culture and traditions.

the reforms introduced in Alexander II's reign (1855–81). His accession coincided with the defeat of Russia at the hands of France and Britain in the Crimean War (1854–6). The shock of this reverse prompted the new tsar into adopting a reform programme.

Local government reform

Alexander II's reforms began with the emancipation of the serfs in 1861, followed three years later by the setting up of a network of elected rural councils, known as *zemstva*. Although these were not truly democratic, they did provide Russia with a form of representative government, no matter how limited, which offered some hope to those who longed for an extension of political rights. The authorities also emphasised the valuable role played in the countryside by the *mir*, which they saw as a local organisation which would help keep order and provide a cheap means of collecting taxes and mortgage repayments.

Legal reforms

In addition, a number of legal reforms were introduced with the aim of simplifying the notoriously cumbersome court procedures, whose delays had led to corruption and injustice. Of even greater importance was Alexander II's relaxation of controls over the press and the universities. Greater freedom of expression encouraged the development of an **intelligentsia**.

Limited nature of the reforms

Alexander II was not a supporter of reform simply for its own sake. He saw it as a way of lessening opposition to the tsarist system. He said that his intention was to introduce reform from above in order to prevent revolution from below. His hope was that his reforms would attract the support of the intelligentsia. In this he was largely successful. Emancipation, greater press and university freedoms and the administrative and legal changes were greeted with enthusiasm by progressives.

However, no matter how progressive Alexander II himself may have appeared, he was still an autocrat. It was unthinkable that he would continue with a process that might compromise his power as tsar. Fearful that he had gone too far, he abandoned his reformist policies and returned to the tsarist tradition of oppression. His successor, Alexander III (1881–94), continued this, becoming notorious for the severity of his rule. During his reign a series of very restrictive measures known as 'the Reaction' was imposed on the Russian people.

When Nicholas II became tsar in 1894 it appeared that he intended to continue the repressive measures of his predecessor. Many of the intelligentsia felt betrayed. Despairing of tsardom as a force for change, a significant number of them turned to thoughts of revolution.

Key terms

Zemstva
Elected local councils.

Mir
The traditional village community.

Intelligentsia
A cross-section of the educated and more enlightened members of Russian society who wanted to see their nation adopt progressive changes along western lines.

Key dates

Emancipation of the serfs: 1861

Reign of Alexander III: 1881–94

Start of Nicholas II's reign: 1894

Key measures of the Reaction

The Statute of State Security, 1881
- Special government-controlled courts, which operated outside the existing legal system, were set up.
- Judges, magistrates and officials who were sympathetic towards liberal ideas were removed from office.
- The powers of the *Okhrana*, the tsarist secret police, were extended, and censorship of the press was tightened.

At its introduction in 1881, this Statute was described as a temporary measure brought in to deal with an emergency, but in essentials it remained in place until 1917.

The University Statute, 1887
Brought the universities under strict government control.

The Zemstva Act, 1890
Decreased the independence of the local councils and empowered government officials to interfere in their decision making.

Key question
What problems confronted Nicholas II?

The early reign of Nicholas II, 1894–1905

It is one of the ironies of Russian history that, at a time when the nation most needed a tsar of strength and imagination, it was a man of weakness and limited outlook who came to the throne. There are two main aspects to Nicholas II's reign:

- the problems he faced as tsar at a particularly critical stage in Russian history
- the growth of opposition in Russia to the tsarist system.

The most pressing question was whether imperial Russia could modernise itself sufficiently to be able to compete with the other European nations. Would the new tsar be a reformer or a reactionary? There was little doubt what the answer would be. Reform had a bad name by the time Nicholas became tsar. Furthermore, his upbringing and education made him suspicious of change. It was no surprise that he continued the repressive policies he had inherited. This further angered the intelligentsia and the critics of the tsarist regime; they began to prepare to challenge tsardom.

Key figure

Konstantin Pobedonostsev (1827–1907)
In addition to being chief minister, he was also the Procurator (lay head) of the Synod, the governing body of the Russian Orthodox Church.

The role of Pobedonostsev

As a young man, Nicholas had been tutored at court by **Konstantin Pobedonostsev**, a man of enormous influence in late imperial Russia. Pobedonostsev was the chief minister in the Russian government from 1881 to 1905. His thin frame and pale skin stretched almost transparently across his bony features gave him the appearance of a living corpse. In a macabre way this was wholly fitting, since his fearful appearance was matched by the frightening nature of his ideas.

Known as 'the Grand Inquisitor' because of his repressive attitudes, Pobedonostsev was an arch-conservative who had a deep distaste for all forms of liberalism and democracy. He dismissed the idea of **representative government** as 'the great lie of our time'. To his mind, **autocracy** was the only possible government for imperial Russia. The Russian masses were too uneducated, vulgar and uninformed to be able to govern themselves. They had to be controlled and directed. For the same reason, he rejected the notions of trial by jury and a free press. Such concessions would simply allow the ignorant and the troublemakers to cause disruption. Russia's rulers had a duty to govern with vigour and harshness, using the legal, religious and educational institutions to inculcate obedience in the people. Pobedonostsev was behind many of the **pogroms**, part of the organised attempt to enforce religious conformity in Russia. Nicholas took to heart the lessons he learned from Pobedonostsev.

Nicholas II's policies

Nicholas II's character is important in any analysis of revolutionary Russia. The evidence suggests that he was far from being as unintelligent as his detractors asserted. Nevertheless, his limited imagination was evident in the reactionary policies he followed. He seemed not to understand the real nature of the problems his nation and his dynasty faced.

Russification

A policy of particular note that had begun under Alexander III and which Nicholas II carried on was Russification. This was a severely enforced policy of restricting the influence of the non-Russian national minorities within the empire by emphasising the superiority of all things Russian. Russian was declared to be the official first language; this meant that all legal proceedings, such as trials, and all administration had to be conducted in Russian. Public office was closed to those not fluent in the language. The aim was to impose Russian ways and values on all the peoples within the nation.

   Officials everywhere in the empire now had a vested interest in maintaining the dominance of Russian values at the expense of the other national cultures. Discrimination against non-Russians, which had previously been a hidden feature of Russian public life, became more open and vindictive in the 1890s. The nationalities that suffered most from this were the Baltic Germans, the Poles, the Finns, the Armenians and the Ukrainians. State interference in their education, religion and culture became widespread and systematic.

Anti-Semitism

Undoubtedly, the greatest victims of Russification were the Jews. Over 600 new measures were introduced, imposing heavy social, political and economic restrictions on the Jewish population.

Key question
What were Nicholas II's policies and what were they intended to achieve?

Key terms

Representative government
A form of rule in which ordinary people choose their government and have the power to replace it if it does not serve their interests.

Autocracy
The absolute rule of one person. In Russia, this meant the tsar.

Pogroms
Fierce persecution of the Jews, which often involved wounding or killing them and destroying their property.

Ghettos
Particular areas
where Jews were
concentrated and to
which they were
restricted.

Since the majority of Jews lived in discrete districts or '**ghettos**', they were easily identifiable scapegoats who could be blamed for Russia's difficulties. Anti-Semitism was deeply ingrained in tsarist Russia. Pogroms had long disfigured Russian history. A group of ultra-conservative Russian nationalists, known as the 'Black Hundreds', were notorious for their attacks upon Jews. During the reign of Nicholas II the number of pogroms increased sharply. This was proof of the tsarist regime's active encouragement of the terrorising of the Jews. But what was disturbingly noticeable was the eagerness with which local communities followed the lead from above in organising the bloodlettings.

The response to Nicholas II's policies

The tight controls that Nicholas II tried to impose did not lessen opposition to tsardom. The reverse happened: despite greater police interference, opposition became more organised. A number of political parties, ranging from moderate reformers to violent revolutionaries, came into being (see page 18). The government's policies of reaction and Russification produced a situation in which many political and national groups grew increasingly frustrated by the mixture of coercion and incompetence that characterised the tsarist system.

Russification proved remarkably ill-judged. At a critical stage in its development, when cohesion and unity were needed, Russia chose to treat half its population as inferiors or potential enemies. The persecution of the Jews was especially crass. It alienated the great mass of the 5 million Jews in the Russian population, large numbers of whom fled in desperation to western Europe and North America, carrying with them an abiding hatred of tsardom. Those who could not escape stayed to form a large and disaffected community within the empire. It is no coincidence that the 1890s witnessed a large influx of Jews into the various anti-tsarist movements in Russia. In 1897, Jews formed their own revolutionary 'Bund' or union.

Yet the remarkable fact was that, for all the bitterness created by these policies, the period was one of rapid economic expansion. For a time it seemed that Russia might become a modern industrial nation. This was largely due to the work of two outstanding ministers – **Sergei Witte**, who served during the early part of Nicholas II's reign, and **Peter Stolypin**, who held office during the middle years (see pages 41–3). In the face of resistance from the very regime they were trying to serve, Witte and Stolypin sought to modernise Russia.

While it is helpful to regard the work of these two ministers as complementary, Witte being concerned with the development of industry in Russia and Stolypin with agriculture, it should not be thought that the two men co-operated in a common economic policy. Indeed, Witte was deeply jealous of Stolypin, and the two men did not get on. However, they did share a basic aim – the strengthening and preservation of the tsarist system.

Jewish Bund formed: 1897

Sergei Witte (1849–1915)
Minister of Finance (equivalent to the British Chancellor of the Exchequer) from 1893 to 1903 and Chief Minister from 1903 to 1906.

Peter Stolypin (1862–1911)
A political conservative but a progressive in agricultural matters. Chief Minister from 1906 to 1911.

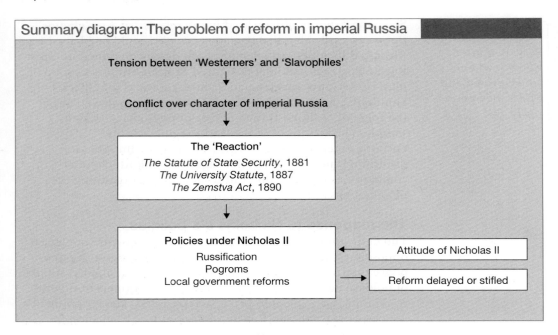

Summary diagram: The problem of reform in imperial Russia

Tension between 'Westerners' and 'Slavophiles'

↓

Conflict over character of imperial Russia

↓

The 'Reaction'
The Statute of State Security, 1881
The University Statute, 1887
The Zemstva Act, 1890

↓

Policies under Nicholas II
Russification
Pogroms
Local government reforms

← Attitude of Nicholas II

→ Reform delayed or stifled

3 | Economic Reform under Witte, 1893–1903

In the 1890s, Russian industry grew so rapidly that the term the **'great spurt'** was used to describe the period. A major reason for the exceptional growth was the increase in the output of coal in Ukraine and of oil in the Caucasus. Economic historians are agreed that although this sudden acceleration was the result of **private enterprise**, it was sustained by deliberate government policy.

However, the motives of the tsarist government were military rather than economic. It is true that the **capitalists** did well out of the spurt, but it was not the government's primary intention to help them. Economic expansion attracted the tsar and his ministers because it was a means of improving the strength of the Russian armed forces. A growing industry would produce more and better guns, equipment and ships.

As Minister of Finance and the outstanding individual involved in Russia's development at this time, Witte set himself the huge task of modernising the Russian economy to a level where it could compete with the advanced nations of the West. To help bring this about, he invited foreign experts and workers to Russia to advise on industrial planning. Engineers and managers from France, Belgium, Britain, Germany and Sweden played a vital role in 'the great spurt'.

State capitalism

It was Witte's belief that modernisation could be achieved only through **state capitalism**. He was impressed by the results of the industrial revolutions in western Europe and the USA, and argued that Russia could successfully modernise by planning along the

Key question
What methods did Witte use to develop the Russian economy?

Key terms

'Great spurt'
The spread of industry and the increase in production that occurred in the 1890s.

Private enterprise
Economic activity organised by individuals or companies, not the government.

Capitalists
Russia's financiers and industrialists.

State capitalism
The direction and control of the economy by the government, using its central power and authority.

Key terms

Tariffs
Duties imposed on foreign goods to keep their prices high and therefore discourage importers from bringing them into the country.

Gold standard
The system in which the rouble, Russia's basic unit of currency, had a fixed gold content, thus giving it strength when exchanged with other currencies.

Key date

Sergei Witte's economic reforms: 1894–1906

same lines. He admitted that, given the backwardness of Russia, this presented particular difficulties. He likened the current relationship of Russia to the advanced economies of Europe to that of a colony and its mother country. It was Russia's task, therefore, to decolonise itself and begin to produce and trade as an equal. 'Russia has the right and the strength not to want to remain the handmaiden of states that are more developed economically.'

Witte judged that Russia's greatest need was to acquire capital for investment in industry. To raise this, he adopted a number of connecting policies. He negotiated large loans and investments from abroad, while imposing heavy taxes and high interest rates at home. At the same time as he encouraged the inflow of foreign capital, Witte limited the import of foreign goods. Protective **tariffs** were set up as a means of safeguarding Russia's young domestic industries. In 1897 the Russian currency was put on the **gold standard**. The hope was that this would create financial stability and so encourage international investment in Russia. The aim was largely successful but it penalised consumers at home since the higher-value rouble raised prices for goods already made scarce by tariff restrictions.

Importance of the railways

Much of the foreign capital that Witte was successful in raising was directly invested in railways. He believed that the modernisation of the Russian economy ultimately depended on developing an effective railway system. His enthusiasm was an important factor in the extraordinary increase in lines and rolling stock that took place between 1881 and 1913. It would not be an exaggeration to describe this as a transport revolution (see Figure 1.3).

1881 ++++++++++ 13,270
1891 +++++++++++++++++ 19,510
1900 ++++++++++++++++++++++++++++++ 33,270
1913 +++ 43,850

Figure 1.3: The growth of Russian railways (in miles of track).

Witte's special prestige project was the Trans-Siberian Railway, which was constructed between 1891 and 1902. The line stretched for 3750 miles from Moscow to Vladivostok (see the map on page 3) and was intended to connect the remoter regions of the central and eastern empire with the industrial west, and so encourage the migration of workers to the areas where they were most needed. However, it promised more than it delivered. Sections of it were still incomplete in 1914 and it did not greatly improve east–west migration. The Trans-Siberian Railway proved more impressive as a symbol of Russian enterprise than as a project of real economic worth.

One of Witte's main hopes was that the major improvements in transport would boost exports and foreign trade. The trade figures suggest that his hopes were largely fulfilled (see Table 1.2 and Figure 1.4).

Table 1.2: The Russian economy: annual production (in millions of tons)

	Coal	Pig iron	Oil	Grain*
1890	5.9	0.89	3.9	36
1900	16.1	2.66	10.2	56
1910	26.8	2.99	9.4	74
1913	35.4	4.1	9.1	90
1916	33.8	3.72	9.7	64

* European Russia only

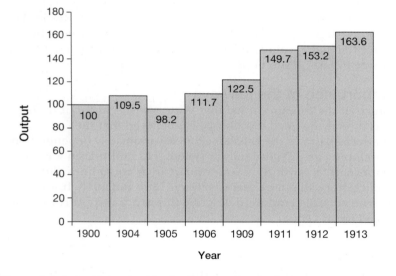

Figure 1.4: Industrial output in the Russian Empire (base unit of 100 in 1900).

These figures of increased production are not so impressive when it is remembered that Russia was experiencing a massive growth in population (see Table 1.3). Production per head of population was lower than the aggregate figures suggested.

Table 1.3: Population of imperial Russia, 1885–1913

	1885	1897	1913
European Russia	81,725,200	93,442,900	121,780,000
Caucasus	7,284,500	9,289,400	12,717,200
Siberia	4,313,700	5,758,800	9,894,500
Steppes and Urals	1,588,500	2,465,700	3,929,500
Central Asia	3,738,600	5,281,000	7,106,000
Total	98,650,500	116,237,800	155,422,200

Nevertheless, Russia was enjoying real economic growth. Figure 1.5 shows how favourably its increase in industrial output compared with that of other European countries. Again, one has to be cautious in interpreting the data. Given its backwardness, Russia was starting from a much lower level of production. For example, although its 96.8 per cent growth looks to be over twice that of Britain's, it was playing catch-up and had a long way to go.

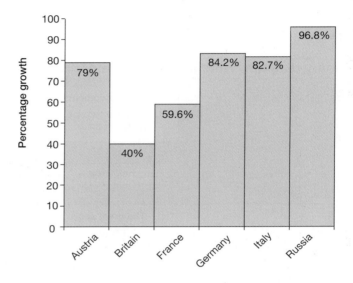

Figure 1.5: Growth in national product, 1898–1913.

Witte's problems

Key question
How successful were Witte's policies?

There is no doubt that Witte's policies had a major impact on the expansion of the Russian economy. However, what can be questioned is whether the results were wholly beneficial for Russia. Critics have pointed to three drawbacks in his economic reforms:

- He made Russia too dependent on foreign loans and investments.
- In giving priority to heavy industry, he neglected vital areas such as light engineering.
- He paid no attention to Russia's agricultural needs.

Yet any criticism of Witte should be balanced by reference to the problems he faced. The demands of the military commanders too often interfered with his plans for railway construction and the building of new industrial plants. Moreover, his freedom of action was restricted by the resistance to change that he met from the court and the government. The main purpose of his economic policies was to make the nation strong and thus protect tsardom against the disruptive forces in Russian society, but he was disliked by the royal court and the government, which seldom gave him the support he needed. In 1906, shortly after he had successfully negotiated a substantial loan from France, the tsar forced him to resign.

Witte was not an easy man to get on with and he made enemies easily, but in ability he towered above all the other ministers and officials in the government. His tragedy was that despite his great talents, which, if properly recognised, might have led Russia towards peaceful modernisation, he was never fully trusted by the people of the tsarist court and system he was trying to save.

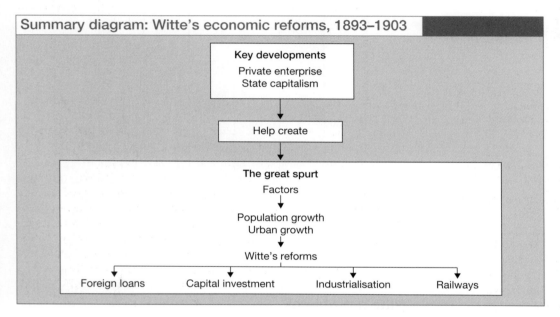

Summary diagram: Witte's economic reforms, 1893–1903

Key developments
Private enterprise
State capitalism

↓

Help create

↓

The great spurt
Factors
↓
Population growth
Urban growth
↓
Witte's reforms

Foreign loans   Capital investment   Industrialisation   Railways

4 | The Opponents of Tsardom

Two main groups opposed to tsardom can be identified in Nicholas II's reign: reformers (liberals) and revolutionaries. Within each of these groups there were many sub-divisions. The opposition never formed a single coherent movement and rarely acted in unison.

Key question
What form did opposition to tsardom take?

The reformers

Until the issuing of the October Manifesto in 1905 (see page 38), political parties had been illegal in Russia. This had not prevented their formation but it had made it very difficult for them to develop as genuinely democratic bodies. There was no tradition of open debate. Since they were denied legal recognition, they often resorted to extreme methods in order to spread their ideas. As a result, during the brief period of their permitted existence from 1905 to 1921, before they were again outlawed, the Russian

Key question
What had encouraged the growth of a liberal movement in tsarist Russia?

political parties proved to be suspicious and intolerant of each other. This made co-operation and collective action difficult to organise and sustain. Yet although they were to have a short and inglorious life, the Russian liberal parties should not be ignored. In historical study, losers deserve as much attention as winners.

The economic boom of the 1890s (see page 14) saw the rapid development of a small but ambitious class of industrialists, lawyers and financiers. It was among such social groups that liberal ideas for the modernising of Russia began to take hold. There was also often a strong national element in Russian liberalism. The national minorities viewed the liberal movement as a means of expressing their wish to be independent of Russian imperial control. Two principal liberal parties came to prominence in the pre-1914 period – the Octobrists and the Kadets.

The Octobrists

This group, which dated from the issuing of the tsar's manifesto of October 1905 (see page 38), were moderates who were basically loyal to the tsar and his government. They believed in the maintenance of the Russian Empire and regarded the manifesto and the establishment of the **duma** as major constitutional advances. The Octobrists were mainly drawn from the larger commercial, industrial and landowning interests. Their leading members were **Alexander Guchkov**, a factory owner, and **Mikhail Rodzianko**, a large landowner, both of whom were later to play a leading part in the Provisional Government of 1917 (see page 88). How relatively restricted the Octobrists were in their aims can be gauged from their programme, issued in November 1905, which called for 'peaceful renewal, the triumph of law and order and the establishment of a strong and authoritative regime'.

The limited aims of the Octobrists led to their being dismissed by revolutionaries as reactionaries who were unwilling to challenge the existing system. This was not wholly accurate. In the dumas the Octobrists frequently voiced serious criticisms of the short-sightedness or incompetence of the tsarist government. They may not have wanted the overthrow of tsardom, but they were very willing to point out its failings.

The Constitutional Democrats (Kadets)

The Constitutional Democrats (known by the shortened title Kadets) also came into being as a party at the time of the 1905 Revolution. The Kadets, the largest of the liberal parties, wanted Russia to develop as a constitutional monarchy in which the powers of the tsar would be restricted by a democratically elected constituent (national) assembly. They believed that such a body, representative of the whole of Russia, would be able to settle the nation's outstanding social, political and economic problems.

Key term

Duma
The Russian parliament, which existed from 1906 to 1917.

Key question
How critical were the Octobrists of the tsarist system?

Key dates

Formation of the Octobrists: 1905

Creation of the duma: 1905

Key figures

Alexander Guchkov (1862–1936)
A successful industrialist who became a prominent figure in the duma, but went into exile after the 1917 Revolution.

Mikhail Rodzianko (1859–1924)
A prosperous landowner who by 1917 had despaired of the tsar, but fled Russia after the 1917 Revolution.

Key question
How sweeping was the Kadet programme for the reform of tsarist Russia?

Although revolutionaries rejected this as wholly unrealistic, there is no doubt that the dream of a constituent assembly remained a source of inspiration to all Russian reformers in the period before the 1917 Revolution.

The Kadet programme
- An All-Russian Constituent Assembly.
- Full equality and civil rights for all citizens.
- The ending of censorship.
- The abolition of the mortgage repayments on land.
- The recognition of trade unions and the right to strike.
- The introduction of universal free education.

Key date

Formation of the Kadets: 1905

The Kadets were the party of the liberal intelligentsia, containing progressive landlords, the smaller industrial entrepreneurs, and members of the professions. Academics were prominent in the party, as typified by the Kadet leader, **Paul Milyukov**, who was a professor of history. In the duma the Kadets proved to be the most outspoken critics of the tsarist system. They were to play a significant part in the events leading to the February Revolution (see page 71).

Key figure

Paul Milyukov (1859–1943)
Struggled to unite the progressive forces in Russia, but came eventually to accept that tsardom was beyond saving.

Revolutionaries
The revolutionary forces in Russia comprised three major elements:

- the Populists
- the Social Revolutionaries
- the Social Democrats.

The Populists
As a revolutionary movement, Populism dated from the 1870s. The **Populists** regarded the future of Russia as being in the hands of the peasants, who made up the overwhelming mass of the population. They argued that the peasants must take the lead in the transforming of Russia, beginning with the overthrow of the tsarist system itself.

Key question
How did Populism help to stimulate a revolutionary atmosphere in late imperial Russia?

As with all the significant political movements that came into being in this period, the Populist leaders were drawn not from the peasants, but from the middle and upper classes. The Populists regarded it as their duty to educate the uninformed peasantry into an awareness of its revolutionary role. This involved 'going to the people', a policy by which the educated Populists went from the universities into the countryside to live for a period with the peasants in an attempt to turn them into revolutionaries.

The policy was seldom a success. The peasants tended to regard the students as airy-fairy thinkers and prattlers who had no knowledge of real life. In desperation, some Populists turned to terrorism as the only way of achieving their aims. In 1879 a group calling itself **'The People's Will'** was founded with the declared intention of murdering members of the ruling class.

Key terms

Populists or Narodniks
From the Russian word for 'the people'.

The People's Will
Reckoned to be no more than 400 strong, this group represented the most extreme element in pre-revolutionary Russia.

The assassination of
Alexander II: 1881

Formation of the
Socialist Revolutionary
Party: 1901

Key question
What were the main
ideas of the Social
Revolutionaries (SRs)?

Key terms

'The people'
The section of the
population who
truly represent the
character and will of
the Russian nation.

**Left Social
Revolutionaries**
The faction of the
SRs that wanted to
continue the policy
of terrorism
inherited from 'the
People's Will'.

Key figures

**Victor Chernov
(1873–1952)**
Founder of the
Social
Revolutionary Party
in 1901.

**Leon Trotsky
(1879–1940)**
Later to be the
organising genius of
the 1917 October
Revolution.

This group gained notoriety two years later when it successfully
planned the assassination of Alexander II, who was blown to pieces
by a bomb. However, this act weakened rather than strengthened
the Populist movement. The murder of a tsar who had initiated
many reforms seemed to discredit the idea of reform itself and so
justified the repression imposed in the wake of the assassination.

The importance of Populism lay in its methods rather than in
its ideas. Its concept of a peasant-based revolution was unrealistic;
the Russian peasantry were simply not interested in political
revolution. What was lasting about Populism was the part it played
in establishing a violent anti-tsarist tradition. All the
revolutionaries in Russia after 1870 were influenced, if not
inspired, by the example of the Populist challenge to tsardom.

The Socialist Revolutionaries (SRs)

The Socialist Revolutionary Party grew directly out of the Populist
movement. The economic spurt of the 1890s (see page 14) had
produced a quickening of interest in political and social issues.
Seeing this as an opportunity to gain recruits from the rapidly
growing urban workforce, the Populists began to agitate among the
workers. The intention was to widen the concept of **'the people'**, so
that it encompassed not simply the peasants but all those in society
who had reasons for wishing to see the end of tsardom.

An important figure in the reshaping of Populist strategy was
Victor Chernov. He was a member of the intelligentsia and sought
to provide a firmer base for Populism than its previous passionate
but vague ideas had produced. However, like all the revolutionary
groups in tsarist Russia, the SRs were weakened by disagreements
among themselves. **Leon Trotsky** pointed to this division when he
described the SRs as being made up of two competing groups:
'**Left Social Revolutionaries** and the **Right Social Revolutionaries**'.

Between 1901 and 1905 it was the terrorist faction that
dominated. During those years the SRs were responsible for over
2000 political assassinations, including the killing of **Vyacheslav
Plehve** and the **Grand Duke Sergei**. These were spectacular
successes but they did little to bring about the desired link with the
urban workers.

The 1905 Revolution, which saw the first serious open challenge
to tsardom in Nicholas II's reign (see page 33), brought more
gains to the liberals than to the revolutionaries. One effect of this
was that the more moderate Right SRs gained greater influence
over party policy. This began to show dividends. From 1906, the
SRs experienced growing support from the professional classes,
from the trade unions and from the All-Russian Union of Peasants,
which had been set up in 1905. At its first congress in 1906, the SR
Party committed itself to **'revolutionary socialism'** and gave a
special pledge to the peasants that it would end 'the bourgeois
principle of private ownership by returning the land to those who
worked it'.

It was their land policy that largely explains why the SRs remained the most popular party with the peasants. However, at the time, the congress decisions brought disruption rather than unity. The left wing protested that the party's programme ignored the industrial proletariat, while the right asserted that congress policy was unworkable in current Russian conditions. Chernov tried to hold the factions together, but from 1906 onwards the SRs constituted a collection of radical groups rather than a united party. Nevertheless, until they were outlawed by the Bolsheviks after the 1917 Revolution (see page 127) the SRs remained the party with the largest popular following in Russia.

The Social Democrats (SDs)
The appeal of Marxism in Russia
The Social Democrats (short for the All-Russian Social Democratic Labour Party) came into being in 1898. Their aim was to achieve revolution in Russia by following the ideas of **Karl Marx**, who had advanced the notion that human society operated according to scientific principles that could be studied and then applied. He claimed that history was a continuous series of class struggles between those who possessed economic and political power and those who did not. Marx referred to this process as **the dialectic** (see Figure 1.6).

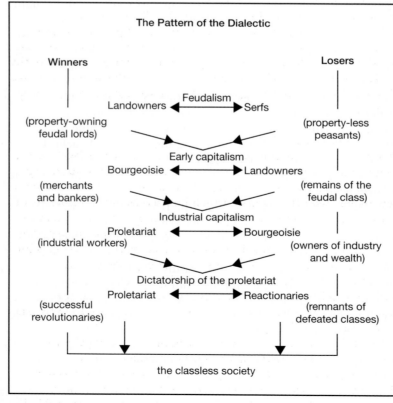

Figure 1.6: The workings of the dialectic.

Key terms

Right Social Revolutionaries
The more moderate members, who believed in revolution as the ultimate goal but were prepared to work with other parties to improve the conditions of the workers and peasants.

'Revolutionary socialism'
The takeover of the state by the peasants and workers.

Key question
Why was Marxism adopted by so many Russian revolutionaries?

Key figures

Vyacheslav Plehve (1846–1904)
The tsar's Minister of the Interior and former head of the Russian police.

Grand Duke Sergei Alexandrovich (1858–1905)
Nicholas II's uncle.

Karl Marx (1818–83)
German radical whose ideas dominated socialist revolutionary thinking in the nineteenth and twentieth centuries.

Key dates

Formation of the All-Russian Social Democratic Labour Party: 1898

All-Russian Union of Peasants set up: 1905

Key terms

The dialectic
The shaping force of history that, according to Marx, leads in every historical period to a violent struggle between the exploiting and the exploited classes of the day.

Proletariat
The exploited industrial workers, who according to Marx would triumph in the last great class struggle.

Bourgeoisie
The owners of capital, the boss class, who exploited the workers but who would be overthrown by them in the revolution to come.

The dictatorship of the proletariat
The last but one stage of history, in which the victorious workers would hunt down and destroy all the surviving reactionaries.

Economism
Putting the improvement of the workers' conditions before the need for revolution.

For revolutionaries in the nineteenth century, the most exciting aspect of Marx's analysis was his conviction that the contemporary industrial era marked the final stage of the dialectical class struggle. Human history was about to reach its culmination in the revolutionary victory of the **proletariat** over the **bourgeoisie**, which would usher in **the dictatorship of the proletariat**, the prelude to the creation of the perfect society.

The attraction of Marx for Russian revolutionaries is easy to understand. His ideas had been known in Russia for some time, but what gave them particular relevance was the 'great spurt' of the 1890s (see page 14). This promised to create the industrial conditions in Russia that would make a successful revolution possible. The previously unfocused hopes for revolution could now be directed on the industrial working class.

Plekhanov and Lenin
The first Marxist revolutionary of note in Russia was **George Plekhanov**, sometimes referred to as 'the founding father of Russian Marxism'. He had translated Marx's writings into Russian and had worked to promote the interests of the industrial workers. It was under his leadership that the SD Party was formed in 1898.

Despite Plekhanov's standing as an interpreter of Marx, a number of the party members soon became impatient with him. They found him too theoretical in his approach, and they wanted a much more active revolutionary programme. They were particularly irritated by his suggestion that Russia was not yet sufficiently advanced politically for a successful proletarian rising to take place in the immediate future, and that, therefore, the way ahead lay in all the revolutionary parties combining to improve the workers' conditions. The outstanding critic of Plekhanov's line was Vladimir Ulyanov, better known as Lenin, the revolutionary name he adopted.

Lenin's impact on the SDs
When Lenin returned from exile to western Russia in 1900, he set about turning the SDs into his idea of what a truly revolutionary party must be. With a colleague, Julius Martov, he founded a party newspaper, *Iskra* (the Spark), which he used as the chief means of putting his case to the party members. Lenin criticised Plekhanov for being more interested in reform than revolution. He said that under Plekhanov the SDs, instead of transforming the workers into a revolutionary force for the overthrow of capitalism, were following a policy of '**economism**'. Lenin wanted living and working conditions to get worse, not better. In that way the bitterness of the workers would increase, and so drive the Russian proletariat to revolution.

In 1902, Lenin wrote his strongest attack yet on Plekhanov. In a pamphlet entitled *What Is to Be Done?* he berated him for continuing to seek allies among as broad a group of anti-tsarist elements as possible. Lenin insisted that this would get nowhere. Revolution in Russia was possible only if it was organised and led by a party of dedicated professional revolutionaries. For Lenin, revolution was not a haphazard affair; it was a matter of applied science. Marx had already provided the key to understanding how revolutions operated. It was the task of those select members of the SD Party who understood scientific Marxism to lead the way in Russia. The workers could not be left to themselves; they did not know enough. They had to be directed. It was the historical role of the informed members of the SD Party to provide that direction. Only they could rescue the Russian working class and convert it to true socialism.

George Plekhanov (1856–1918)
A much-travelled revolutionary who believed that for a true revolution to occur, all the stages of the dialectic had to be worked through.

Key figure

Profile: V.I. Lenin (1870–1924)

1870	– Lenin born as Vladimir Ilyich Ulyanov to a minor aristocratic family of Jewish ancestry
1887	– His brother's execution intensifies Lenin's revolutionary attitude
1897	– Exiled to Siberia; takes the name Lenin (the most famous of the 160 aliases he used as a revolutionary)
1900	– Joins the SD Party
1902	– Writes *What Is to Be Done?*
1903	– Leads the Bolshevik breakaway movement in the SD
1905	– Returns to Russia in December but plays no part in the Revolution
1906–17	– In exile abroad
1917	– Returns to Petrograd following the February Revolution
	– Leads the Bolsheviks in a successful coup in October
1917–20	– Leads the Bolsheviks in consolidating their hold on Russia
1918	– Injured in an SR attempt on his life
1921	– Introduces the New Economic Policy to save Russia from starvation
1922–3	– Suffers a number of severe strokes that leave him speechless
1924	– Dies

Lenin had been on the tsarist authorities' list of 'dangerous persons' since he was 17. The execution of his elder brother in 1887 for his part in an attempted assassination of Alexander III had made Lenin himself politically suspect. He lived up to his reputation. By the time he was 20, his study of Marx's writings had turned him into a committed Marxist for whom revolution was a way of life. By the time he was 30, his dedication to the cause of revolution in Russia had led to arrest, imprisonment and internal exile. Indeed, he was in exile in Siberia when the SD Party was formed in 1898.

Key question
What led to the divide in the SD Party?

Key date

The SD Party splits into Menshevik and Bolshevik factions: 1903

The Bolshevik–Menshevik split

The dispute between Lenin and Plekhanov came to a head during the second congress of the SD Party in 1903. Plekhanov tried to avoid confrontation, but Lenin deliberately made an issue of how the Socialist Democratic Party should recruit its members. His aim was to force the SDs to choose between Plekhanov's idea of a broad-based party, open to all revolutionaries, and his own concept of a small, tightly knit and exclusive party. The congress, which met in a number of different places, including Brussels and London, was a heated affair that frequently descended into a series of slanging matches over points of procedure. The London police, who had been asked by the Russian authorities to keep an eye on proceedings, tended to find the SDs a comical bunch. Their reports spoke of funny foreign gentlemen all speaking at the same time and trying to out-shout each other.

No matter how much the SDs may have amused the London bobbies, they took themselves very seriously. A deep divide developed between Lenin and his *Iskra* co-editor Julius Martov, who shared Plekhanov's viewpoint about membership. Their quarrel was as much to do with personality as with politics. Martov believed that behind Lenin's tactics was a fierce determination to become dictator of the party. The following was typical of their exchanges:

> *Martov* – The more widely the title of 'member of the party' is spread, the better. We can only rejoice if every striker, every demonstrator, is able to declare himself a party member.

> *Lenin* – It is better that ten real workers should not call themselves party members than that one chatterbox should have the right and opportunity to be a member.

In a series of votes, the SD congress showed itself to be evenly divided between Lenin and Martov. However, after a particular set of divisions had gone in his favour, Lenin claimed that he and his supporters were the majority. This led to their being called **Bolsheviks** while Martov's group became known as **Mensheviks**.

Initially, the main point dividing Bolsheviks and Mensheviks was simply one of procedure. However, following the split in 1903 the differences between them hardened into a set of opposed attitudes. These can be illustrated in tabulated form (see Figure 1.7).

By 1912 the Bolsheviks and Mensheviks had become two distinct and opposed Marxist parties. Lenin deliberately emphasised the difference between himself and Martov by resigning from the editorial board of *Iskra* and starting his own journal, *Vyperod* (Forward), as an instrument for Bolshevik attacks upon the Mensheviks. A Bolshevik daily paper, ***Pravda***, was first published in 1912.

Key terms

Bolsheviks
From *bolshinstvo,*
Russian for majority.

Mensheviks
From *menshinstvo,*
Russian for minority.

Pravda
Russian for 'truth'.

Menshevik view	Issue	Bolshevik view
Russia not yet ready for proletarian revolution – the bourgeois stage had to occur first	*Revolution*	The bourgeois and proletarian stages could be telescoped into one revolution
A mass organisation with membership open to all revolutionaries	*The party*	A tight-knit, exclusive organisation of professional revolutionaries
Open, democratic discussion within the party – decisions arrived at by votes of members	*Decision-making*	Authority to be exercised by the Central Committee of the party – this was described as 'democratic centralism'.
• Alliance with all other revolutionary and bourgeois liberal parties • Support of trade unions in pursuing better wages and conditions for workers (economism)	*Strategy*	• No co-operation with other parties • Economism dismissed as playing into the hands of the bourgeoisie • The aim was to turn workers into revolutionaries

Figure 1.7: Main differences between the Mensheviks and the Bolsheviks.

'Democratic centralism'

Democratic centralism was the notion, developed by Lenin, that true democracy in the Bolshevik Party lay in the obedience of the members to the authority and instructions of the leaders. The justification for this was that while, as representatives of the workers, all Bolsheviks were genuine revolutionaries, only the leaders were sufficiently educated in the science of revolution to understand what needed to be done. In practice, democratic centralism meant the Bolsheviks doing what Lenin told them to do.

Lenin and the Bolsheviks

The later success of Bolshevism in the October Revolution has tempted writers to overstate the importance of Lenin in the period before 1917. For example, Trotsky, who joined Lenin in 1917 after having been a Menshevik, argued in his later writings that the Bolsheviks had been systematically preparing the ground for revolution from 1903 onwards. But the fact was that during the years 1904 to 1917 Lenin was largely absent from Russia. He lived variously in Finland, France, Switzerland and Austria, and his visits to Russia were rare and fleeting. Although he continued to issue from exile a constant stream of instructions to his followers, he and they played only a minor role in events in Russia before 1917.

Key question
How strong were the Bolsheviks before 1917?

Bolshevik tactics before 1917

Lenin and his fellow exiles set up training schools for revolutionaries, who were then smuggled back into Russia with the

Key figure

Joseph Stalin
(1879–1953)
Later to be ruler of
Communist Russia
from 1929 to his
death in 1953.

main intention of infiltrating workers' organisations such as the
trade unions. The Bolsheviks who remained in Russia spent their
time trying to raise money for their party. This frequently involved
direct terrorism and violence. Post offices were favourite targets
for Bolshevik attack. In one notorious episode in Tiflis in Georgia,
a Bolshevik gang, organised by **Joseph Stalin**, bomb-blasted their
way into a post office, killing some 50 people before making off
with the equivalent of £1.7 million. The money stolen in such raids
was used to finance the printing of masses of handbills, leaflets
and newspapers attacking the tsarist regime and calling for
revolution.

Yet the truth was that, despite such activities, Lenin's
revolutionaries were regarded by the authorities during this period
as merely a fringe group of extremists. Interestingly, the Bolsheviks
were not listed by the police as a major challenge to the tsarist
system. In the pre-1914 period the numerical strength of the
Bolsheviks varied between 5000 and 10,000; even in February 1917
it was no more than 25,000. Before 1917 the Mensheviks invariably
outnumbered them. Numbers, of course, are not everything.
Determination is arguably more important. Whatever the apparent
lack of influence of Lenin's Bolsheviks before 1917, the fact was
that when a revolutionary situation developed in 1917 it was they
who proved the best prepared to seize the opportunity to take over
government (see page 108). The Bolsheviks' readiness was one of
Lenin's major political achievements.

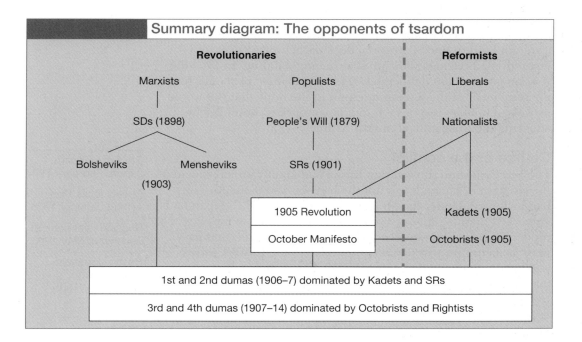

Summary diagram: The opponents of tsardom

5 | The Russo-Japanese War, 1904–5

The foreign policy that Nicholas II inherited and continued was largely determined by the size of the Russian Empire. The protection of its many frontiers was a constant preoccupation. In 1904, Nicholas II faced his first major test in foreign affairs when his country clashed with its Far Eastern neighbour, Japan. It was a war largely of Russia's own making.

The Russian government had three main motives in going to war with Japan in 1904:

- to pursue an expansionist policy in the Far East, to make up for what it saw as its relative decline in Europe (see page 57)
- to obtain an ice-free port – all Russia's major ports on its northern coastline were frozen up for some part of the year
- to distract attention from Russia's domestic troubles by rallying the nation in a patriotic struggle.

In regard to the last point, it used to be thought that Vyacheslav Plehve, the **Interior Minister**, was the main force pushing for war. His words 'We need a small, victorious war to avert a revolution' were often quoted. However, recent research has shown that Plehve was deliberately misrepresented by his political opponent Sergei Witte. We now know that Plehve was reluctant to go to war, whereas Witte, wishing to see Russia expand economically into the Far East (see page 15), knew full well that this made conflict with Japan a very strong possibility.

The path to war

The Russians looked on Japan as an inferior nation and no match for themselves. They expected an easy victory. Pretexts for war were not hard to find. Territorial disputes between Russia and Japan over Korea and Manchuria were long-standing. In 1904 the Russian government deliberately rejected Japanese proposals for the settlement of the Korean question in the hope that this would provoke a military response. It did: Japan opened hostilities by attacking the Russian fleet in Port Arthur.

Course of the conflict

The war itself soon showed that Russia had greatly underestimated the strength of Japan. It was not the backward state the Russians had imagined. Under the Meiji emperors (1869–1912), Japan had embarked upon a series of sweeping reforms aimed at rapid modernisation along western lines. The Japanese army and navy were far better prepared and equipped than the Russian forces and won a series of major victories. For Russia the conflict was a tale of confusion and disaster. After a long siege, Port Arthur fell to Japan in January 1905. The following month the Japanese exploited their advantage by seizing the key Manchurian town of Mukden.

Key question
Why did Russia go to war with Japan in 1904?

Interior Minister
Equivalent to Britain's Home Secretary.

Key term

Key dates

Start of war with Japan: February 1904

Russia loses Port Arthur: January 1905

Russian fleet sunk at Tsushima: May 1905

Russo-Japanese peace treaty: September 1905

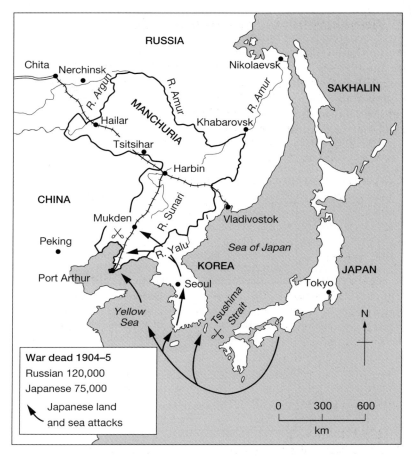

Figure 1.8: Map showing the main areas of the Russo-Japanese war.

The final humiliation for Russia came at sea. The Russian Baltic fleet, dispatched to the Far East in 1904, took eight months to reach its destination, only to be blown out of the water immediately on its arrival by the Japanese fleet at Tsushima in May 1905. Such defeats obliged the tsarist government to make peace. In the Treaty of Portsmouth (USA), Russia agreed to withdraw its remaining forces from Manchuria and accepted Japanese control of Korea and Port Arthur.

Key question
Why did Russia perform so badly in the war?

Russia's defeat
Russia lost the war not because its troops fought badly, but because its military commanders had not prepared effectively. They understood neither the enemy they were fighting nor the territory in which the struggle took place. Their unimaginative strategy allowed the Japanese to outmanoeuvre the Russian forces. Moreover, the distance over which men and materials had to be transported from western Russia made it impossible to provide adequate reinforcements and supplies. The Trans-Siberian Railway, still incomplete in a number of sections, proved of little value.

Effects at home

Russia's defeat at the hands of a small, supposedly inferior Asian country was a national humiliation. Within Russia, the incompetence of the government, which the war glaringly revealed, excited the social unrest that it had been specifically designed to dampen. Russia's dismal performance contributed considerably to the build-up of tension that led to a direct challenge to tsardom – the 1905 Revolution.

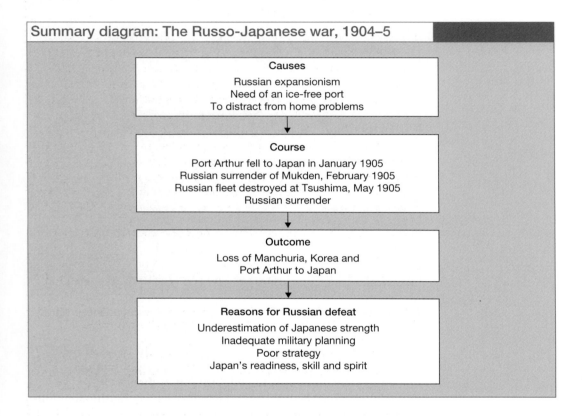

Summary diagram: The Russo-Japanese war, 1904–5

Causes

Russian expansionism
Need of an ice-free port
To distract from home problems

Course

Port Arthur fell to Japan in January 1905
Russian surrender of Mukden, February 1905
Russian fleet destroyed at Tsushima, May 1905
Russian surrender

Outcome

Loss of Manchuria, Korea and
Port Arthur to Japan

Reasons for Russian defeat

Underestimation of Japanese strength
Inadequate military planning
Poor strategy
Japan's readiness, skill and spirit

Study Guide: AS Question

In the style of OCR

How effectively did Nicholas II deal with the problems facing Russia in the period 1894–1905?   (50 marks)

Exam tips

The cross-references are intended to take you straight to the material that will help you to answer the question.

This question requires an evaluation of the effectiveness with which Nicholas dealt with his problems before 1905. You need to establish clear criteria by which 'effectively' can be judged. This can best be achieved by examining his aims, the nature of the problems he faced, his policies and their outcome. It does not want a description of the problems or his policies. The period after 1905, including the 1905 Revolution, may be discussed by way of establishing reference points, but it is important that your answer focuses on the problems before 1905 and analyses Nicholas's successes and failures in addressing them. To gain the highest marks, you need to determine a hierarchy of successes and failures in relation to the problems, and present a balanced assessment. Points that you might consider are:

- political and imperial problems – how much success did Nicholas achieve? (pages 4–13)
- opposition groups – reformers (pages 18–24) and revolutionaries (pages 20–3); does their influence in the October 1905 Revolution suggest that Nicholas failed?
- economic problems – agriculture, industry, transport, and the work of Witte (pages 14–18); do his achievements outweigh the failures?
- the Russo-Japanese War – did it reveal weaknesses in the Russian army, navy and commanders, or demonstrate the strength of Japanese forces? (pages 28–30)

2

The 1905 Revolution and Its Aftermath

POINTS TO CONSIDER

The period 1905–14 was a testing time for imperial Russia. At issue was the question of whether it could become a modern state. In 1905 the tsarist system was shaken by the most open challenge it had yet faced. It survived, but only by making concessions to its opponents. A parliament was granted and political parties were legalised. Whether such concessions weakened or strengthened tsardom is the underlying theme of this chapter, which examines imperial Russia's wrestling with its internal and external enemies. The key areas examined are:

- the 1905 Revolution
- the Stolypin land reforms
- the dumas
- Witte's economic reforms
- growing tensions, 1911–14.

Key dates

1905	January	Revolution begins with Bloody Sunday
	May	'Union of Unions' formed
	June	The *Potemkin* mutiny
	October	October Manifesto creates a Russian duma
		St Petersburg Soviet formed
	November	Moscow Soviet formed
1906		Fundamental Laws issued
		First duma
1906–11		Stolypin's years as Chief Minister
1907		Second duma
1907–12		Third duma
1911		Stolypin asassinated
1912		Lena Goldfields episode
1912–14		Fourth duma
1914		Germany declares war on Russia

1 | The 1905 Revolution

Reasons for the Revolution

The situation created by the tsarist government's policy of political repression was graphically described by **Leo Tolstoy** in 1902 in an 'Open address to Nicholas II':

> Russia lives under emergency legislation, and that means without any lawful guarantees. The armies of the secret police are continuously growing in numbers. The prisons and penal colonies are overcrowded with thousands of convicts and political prisoners, among whom the industrial workers are now included. The censorship issues the most meaningless interdictions [prohibitions or bans].
>
> At no previous time have the religious persecutions been so frequent and so cruel as they are today. In all the cities and industrial centres soldiers are employed and equipped with live ammunition to be sent out against the people. Yet this strenuous and terrible activity of the government results only in the growing impoverishment of the rural population, of those 100 million souls on whom the power of Russia is founded, and who, in spite of ever-increasing budgets, are faced with famine, which has become a normal condition. A similar normal condition is the general dissatisfaction of all classes with the government and their open hostility against it. Autocracy is a superannuated [hopelessly outdated] form of government that may suit the needs of a Central African tribe, but not those of the Russian people, who are increasingly assimilating the culture of the rest of the world. That is why it is impossible to maintain this form of government except by violence.

The bleak picture that Tolstoy painted did not necessarily mean that confrontation, still less revolution, had to come. After all, if oppression is applied firmly enough, it prevents effective challenges to government. What weakened the tsarist regime in the period before 1917 was not its tyranny but its incompetence. It is certainly true that the crisis that occurred in Russia in 1905 was in large measure due to the mishandling of the situation by the tsar and his government. This was shown by the speed with which the government reasserted its authority once it had recovered its nerve.

The groups that led the Revolution

The year 1905 marked the first time the tsarist government had been faced by a combination of the three main opposition classes in Russia:

- the industrial workers
- the peasantry
- the reformist middle class.

Key question
How far was the tsarist government responsible for the 1905 Revolution?

Key figure

Leo Tolstoy (1828–1910)
Outstanding Russian novelist and critic of the tsarist system.

This was the broad-based revolt that most revolutionaries had been awaiting. Yet when it came, it was accidental rather than planned. Despite the efforts of the various revolutionary parties to politicise events, the strikes and demonstrations in the pre-1905 period had been the result of economic rather than political factors. They had been a reaction to industrial recession and bad harvests. It was the tsarist regime's ill-judged policies that turned the disturbances of 1905 into a direct challenge to its own authority.

The course of events
Bloody Sunday
The 1905 Revolution began with what has become known as Bloody Sunday. On 22 January, Father Georgi Gapon, an Orthodox priest, attempted to lead a peaceful march of workers and their families to the Winter Palace in St Petersburg. The marchers' intention was to present a loyal petition to the tsar, begging him to use his royal authority to relieve their desperate conditions.

However, the march induced panic in the police forces in the capital. The marchers were fired on and charged by cavalry. There are no precise casualty figures, but estimates suggest that up to 200 marchers may have been killed, with hundreds more being injured. The deaths were depicted by opponents of the tsarist regime as a deliberate massacre of unarmed petitioners. Although Nicholas II was in fact absent from St Petersburg when these events took place, they gravely damaged the traditional image of the tsar as the 'Little Father', the guardian of the Russian people. In the midst of the death and confusion, Gapon had repeatedly cried out: 'There is no God any longer. There is no tsar.'

Disorder spreads
The immediate reaction to Bloody Sunday in Russia at large was a widespread outbreak of disorder, which increased as the year went on. Strikes occurred in all the major cities and towns. Terrorism against government officials and landlords, much of it organised by the Socialist Revolutionaries, spread to the countryside.

The situation was made worse by Russia's humiliation in the war against Japan (see page 28). The government was blamed for Russia's defeat, which led to further outrages, including the assassination of Plehve by SR terrorists. Public buildings in towns and large private estates in the country were attacked. Land and properties were seized by the peasants, who then squatted in the landlords' houses. An important factor motivating the peasants was the fear that the government was about to repossess the homes of those families who had failed to pay off the mortgages taken out in the post-emancipation years (see page 7).

The unrest and the government's difficulties in containing it encouraged the non-Russian minorities to assert themselves. Georgia declared itself an independent state, the Poles demanded **autonomy** and the Jews pressed for equal rights.

Key question
What pattern did the 1905 Revolution follow?

Revolution begins with Bloody Sunday: January 1905

Key date

Autonomy
National self-government.

Key term

Profile: Father Georgi Gapon (1876–1906)

1876 – Born
1903 – Helped found the Assembly of Russian Workers
1904 – Involved in organising a mass strike
1905 – January – Led workers' march to present a petition to the tsar
– February – Fled to Geneva after Bloody Sunday massacre
– December – Returned to St Petersburg
1906 – March – Murdered

Gapon himself remains an intriguing character about whom mystery still hangs. There were strong suspicions that he was an *Okhrana* **double agent**. Sometimes he genuinely sympathised with the workers, as suggested by his efforts in organising the Assembly of Russian Factory and Plant Workers. He said he wanted to 'build a nest among the factory and mill workers where a truly Russian spirit would prevail'. Yet on other occasions he was willing to inform on those he led and betray them to the authorities.

Exile and meeting with Lenin

At the time of Bloody Sunday, he appeared sincere in his wish to lead the workers in protest; indeed, he ignored a direct order from the authorities to call off the march. Having escaped serious injury or arrest during the suppression of the protest, he immediately fled from Russia to join a group of Social Democratic revolutionaries in Geneva. It was there that he met Lenin, with whom he had a series of intense discussions. Lenin's wife, Krupskaya, recorded that her husband learned a great deal about Russian peasant problems from his talks with Gapon. For his part, Lenin tried to convert Gapon to Marxism.

Return to St Petersburg

Yet by the end of 1905, Gapon had returned to St Petersburg, declaring that he no longer believed in revolution and that he wished to help the government track down its enemies. This may have been a ruse; perhaps he intended to infiltrate government circles as an SD spy. His exact intentions will never be known. The only hard fact is that in March 1906 he was murdered, apparently by *Okhrana* agents, though even this is unclear.

Gapon's significance

Modern historians tend to agree that Gapon was naïve politically and became involved in events he never fully grasped. A contemporary was once asked whether Gapon was a supporter of constitutionalism. He replied, 'Support it? He can't even say it.' Whatever Gapon's real intentions may have been, his lack of understanding of political realities made him a fascinating but ultimately powerless participant in the 1905 Revolution.

Key term

Double agent
A government spy who pretends to be spying for the opposition against the authorities but who reports plans and secrets back to the authorities.

In May, the Kadets, led by Milyukov, persuaded the majority of the liberal groups to join them in forming a 'Union of Unions' with the aim of organising a broad-based alliance that would include the peasants and the factory workers. A 'Union of Unions' declaration was issued, which referred to the government as 'a terrible menace' and called for a constituent assembly to replace 'the gang of robbers' now in power.

'Union of Unions' formed: May 1905

The *Potemkin* mutiny: June 1905

Key dates

The *Potemkin* mutiny

The summer of 1905 brought the still more disturbing news for the tsarist authorities of mutinies in the army and navy. The rank-and-file soldiers in the army were peasants who were naturally reluctant to attack their own kind: workers on strike or rebellious peasants in the countryside. There were several instances of troops disobeying orders to shoot unarmed strikers or to use force to drive peasants from the properties they had occupied.

Key question
Why was mutiny such a serious threat to the tsarist regime?

In June there were even worse tidings for the government. The crew of the battleship *Prince Potemkin*, of the Black Sea naval squadron, mutinied while at sea. The incident began as a protest by the sailors at having to eat rotting food and drink foul water; particular horrors were **borsch** and putrid, maggot-infested scraps of meat. The sailors elected a representative, Peter Vakulenchuk, to approach the captain with their complaints. The captain's immediate response was to have the man shot. In retaliation, the crew attacked the officers, killed several of them and then took over the ship. This was a desperate act and could have worked only if the other ships in the squadron had joined the mutiny. But they did not; despite the equally grim conditions in the other ships, the captains managed to maintain control. The crew of the *Potemkin* were on their own.

Borsch
A thin soup made from mouldy beetroots.

Key term

Hoping to arouse support on land, they sailed to the port of Odessa, where a serious anti-government strike was taking place. The strikers welcomed the crew as heroes and formally honoured the body of Vakulenchuk by laying it on an elevated platform and surrounding it with flowers. It was a defiant gesture of solidarity but it enraged the authorities, who could not tolerate strikers and mutineers making common cause. Troops were ordered to disperse the crowds who had gathered in the harbour at the foot of a deep and wide flight of steps. With bayonets fixed, the soldiers marched resolutely down the steps, trampling on those who fell in front of them and driving hundreds into the sea. The civilian death toll ran into thousands.

The massacre forced the *Potemkin* to leave Odessa. Since no other ships had sided with them, the crew decided to cut their losses. They abandoned their ship in a Romanian port, hoping to find sanctuary for themselves in this remoter part of the Russian Empire.

Left, the captain of the *Potemkin* holding the rifle with which he is about to shoot Vakulenchuk. Right, the battleship *Potemkin* itself. There are no photographs of the *Potemkin* mutiny. These two stills are taken from the feature film *Battleship Potemkin*, made in 1925 by Sergei Eisenstein, the pro-Bolshevik director. The images from his silent film are so powerful that they have conditioned the way we visualise the actual event itself.

Although the mutiny was restricted to one ship, there is no doubt that the affair was deeply troubling to the Russian authorities. A government that cannot rely on the loyalty of its armed services, particularly in time of war, is in a very vulnerable position. The end of the Russo-Japanese War in August did little to ease the situation. Indeed, Witte feared that the returning troops would join the Revolution. If this happened, he said, 'then everything would collapse'.

Despite being the tsar's most able minister (see page 13), Witte was not liked by Nicholas II, who found his reformist views far too progressive. Nevertheless, the dangerous situation obliged the government to rely heavily on Witte to steer them through the crisis. Witte's first task was to negotiate peace terms with the Japanese. With this successfully completed, he then became chairman of the Council of Ministers, the effective head of the tsar's government. Yet Witte remained frustrated by the inability of the tsar and his ministers to understand how much they were the authors of their own difficulties. He referred to government policy as a 'mixture of cowardice, blindness and stupidity'. Nevertheless, he remained at his post, driven by a sense of duty to do his best to guide the regime through its difficulties.

Soviets formed

By the autumn of 1905 the industrial unrest had grown into a general strike. It was in this atmosphere that a development of particular moment occurred. In a number of cities, most notably

Key dates

St Petersburg Soviet formed: Oct 1905

Moscow Soviet formed: Nov 1905

in St Petersburg and Moscow, workers formed themselves into an elected **soviet**. The soviets began as organisations to represent the workers' demands for better conditions, but their potential as bases for political agitation was immediately recognised by revolutionaries. Leon Trotsky, who was a leading Menshevik at this time, became chairman of the St Petersburg soviet and organiser of several strikes in the capital.

The October Manifesto, 1905

Key question
What steps did the government take to deal with the challenge facing it?

By October, the tsar was faced by the most united opposition in Romanov history. But at this critical juncture the regime began to show a sense of purpose that it had so far lacked. Concession was unavoidable, but by giving ground, the government intended to divide the opposition forces that confronted it: liberals, peasants and workers.

The liberals were the first to be appeased. The tsar issued the October Manifesto, a document drafted by Witte, in which the following concessions were granted:

- the creation of a **legislative duma**
- freedom of speech, assembly and worship
- the right of political parties to exist
- the legalising of trade unions.

Soviet
A council made up of elected representatives.

Legislative duma
A parliament with law-making powers.

Given the tsar's earlier resistance to the granting of political freedoms, these were substantial gains for the liberals, who felt they had achieved a genuine advance. Their appetite for reform was satisfied, at least temporarily.

October Manifesto creates a Russian duma: 1905

The peasants were the next to be pacified by an announcement in November that the mortgage repayments that had so troubled them were to be progressively reduced and then abolished altogether. The response was an immediate drop in the number of land seizures by the peasants and a decline in the general lawlessness in the countryside.

Having won over the liberals and peasants, the government was now seriously opposed by only one major group – the industrial workers. Here the policy was one not of concession but of suppression. The government felt strong enough to attempt to crush the soviets. Despite the mutinies earlier in the year, the troops who returned from the Far East at the end of the war proved loyal enough to be used against the strikers. After a five-day siege, the headquarters of the St Petersburg soviet were stormed and the ringleaders, including Trotsky, were arrested. The destruction of the Moscow soviet was even more violent. Lenin, who had been slow to take advantage of the 1905 Revolution, arrived in Moscow in December, only in time to witness the flames of the gutted soviet buildings, set ablaze by government troops.

With the worst of the troubles clearly over by the spring of 1906, Nicholas II again revealed his distaste for Witte by summarily dismissing him. Witte was to live another nine years but he was never again to hold a prominent position in Russian public affairs. That the tsar believed he could dispense with the services of one of the few truly able men in the government was another indication of how out of touch Nicholas was with Russia's real needs.

Significance of the 1905 Revolution

A notable feature of the 1905 Revolution was how minor a part was played by the revolutionaries. Hardly any of them were in St Petersburg or Moscow when it began. Revolution occurred in spite of them, rather than because of them. With the exception of Trotsky, none of the SDs made an impact on the course of events. This throws doubt on the notion of 1905 as a revolution.

There is the further fact that in a number of important respects, tsardom emerged from the disturbances stronger rather than weaker. Despite its humiliating failure to win the war against Japan, which produced protest throughout Russia and united the classes in opposition, the tsarist regime survived 1905 remarkably unscathed. The mutinies in the armed services did not spread and did not continue after the war. Loyal troops returned to destroy the soviets. The readiness of the liberals and the peasants to accept the government's political and economic bribes indicated that neither of those groups was genuinely ready for revolution.

It is true that the tsar appeared to grant significant concessions in the October Manifesto, but these were expedients rather than real reforms. The duma was not intended to be, nor did it become, a limitation on the tsar's autocratic powers. This was evident from the Fundamental Laws, which Nicholas II promulgated in April 1906:

Key date | Tsar promulgates the Fundamental Laws: April 1906

> The Sovereign Emperor possesses the initiative in all legislative matters. The Fundamental Laws may be subject to revision in the State Council and the State Duma only on his initiative. The Sovereign Emperor ratifies the laws. No law can come into force without his approval.

The lesson of the 1905 Revolution

What 1905 showed was that as long as the tsarist government kept its nerve and the army remained loyal, the forces of protest would find it very difficult to mount a serious challenge.

The events of 1905 also raised questions about the extent to which the liberals wanted change in Russia. Few of them enjoyed their experience of mixing with the workers during the Revolution. They found proletarian coarseness unattractive and were frightened by the primitive forces they had helped to unleash. One middle-class proprietor who had thrown his house open to the strikers remarked on the difficulty of sustaining his belief in the goodness of people who abused his hospitality by molesting his daughters, urinating on his carpets and stealing everything they could carry. **Peter Struve**, who had been a Marxist before joining the Kadets in 1905, spoke for all frightened liberals when he said: 'Thank God for the tsar, who has saved us from the people.'

Leon Trotsky reflected that while the Russo-Japanese War 'had made tsarism totter', the revolution that followed in 1905 had failed because the protestors were disunited and inexperienced. 'The workers had organised independently of the bourgeoisie in soviets.'

Key figure

Moreover, the liberals had backed out of the revolution and betrayed the workers by leaving them to be crushed by government troops. He concluded that the tsarist system, 'although with a few broken ribs, had come out of the experience of 1905 alive and strong'.

Summary diagram: The 1905 Revolution

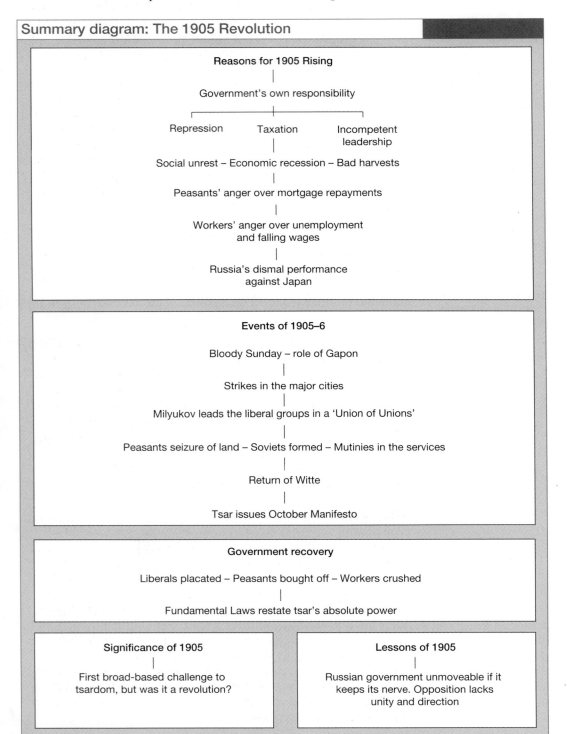

Reasons for 1905 Rising
|
Government's own responsibility
|
Repression   Taxation   Incompetent leadership
|
Social unrest – Economic recession – Bad harvests
|
Peasants' anger over mortgage repayments
|
Workers' anger over unemployment and falling wages
|
Russia's dismal performance against Japan

Events of 1905–6

Bloody Sunday – role of Gapon
|
Strikes in the major cities
|
Milyukov leads the liberal groups in a 'Union of Unions'
|
Peasants seizure of land – Soviets formed – Mutinies in the services
|
Return of Witte
|
Tsar issues October Manifesto

Government recovery

Liberals placated – Peasants bought off – Workers crushed
|
Fundamental Laws restate tsar's absolute power

Significance of 1905
|
First broad-based challenge to tsardom, but was it a revolution?

Lessons of 1905
|
Russian government unmoveable if it keeps its nerve. Opposition lacks unity and direction

2 | Stolypin and Land Reform

Key question
What was Stolypin aiming to achieve in his dealings with the peasants?

Peter Stolypin was appointed president of the Council of Ministers in July 1906 in the aftermath of the 1905 Revolution. Like Witte before him, he was dedicated to strengthening tsardom in a time of crisis. He was a political conservative whose attitude was clearly expressed in the coercive measures he introduced between 1906 and 1911. He declared his guiding principle to be 'suppression first and then, and only then, reform'. However, he also considered that, where possible, reform should be introduced as a way of reducing the social bitterness on which opposition fed. It was in this spirit that he approached the land problem in Russia.

Stolypin started from the conviction that industrial progress by itself could not solve Russia's most pressing need: how to feed the nation's rapidly growing population. Russia had undergone a **'rural crisis'** in the late nineteenth century. The problem had been deepened by a series of bad harvests in the 1890s that left millions hungry; the years 1891 and 1897 had witnessed especially severe famines.

The government's land policies following the emancipation of the serfs in 1861 had not helped. The scheme under which state mortgages were advanced to the freed serfs to enable them to buy their properties had not created the peace and harmony for which the government had hoped.

Key date
Stolypin's years as Chief Minister: 1906–11

Key term
'Rural crisis'
The problem of land shortage and overpopulation in the countryside produced by the huge increase in the number of people living in Russia in the late nineteenth century.

'De-revolutionising' the peasantry

The high price of land, which led to heavy mortgage repayments, had impoverished the peasants. They felt very insecure, which meant that they farmed inefficiently and were a dangerous social force. One of the reasons why the peasants joined the Revolution in 1905 was their fear that the government was about to seize the land of those many mortgage-holders who had fallen behind in their payments. When the government came to understand this fear, it bought off the peasants by announcing that the outstanding repayments would be cancelled. This tactic has been called 'de-revolutionising' the peasants.

The 'wager on the strong'

Stolypin planned to build upon this successful treatment of the peasantry. In 1906–7, he introduced measures to restore the peasants' sense of security. Farmers were urged to replace the inefficient strip system (see page 43) with fenced fields, based on the pattern that existed in western Europe. A special Land Bank was established to provide funds for the independent peasant to buy his land. Stolypin defined his policy as 'a wager on the strong'. His intention was to create a layer of prosperous, productive peasants whose new wealth would turn them into natural supporters of the tsarist system. His reforms also included schemes for large-scale voluntary resettlement of the peasants, the aim being to populate the empire's remoter areas, such as Siberia, and turn them into food-growing areas.

Key debate

Did Stolypin's land reforms have any realistic chance of success?

Historians disagree over how realistic Stolypin's policies were. The standard view of most scholars in this field has been that he had little real chance of reforming agriculture since the Russian peasantry was so backward and he had so little time to change things.

Others, however, have argued that while it is true that the **conservatism** of most peasants prevented them from embracing progressive change, Stolypin was right, nonetheless, in thinking that he could wager on 'the strong' since there was indeed a layer of strong peasant farmers. This argument is based on evidence drawn from tsarist tax returns, which show that a significant minority of peasants were paying increasingly higher taxes in the 1890s, a sign that their farming was producing high profits. The conclusion, therefore, is that the traditional picture of a totally depressed peasantry is misleading since it takes too little notice of the agricultural advances being made in parts of Russia.

The problem is that even if one accepts as fact that there was a progressive element among the peasants, there is no certainty that this would have been enough to modernise Russian agriculture. Even in advanced economies, land reform takes time to work. Stolypin was well aware that in a country as relatively backward as Russia, the changes would take even longer to become effective. He spoke of needing 20 years for his 'wager on the strong' to bring results. In the event, his assassination in 1911 allowed him personally only five, and the coming of the war in 1914 allowed Russia only eight.

However, there remains doubt as to whether, even without the interruption of murder and war, his peasant policy would have succeeded. The deep conservatism of the mass of the Russian peasants made them slow to respond. In 1914 the strip system (see Figure 2.1) was still widespread. As Table 2.1 shows, only about 10 per cent of the land had been consolidated into farms. Most peasants were reluctant to leave the security of the commune for the uncertainty of individual farming. Furthermore, by 1913 the government's own Ministry of Agriculture had itself begun to lose confidence in the policy.

One notable feature of Stolypin's land policy was his effective working relations with the duma. The understanding which he developed with the Octobrists, the largest party in the third duma (see page 47), allowed him to pursue his reforms with little obstruction from the other deputies. His success here hinted at how much co-operation might have developed between government and progressive opinion had the tsarist regime been willing to trust its own ministers.

Conservatism
Suspicion of change, and, therefore, resistance to it.

Key term

Table 2.1: Number of peasant households that opted to set up
independent farms (out of an estimated total of 10–12 million households)

1907	48,271
1908	508,344
1909	579,409
1910	342,245
1911	145,567
1912	122,314
1913	134,554

Total area:
215 hectares
19 households

1 hectare = 100 acres

The black shaded areas
represent the land farmed
by one family

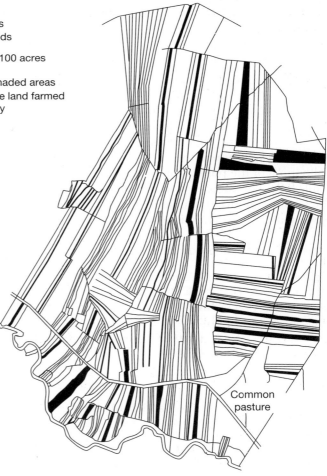

Common
pasture

Figure 2.1: Strip
farming as practised
in central Russia,
c.1900. The land was
divided into small,
individually cultivated
sections. The
weakness of the
system was that the
lack of space and
closeness to other
strips prevented the
farmer from being
efficient; he could not
protect or improve his
crops and livestock or
expand his output.

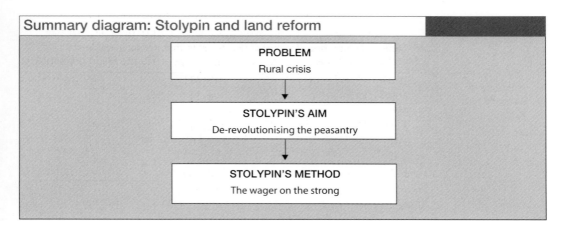

Summary diagram: Stolypin and land reform

PROBLEM
Rural crisis

↓

STOLYPIN'S AIM
De-revolutionising the peasantry

↓

STOLYPIN'S METHOD
The wager on the strong

3 | The Russian Economy after Witte, 1903–14

The issue raised in the previous section of whether Stolypin's policies could have worked ties in with the question of how much likelihood there was of the Russian economy modernising overall. Russia's economic improvement in the 1890s had not simply been the result of the work of Witte. It had been part of a worldwide industrial boom. However, by the turn of the century the boom had ended and a serious international **trade recession** had set in.

The consequences for Russia were especially serious. The industrial expansion at the end the century had led to a ballooning of the population of the towns and cities (see Table 2.2). This increase had not been organised or supervised; the facilities for accommodating the influx of workers were wholly inadequate. The result was acute overcrowding.

Key question
What problems followed Russia's falling back into recession?

Trade recession
A marked fall in the demand for goods, resulting in a cutback in production and the laying off of workers.

Table 2.2: Growth of population in Russia's two main cities

	St Petersburg	Moscow
1881	928,000	753,500
1890	1,033,600	1,038,600
1897	1,264,700	1,174,000
1900	1,439,600	1,345,000
1910	1,905,600	1,617,700
1914	2,217,500	1,762,700

Initially, the peasants who had left the land to take work in the urban factories accepted their grim conditions because of the higher wages they received. But when boom turned to recession there was widespread unemployment. The authorities in the towns and cities found themselves facing large numbers of rootless workers who had had their expectations of a better life raised, only to have them dashed by harsh economic realities.

The presence of thousands of disaffected workers on the streets of St Petersburg and Moscow played an important part in the growth of serious social unrest in Russia between 1900 and 1917.

Despite the recession, the period from 1908 to 1914 saw an overall increase in industrial output of 8.5 per cent. The figures shown in Table 2.3 also indicate continued growth.

Table 2.3: Economic growth in Russia, 1908–14

	1908	1914
State revenues (in roubles)	2 billion	4 billion
Number of banks	1,146	2,393
Number of factories	22,600	24,900
Number of workers	2,500,000	2,900,000

Table 2.4: Strikes in Russia, 1905–14

Year	Number of strikes
1905	13,995
1908	892
1910	222
1911	466
1912	2,032
1913	2,404
1914	3,574

Nevertheless, against the bright picture these figures paint has to be set the darker aspect. Few workers gained from the industrial and financial expansion. Weak trade unions and minimal legal protection left the workforce very much at the mercy of the employers. Little of the greater amount of money in circulation reached the pockets of the workers. Although the rate of inflation rose by 40 per cent between 1908 and 1914, the average industrial wage rose from 245 to only 264 roubles per month in the same period.

Of course, a national average does not tell the whole story. Some workers did better than others; for example, wages were a third higher in St Petersburg than in Moscow. Nonetheless, the strike statistics compiled by the Ministry of Trade (Table 2.4) show the scale of the industrial unrest.

The key debate

There is a lively discussion among historians over the question:

How strong had the Russian economy become by 1914?

Key term

Modern industrial state
A nation whose economic development enables it to compete on equal terms with other advanced economies. This invariably means having a strong industrial base and sufficient capital to undertake progressive social reforms.

There are those who suggest that until the First World War intervened, Russia was in the process of developing into a **modern industrial state**. They cite the figures of increased industrial production, growth of the labour force and expansion of foreign investment.

Other historians, while accepting these figures, argue that, compared to developments in other countries, Russian growth was too limited to provide a genuine industrial base. They further stress that in 1914, four-fifths of the population were still peasants, a fact that undermines the claim that there had been significant industrial development.

In the end, no final answer can be given to the question as to how the economy would have developed had the war and the 1917 Revolution not intervened. There are too many ifs and buts. The comment of Alex Nove, a major western authority on the subject, is particularly telling in this context. He says that there are convincing arguments on either side of the question as to whether Russia would have become a modern industrial state:

> If the growth rates characteristic of the period 1890–1913 for industry and agriculture were simply projected over the succeeding 50 years, no doubt citizens would be leading a reasonable existence. However, this assumes that the imperial authorities would have successfully made the adjustment necessary to govern in an orderly manner a rapidly developing and changing society.

However, Nove wisely adds that, fascinating though the debate is, 'there must surely be a limit to the game of what-might-have-been'.

Some key books in the debate:
David Christian, *Imperial and Soviet Russia: Power, Privilege and the Challenge of Modernity* (Macmillan, 1997)
R.W. Davies, *From Tsarism to the New Economic Policy* (Cornell University Press, 1991)
Peter Gatrell, *The Tsarist Economy* (Batsford, 1986)
P.R. Gregory, *Before Command* (Princeton University Press, 1994)
W.E. Mosse, *An Economic History of Russia 1856–1914* (Tauris, 1996)
Alec Nove, *An Economic History of the USSR* (Penguin, 1976)
Richard Pipes, *Russia under the Old Regime* (Penguin, 1987)
Richard Pipes, *The Russian Revolution 1899–1919* (Collins Harvill, 1990)

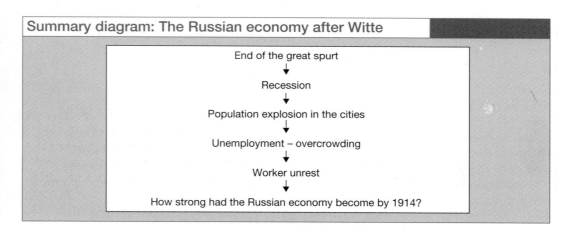

Summary diagram: The Russian economy after Witte

End of the great spurt
↓
Recession
↓
Population explosion in the cities
↓
Unemployment – overcrowding
↓
Worker unrest
↓
How strong had the Russian economy become by 1914?

4 | The Dumas, 1906–14

The tsar's granting of a duma in the October Manifesto was the most striking of the concessions made to the liberals. It remained to be seen what role this new parliament, the first in Russian history, would play. There were four dumas in the years between the 1905 Revolution and the February Revolution of 1917 (see page 47). The four elections produced the results shown in Table 2.5.

Table 2.5: Duma election results

Party or group	1st Duma 1906	2nd Duma 1907	3rd Duma 1907–12	4th Duma 1912–17
SDs (Mensheviks)	18	47	–	–
SDs (Bolsheviks)	–	–	19	15
SRs	–	37	–	–
Labourists	136	104	13	10
Kadets	182	91	54	53
Octobrists	17	42	154	95
Progressists	27	28	28	41
Rightists	8	10	147	154
National parties	60	93	26	22
Others	–	50	–	42
Total	448	502	441	432

Key question
Why was the first duma unsuccessful?

Key terms

Labourists
Name adopted by the SRs, who as a party officially boycotted the elections to the first duma.

Progressists
A party of businessmen who favoured moderate reform.

Rightists
Not a single party; they represented a range of conservative views from right of centre to extreme reaction.

Bi-cameral
A parliament made up of two chambers or houses, an upper and a lower.

Key date

The first duma: April–June 1906

The first duma, April–June 1906

The high hopes of the liberals that the granting of the duma marked a real constitutional advance were dashed even before it first met. Having survived the challenge of the 1905 Revolution, the tsarist regime quickly recovered its confidence. Early in 1906 it successfully negotiated a substantial loan from France. This lessened the likelihood of the duma's being able to exercise a financial hold over the government.

A still greater limitation on the duma's influence was the tsar's promulgation of the Fundamental Laws, which was timed to coincide with the opening of the duma. In addition to declaring that 'Supreme Autocratic Power' belonged to the tsar, the Laws announced that the duma would be **bi-cameral**:

- one chamber would be an elected lower house
- the other would be a state council, the majority of whose members would be appointed by the tsar.

The existence of a second chamber with the right of veto deprived the elected duma of any real power. Taken together with the declaration that no law could come into being without the tsar's approval, these restrictions made it clear that the tsarist regime had no intention of allowing the concessions it had made in 1905 to diminish its absolute authority.

The Vyborg appeal

The result was that the duma met in a mood of bitterness. The elections had returned an assembly that was dominated by the reformist parties. They immediately voiced their anger at what they regarded as the government's going back on its promises. They demanded that the rights and powers of the duma be increased. Ivan Goremykin, the chief minister, told them that their demands were 'inadmissible' and Nicholas II was reported as saying: 'Curse the duma. It is all Witte's doing.' After two months of bitter wrangling, the tsar ordered the duma to be dissolved.

In frustration, 200 Kadet and Labourist deputies reassembled at Vyborg in Finland, where they drew up an 'Appeal' urging the people of Russia to defy their government in two main ways by:

* refusing to pay taxes
* disobeying conscription orders.

However, the rebellious Kadets who issued the Appeal had made a serious tactical error. The response from the Russian people was not widespread **passive disobedience** but scattered violence. This provided the government with a ready excuse for retaliation. The tsar appointed Stolypin as chief minister to act as his strongman. The Vyborg group of deputies was arrested and debarred from re-election to the duma.

This was the prelude to Stolypin's introduction of a policy of fierce repression, which he sustained until his assassination in 1911. **Martial law** was proclaimed and a network of military courts, with sweeping powers, was used to quell disturbances wherever they occurred. Between 1906 and 1911 there were over 2500 executions in Russia, a grim detail that, in a piece of black humour, led to the hangman's noose being nicknamed 'Stolypin's necktie'.

Peter Stolypin was fatally shot in the presence of Nicholas on 14 September 1911 while attending the opera at the Kiev Theatre. His last words were reported to be 'It's all over. I am happy to die for the tsar.' There were rumours that his assassin, **Dmitri Bogrov**, who was hanged for his crime ten days later, was a secret government agent. What grounds are there for thinking that government agents might have been involved in the assassination?

'Mother Russia weeping over the death of the first-born'. A dramatic representation of the failure of the first duma. Which group in Russian society would be the target audience for the cartoon's message?

THE DEATH OF THE FIRST-BORN.

The Kadets' failure in 1906 had serious long-term effects. Although the Kadet Party survived under the leadership of Milyukov, it never really recovered from its humiliation. The liberal cause had discredited itself, thus allowing both the left and the right to argue from their different standpoints that Russia's salvation could not be gained through moderate policies but only by revolution or extreme reaction.

The second duma, February–June 1907

Key question
Why was the second duma even more critical of the government than the first?

The immediate result of the Vyborg fiasco was that in the elections for the second duma, the Kadets lost half their seats. These were filled by the SDs and the SRs, who between them returned over 80 deputies. This made the new assembly strongly anti-government. Indeed, the SRs proclaimed dramatically that it was 'the duma of the people's wrath'. However, since the right-wing parties had also increased their numbers, there was considerable disagreement within the duma, as well as between it and the government.

Key date
The second duma: February–June 1907

Whatever the internal divisions among the parties, the mood of the duma was undeniably hostile to the government. Stolypin, who, despite his stern repression of social disorder, was willing to work with the duma in introducing necessary reforms, found his land programme strenuously opposed. The tsar was particularly incensed when the duma directed a strong attack on the way the imperial army was organised and deployed. The SD and SR deputies were accused of engaging in subversion, and Nicholas ordered that the assembly be dissolved. Deputies scuffled and shouted out in protest as the session was duly brought to an end.

The third duma: November 1907–June 1912

The fourth duma: November 1912–August 1914

Key dates

The third duma, November 1907–June 1912

Despite the opposition shown by the first two dumas, the tsar made no attempt to dispense with the duma altogether. There were two main reasons for this. The first related to foreign policy. The tsar was keen to project an image of Russia as a democratic nation. He was advised by his Foreign Ministers, who at this time were in trade talks with France and Britain, that Russia's new commercial allies were considerably impressed by the tsar's creation of a representative national parliament.

The second reason was that the duma had been rendered docile by the government's doctoring of the electoral system. Stolypin introduced new electoral laws that restricted the vote to the propertied classes. The peasants and industrial workers lost the franchise. The consequence was that the third and fourth dumas were heavily dominated by the right-wing parties (as Table 2.5 on page 47 shows), a reversal of the position in the first two dumas in which the radical parties had held a large majority. Any criticisms of tsardom were now much more muted.

With the balance of the parties redressed in this way, Stolypin found the third duma more co-operative, which enabled him to pursue his land reforms without opposition from the deputies (see page 42). This is not to say that the duma was entirely subservient. It exercised its right to question ministers and to discuss state finances. It also used its **committee system** to make important proposals for modernising the armed services. Among the 2571 bills it approved were social reform measures that included the setting up of schools for the children of the poor and **national insurance** for industrial workers.

> **Key question**
> Why was the third duma less hostile to the government?

> **Committee system** A process in which the deputies of the third duma formed various committees to discuss and advise on particular issues.
>
> **National insurance** A system of providing workers with state benefits, such as unemployment pay and medical treatment, in return for regular contributions to a central fund.
>
> Key terms

The fourth duma, November 1912–August 1914

After 1917 it was usual for historians to follow the lead of the Bolsheviks in dismissing the later dumas as having been merely rubber stamps of government policy. However, modern scholars tend to be less critical. Although the fourth duma was less openly obstructive than the earlier ones had been, it still voiced criticism of the tsar's government.

Interestingly, a Moscow *Okhrana* report in 1912 blamed the tension in Russia on the awkward and searching questions continually being asked in the duma about government policy:

> **Key question**
> Did the fourth duma serve any real purpose?

People can be heard speaking of the government in the sharpest and most unbridled tones. Influenced by questions in the duma and the speeches which they called forth there, public tension is increasing still more. It is a long time since even the extreme left has spoken in such a way, since there have been references in the duma to 'the necessity of calling a Constituent Assembly and overthrowing the present system by the united strength of the proletariat'.

Historians also emphasise the progressive work of the duma in providing state welfare and suggest that it was only the blindness of the tsarist government that prevented the dumas from making a greater contribution to the development of Russia. A strong supporting piece of evidence is a duma resolution of 1913 pointing out how seriously the government was damaging its own position by refusing to acknowledge what was happening in Russia:

The Ministry of the Interior systematically scorns public opinion and ignores the repeated wishes of the new legislature. The duma considers it pointless to express any new wishes in regard to internal policy. The Ministry's activities arouse dissatisfaction among the broad masses who have hitherto been peaceful. Such a situation threatens Russia with untold dangers.

Summary diagram: The dumas, 1906–14

	Character	Achievements
1st duma 1906	Dominated by reformist parties	Short lived – little achieved
2nd duma 1907	Clash between revolutionaries and right-wing parties	Dissolved in disorder – little achieved
3rd duma 1907–12	Election rigged by Stolypin to produce more co-operative deputies from moderate parties	Committees did achieve effective work in social reform
4th duma 1912–14	Dominated by right-wing parties again willing to co-operate	Social reform work continued, but prepared to criticise government

The debate on the role of the dumas

Were they ever more than a talking shop?

How valuable was their committee work?

How significant were they as critics of tsardom?

5 | Growing Tensions in Russia, 1911–14

Key question
Why were there
mounting political and
social strains in this
period?

It was Stolypin's tragedy, as it had been Witte's, that his abilities
were never fully appreciated by the regime he tried to serve.
Following his murder in 1911, the various ministers the tsar
appointed were distinguished only by their incompetence. Since
they lacked political imagination, their only course was further
repression. An intensification of the anti-Jewish pogroms was one
expression of this. Between 1911 and 1914 the regime's terror
tactics were part cause, part effect, of a dramatic increase in public
disorder, which gradually returned to the proportions of 1905.
The number of strikes listed as 'political' by the Ministry of Trade
and Industry rose from 24 in 1911 to 2401 in 1914.

Stolypin assassinated:
September 1911

The Lena Goldfields
incident: 1912

Key dates

More seriously still, there had in that same period been over
17,000 victims of acts of terrorism perpetrated by radicals and
revolutionaries. It is important to note that an atmosphere of
violence prevailed in Russia in the decade before 1914 which was not
necessarily a product of government policies. Not all revolutionaries
were inspired by high ideals. A modern Russian historian, Anna
Geifman, has observed that a new type of brutal extremist entered
the ranks of the revolutionary parties in the two decades before
1914. The new revolutionaries were little concerned with political or
social theory; they often had a love of violence for its own sake. She
writes that the new activists 'exhibited a considerably inferior level of
intellectual and ideological awareness, as well as less inclination
towards selfless idealism' than the older members. It was these
pathological types, she concludes, who, having infiltrated all the
revolutionary groups, 'bore primary responsibility for the pervading
atmosphere of anti-government violence and bloodshed in the
empire in the first decade of the century'.

Geifman is quick to add that none of this exempts the tsarist
government 'from a large share of the responsibility for the acute
domestic crisis in the empire and the eventual collapse of its
political order in 1917'.

The Lena Goldfields incident, 1912

The Moscow *Okhrana* report that had referred to the role of the
duma in creating tension went on to cite the 'shooting of the Lena
workers' as the major reason why the 'people can be heard
speaking of the government in the sharpest and most unbridled
tones'. The mention of the Lena workers was a reference to a
notorious incident that occurred in 1912 in the Lena Goldfields in
Siberia. Demands from the miners there for better pay and
conditions were resisted by the employers, who appealed to the
police to arrest the strike leaders as criminals.

The issue thus became the much larger one of trade union
rights in Russia. When the police moved into Lena, the strikers
closed ranks and the situation rapidly worsened, resulting in
troops firing on and killing or injuring a large number of miners.
The *Okhrana* appeared to have acted as **agents provocateurs** in order
to identify the organisers of the strike.

Agents provocateurs
Government agents
who infiltrate
opposition
movements with the
deliberate aim of
stirring up trouble
so as to expose the
ringleaders.

Key term

Anger among the moderates

Even the moderate parties began to despair of the government's dealing effectively with the problems that confronted Russia. The Octobrist leader, Alexander Guchkov, told his party conference in 1913 that their attempts to achieve 'a peaceful, painless transition from the old condemned system to a new order' had failed. He warned that the blindness of the tsar's government was daily driving the Russian people closer to revolution.

Guchkov's warning was to come true in 1917. What delayed by four years the revolution he forecast was Russia's entry into the First World War in 1914 (see Chapter 3).

6 | The Key Debate

An absorbing question which continues to occupy historians is:

> Did the two decades between the accession of Nicholas II and the start of the First World War mark the period when the tsarist regime threw away its last chance of escaping revolution?

Of crucial importance in this question are the attempted reforms of Sergei Witte and Peter Stolypin. What makes their attempted reforms so important is that, had the tsarist government and bureaucracy been willing to support Witte and Stolypin in their efforts to modernise Russian industry and agriculture, this might have prevented the build-up of the social and political tensions that culminated in the 1917 Revolution.

'Might' is the key word here, because it is never possible to be absolutely certain how history would have developed had things occurred differently. Nevertheless, there is a strong case for suggesting that Witte and Stolypin represented the last hope that tsardom could save itself by its own efforts.

Resistance to reform

The economic policies of Witte and Stolypin and the introduction of the duma were important advances, but they were not enough to alter the essentially reactionary character of the tsarist system. The government remained hostile towards reform. The industrial spurt of the 1890s had offered an opportunity for Russia to modernise itself, but a sustained policy of modernisation required not simply economic progress but a willingness to accept political change as well. This the tsar was never willing to give. His resistance to change would have mattered less if the system had operated efficiently. But the tsarist autocracy was both oppressive and inefficient, thereby alienating the progressive elements in society, which could see no possibility of real advance in Russia as long as government and administration remained in the hands of incompetents.

It was this that undermined the work of the few enlightened ministers, such as Witte and Stolypin, within the government. They were reformers but they were also loyalists. Indeed, it was their loyalty to the system that led them to consider reform as a way of lessening the opposition to it. The irony was that they were not trusted by the representatives of the very system they were trying to preserve. It is for this reason that historians have suggested that in failing to recognise the true worth of reformers within the government, the tsarist regime unwittingly destroyed its last chance of survival.

Germany declares war on Russia: August 1914 **Key date**

By 1914, all the signs were that imperial Russia was heading towards a major confrontation between intransigent tsardom and the forces of change. It was to be the war of 1914–17 that would determine what form that conflict would take.

Some key books in the debate:
David Christian, *Imperial and Soviet Russia: Power, Privilege and the Challenge of Modernity* (Macmillan, 1997)
Anna Geifman (ed.), *Russia under the Last Tsar: Opposition and Subversion 1894–1917* (Blackwell, 1999)
Anna Geifman, *Thou Shalt Kill: Revolutionary Terrorism in Russia, 1894–1917* (Princeton University Press, 1993)
Hans Rogger, *Russia in the Age of Modernisation and Revolution* (Longman, 1983)
Ian D. Thatcher (ed.), *Late Imperial Russia: Problems and Perspectives* (Manchester University Press, 2005)

Summary diagram: Growing tensions in Russia, 1911–14

Increasing social disorder
↓
Violent extremism grows in the ranks of the revolutionaries
↓
Industrial unrest – the Lena Goldfields incident, 1912
↓
Moderates turning against the government
↓
Key issue: had imperial Russia lost its last chance of survival?

Study Guide: AS Question

In the style of OCR

'The 1905 Revolution never seriously threatened the position of the tsar or his government.' How far do you agree with this view?

(50 marks)

Exam tips

The cross-references are intended to take you straight to the material that will help you to answer the question.

The question requires an assessment of the impact of the revolutionary events of 1905. You need to consider a range of factors that will enable you to reach a balanced judgement. Focus on the term 'seriously' and decide how this can be assessed. It might be sensible to group the tsar and his government together rather than treat them separately. Arguments that agree with the assertion may include:

- the aims of the revolutionaries; did they plan to overthrow the tsar or his government? (pages 33–4)
- the rebels were politically and socially divided and the liberals and peasants readily accepted government bribes (page 39)
- Nicholas lost none of his power, and emerged stronger after the uprising (page 39–40)
- mutinies in the armed forces failed to spread and the forces rallied in defence of the tsar (page 36–7).

A counter-argument, however, is that:

- the events of 1905 were very violent and threatening (pages 34–7)
- Nicholas made several concessions, including setting up the Duma and introducing liberal reforms (page 46)
- Nicholas's image as the 'Little Father' was irrevocably damaged (page 34)
- Plehve was assassinated and Witte fell from office (although the latter was a casualty of the tsar's anger rather than the rebels' opposition) (page 34).

3 War and Revolution, 1914–17

POINTS TO CONSIDER
This chapter considers five main interlocking themes:

- the long-term reasons why Russia went to war in 1914
- the short-term reasons for war
- the effect that the war had on the internal situation in Russia
- the growth of opposition to tsardom
- the February Revolution in 1917.

There is also a concluding section that looks at the historical debate over the fall of tsardom.

Key dates
1914

June 28	Assassination of Franz Ferdinand in Bosnia
July 28	Austria-Hungary declares war on Serbia
July 30	Russian full mobilisation orders given
August 1	Germany declares war on Russia Suspension of fourth duma

1915

June–July	Fourth duma reconvened
June 25	Progressive Bloc formed in the duma
August 22	Nicholas II makes himself commander-in-chief of the Russian armies

1916

December 1	Rasputin murdered by a group of aristocrats

1917	
February 18–	
March 4	February Revolution
February 18	Strike begins at the Putilov factories in Petrograd
February 23	International Women's Day sees the beginning of widespread workers' demonstrations
February 25	City-wide strike begins in Petrograd
February 27	Unofficial meeting of duma coincides with the first meeting of the Petrograd Soviet
February 28	Nicholas II prevented from returning to Petrograd
March 2	Provisional Government formed from the duma committee
	Tsar signs abdication decree
March 4	Tsar's abdication publicly proclaimed

1 | Russia's Entry into the First World War: Long-Term Reasons

Key question
What shaped Russia's attitude towards the outside world?

As an empire covering a huge land mass, tsarist Russia had always been concerned about the security of its borders, but its greatest anxiety was in regard to its European frontiers. Russia believed that the greatest potential threat came from its neighbours in central and south-eastern Europe.

Three particular developments had occurred in Europe in the second half of the nineteenth century which alarmed Russia:

Key term

The Balkans
The area of south-eastern Europe (fringed by Austria-Hungary to the north, the Black Sea to the east, Turkey to the south and the Adriatic Sea to the west) that had largely been under Turkish control.

- The growth of a united Germany – Russia feared that the unification of Germany in 1871 had left central Europe dominated by a powerful and ambitious nation eager to expand eastwards.
- The formation of the Austro-Hungarian Empire in 1867 – Russia was concerned that Austria would build on its new strength as a joint empire by an expansionist policy in south-east Europe.
- The decline of the Ottoman (Turkish) Empire. Russia's worry was that as Turkey weakened it would be increasingly challenged by aggressive national movements seeking independence from Turkish rule. This threatened Russian interests in **the Balkans**.

Figure 3.1: Russia and its neighbouring states of Germany, Austria-Hungary and Turkey.

Two main considerations influenced Russia's attitude towards the Balkans.

- The first had a long tradition attaching to it. As a predominantly Slav nation, Russia had always regarded it as its duty to protect the Slav Christian peoples of the Balkans from oppression by their Turkish Islamic masters.
- The second was a commercial concern. Seventy-five per cent of Russia's grain exports (which accounted for 40 per cent of its total foreign trade) were shipped through the Straits of the Dardanelles. It was therefore necessary to ensure that the Straits did not come under the control of a hostile power capable of interrupting the passage of Russian ships from the Black Sea into the Mediterranean.

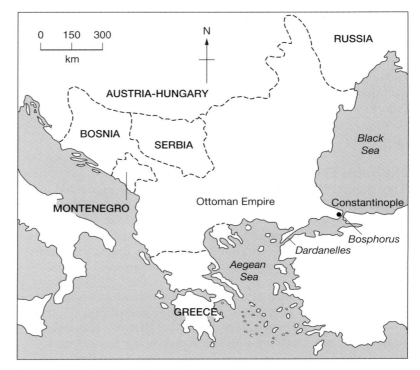

Figure 3.2: The Dardanelles and the Balkans.

Key question
What factors drew Russia away from Germany but closer to France and Britain?

Key term

Buffer state
An area that lies between two states and so provides a form of protection for each against the other.

Key figures

Otto von Bismarck (1815–98)
Creator of the new nation of Germany in the early 1870s.

William II (1859–1941)
Kaiser (emperor) of Germany from 1888 to 1918.

Russia's relations with Germany, France and Britain

In the quarter-century before 1914, Russia's response to the shifts and turns of European diplomacy was consistently defensive. Russia was reluctant to take the diplomatic initiative, but was willing to enter into alliances that protected her western borders and possessions. In particular, it was concerned that its traditional control over Poland, a **buffer state** between Russia and Germany, should not be weakened.

The unified Germany that came into being in 1871 dominated the European scene for a generation. Chancellor **Otto von Bismarck** achieved this largely by developing an alliance system. In order to encourage the European powers to make agreements with Germany, he played upon their fears of their becoming isolated. All the major powers came to accept the need for a diplomacy that guaranteed that they would not be left friendless should war threaten.

However, in 1890, Bismarck was dismissed by the new German Kaiser, **William II**. Under its new ruler, Germany adopted a more aggressive form of diplomacy that hardened international attitudes and led eventually to the splitting of Europe into two opposed armed camps. William II showed every intention of joining with Austria in asserting German influence in the Balkans and the Near East. This frightened the Russian government into looking for agreements with other powers so as to counterbalance the Austro-German threat.

The Franco-Russian Convention, 1892

To avoid isolation, Russia turned first to France. These two countries had not been on good terms, but a common fear of German aggression now outweighed their traditional dislike of each other. In the Franco-Russian Convention, signed in 1892, each partner promised to give military support to the other should it go to war with Germany. Economic co-operation also brought them closer. France was the major foreign investor in Russia's 'great spurt' in the 1890s (see page 14).

The Triple Entente, 1907

The original alliance between France and Russia expanded into a **Triple Entente** with the inclusion of Britain in 1907. This, too, was something of a diplomatic revolution. Anglo-Russian relations had been strained for decades. Imperial rivalries in Asia and Britain's resistance to what it regarded as Russia's attempts to dominate the eastern Mediterranean had aroused mutual animosity.

However, by the turn of the century Germany had embarked on an expansive naval programme that Britain interpreted as a direct threat to its own security and to its empire. Britain's response was to form an understanding with Germany's major western and eastern neighbours, France and Russia. In the Anglo-French Entente of 1904, Britain and France had already agreed to abandon their old rivalry. It made diplomatic sense for Russia and Britain to do the same.

Consequently, in 1907 they agreed to settle their past differences by recognising each other's legitimate interests in Afghanistan, Persia and Tibet. No precise agreement was reached regarding military co-operation but there was a broad, if imprecise, general understanding that such co-operation would follow in the event of war.

A key experience that had helped convince Russia of the wisdom of entering into foreign alliances had been its defeat in the 1904–5 war against Japan. This strongly suggested that Russia's plans for eastward expansion had been misplaced. It redirected Russia's attention towards the west and made the country keener still to form protective agreements with friendly European powers.

> **Triple Entente, 1907**
> Not a formal alliance, but a declared willingness by France, Britain and Russia to co-operate with each other.
>
> *Key term*

Russia's relations with Austria-Hungary

In 1908, Austria-Hungary made a startling move by annexing the Balkan states of Bosnia and Herzegovina. When Izvolski, the Russian Foreign Minister, protested, he was urged by his Austrian counterpart, Aehrenthal, to accept the takeover as a means of creating greater stability in the Balkan region. Izvolski eventually agreed, in return for Austria-Hungary's promise that it would acknowledge Russia's unrestricted right to the use of the

> **Key question**
> Why did Russia's relations with Austria-Hungary become increasingly strained?

Straits, and would persuade the other European powers to do the same. Russia kept its side of the bargain by recognising Austria-Hungary's takeover of Bosnia and Herzegovina. The Austrians, however, did not honour their promise; they made no effort to encourage the international recognition of Russian rights in the Straits.

The question of Serbia

From this time onwards, relations between Russia and Austria-Hungary steadily deteriorated. A key issue dividing them was the position of Serbia. Bosnia contained many Serbs, and its annexation by Austria-Hungary in 1908 aroused fierce Serbian nationalism. Russia, viewing itself as the special defender of Serbia and its Slav people, backed it in demanding compensation. Germany sided aggressively with Austria-Hungary and warned Russia not to interfere.

The crisis threatened for a time to spill over into war. However, in 1909 none of the countries involved felt ready to fight. Russia backed off from an open confrontation, while at the same time stating clearly that it regarded Germany and Austria-Hungary as the aggressors.

The Balkan Wars

Between 1909 and 1914, Russia continued to involve itself in the complexities of Balkan nationalist politics. The aim was to prevent Austria-Hungary from gaining a major advantage in the region. The tactic was to try to persuade the various nationalities in the region to form a coalition against Austria-Hungary. Russia had some success in this. Balkan nationalism led to a series of conflicts, known collectively as the Balkan Wars (1912–13). These were a confused mixture of anti-Turkish uprisings and squabbles between the Balkan states themselves over the division of the territories they had won from the Turks.

On balance, the outcome of these wars favoured Russian rather than Austro-Hungarian interests. Serbia had doubled in size and felt itself more closely tied to Russia as an ally and protector. However, such gains as Russia had made were marginal. The international issues relating to Turkish decline and Balkan nationalism had not been resolved. The events of 1914 were to show how vulnerable imperial Russia's status and security actually were.

Summary diagram: Russia's entry into the First World War: long-term reasons

Russia's chief concerns
- The growth of a united Germany
- The formation of the Austro-Hungarian Empire
- The decline of the Ottoman (Turkish) Empire threatened Russian interests in the Balkans where Russia saw herself as the defender of Slav nationalism

Consequences of Russia's concerns
Russia:
- draws away from Germany
- forms alliances with France and Britain
- competes with Austria-Hungary for influence in the Balkans

The Serbia question and the Balkan Wars heighten tension

Critical factors making the Balkans a flash point
Russia's:
- role as champion of Slav culture
- commercial interest in the area

---

2 | Russia's Entry into the First World War: Short-Term Reasons

None of the long-term causes made war inevitable. Their importance is that they maintained Russia's anxieties and predisposed the Russians to regard Germany and Austria-Hungary with deep suspicion. When crises occurred, therefore, they were more likely to lead to conflict. This is not to say that the tsarist government was looking for war in 1914. Russia's experience ten years earlier against Japan had made the country wary of putting itself at risk again, and Russia's foreign policy after 1905 had been essentially defensive. Russia had joined France and Britain in the Triple Entente as a means of safeguarding itself against the alliance of the **Central Powers**. However, the events that followed the assassination in June 1914 of Archduke **Franz Ferdinand** by **Serbian nationalists** made it virtually impossible for Russia to avoid being drawn into a European conflict.

A critical factor at this point was Russia's perception of itself as the protector of the Slav peoples of the Balkans. **Sazonov**, the tsar's foreign Secretary in 1914, described the link between the commitment to defend Slav nationalism in the Balkans and Russia's long-standing strategic interests. He claimed that:

> Russia's sole and unchanging object was to see that those Balkan peoples should not fall under the influence of powers hostile to her.

Key question
How was Russia drawn into war in 1914?

Central Powers
Germany, Austria-Hungary, Turkey.

Serbian nationalists
Activists struggling for Serbia's independence from Austria-Hungary.

Franz Ferdinand (1863–1914)
Heir to the Austro-Hungarian throne.

Assassination of Franz Ferdinand: 28 June 1914

Key terms

Key figure

Key date

Sergei Sazonov (1860–1927)
Russian Foreign Secretary from 1908 to 1916, disliked by conservatives in the government.

Bosphorus
The narrow waterway linking the Black Sea with the Dardanelles (see the map on page 59).

The ultimate aim of Russian policy was to obtain free access to the Mediterranean, and to be in a position to defend her Black Sea coasts against the threat of the irruption of hostile naval forces through the **Bosphorus**.

A month after Franz Ferdinand's murder, Austria-Hungary, with German encouragement, declared war on Serbia. Russia still expected to be able to force the Austrians to withdraw without itself having to go to war. Russia hoped that if it mobilised, this would act as a deterrent to Austria. This was not unrealistic. Despite Russia's defeat by Japan, its armies were still regarded as formidable. In pre-1914 Germany and Austria-Hungary, the image of Russia as a steamroller that could crush their armies was a powerful and frightening one. German generals often spoke in awe of the immense reserves of manpower on which, they believed, Russia could draw.

A British cartoon of 1914 showing Franz Joseph, the Austro-Hungarian emperor, fleeing from the chasing Russian 'steamroller'.
What influence did fear of the Russian steamroller have on the preparation of German war plans down to August 1914?

"THE STEAM-ROLLER."
Austria. "I SAY, YOU KNOW, YOU'RE EXCEEDING THE SPEED LIMIT!"

With tension building, Nicholas II made a personal move to avoid war with Germany. In July he exchanged a series of personal telegrams with his cousin, Kaiser William II, regretting the growing crisis in Russo-German relations and hoping that conflict could be avoided. But although these 'Willy–Nicky' exchanges, written in English, were friendly, there was a sense in which the two emperors were being carried along by events beyond their control.

Russia's mobilisation plans

It was at this stage that the great length of Russia's western frontier proved to be of momentous significance. The Russian military high command had two basic mobilisation schemes:

- partial – based on plans for a limited campaign in the Balkans against Austria-Hungary
- full – based on plans for a full-scale war against Germany and Austria-Hungary.

Both forms of mobilisation depended on detailed and precise railway timetabling aimed at transporting huge numbers of men and vast amounts of material. The complexity of the timetables meant that the adoption of one type of mobilisation ruled out the use of the other. Horse-drawn wagons and marching men can change direction in an instant; trains cannot. Russia's fear in July 1914 was that if it mobilised only partially, it would be left defenceless should Austria's ally Germany strike at Russia's Polish borders (see map on page 58).

On the other hand, full mobilisation might well appear to Germany as a deliberate provocation. The German government did indeed warn Sazonov that if Russia mobilised, Germany would have to do the same.

Germany's mobilisation plans

Here a vital fact intervened and made war unstoppable. Germany had no room for manoeuvre. According to German contingency plans, if Russia mobilised, Germany would have to go to war. There would no longer be a choice. The '**Schlieffen Plan**' on which German strategy was built required it. Speed was of the essence. Germany could not play a game of diplomatic bluff; it had to strike first.

When, therefore, on 30 July, after a long hesitation, Nicholas chose to sign the Russian full mobilisation order, he had taken a more fateful decision than he could have realised. What had been intended as a diplomatic move that would leave Russia free to hold back from war was the step that precipitated war. On 31 July, Germany demanded that the Russians cease their mobilisation. On 1 August, having received no response, Germany declared war on Russia. Four days later, Austria-Hungary did the same.

Key dates

Austria-Hungary declares war on Serbia: 28 July 1914

Russian full mobilisation orders given: 30 July 1914

Germany declares war on Russia: 1 August 1914

Fourth duma suspended: 1 August 1914

Key term

Schlieffen Plan Dating from 1905, the plan was aimed at eliminating the danger to Germany of a two-front war against France and Russia by a lightning knock-out blow against France first.

Summary diagram: Russia's entry into the First World War: short-term reasons	
Line-up of opposed alliances *Central Powers* *Triple Alliance* Germany Russia Austria-Hungary France Turkey Britain	**Events in Serbia** Austro-Hungarian ultimatum to Serbia following Franz Ferdinand's assassination in June 1914 resisted by Russia ↓ Germany backed Austria-Hungary ↓ The crisis did not make war unavoidable but Russian and German mobilisation plans did
Mobilisation plans **Russian** **German** Choice between Schlieffen Plan ruled partial or full that if it mobilised it mobilisation went to war	**Consequence** When tsar signed full mobilisation order, Germany had no choice but to declare war on Russia

Key question
How did Russia respond to the demands of war?

3 | Russia at War

Whatever the tsar's previous uncertainties may have been, once war was declared he became wholly committed to it. By 1917 the war would prove to be the undoing of tsardom, but in 1914 the outbreak of hostilities greatly enhanced the tsar's position. Nicholas II became the symbol of the nation's resistance in its hour of need. Watching the great crowds cheering the tsar as he formally announced that Russia was at war, the French ambassador remarked: 'To those thousands the tsar really is the autocrat, the absolute master of their bodies and souls.' At a special session of the duma, all the deputies, save for the five Bolshevik representatives, fervently pledged themselves to the national struggle.

Setback for the Bolsheviks

It was the same story in all the warring countries. The socialist parties abandoned their policies and committed themselves to the national war effort. Lenin was bitter in his condemnation of 'these class traitors'. He called on all true revolutionaries 'to transform the imperialist war everywhere into a civil war'. But the prevailing mood in Russia and Europe was all against him.

The early stages of the war were dark days for Lenin's Bolsheviks. Vilified as traitors and German agents for their opposition to the war, they were forced to flee or go into hiding. Lenin, who was already in Poland, made his way with Austrian help into neutral Switzerland. Had the war gone well for Russia, there is every reason to think that the Bolshevik Party would have disappeared as a political force.

Russia's problems

But the war did not go well for Russia, and the reason was only partly military. The basic explanation for Russia's decline and slide into revolution in 1917 was an economic one. Three years of **total war** were to prove too great a strain for the Russian economy to bear. War is a time when the character and structure of a society are put to the test in a particularly intense way. The longer the war lasts, the greater the test. During the years 1914–17, the political, social and economic institutions of Russia proved increasingly incapable of meeting the demands that war placed upon them.

This does not prove that Russia was uniquely incompetent. The pressure of total war on all countries was immense, and it should be remembered that of the six empires engaged in the First World War – Germany, Austria, Turkey, Russia, France and Britain – only the last two survived.

Differing estimates have been made of Russia's potential for growth in 1914. But however that is assessed, the fact remains that the demands of the 1914–18 war eventually proved too heavy for Russia to sustain. The impact of the war on Russia can be conveniently studied under six headings:

- inflation
- food supplies
- transport
- the army
- the role of the tsar
- morale.

Inflation

Russia had achieved remarkable financial stability by 1914. Its currency was on the gold standard (see page 15) and it had the largest gold reserves of any European country. This happy position was destroyed by the war. Between 1914 and 1917, government spending rose from 4 million roubles to 30 million. Increased taxation at home and heavy borrowing from abroad were only partially successful in raising the capital Russia needed. The gold standard was abandoned, which allowed the government to put more notes into circulation. In the short term this enabled wages to be paid and commerce to continue, but in the long term it made money practically worthless. The result was severe inflation, which became particularly acute in 1916. In broad terms, between 1914 and 1916 average earnings doubled while the price of food and fuel quadrupled (see Table 3.1).

Key term

Total war
A struggle in which a whole nation, its people, resources and institutions, is involved.

Key question
How was Russia's financial position damaged by the war?

Table 3.1: Wartime inflation

	Prices (to a base unit of 100)	Notes in circulation (to a base of 100)
July 1914	100	100
January 1915	130	146
January 1916	141	199
January 1917	398	336

Key question
How did the war
disrupt the supply of
food?

Key terms

Requisitioning
State-authorised
takeover of property
or resources.

Petrograd
For patriotic
reasons, the German
name for the capital,
St Petersburg, was
changed to the
Russian form,
Petrograd, in 1914.

Key question
Why did the Russian
transport system
prove inadequate in
wartime?

Food supplies

The **requisitioning** of horses and fertilisers by the military for the war effort made it difficult for peasants to sustain agricultural output. However, the decline in food production should not be exaggerated. It was not an immediate problem. Indeed, during the first two years of the war Russia's grain yield was higher than it had been between 1912 and 1914. It was not until 1916 that it began to fall. Part of the reason was that inflation made trading unprofitable and so the peasants stopped selling food and began hoarding their stocks.

What increased the problems for the ordinary Russian was that the army had first claim on the more limited amount of food being produced. The military also had priority in the use of the transport system. They commandeered the railways and the roads, with the result that the food supplies that were available could not be distributed easily to the civilian areas.

Hunger bordering on famine was a constant reality for much of Russia during the war years. Shortages were at their worst in the towns and cities. **Petrograd** suffered particularly badly because of its remoteness from the food-producing regions and because of the large number of refugees who swelled its population and increased the demand on its dwindling resources. By early 1917, bread rationing meant that Petrograd's inhabitants were receiving less than a quarter of the amount that had been available in 1914.

Transport

It was the disruption of the transport system rather than the decline in food production that was the major cause of Russia's wartime shortages. The growth of the railway lines, from 13,000 to 44,000 miles between 1881 and 1914 (see page 15), had been an impressive achievement, but it did not meet the demands of war. The attempt to transport millions of troops and masses of supplies to the war fronts created unbearable pressures. The signalling system on which the railway network depended broke down; blocked lines and trains stranded by engine breakdown or lack of coal became commonplace.

Less than two years after the war began, the Russian railway system had virtually collapsed. By 1916, some 575 stations were no longer capable of handling freight. A graphic example of the confusion was provided by Archangel, the northern port through which the bulk of the Allied aid to Russia passed. So great was the pile-up of undistributed goods that they sank into the ground beneath the weight of new supplies.

Elsewhere there were frequent reports of food rotting in railway trucks that could not be moved. One of the tsar's wartime prime ministers later admitted: 'There were so many trucks blocking the lines that we had to tip some of them down the embankments to move the ones that arrived later.'

By 1916, Petrograd and Moscow were receiving only a third of their food and fuel requirements. Before the war, Moscow had received an average of 2200 wagons of grain per month; by February

1917 this figure had dropped to below 700. The figures for Petrograd told a similar story; in February 1917 the capital received only 300 wagon-loads of grain instead of the 1000 it needed.

The army

A striking statistic of the First World War is that Russia, in proportion to its population, put fewer than half the troops into the field as compared with either Germany or France (see Table 3.2).

Key question
How well did the organisation of the Russian army adapt to the needs of war?

Table 3.2: Numbers and percentages of the population mobilised

	1914 (million)	1918 (million)	Total population (million)	% of population mobilised
Russia	5.3	15.3	180	8.8
Germany	3.8	14.0	68	20.5
France	3.8	7.9	39	19.9
Britain	0.6	5.7	45	12.7

Yet in total numbers the Russian army was still a mighty force. It had by far the largest army of all the countries that fought in the war. Its crippling weakness, which denied it the military advantage that its sheer size should have given it, was lack of equipment. This was not a matter of Russia's military underspending. Indeed, until 1914 Russia led Europe in the amount and the proportions it spent on defence (see Figure 3.3).

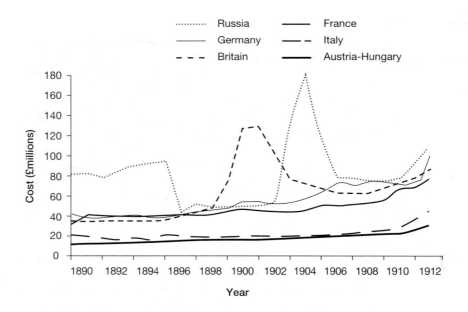

Figure 3.3: Graph showing the comparative defence expenditures of the European powers 1890–1912 (in £million).

Russia's problem was not lack of resources but poor administration and liaison between the government departments responsible for supplies. Despite its takeover of the transport system, the military was as much a victim of poor distribution as the civilian population was. In the first two years of the war the army managed to obtain its supply needs, but from 1916 serious shortages began to occur. Mikhail Rodzianko, the president of the duma, who in 1916 undertook a special fact-finding study of conditions in the army, reported to the duma on the widespread disorganisation and its dismal effects:

> General Ruzsky complained to me of lack of ammunition and the poor equipment of the men. There was a great shortage of boots. The soldiers fought barefooted. The hospitals and stations of the Red Cross, which came under my notice, were in excellent condition; but the war hospitals were disorganised. They were short of bandages and such things.
>
> The great evil was, of course, the lack of co-operation between the two organisations. At the front, one had to walk about ten or more **versts** from the war hospitals to those of the Red Cross. The Grand Duke stated that he was obliged to stop fighting, temporarily, for lack of ammunition and boots.
>
> There was plenty of material and labour in Russia. But as it stood then, one region had leather, another nails, another soles, and still another cheap labour. The best thing to do would be to call a congress of the heads of the zemstva and ask for their co-operation.

Key term

Verst
Approximately two-thirds of a mile, or just over a kilometre.

Key question
How did Nicholas II respond to the war?

The role of the tsar

The clear implication in Rodzianko's account was that the strong central leadership that the war effort desperately needed was not being provided. It was a view that became increasingly widespread, and it was against the tsar that criticisms began to mount.

This was Nicholas II's own fault; in 1915 he had formally taken over the direct command of Russia's armed services. It was a critical decision. The intention was to rally the nation around him as tsar and representative of the Russian people. But it also made him a hostage to fortune. Nicholas II was now personally responsible for Russia's performance in the war. If things went well, he would take the credit, but if they went badly, he would be to blame. Lack of success could no longer be blamed upon his appointees.

Key date

Nicholas takes personal command of the Russian army: 22 August 1915

Key question
How was Russian morale affected during the course of the war?

Morale

The suffering that the food shortages and the dislocated transport system brought to both troops and civilians might have been bearable had the news from the war front been encouraging or had there been inspired leadership from the top. There were occasional military successes, such as those achieved on the south-western front in 1916, when a Russian offensive under General Brusilov killed or wounded half a million Austrian troops and brought Austria-Hungary to the point of collapse. But the gains made were never enough to justify the appalling casualty lists.

The enthusiasm and high morale of August 1914 had turned by 1916 into pessimism and defeatism. Ill-equipped and underfed, the 'peasants in uniform' who composed the Russian army began to desert in increasing numbers.

Care should be taken not to exaggerate the effect of the breakdown in morale. Modern research, such as that undertaken by E. Mawdsley and Norman Stone, has shown that the Russian army was not on the verge of collapse in 1917. Mutinies had occurred but these were not exclusive to Russia; the strains of war in 1917 produced mutinies in all the major armies, including the French and British. Stone dismisses the idea of a disintegrating Russian army as a Bolshevik 'fabrication'. With all their problems, the Russian armies were still intact as a fighting force in 1917.

Stone also emphasises the vital role that Russia played as an ally of Britain and France in tying down the German army for over three years on the eastern front. An interesting detail, indicating how far Russia was from absolute collapse in 1916, is that in that year Russia managed to produce more shells than Germany. To quote these findings is not to deny the importance of Russia's military crises, but it is to recognise that historians have traditionally tended to overstate Russia's military weakness in 1917.

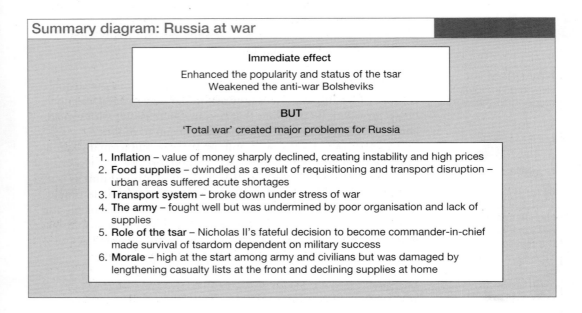

Summary diagram: Russia at war

Immediate effect

Enhanced the popularity and status of the tsar
Weakened the anti-war Bolsheviks

BUT

'Total war' created major problems for Russia

1. **Inflation** – value of money sharply declined, creating instability and high prices
2. **Food supplies** – dwindled as a result of requisitioning and transport disruption – urban areas suffered acute shortages
3. **Transport system** – broke down under stress of war
4. **The army** – fought well but was undermined by poor organisation and lack of supplies
5. **Role of the tsar** – Nicholas II's fateful decision to become commander-in-chief made survival of tsardom dependent on military success
6. **Morale** – high at the start among army and civilians but was damaged by lengthening casualty lists at the front and declining supplies at home

4 | The Growth of Opposition to Tsardom

By 1916, all important sections of the population shared the view that the tsar was an inept political and military leader, incapable of providing the inspiration that the nation needed. It is significant that the first moves in the February Revolution in 1917, the event that led to the fall of tsardom, were not made by the revolutionary parties. The Revolution was set in motion by those members of Russian society who at the outbreak of the war in 1914 had been the tsar's strongest supporters, but who by the winter of 1916 were too wearied by his incompetence to wish to save him or the barren system he represented.

The duma recalled

In August 1914 the duma had shown its total support for the tsar by voting for its own suspension for the duration of the war. But within a year, Russia's poor military showing led the duma to demand that it be recalled. Nicholas II bowed before the pressure and allowed the duma to reassemble in July 1915.

One major political mistake of the tsar and his ministers was their refusal to co-operate fully with the non-governmental organisations such as the **Union of *Zemstva*** and the **Union of Municipal Councils**, which at the beginning of the war had been wholly willing to work with the government in the national war effort. These elected bodies formed a joint organisation, *Zemgor*. The success of this organisation both highlighted the government's own failures and hinted that there might be a workable alternative to tsardom.

Formation of a 'Progressive Bloc'

A similar political blindness characterised the tsar's dismissal of the duma's urging that he replace his incompetent cabinet with 'a ministry of national confidence' with its members drawn from the duma. Nicholas's rejection of this proposal destroyed the last opportunity he would have of retaining the support of the politically progressive parties. Milyukov, the Kadet leader, complained that the tsar and his advisers had 'brushed aside the hand that was offered them'.

Denied a direct voice in national policy, 236 of the 422 duma deputies formed themselves into a 'Progressive Bloc' composed of the Kadets, the Octobrists, the Nationalists and the Party of Progressive Industrialists. The SRs did not formally join the Bloc but voted with it in all the duma resolutions criticising the government's handling of the war. Initially, the Bloc did not directly challenge the tsar's authority, but tried to persuade him to make concessions. Nicholas, however, would not budge. He was not willing to listen to the Bloc. It was part of that stubbornness that he mistook for firmness.

One of the Bloc's members, **Vasily Shulgin**, sorrowfully pointed out how short-sighted the tsar was in viewing the Bloc as an enemy, not a friend. 'The whole purpose of the Progressive Bloc was to

Key question
How did the war encourage the development of opposition to the tsar and his government?

Key dates

Duma reconvened: 19 July 1915

The Progressive Bloc formed in the duma: 25 June 1915

Key terms

Union of *Zemstva*
A set of patriotic rural local councils.

Union of Municipal Councils
A set of patriotic urban local councils.

Zemgor
The joint body that devoted itself to helping Russia's war wounded, 1914–17.

Key figure

Vasily Shulgin (1878–1976)
Originally a strong defender of tsarist rule, he became embittered by the failure of Nicholas II's wartime leadership.

prevent revolution so as to enable the government to finish the war.' The tragedy for the tsar was that as he and his government showed themselves increasingly incapable of running the war, the Bloc, from having been a supporter, became the focal point of political resistance. It was another of tsardom's lost opportunities.

Profile: Nicholas II (1868–1918)

1868 – Born into the Romanov house
1894 – Becomes tsar on the death of his father, Alexander III
    – Marries Princess Alexandra, the German granddaughter of Queen Victoria
1905 – Grants the October Manifesto (see page 38)
1906 – Opens the first duma (see page 47)
1913 – Leads the celebrations of 300 years of Romanov rule
1914 – Signs the general mobilisation order that led to Russia's entry into the First World War
1915 – Takes over personal command of the Russian armed forces
1917 – Tries to return to Petrograd but prevented by rebellious soldiers and workers
    – Advised by the military high command and duma to stand down
    – Abdicates on behalf of the Romanov dynasty
1918 – Murdered with his family in Yekaterinburg on Lenin's orders

War errors
The tsar made a number of crucial errors in his handling of the war, the most significant being his decision in 1915 to take direct command of Russia's armed forces. This in effect tied the fate of the Romanov dynasty to the success or otherwise of Russia's armies.

Nicholas's fall from power
In 1914 there had been a very genuine enthusiasm for the tsar as representative of the nation. Within three years that enthusiasm had wholly evaporated, even among dedicated tsarists. The fall of Nicholas was the result of weak leadership rather than of savage oppression. He was not helped by his wife's German nationality or by court scandals, of which Rasputin's was the most notorious (see page 74). But these were minor affairs that by themselves would not have been sufficient to bring down a dynasty.

Views of contemporaries
It is interesting to note the range of comments made about Nicholas by those who knew him personally:

'His character is the source of all our misfortunes. His outstanding weakness is a lack of willpower.' (Sergei Witte)

'The tsar can change his mind from one minute to the next; he's a sad man; he lacks guts.' (Rasputin)

'My poor Nicky's cross is heavy, all the more so as he has nobody on whom he can thoroughly rely.' (Empress Alexandra)

'His mentality and his circumstances kept him wholly out of touch with his people. From his youth he had been trained to believe that his welfare and the welfare of Russia were one and the same thing, so that "disloyal" workmen, peasants and students who were shot down, executed or exiled seemed to him mere monsters who must be destroyed for the sake of the country.' (Alexander Kerensky)

'He has a naturally good brain. But he only grasps the significance of a fact in isolation without its relationship to other facts.' (Pobedonostsev)

'He kept saying that he did not know what would become of us all, that he was wholly unfit to reign. He was wholly ignorant about governmental matters. Nicky had been trained as a soldier. He should have been taught statesmanship and he was not.' (Grand Duchess Olga, Nicholas II's sister)

The government continued to shuffle its ministers in the hope of finding a successful team. In the year 1915–16 there were four prime ministers, three Foreign Secretaries, three Ministers of Defence and six Interior Ministers. It was all to no avail. None of them was up to the task. The description by the British ambassador in Petrograd of one of the premiers, **Boris Sturmer**, might have been fairly applied to all the tsar's wartime ministers:

> Possessed of only a second-class mind, having no experience of statesmanship, concerned exclusively with his own personal interests, and distinguished by his capacity to flatter and his extreme ambition, he owed his appointment to the fact that he was a friend of Rasputin and enjoyed the support of the crowd of intriguers around the empress.

Key figure

Boris Sturmer (1848–1917)
Previously a court official, he came to hold the posts of Foreign Secretary and premier during the war.

The role of Rasputin

Gregory Efimovich **Rasputin** was the individual on whom much of the hatred of the tsarist system came to be focused. By any measure his rise to prominence in Russia was an extraordinary story, but its true significance lay in the light it shed on the nature of tsarist government.

Rasputin was a self-ordained holy man from the Russian steppes who was notorious for his sexual depravity. This made him fascinating to certain women, who threw themselves at him. Many fashionable ladies in St Petersburg, including the wives of courtiers, boasted that they had slept with him. His reluctance to wash himself or change his clothes seemed to add to the attraction he had for them. In colloquial terms, it is known as 'liking a bit of rough'.

His behaviour made him bitterly hated at the imperial court, to which he was officially invited. Outraged husbands and officials detested this upstart from the steppes. But they could not get rid of him; he enjoyed royal favour. As early as 1907, Rasputin had won himself a personal introduction to the tsar and his wife, Alexandra. The Empress Alexandra was desperate to cure her son, Alexei, the heir to the throne, of his **haemophilia**. Hearing that Rasputin had extraordinary gifts of healing, she invited him to court. Rasputin did indeed prove able to help Alexei, whose condition eased considerably when the *starets* was with him.

Rasputin did not, of course, have the magical or devilish powers that the more superstitious claimed for him, but he was a very good amateur psychologist. He realised that the pushing and prodding to which Alexei was subjected when being examined by his doctors only made the boy more anxious and feverish. Rasputin's way was to speak calmly to him, stroking his head and arms gently so that he relaxed. This lowered Alexei's temperature and eased his pain. It was not a cure, but it was the most successful treatment he had ever had. Alexandra, a deeply religious woman, believed it was the work of God and that Rasputin was His instrument. She made 'the mad monk', as his enemies called him, her **confidant**.

Scandal inevitably followed. Alexandra's German nationality had made her suspect and unpopular since the outbreak of war, but she had tried to ride out the storm. She would hear no ill of 'our dear friend', as she called Rasputin in letters to Nicholas, and obliged the tsar to maintain him at court. Since Nicholas was away at military headquarters for long periods after 1915, Alexandra and Rasputin effectively became the government of Russia. Even the staunchest supporters of tsardom found it difficult to defend a system that allowed a nation in the hour of its greatest trial to fall under the sway of **'the German woman'** and a debauched monk.

Alexandra was indeed German, having been born a princess in the house of Hesse. However, after marrying Nicholas she had made sincere efforts to make Russia her adopted country. She converted to the Orthodox Church and endeavoured to learn and apply Russian customs and conventions. This accounted for little

Key question
Why did Rasputin prove such an influential figure in the build-up to revolution?

Key figure

Gregory Efimovich Rasputin (1872–1916)
By a strange coincidence, the word rasputin can also mean 'lecher' in Russian.

Key terms

Haemophilia
A condition in which the blood does not clot, leaving the sufferer with heavy, painful bruising and internal bleeding, which can be life-threatening.

Starets
Russian for holy man, the nickname Rasputin was given by the impressionable peasants, who believed he had superhuman powers.

Confidant
A person to whom one confides intimate secrets and a special trust.

'The German woman'
The term used by anti-tsarists to suggest that Alexandra was spying for Germany.

after 1914, when, despite her undoubted commitment to the Russian cause, her enemies portrayed her as a German agent.

Rodzianko, desperate to prevent Russia sliding into political chaos and military defeat, warned the tsar that Rasputin's presence at court and influence over the government threatened disaster:

> I must tell your majesty that this cannot continue much longer. No one opens your eyes to the true role this man Rasputin is playing. His presence in Your Majesty's Court undermines confidence in the supreme power and may have an evil effect on the fate of the dynasty and turn the hearts of the people from their Emperor.

It was an appeal that went unheeded. Nicholas's long absences at military headquarters away from Petrograd after he became commander-in-chief allowed Rasputin to interfere with, if not direct, government policy. This had the result against which Rodzianko had warned. The tsar's reputation declined further and his government fell into increasing disrepute.

The death of Rasputin

In December 1916, in a mixture of spite, resentment and a genuine wish to save the monarchy, a group of aristocratic conspirators murdered Rasputin. His death was as bizarre as his life. Poisoned with arsenic, shot at point-blank range, battered over the head with a steel bar, he was still alive when he was thrown, trussed in a heavy curtain, into the River Neva. His post-mortem showed that he had water in his lungs, and so must have still been breathing when finally sucked into the icy waters.

Key date

Rasputin murdered by a group of aristocrats: 1 December 1916

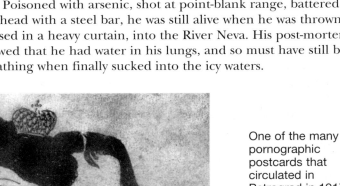

One of the many pornographic postcards that circulated in Petrograd in 1917. The Russian word on the card, 'samoderzhavie', means 'holding'. It is used here as a pun to suggest Rasputin's hold on Russia as well as his physical holding of the Empress. Despite this cartoon and all the scurrilous things said about Rasputin and Alexandra then and since, it is highly unlikely they were ever lovers in a sexual sense. There is certainly no reliable evidence for it.

Rasputin's importance

From time to time there have been various attempts to present Rasputin in a more sympathetic light, but any new evidence that appears seems to bear out the description given of him above. Where he does deserve credit is for his achievement in reorganising the army's medical supplies system. He showed the common sense and administrative skill that Russia so desperately needed and which his aristocratic superiors in government so lamentably lacked. It was his marked competence that infuriated those who wanted him out of the way.

Yet no matter how much the reactionaries in the court and government might rejoice at the death of the upstart, the truth was that by the beginning of 1917 it was too late to save tsardom. Rasputin's extraordinary life at court and his murder by courtiers were but symptoms of the fatal disease affecting the tsarist system.

Summary diagram: The growth of opposition to tsardom

- The most significant opposition comes from those who had been the tsar's keenest supporters in 1914.
- Duma recalled in July 1915 but tsar not willing to co-operate with it.
- Government also declines to work with patriotic non-government organisations, e.g. *Zemgor* who called for a united national war effort.
- Key significance of Nicholas II's character – mixture of naivety, stubbornness and political myopia – the wrong man in the wrong time.
- Tsar's ministers staggeringly incompetent.
- Tsar rejects notion of working with the Progressive Bloc.
- Tsar's limited powers of judgement blind him to the need to make an accommodation with his natural supporters.
- Another lost opportunity for tsardom.

Rasputin and Alexandra became the focal point of the growing hatred of tsardom. The very fact of Rasputin becoming so prominent within the tsarist system convinced many that the system was not worth saving.

---

5 | The February Revolution

Background to the Revolution

The rising that came in February 1917 was not the first open move against the tsar or his government. During the preceding year there had been a number of challenges. The Octobrists in the duma had frequently demanded the removal of unwanted ministers and generals. What made February 1917 different was the range of the opposition to the government and the speed with which events turned from a protest into a revolution. Rumours of the likelihood of serious public disturbances breaking out in Petrograd had been widespread since the beginning of the year.

Key question
Were the events of February 1917 a collapse at the top or a revolution from below?

February Revolution: 18 February–March 4 1917

Key date

Key date
Strike begins at the Putilov factories in Petrograd: 18 February 1917

Key terms

System of dating
Until February 1918, Russia used the Julian calendar, which was 13 days behind the Gregorian calendar, the one used in most western countries by this time.

International Women's Day
A demonstration organised by socialist groups to demand female equality: 23 February 1917.

An *Okhrana* report in January 1917 provides an illuminating summary of the situation:

> There is a marked increase in hostile feelings among the peasants not only against the government but also against all other social groups. The proletariat of the capital is on the verge of despair. The mass of industrial workers are quite ready to let themselves go to the wildest excesses of a hunger riot. The prohibition of all labour meetings, the closing of trade unions, the prosecution of men taking an active part in the sick benefit funds, the suspension of labour newspapers, and so on, make the labour masses, led by the more advanced and already revolutionary-minded elements, assume an openly hostile attitude towards the Government and protest with all the means at their disposal against the continuation of the war.

On 14 February, Rodzianko, the duma's president, in the first of a series of telegrams to the tsar, warned him that 'very serious outbreaks of unrest' were imminent. He added ominously: 'There is not one honest man left in your entourage; all the decent people have either been dismissed or left.' It was this desertion by those closest to the tsar that unwittingly set in motion what proved to be a revolution.

According to the **system of dating** in use in imperial Russia, the Revolution occupied the period from 18 February to 4 March 1917. A full-scale strike was started on 18 February by the employees at the Putilov steel works, the largest and most politically active factory in Petrograd. During the next five days the Putilov strikers were joined on the streets by growing numbers of workers, who had been angered by rumours of a further cut in bread supplies. It is now known that these were merely rumours and that there was still enough bread to meet the capital's basic needs. However, in times of acute crisis, rumour often has the same power as fact.

Key question
What steps led to Nicholas II's abdication?

Key dates
A city-wide strike begins: 25 February 1917

International Women's Day sees beginning of widespread worker's demonstrations: 23February 1917

The course of events

It so happened that 23 February was **International Women's Day**. This brought thousands of women on to the streets to join the protesters in demanding food and an end to the war. By 25 February, Petrograd was paralysed by a city-wide strike, which again had begun at the Putilov works. Factories were occupied and attempts by the authorities to disperse the workers were hampered by the growing sympathy among the police for the demonstrators.

There was a great deal of confusion and little clear direction from the top. Events that were later seen as having had major political significance took place in an atmosphere in which political protests were indistinguishable from the general outcry against food shortages and the miseries brought by war.

Some of the demonstrators at the International Women's Day. On the banner is written: 'As long as women are slaves, there will be no freedom. Long live equal rights for women.'

The breakdown of order

The tsar, at his military headquarters at Mogilev, 400 miles from Petrograd, relied for news largely on the letters received from Empress Alexandra, who was still in the capital. When he learned from her about the disturbances, Nicholas ordered the commander of the Petrograd garrison, General Khabalov, to restore order. Khabalov cabled back that, with the various contingents of the police and militia either fighting each other or joining the demonstrators, and his own garrison troops disobeying orders, the situation was uncontrollable.

Khabalov had earlier begged the government to declare martial law in Petrograd, which would have given him the power to use unlimited force against the demonstrators. But the breakdown of ordinary life in the capital meant that the martial law proclamation could not even be printed, let alone enforced. More serious still, by 26 February all but a few thousand of the original 150,000 Petrograd garrison troops had deserted. Desertions also seriously depleted a battalion of troops sent from the front under General Ivanov to reinforce the garrison.

Faced with this near-hopeless situation, Rodzianko on behalf of the duma informed the tsar that only a major concession on the government's part offered any hope of preserving the imperial power. Nicholas, again with that occasional obduracy that he showed, then ordered the duma to dissolve. It did so formally as an assembly, but a group of 12 members disobeyed the order and remained in session as a 'Provisional Committee'. This marked the first open constitutional defiance of the tsar. It was immediately followed by the boldest move so far, when Alexander Kerensky, a lawyer and a leading SR member in the duma, called for the tsar to stand down as head of state or be deposed.

Key dates

Formation of the Petrograd Soviet: 27 February 1917

Nicholas II prevented from returning to Petrograd: 28 February 1917

The duma Provisional Committee declares itself a Provisional Government: 2 March 1917

The tsar signs the abdication decree: 2 March 1917

The tsar's abdication publicly proclaimed: 4 March 1917

Key terms

De facto
A term used to denote the real situation, as compared to what it should or might be in theory or in law.

Dual authority
Lenin coined this term to describe the uneasy alliance and balance of power between the Provisional Government and the Petrograd Soviet (see page 00).

Universal suffrage
An electoral system in which all adults have the right to vote.

Stavka
The high command of the Russian army.

The Petrograd Soviet

On that same day, 27 February, another event took place that was to prove as significant as the formation of the Provisional Committee. This was the first meeting of the 'Petrograd Soviet of Soldiers', Sailors' and Workers' Deputies', which gathered in the Tauride Palace, the same building as housed the Provisional Committee. The moving force behind the setting up of the Soviet was the Mensheviks, who, under their local leader, Alexander Shlyapnikov, had grown in strength in Petrograd during the war.

These two self-appointed bodies – the Provisional Committee, representing the reformist elements of the old duma, and the soviet, speaking for the striking workers and rebellious troops – became the *de facto* government of Russia. This was the beginning of what Lenin later called the '**dual authority**', an uneasy alliance that was to last until October. On 28 February the soviet published the first edition of its newspaper, *Izvestiya* (the Times), in which it declared its determination 'to wipe out the old system completely' and to summon a constituent assembly, elected by **universal suffrage**.

The tsar abdicates

The remaining ministers in the tsar's cabinet were not prepared to face the growing storm. They used the pretext of an electricity failure in their government offices to abandon their responsibilities and to slip out of the capital. Rodzianko, who up to this point had struggled to remain loyal to the official government, then advised Nicholas that only his personal abdication could save the Russian monarchy. On 28 February, Nicholas decided to return to Petrograd, apparently in the belief that his personal presence would have a calming effect on the capital. However, the royal train was intercepted on its journey by mutinous troops, who forced it to divert to Pskov, a depot 100 miles from Petrograd.

It was at Pskov that a group of generals from *stavka*, together with the representatives of the old duma, met the tsar to inform him that the seriousness of the situation in Petrograd made his return both futile and dangerous. They, too, advised abdication.

Nicholas tamely accepted the advice. His only concern was whether he should also renounce the throne on behalf of his son, Alexei. This he eventually decided to do. The decree of abdication that Nicholas signed on 2 March nominated his brother, the Grand Duke Michael, as the new tsar. However, Michael, unwilling to take up the poisoned chalice, refused the title on the pretext that it had not been offered to him by a Russian constituent assembly.

By default, the Provisional Committee, which had renamed itself the Provisional Government, thus found itself responsible for governing Russia. On 3 March the new government officially informed the rest of the world of the revolution that had taken place.

On the following day, Nicholas II's formal abdication was publicly announced. Thus it was that the house of Romanov, which only four years earlier in 1913 had celebrated its tri-centenary as a divinely appointed dynasty, came to an end not with a bang but a whimper.

Character of the February Revolution

It is difficult to see the events of 18 February to 3 March as an overthrow of the Russian monarchy. What does stand out is the lack of direction and leadership at the top and the unwillingness at the moment of crisis of the tsarist generals and politicians to fight to save the system. Tsardom collapsed from within. Revolutionary pressure from outside had no direct effect.

Key question
Were the events of February really a revolution?

The role of the Bolsheviks

It would be more accurate to speak of the 'non-role' of the Bolsheviks. The Bolsheviks, absent from the 1905 Revolution, were also missing when the February Revolution took place. Practically all their leaders were in exile. Lenin, who was in Switzerland at the time, had not been in Russia for over a decade. With so many of the leading Bolsheviks out of the country for so long before 1917, and given the difficulties of communication created by the war, their knowledge of the situation in Petrograd in 1917 was fragmentary and unreliable.

It is small wonder, therefore, that the events of February took them by surprise. This is borne out by a statement Lenin made to a group of students in Zurich in December 1916, only two months before the February Revolution. He told his audience of youthful Bolshevik sympathisers that although they might live to see the proletarian revolution, he, at the age of 46, did not expect to do so.

The role of Petrograd

One remarkable feature of the revolution was that it had been overwhelmingly the affair of one city, Petrograd. Another was the willingness of the rest of Russia to accept it. Trotsky observed:

> It would be no exaggeration to say that Petrograd achieved the February Revolution. The rest of the country adhered to it. There was no struggle anywhere except in Petrograd. There was not to be found anywhere in the country any groups of the population, any parties, institutions, or military units which were ready to put up a fight for the old regime. Neither at the front nor at the rear was there a brigade or regiment prepared to do battle for Nicholas II.

The February Revolution was not quite the bloodless affair that some of the liberal newspapers in Petrograd claimed. Modern estimates suggest that between 1500 and 2000 people were killed or wounded in the disturbances. But by the scale of the casualties regularly suffered by Russian armies in the war this figure was small, which further supports Trotsky's contention that the nation was unwilling to fight to save the old regime.

It should be re-emphasised that it was among tsardom's hitherto most committed supporters that the earliest rejection of the tsar occurred. It was the highest-ranking officers who first intimated to Nicholas that he should stand down. It was the aristocratic members of the duma who took the lead in refusing to disband on the tsar's orders. It was when the army and the police told

Nicholas that they were unable to carry out his command to keep the populace in order that his position became finally hopeless.

The strikes and demonstrations in Petrograd in February 1917 did not in themselves cause the Revolution. It was the defection of the tsar's previous supporters at the moment of crisis, compounded by Nicholas II's own failure to resist, that brought about the fall of the Romanov dynasty.

Lenin once observed that a true revolution can occur only when certain preconditions exist; one essential is that the ruling power loses the will to survive. Some time before he formally abdicated, Nicholas had given up the fight. It was not the fact but the speed and completeness of the collapse of tsardom that was so remarkable.

Summary diagram: The February Revolution

Background

A general unrest and anger in Petrograd but this was not led or directed
↓
The Revolution began as a challenge not by revolutionaries but by traditional supporters of tsardom

Course

Strikes in major factories
↓
International Women's Day protest becomes a bread riot
↓
Disorder spreads throughout the city
↓
Police and garrison troops declare the situation uncontrollable
↓
12 rebellious duma members create the Provisional Committee
↓
Mensheviks set up the Petrograd Soviet
↓
Nicholas tries to return to Petrograd but is prevented by mutinous troops
↓
Army high command advise tsar to abdicate
↓
Nicholas tamely abdicates
↓
Dual authority becomes *de facto* government

Character

Not a revolution from below
↓
Bolsheviks played no part
↓
Revolution started by tsardom's traditional supporters
↓
A failure of leadership and nerve at the top
↓
A revolution of one city – Petrograd
↓
Not the result of a social or political movement but a consequence of war
↓
An institutional crisis?

6 | The Key Debate: Why Did the Tsarist System Collapse in February 1917?

Effect of the war

An outstanding feature of the major wars of the twentieth century was that they put immense pressures on the nations that fought them. The question arose for each of them: could their internal structures withstand the strain of war? The war that Russia entered in 1914 intensified all the problems from which it had traditionally suffered.

It is possible to argue that what destroyed tsardom was the length of the war. A short war, even if unsuccessful, might have been bearable, as Russia's defeat by Japan 12 years earlier had shown. But the cumulative effect of a prolonged struggle proved overwhelming. Deaths and casualties by the million, soaring inflation, a dislocated communications system, hunger and deprivation, all presided over by a series of increasingly bewildered and ineffectual ministries under an incompetent tsar: this was the lot of the Russian people between 1914 and 1917.

The consequence was a loss of morale and a sense of hopelessness that fatally undermined the once-potent myth of the tsar's God-given authority. By 1917 the tsarist system had forfeited its claim to the loyalty of the Russian people.

'Institutional crisis'

However, many historians now interpret the February Revolution as the climax of an 'institutional crisis' in Russia. What they mean by this is that it was not military failure that finally brought down tsardom. The wartime difficulties were certainly important but they were symptoms rather than the cause. What produced the 1917 crisis in Russia was the failure of its **institutions** to cope with the problems it faced.

While this line of thought does not absolve the tsar and his ministers from responsibility for the collapse of February 1917, it does put their failure in a more sympathetic light. If the institutions of which they were a part were inadequate to meet the challenges, then no matter what efforts they might have made, the problems would have overwhelmed them.

The doubters

The debate can be expressed as two broad lines of argument between those who might be termed the doubters and the believers respectively. The doubters argue that the February Revolution was simply the concluding sequence in the collapse of old imperial Russia, which had been tottering ever since it had failed to introduce the changes necessary for its modernisation. It had the potential for genuine growth but had failed to use it; to Russia's great loss, the conservatives had defeated the progressives. Norman Stone puts it in these terms:

Key question
Was tsardom already doomed by 1914?

Institutions
The formal structures on which a society depends, such as the government, the administrative system, the law, education, the economy.

Key term

Russia was not advanced enough to stand the strain of war, and the effort to do so plunged her economy into chaos. But economic backwardness did not alone make for revolution. The economic chaos came more from a contest between the old and the new in the Russian economy. There was a crisis, not of decline … but rather of growth.

The doubters suggest that even without the war of 1914–17, the tsarist system was already beyond recovery. Imperial Russia simply was not capable of making the adjustments necessary for it to become a modern state. It was so backward, politically and economically, that whatever efforts it made, it could not catch up with the advanced nations. Its underlying weaknesses were:

- a rapidly growing population
- urban overcrowding and poverty
- land hunger
- food shortage
- an uneducated peasantry who made up four-fifths of the nation
- an economic system that stifled initiative
- a repressive political system that, regarding all reform with suspicion, rewarded incompetence
- a government run by inept courtiers from a corrupt court headed by a weak tsar who lacked understanding of his nation's real needs
- a social system that, with its tiny middle class, its unenterprising aristocracy and undermanned workforce, was not equipped to embrace progress
- the presence within the empire of national minorities seeking independence.

One of the points stressed by the doubters is the crippling lack of leadership from which Russia suffered. Nicholas II and his ministers led the nation so ineptly that Russia was unable to use the strengths it possessed. It is true that on occasion, as under Witte and Stolypin, tsardom had dallied with reform. But too often reaction prevailed. In the end, the tsarist system showed itself unwilling to make the political adjustments needed to accommodate the social and economic changes that were occurring. It seemed to have overcome the challenge of 1905, but later events suggested this had been no more than a reprieve. Richard Pipes describes imperial Russia in 1917 as

a power that, however dazzling its external glitter, was internally weak and quite unable to cope effectively with the strains – political, economic, and psychological – which the war brought in its wake … the principal causes of the downfall in 1917 were political, and not economic or social.

The believers
While not denying the political failings of the tsarist leaders, believers suggest that Russia in 1914, far from being in irrecoverable decline, was on an upward path. They point to the fact that other

nations in other periods of history had surmounted what seemed like crippling disadvantages. An outstanding contemporary example was Japan, which, as Russia learned to its cost in 1904–5 (see pages 28–30), turned itself from a feudal to a modern society in scarcely more than a generation. It is equally possible, therefore, to argue from an optimistic angle that Russia had the potential to overcome its problems and become a modern state. A list of Russia's strengths might include:

- a growing population, which all societies need if they are to modernise successfully
- rich natural resources, such as oil, which, if fully exploited, could have earned her huge foreign revenues
- growing commercial and financial dealings with the outside world
- the great industrial spurt of the 1890s, which, despite the temporary recession that followed, showed the potential for long-term sustained economic growth
- the beginnings of a parliamentary democracy in the form of the duma.

These, of course, did not guarantee modernisation, but they did hint that, given time and stability, Russia had the means to overcome its backwardness. Arguably, therefore, it was the intrusion of the disruptive war of 1914–17 that denied Russia the time and stability it needed and created the disturbed and confused situation that resulted in the collapse of tsardom.

Reflecting on the arguments of the doubters and believers, it has to be said that whether tsardom would have survived but for the onset of war in 1914 must remain an open question. What is clear is that the war revealed both the fragility of the economic advance made since the 1890s and the weakness of the tsarist state as an organisation.

The war also finally destroyed the myth of the tsar as the protector of the Russian people. The lack of character that Nicholas II revealed when faced by the military and political crises that confronted Russia after 1914 eroded the loyalty of the people. By February 1917 not even the tsar's traditional supporters were prepared to save him. It was not the demonstrators in Petrograd but the army high command and the aristocratic members of the duma who advised him to abdicate. The February Revolution was not an overthrow of tsardom by outside forces but a collapse from within.

Some key books in the debate:

Edward Acton, *Critical Companion to the Russian Revolution* (Edward Arnold, 1990)

Edward Acton, *Rethinking the Russian Revolution* (Edward Arnold, 1990)

Orlando Figes, *A People's Tragedy: The Russian Revolution 1891–1924* (Jonathan Cape, 1996)

Anna Geifman (ed.), *Russia under the Last Tsar: Opposition and Subversion 1894–1917* (Blackwell, 1999)

Richard Pipes, *The Russian Revolution 1899–1919* (Collins Harvill, 1990)

Richard Pipes, *Three Whys of the Russian Revolution* (Pimlico, 1998)

Norman Stone, *The Eastern Front, 1914–1917* (Penguin, 1998)

Ian D. Thatcher (ed.), *Late Imperial Russia: Problems and Perspectives* (Manchester University Press, 2005)

Dimitri Volkogonov, *The Rise and Fall of the Soviet Empire* (HarperCollins, 1998)

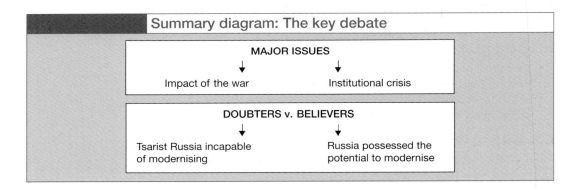

Summary diagram: The key debate

MAJOR ISSUES

Impact of the war   Institutional crisis

DOUBTERS v. BELIEVERS

Tsarist Russia incapable of modernising   Russia possessed the potential to modernise

Study Guide: AS Question

In the style of OCR

Assess the reasons for the outbreak of revolution in February 1917.

(50 marks)

Exam tips

The cross-references are intended to take you straight to the material that will help you to answer the question.

In this question, try to avoid giving a list of reasons. Instead, you should explain how a revolution occurred by linking different factors together, establishing a hierarchy, and perhaps distinguishing between short- and long-term causes. Some of the arguments you might include are:

- the effects of the First World War – economic, social and political; the failure of Nicholas as commander-in-chief and of his generals and politicians to defend tsarism in 1917 (pages 65–70, 82)
- institutional paralysis – arguments for and against (pages 82–3, 83–4)
- Nicholas's decision to abdicate under pressure from opposition groups (pages 71–2, 76–8, 79)
- the role of government and palace officials, e.g. Alexandra, Rasputin and Sturmer (pages 73–6)
- industrial action by Petrograd workers, especially the Putilov factory (pages 76–8).

1917: The October Revolution

Key dates

1917

March 2	Formation of the Provisional Government
March 12	Stalin and Kamenev arrive in Petrograd
March 14	The Petrograd Soviet issues its 'Address to the people of the whole world'
April 3	Lenin returns to Petrograd
April 4	Lenin issues his *April Theses*
April 20	Bolshevik Red Guards formed
May 10	Trotsky returned to Russia
June 16	Start of Russian offensive against Austria
June 29	Lenin fled to Finland
July 3–6	Failure of the 'July Days' Bolshevik uprising
July 4	Lenin returned to Petrograd
July 8	Kerensky becomes Prime Minister
July 18	Kornilov becomes commander-in-chief
August 30	Provisional Government released Bolsheviks held since July days

September 1	Kornilov march on Petrograd abandoned
September 25	The Bolsheviks gain a majority in the Petrograd Soviet
October 9	The Petrograd Soviet sets up the Military Revolutionary Committee
October 20	MRC deploys armed units in and around Petrograd
October 23	Kerensky moves against the Bolsheviks by attempting to close down *Pravda* and *Izvestiya*
October 23	Lenin instructs the Bolsheviks to begin the rising against Kerensky's government
October 25	First session of the All-Russian Congress of Soviets
	Lenin declared Provisional Government was deposed
October 24–25	Bolsheviks take control of Petrograd
October 25–26	Kerensky flees Petrograd
	Bolsheviks seize the Winter Palace
October 26	Bolsheviks establish *Sovnarkom*
	Congress of Soviets passed Lenin's decrees on land and peace
October 27	Lenin claims power in the name of Congress of Soviets

1 | The Dual Authority

The Provisional Government, led by **Prince Lvov**, which picked up the reins of authority after the tsar's abdication, was really the old duma in a new form. When Paul Milyukov, the Foreign Minister, read out the list of ministers in the newly formed government, someone in the listening crowd called out: 'Who appointed you lot, then?' Milyukov replied: 'We were appointed by the Revolution itself.'

In that exchange were expressed the two crippling weaknesses of the Provisional Government throughout the eight months of its existence:

- It was not an elected body, having come into being as a rebellious committee of the old duma, refusing to disband at the tsar's order. As a consequence, it lacked legitimate authority and had no constitutional claim upon the loyalty of the Russian people. Lacking a natural fund of goodwill, it would be judged entirely on how well it dealt with the nation's problems.
- Its authority was limited by its unofficial partnership with the Petrograd Soviet. It was not that the Soviet was initially hostile. Indeed, at first, there was considerable co-operation between them.

Key question
Was the Provisional Government fatally weakened from the first?

Prince Lvov (1861–1925)
A large landowner and progressive reformer, he headed the Provisional Government from March to July 1917.

Key figure

Key figure

Alexander Kerensky (1881–1970)
A lawyer and leading member of the SR party, he was to be Prime Minister of the Provisional Government from July until its fall in October 1917.

Some individuals were members of both bodies. For example, **Alexander Kerensky**, the SR leader, was for a time chairman of the Soviet as well as a minister in the Provisional Government.

Role of the Petrograd Soviet

The Soviet did not set out to be an alternative government. It regarded its role as supervisory, checking that the interests of the soldiers and workers were fully understood by the new government. However, in the uncertain times that followed the February Revolution, the Provisional Government often seemed unsure of its own authority. This uncertainty tended to give the Soviet greater prominence.

There was also the impressive fact that in the aftermath of the February Revolution, Soviets were rapidly set up in all the major cities and towns of Russia. Yet although the Soviets were to play an increasingly important role in the development of the Revolution, in the early stages the Bolsheviks did not dominate them. They were not, therefore, necessarily opposed to the Provisional Government. It was significant, however, that even before the Bolshevik influence became predominant, the ability of the Petrograd Soviet to restrict the Provisional Government's authority had been clearly revealed. In one of its first moves as an organisation it had issued its 'Soviet Order Number 1', which read:

> The orders of the military commission of the state duma are to be obeyed only in such instances as they do not contradict the orders and decrees of the Soviet.

An overflowing meeting of the Petrograd Soviet in March 1917. Huge numbers of soldiers and workers, sometimes as many as 3000, attended the early meetings. By the autumn this had dropped to a few hundred but the Bolsheviks kept up their numbers, which gave them a disproportionate influence in the Soviet. Why was the presence of the Bolsheviks in the meetings of the Petrograd Soviet so politically important between March and October 1917?

Importance of the Order

What the Order meant was that the decrees of the Provisional Government in regard to military affairs were binding only if they were approved by the Petrograd Soviet. History shows that unless a government has control of its army, it does not hold real power. Order Number 1 made it clear that the Provisional Government did not have such power. It therefore had to compromise with the Soviet. Between February and April 1917 this arrangement worked reasonably well; there were no serious disputes between the two bodies in the 'dual authority'.

Early political co-operation

An important factor that helped lessen party differences was the widespread elation in Petrograd in the weeks following the February Revolution. There was an excitement in the air; people on the streets greeted each other enthusiastically as if a new era had dawned. This encouraged a genuine feeling across all the political groups that Russia had entered a period of real freedom. For a time, co-operation between opposing parties became much easier to achieve.

There was also a general acceptance that the new liberty that had come with the collapse of tsardom should not be allowed to slip into **anarchy**. This created a willingness to maintain state authority at the centre of affairs. Furthermore, at the beginning, both the Provisional Government and the Soviet contained a wider range of political representation than was the case later. Moderate socialists had a bigger influence than the Social Revolutionaries (SRs) or Social Democrats (SDs) in the first meetings of the Soviet, while all parties, apart from the Bolsheviks and the **monarchists**, were represented in the Provisional Government during its early weeks. As the year wore on and the problems mounted, the Provisional Government moved increasingly to the right and the Soviet increasingly to the left. But before that shift occurred there had been considerable harmony.

Early achievements of the Provisional Government

The fruits of this harmony were shown in a set of progressive measures adopted by the Provisional Government:

- an amnesty for political prisoners
- trade unions legally recognised
- an eight-hour day for industrial workers
- replacement of the tsarist police with a '**people's militia**'
- granting of full civil and religious freedoms
- preparations made for the election of a constituent assembly.

Noticeably, however, these changes did not touch on the critical issues of the war and the land. It would be these that would destroy the always tenuous partnership of the dual authority, and it would be Lenin who would begin the process of destruction.

Key question
Why was there so little political conflict in the period immediately after the February Revolution?

Key terms

Anarchy
Absence of government or authority, leading to disorder.

Monarchists
Reactionaries who wanted a restoration of tsardom.

People's militia
Volunteer law-enforcement officers drawn from ordinary people.

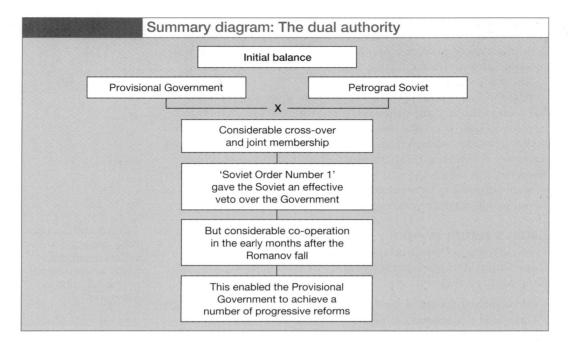

Summary diagram: The dual authority

Initial balance

Provisional Government — Petrograd Soviet

X

Considerable cross-over and joint membership

'Soviet Order Number 1' gave the Soviet an effective veto over the Government

But considerable co-operation in the early months after the Romanov fall

This enabled the Provisional Government to achieve a number of progressive reforms

2 | The Bolsheviks Return

The impact of Stalin and Kamenev

Key question
What did Stalin and Kamenev think Bolshevik policy should be after the February Revolution?

Once the exiled Bolsheviks learned of Nicholas's abdication, they rushed back to Petrograd. Those who, like Stalin, had been in Siberia were the first to return in March. Stalin's return was significant. Because of their standing in the Party, he and his fellow returnee **Lev Kamenev** became the leading voices among the Petrograd Bolsheviks. Initially this duo took an anti-Lenin line. Lenin, who did not reach Petrograd until nearly a month later, still tried to direct things from exile. In his *Letters from Afar* he urged that the war that Russia was fighting should be turned into a class war; Bolsheviks should infiltrate the armies of the warring nations and encourage the soldiers to turn their weapons against their officers as the first step towards overthrowing their governments. Lenin also instructed the Bolsheviks not to co-operate with the Provisional Government or with the other parties.

Key figure

Lev Kamenev (1883–1936)
Was to hold various key positions under Lenin between 1917 and 1924.

Stalin and Kamenev ignored Lenin's instructions. On the war issue, they argued that the best policy was to press for international negotiations to be started. Stalin wrote to the Bolsheviks in Petrograd telling them to 'put pressure on the Provisional Government to announce its willingness to start peace talks at once'.

On the question of the Bolsheviks' relations with the Provisional Government, Kamenev insisted that circumstances made co-operation with it essential, at least for the time being,

Key date

Stalin and Kamenev arrive in Petrograd: 12 March 1917

since it was 'genuinely struggling against the remnants of the old regime'. As to the other parties, Kamenev believed co-operation with them made perfect sense. He backed a proposal that it was 'possible and desirable' for the Bolsheviks to consider linking again with the Mensheviks.

Clearly, at this juncture there was a wide divergence of view between Lenin and the other two men. Interestingly, Kamenev appears to have been the dominant partner in his relations with Stalin, who later admitted that in the period before Lenin arrived, Kamenev dominated Bolshevik discussions in Petrograd. What Kamenev was advancing and what Stalin went along with was what is often referred to as **accommodationism**. It was an approach that Lenin would totally reject once he was back in Petrograd.

Lenin's return in April

Lenin arrived in Petrograd on 3 April. The manner of his return from Switzerland is a remarkable story in itself. His wife, Krupskaya, recorded it:

> The moment the news of the February Revolution was received, Ilyich [Lenin] was all eagerness to get back to Russia. As there were no legal ways of travelling, illegal ways would have to be used. But what ways? From the moment the news of the Revolution was received, Ilyich had no sleep. His nights were spent building the most improbable plans. Naturally the Germans gave us permission to travel through Germany in the belief that Revolution was a disaster to a country, and that by allowing **emigrant internationalists** to return to their country they were helping to spread the Revolution in Russia. The Bolsheviks, for their part, considered it their duty to bring about a victorious proletarian revolution. They did not care what the German bourgeois government thought about it.

Krupskaya's account was wholly accurate. In the hope that the tsar's fall would be the prelude to the collapse of the Russian armies, the German government arranged for Lenin to return to Russia in a sealed train across occupied Europe. Norman Stone has waggishly referred to it as 'the first no-smoking train in history', Lenin being a fanatical anti-smoker.

Was Lenin a German agent?

Since the outbreak of war in 1914, Lenin's opponents had continually accused him of being in the pay of the German government. Their charge had weight. Between 1914 and 1917 the German Foreign Office had given regular financial support to Lenin and the Bolsheviks, in the hope that if they achieved their revolutionary aims they would pull Russia out of the war. As Krupskaya observed, Lenin did not really care what the attitude of the Germans was. It just so happened that, for quite different reasons, what they wanted – the withdrawal of the Russian armies from the war – was precisely what he wanted. However, it made no difference to anti-Bolsheviks that the German reasons were military

Key question
What impact did Lenin's return have on the situation in Petrograd?

Key date

Lenin arrives in Petrograd: 3 April 1917

Key terms

Accommodationism The idea that the Bolsheviks should accept the situation that followed the February Revolution in 1917 and co-operate with the Provisional Government, and work with the other revolutionary and reforming parties.

Emigrant internationalists Russian revolutionaries living in exile.

and Lenin's were political. They considered the German government and the Bolshevik Party to be co-operating in a common cause, the defeat of Russia.

Lenin's impact

There is no doubting the great significance of Lenin's return to Petrograd in April 1917. Before then, the Bolsheviks, led by Kamenev and Stalin, had accepted the formation of the dual authority as part of a genuine revolution. They had been willing to work with the other reformist parties. Lenin changed all that. In his speech on his arrival at Petrograd's Finland Station on 3 April, he declared that the events of February, far from giving Russia political freedom, had created a '**parliamentary-bourgeois republic**'. He condemned the Provisional Government and called for its overthrow in a genuine revolution.

The *April Theses*

The following day he issued his *April Theses*, in which he spelt out future Bolshevik policy. To the bewilderment of those Bolsheviks who had been in Petrograd since February and expected to be praised for their efforts in working with the other revolutionary groups, Lenin condemned all that had happened since the fall of the tsar. He insisted that since the Bolsheviks were the only truly revolutionary proletarian party, they must:

- abandon all co-operation with other parties
- work for a true revolution entirely by their own efforts
- overthrow the Provisional Government, which was simply the old, class-ridden duma in a new garb
- struggle, not to extend freedom to all classes, but to transfer power to the workers
- demand that authority pass to the soviets.

Lenin had ulterior motives in demanding the soviets take over government. Although he rejected much of what they had done, he saw the soviets as a power base. In practice they had become an essential part of the structure of post-tsarist government. Lenin calculated that the soviets – the Petrograd Soviet in particular – offered his small Bolshevik Party the means by which it could obtain power in the name of the proletariat. If it could infiltrate and dominate the soviets, the Bolshevik Party would be in a position to take over the state.

The essence of Lenin's argument was summed up in two provocative Bolshevik slogans that he coined: 'Peace, Bread and Land' and 'All Power to the Soviets'. But these were more than slogans. They were Lenin's way of presenting in simple, dramatic headings the basic problems confronting Russia:

- 'Peace' – the continuing war with Germany
- 'Bread' – the chronic food shortage
- 'Land' – the disruption in the countryside.

He asserted that, as long as the Provisional Government stayed in power, these problems could not be solved, because the ministers

Key term

Parliamentary-bourgeois republic Lenin's contemptuous term for the Provisional Government, which he dismissed as an unrepresentative mockery that had simply replaced the feudal control of the tsar with the bourgeois control of the old duma.

Key date

Lenin issues his *April Theses*: 4 April 1917

governed only in the interests of their own class. They had no wish to end the war, which brought them profits, or supply food to the Russian people, whom they despised, or reform the landholding system, which guaranteed their property rights and privileges. That is why Lenin wanted 'All Power to the Soviets'. The current ministers must be swept aside and replaced with a government of the soviets. Only then would the people's needs be addressed.

Lenin's analysis was shrewd and prophetic. The Provisional Government's failure to deal with the three principal issues he had identified would lead to its eventual downfall.

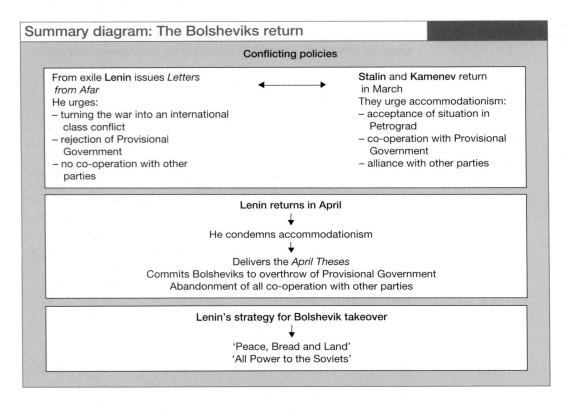

Summary diagram: The Bolsheviks return

Conflicting policies

From exile **Lenin** issues *Letters from Afar*
He urges:
– turning the war into an international class conflict
– rejection of Provisional Government
– no co-operation with other parties

Stalin and **Kamenev** return in March
They urge accommodationism:
– acceptance of situation in Petrograd
– co-operation with Provisional Government
– alliance with other parties

Lenin returns in April
↓
He condemns accommodationism
↓
Delivers the *April Theses*
Commits Bolsheviks to overthrow of Provisional Government
Abandonment of all co-operation with other parties

Lenin's strategy for Bolshevik takeover
↓
'Peace, Bread and Land'
'All Power to the Soviets'

3 | The Provisional Government and Its Problems

The war

From the outset, the Provisional Government was in a troubled position. The main problem was the war. For the Provisional Government after February 1917 there was no choice but to fight on. The reason was not idealistic but financial. Unless it did so, it would no longer receive the supplies and **war credits** from the western allies on which it had come to rely. Tsardom had left Russia virtually bankrupt. No government could have carried on without large injections of capital from abroad. Foreign bankers were among the first to visit Russia after Nicholas's abdication to ensure that the new regime would carry on the war.

Key question
What difficulties beset the Provisional Government?

War credits
Money loaned on easy repayment terms to Russia to finance its war effort.

Key term

The strain that this obligation imposed on the Provisional Government finally proved unsustainable. Its preoccupation with the war prevented the government from dealing with Russia's social and economic problems. It was a paradoxical situation: in order to survive, the Provisional Government had to keep Russia in the war, but in doing so it destroyed its own chances of survival.

Government crisis

The question of the war brought about the first serious rift between the Petrograd Soviet and the Provisional Government. On 14 March the Soviet had issued an 'Address to the people of the whole world', calling for 'peace without annexations or **indemnities**'. The government declared that it accepted the address, but this appeared meaningless when it became known that Milyukov, the Foreign Minister, had made a pledge to the Allies that Russia would fight on until Germany was defeated.

Late in April, a series of violent demonstrations directed against Milyukov occurred in Petrograd. These produced a government crisis. Milyukov and Guchkov, the War Minister, resigned early in May. These resignations were an illustration of the divisions within the government as well as of the outside pressures on it. In the reshuffled cabinet, Alexander Kerensky become the War Minister and places were found for leading Mensheviks and SRs.

It was hoped that this apparent leftward shift of the Provisional Government would ease its relationship with the Soviet. But the opposite happened. The socialists in the government tended to become isolated from the Soviet. This was because in joining the government they had to enter into coalition with the Kadets (see page 109), which opened them to the charge that they were compromising with the bourgeoisie. Lenin wrote of 'those despicable socialists who have sold out to the Government'.

The emergence of Kerensky

Some individuals within the Provisional Government had misgivings about continuing the war, but at no time did the government as a body contemplate withdrawing from it. This would have mattered less had the Russian armies been successful, but the military situation continued to deteriorate, eroding the support the government had initially enjoyed.

Lvov stayed as nominal head of the government but it was Kerensky who became the major influence. As War Minister, he campaigned for Russia to embrace the conflict with Germany as a struggle to save the Revolution, requiring the total dedication of the nation. He made a number of personal visits to the front to deliver passionate speeches to the troops. He later described his efforts:

> For the sake of the nation's life it was necessary to restore the army's will to die. 'Forward to the battle for freedom. I summon you not to a feast but death.' These were the words I used before the troops in the front-line positions.

Key term

Indemnities
Payment of war costs demanded by the victors from the defeated.

Key date

'Address to the people of the whole world' issued by the Petrograd Soviet: 14 March 1917

The government's troubles increase

The attempt to turn the war into a revolutionary crusade took no account of the real situation. The truth was that Russia had gone beyond the point where it could fight a successful war. Yet Kerensky persisted. In June a major offensive was launched on the south-western front. It failed badly. With their already low morale further weakened by Bolshevik agitators who encouraged them to disobey orders, the Russian forces were no match for the Austrians, who easily repulsed them and inflicted heavy losses. Whole Russian regiments mutinied or deserted.

General Kornilov, the commander on the south-western front, called on the Provisional Government to halt the offensive and direct its energies to crushing the **political subversives** at home. This appeal for a tougher policy was taken up by the government. Early in July, Lvov stood down as Prime Minister, to be replaced by Kerensky. Kornilov became commander-in-chief.

The government's troubles were deepened by events on the island of Kronstadt, the naval base situated 15 miles west of Petrograd in the Bay of Finland. Sailors and workers there defied the central authorities by setting up their own separate government. Such developments tempted a number of revolutionaries in Petrograd into thinking that the opportunity had come for them to bring down the Provisional Government. The attempt to do so became known as 'the July Days'.

The July Days

By the summer of 1917 it did indeed seem that the government was no longer in control of events. The most ominous signs were:

- the spread of soviets
- worker control of the factories
- widespread seizure of land by the peasants
- the creation of breakaway **national minority governments** – most notably in Ukraine.

It was the Ukrainian question that helped to provoke the July Days crisis. When the Kadet ministers in the government learned in late June that a Provisional Government deputation in Kiev (the Ukrainian capital) had offered independence to Ukraine, they resigned, protesting that only an all-Russian constituent assembly could properly decide such matters.

This ministerial clash coincided with large-scale street demonstrations in Petrograd. Public protests were not uncommon; they had been almost a daily occurrence since February. But in the atmosphere created by the news of the failure of the south-western offensive and the government's mounting problems, the demonstrations of early July turned into a direct challenge to the Provisional Government.

The rising itself was a confused, disorderly affair. In the course of the three days the demonstrators fell out among themselves; those members of the Soviet who seemed reluctant to make a real bid for power were physically attacked. The disunity made it

Key figure

General Kornilov (1870–1918)
Distinguished by his bravery as a soldier, he was a fierce patriot who hated Russia's revolutionaries.

Key term

Political subversives
The SDs and SRs, as seen by the opponents of the revolutionaries.

◄ **Key question**
How were the Bolsheviks able to survive their failure in the July Days?

Key term

National minority governments
A number of Russia's ethnic peoples exploited the Provisional Government's difficulties by setting up their own governments and claiming independence of central control.

Key date

The abortive 'July Days' rising: 3–6 July 1917

Key term

All-Russian Congress of Soviets
A gathering of representatives from all the soviets formed in Russia between February and October 1917.

Key figure

Nikolai Chkheidze (1864–1926)
The Menshevik chairman of the Petrograd Soviet.

relatively easy for the Provisional Government to crush the rising. Troops loyal to the government were rushed from the front. They duly scattered the demonstrators and restored order.

It is not entirely clear who started the rising of 3–6 July. A month before, at the first **All-Russian Congress of Soviets**, Lenin had declared that the Bolshevik Party was ready to take power, but the delegates had regarded this as a general intention rather than a specific plan. There were also a number of SRs and other non-Bolshevik revolutionaries in the Soviet who, for some time, had been demanding that the Petrograd Soviet take over from the Provisional Government.

Trotsky later referred to the July Days as a 'semi-insurrection' and argued that it had been begun by the Mensheviks and SRs. In saying this, he was trying to absolve the Bolsheviks from the blame for having started a rising that failed. The explanation offered afterwards by the Bolsheviks was that they had come heroically to the aid of the workers of Petrograd and their comrades-in-arms, the sailors of Kronstadt, who had risen spontaneously against the government.

The opposite point of view was put at the time by **Nikolai Chkheidze**. He argued that the Bolsheviks, having been behind the rising from the beginning, later tried to disclaim responsibility for its failure.

Anti-government protesters scattering under rifle-fire during the suppression of the July Days. How were the Bolsheviks able to survive their failure in the July Days?

Consequences of the rising

While the origins of the July Days may have been uncertain, the results were not. The failed rising revealed a number of important facts:

- The opposition movement was disunited.
- The Bolsheviks were still far from being the dominant revolutionary party.
- The Provisional Government still had the strength to be able to put down an armed insurrection.

This last revelation did much to raise the spirits of the Provisional Government and brought particular credit to Kerensky as War Minister. Two days after the rising had been crushed, he became Prime Minister. He immediately turned the heat on the Bolsheviks. *Pravda* was closed down and many of the Bolshevik leaders, including Trotsky and Kamenev, were arrested. Lenin fled to Finland.

Kerensky also launched a propaganda campaign in which Lenin and his party were branded as traitors and agents in the pay of the German high command. A fortnight after the July Days the Bolshevik Party appeared to have been broken as a political force in Russia. What enabled the Bolsheviks to survive, as the next two sections show, was the critical misjudgements by the Provisional Government over the land question (see page 99) and the Kornilov Affair (see page 100).

Key date

Kerensky becomes Prime Minister: 8 July 1917

Photo of Lenin, clean-shaven and be-wigged, in hiding in Petrograd 1917. Throughout the period April–October 1917, Lenin went in constant fear of being arrested and executed by the Provisional Government. He adopted various disguises, kept continually on the move and frequently fled to Finland. Yet, oddly, as Kerensky later regretfully admitted, the authorities made little concerted effort to capture their chief opponent. This raises the interesting question whether Lenin exaggerated, or the government underestimated, his powers of disruption (see page 111).

Key question
Why was the government unable to develop an effective land policy?

The land question

The Provisional Government had misread the public attitude towards the war. It similarly failed to appreciate the common view on the land question. Land shortage was a chronic problem in Russia. It had been a chief cause of peasant unrest since the emancipation of the serfs in 1861 (see page 7). The February Revolution had led the peasants to believe that they would soon benefit from a major land redistribution following a government takeover of the landowners' estates.

When the government failed to carry out such a redistribution, the peasants in many parts of Russia took the law into their own hands and seized the property of local landlords. Disturbances in the countryside occurred daily throughout 1917. It would be appropriate to describe this as a national peasants' revolt.

The Provisional Government had no real answer to the land problem. While it was true that it had set up a Land Commission with the object of redistributing land, this body made little progress in handling a massive task. It is doubtful, moreover, whether the government's heart was ever really in land reform. The majority of its members came from the landed and propertied classes. They were unlikely to be enthusiasts for a policy that would threaten their own position. They had supported the February Revolution as a political change, not as a social upheaval. They were quite willing for the estates of the fallen monarchy to go to the peasants, but they had no intention of losing their own possessions in a state land grab. This had been the strength of Lenin's assertion in the *April Theses* that tsardom had been replaced not by a revolutionary but by a bourgeois regime.

The Bolshevik position on the land question

Interestingly, the land issue was equally difficult for the Bolsheviks. They simply did not have a land policy. As a Marxist party they had dismissed the peasantry as, in Trotsky's words, 'the packhorse' of history, lacking true revolutionary initiative. By definition, the proletarian revolution was an affair of the industrial working class. Lenin, on his return in April, had declared that it would be pointless for the Bolsheviks, the party of the workers, to make an alliance with the backward peasantry.

However, faced with the fact of peasant land seizures throughout Russia, Lenin was quite prepared to make a tactical adjustment. Appreciating that it was impossible to ignore the disruptive behaviour of four-fifths of the Russian population, he asserted that the special circumstances of post-tsarist Russia had produced a situation in which the peasants were acting as a truly revolutionary force. This adaptation of Marxist theory thus allowed Lenin to add the Russian peasants to the proletarian cause.

Lacking a land policy of his own, Lenin simply stole one from the SRs. 'Land to the Peasants', a slogan lifted straight from the SR programme, became the new Bolshevik catchphrase. What this meant in mid-1917 was that the Bolsheviks recognised the peasants' land seizures as perfectly legitimate. This produced a considerable swing to the Bolsheviks in the countryside. It had the further effect of splitting the SRs, a significant number of whom began to align themselves with the Bolsheviks. Known as Left SRs, they sided with the Bolshevik Party on all major issues.

The Kornilov Affair

In August, Kerensky's government became involved in the Kornilov Affair, a crisis that undermined the gains it had made from its handling of the July Days and allowed the Bolsheviks to recover from their humiliation. Parts of the story have been obscured by the conflicting descriptions later given by some of the participants, but there was little doubt as to the intentions of the chief figure in the episode, General Kornilov, the new commander-in-chief.

Kornilov was the type of right-wing army officer who had never accepted the February Revolution. He believed that before Russia could fulfil its patriotic duty of defeating Germany, it must first destroy the socialist enemies within. 'It's time', he said, 'to hang the German supporters and spies, with Lenin at their head, and to disperse the Soviet.' By late August the advance of German forces deeper into Russia began to threaten Petrograd itself. Large numbers of refugees and deserters flocked into the city, heightening the tension there and increasing the disorder. Kornilov declared that Russia was about to topple into anarchy and that the government stood in grave danger of a socialist-inspired insurrection. He informed Kerensky that he intended to bring his loyal troops to Petrograd to save the Provisional Government from being overthrown.

Accounts tend to diverge at this point in their description of Kerensky's response. Those who believe that he was involved in a plot with Kornilov to destroy the Soviet and set up a dictatorship argue that Kerensky had at first fully supported this move. It was only afterwards, when he realised that Kornilov also intended to remove the Provisional Government and impose military rule, that he turned against him.

Other commentators, sympathetic to Kerensky, maintain that he had not plotted with Kornilov and that his actions had been wholly consistent. They also emphasise that a special Commission of Enquiry into the affair in 1917 cleared Kerensky of any complicity. But however the question of collusion is decided, it is certainly the case that Kerensky publicly condemned Kornilov's advance. He ordered him to surrender his post and placed Petrograd under martial law. Kornilov reacted by sending an open telegram, declaring:

> People of Russia! Our great motherland is dying. I, General Kornilov, declare that under pressure of the Bolshevik majority in the Soviets, the Provisional Government is acting in complete accord with the plans of the German General Staff. It is destroying the army and is undermining the very foundations of the country.

Key question
How real a threat was the Kornilov Affair to the Provisional Government?

Kornilov becomes commander-in-chief: 18 July 1917

Key date

Kerensky addressing Russian forces in May 1917. In what ways did Kerensky's commitment to the war weaken the Provisional Government?

Kerensky's response

Fearful that Kornilov would attack, Kerensky called on all loyal citizens to take up arms to defend the city. The Bolsheviks were released from prison or came out of hiding to collect the weapons issued by the Provisional Government to all who were willing to fight. By this strange twist in the story of 1917, the Bolsheviks found themselves being given arms by the very government they were pledged to overthrow.

As it happened, the weapons were not needed against Kornilov. The railway workers refused to operate the trains to bring Kornilov's army to Petrograd. When he learned of this and of a mass workers' militia formed to oppose him, Kornilov abandoned the advance and allowed himself to be arrested. He was to die early in April 1918, killed by a stray shell at the start of the Civil War (see page 127).

Key date

Kornilov abandons march on Petrograd: 1 September 1917

Bolshevik gains

It was the Bolsheviks who benefited most from the failure of the attempted coup. They had been able to present themselves as defenders of Petrograd and the Revolution, thus diverting attention away from their failure in the July Days. What further boosted the Bolsheviks was that despite the obvious readiness of the people of Petrograd to defend their city, this could not be read as a sign of their belief in the Provisional Government. Indeed, the episode had damaged the Provisional Government by revealing its political weakness and showing how vulnerable it was to military threat. Kerensky later admitted that the Kornilov Affair had been 'the prelude to the October Revolution'.

Summary diagram: The Provisional Government and its problems

The war
- Government obliged to continue the war in order to maintain loans from the Allies
- Caused first serious split between Soviet and Provisional Government
- Prevented resources being spent on other needs
- Kerensky emerges as committed supporter of the war

National minorities question
Caused ministerial crisis which led to ...
... The July Days
which saw near-extinction of Bolsheviks

The land question
- Provisional Government not genuinely committed to land reform
- Enabled Bolsheviks to steal a march and gain peasant support

The Kornilov Affair
- Provisional Government survived but gravely weakened
- Bolsheviks begin recovery
- The prelude to the October Revolution

---

4 | The October Revolution
The political shift in Petrograd

The measure of the Bolsheviks' recovery from the July Days and of their gains from the Kornilov Affair was soon apparent. By the middle of September they had gained a majority in both the Petrograd and the Moscow soviets. However, this should not be seen as indicating a large swing of opinion in their favour; rather, it was a reflection of the changing character of the soviets.

In the first few months after the February Revolution the meetings of the soviets had been fully attended. Over 3000 deputies had packed into the Petrograd Soviet at the Tauride Palace. But as the months passed, enthusiasm waned. By the autumn of 1917, attendance was often down to a few hundred. This was a major advantage to the Bolsheviks. Their political dedication meant that they continued to turn up in force while the members of the other parties attended only occasionally. The result was that the Bolshevik Party exerted an influence out of proportion to its numbers. This was especially the case in regard to the composition of the various sub-committees.

Broadly, what happened in Petrograd following the Kornilov Affair was that the Petrograd Soviet moved to the left while the Provisional Government shifted to the right. This made some form of clash between the two bodies increasingly likely. Lenin put it as a matter of stark choice: 'Either a soviet government or Kornilovism. There is no middle course.'

Key question
What factors enabled the Bolsheviks to gain in strength?

Bolsheviks gain a majority in the Petrograd Soviet: 25 September 1917

Key date

Lenin's strategy

From his exile in Finland, Lenin constantly appealed to his party to prepare for the immediate overthrow of Kerensky's government. He claimed that his earlier estimate of what would happen had proved wholly correct: the Provisional Government, incapable of solving the war and land questions, was becoming increasingly reactionary. This left the Soviet as the only hope of true revolutionaries. He further argued that the Bolsheviks could not wait; they must seize the moment while the government was at its most vulnerable. In a sentence that was to become part of Bolshevik legend, Lenin wrote on 12 September: 'History will not forgive us if we do not assume power.'

Lenin's sense of urgency arose from his concern over two events that were due to take place in the autumn, and which he calculated would seriously limit the Bolsheviks' freedom of action:

• the meeting of the All-Russian Congress of Soviets in late October
• the election for the Constituent Assembly in November.

He was convinced that the Bolsheviks would have to take power before these events occurred. If, under the banner 'All Power to the Soviets', the Bolsheviks could topple the Provisional Government before the Congress of Soviets met, they could then present their new authority as a *fait accompli* that the Congress would have no reason to reject.

The elections to the Constituent Assembly presented a different problem. The assembly was the body on which all **progressives** and reformers had set their hopes. Once it came into being, its moral authority would be difficult to challenge. Lenin told his party that since it was impossible to forecast how successfully the Bolsheviks would perform in the elections, they would have to be in power before the results were announced. This would provide them with the authority to undermine the results, should they go against them.

The 'Pre-Parliament'

At the same time as Lenin pressed this policy upon his party, Kerensky tried to make his government less exposed by announcing plans for the creation of a **'Pre-Parliament'** with authority to advise the government. Lenin condemned this as a manoeuvre not to broaden the government's base but to strengthen its grip on power. Acting on his orders, the Bolshevik members of the Soviet who were entitled to attend the Pre-Parliament first derided it and then walked out.

Lenin returns to Petrograd

Emboldened by the Bolsheviks' success in undermining the Pre-Parliament, Lenin now began urging his party to prepare to overthrow the Provisional Government. Despite the passionate conviction with which Lenin put his arguments to his colleagues, there were Bolsheviks on the **Central Committee** of the party who doubted the wisdom of striking against the Provisional Government at this point.

In an effort to enforce his will, Lenin slipped back into Petrograd on 7 October. His personal presence stiffened Bolshevik resolve but did not produce total unity. During the next two weeks he spent exhausting hours at a series of Central Committee meetings trying to convince the waverers. On 10 October the Central Committee pledged itself to an armed insurrection but failed to agree on a specific date. In the end, by another quirk of fate, it was Kerensky and the government, not the Bolsheviks, who initiated the actual rising.

Kerensky makes the first move

Rumours of an imminent Bolshevik coup had been circulating in Petrograd for some weeks, but it was not until an article written by two members of the Bolshevik Central Committee appeared in a journal that the authorities felt they had sure proof. The writers of the article, **Grigor Zinoviev** and Lev Kamenev, argued that it would be a mistake to attempt to overthrow the government in current circumstances.

Kerensky interpreted this as indicating that a date had already been set. Rather than wait to be caught off guard, he ordered a pre-emptive attack on the Bolsheviks. On 23 October the Bolshevik newspapers, *Pravda* and *Izvestiya*, were closed down by government troops and an attempted round-up of the leading Bolsheviks began. The Bolsheviks no longer had a choice; Lenin ordered the planned insurrection to begin.

Trotsky's role

That the Bolsheviks had a plan at all was the work not of Lenin but of Trotsky. While it was Lenin who was undoubtedly the great influence behind the October Rising, it was Trotsky who actually organised it. The key to Trotsky's success in this was his chairmanship of the Petrograd Soviet, to which he had been elected in September. On 9 October the Soviet set up the Military Revolutionary Committee (MRC) to organise the defence of Petrograd against a possible German attack or another Kornilov-type assault from within Russia.

It proved a critical decision. Realising that if the Bolsheviks could control the Military Revolutionary Committee they would control Petrograd, Trotsky used his influence to have himself accepted as one of the **troika** appointed to run the MRC. This meant he had at his disposal the only effective military force in Petrograd. Moreover, it was a legitimate force since theoretically it acted on the authority of the Soviet. Trotsky was now in a position to draft the plans for the overthrow of the Provisional Government. When Lenin gave the order for the uprising to begin, it was Trotsky who directed the **Red Guards** in their seizure of the key vantage points in Petrograd, such as the bridges and the telegraph offices.

Collapse of the Provisional Government

In the three days (25–27 October) that it took for the city to fall under Bolshevik control there was remarkably little fighting. There

Key figure

Grigor Zinoviev (1883–1936)
A close colleague of Lenin since the formation of the Bolshevik Party in 1903.

Key dates

Kerensky attempts to close down *Pravda* and *Izvestiya*; Bolshevik rising against the government begins: 23 October 1917

The Petrograd Soviet sets up the Military Revolutionary Committee: 9 October 1917

Key terms

Troika
A three-man team.

Red Guards
Despite the Bolshevik legend that these were the crack forces of the Revolution, the Red Guards, some 10,000 in number, were largely made up of elderly men recruited from the workers in the factories.

A contingent of Amazons under instruction in 1917. Kerensky had specially recruited these female soldiers, also known as 'the Women's Battalion of Death', as an example of the fighting spirit of the Russian people.

Key date

Bolsheviks take control of Petrograd: 24–25 October 1917

were only six deaths during the whole episode and these were all Red Guards, most probably accidentally shot by their own side. The simple fact was that the Provisional Government had hardly any military forces on which to call. The Petrograd garrison, which had turned out to defend the government on previous occasions, did not come to its aid now. Desertions had reduced the garrison to a few loyal officer-cadets, a small group of **Cossacks** and a unit known as the '**Amazons**'.

When the Red Guards approached the Winter Palace, which housed the Provisional Government, they expected stiff resistance, but there was none. A black-and-white film of the dramatic, death-defying storming of the palace gates often appears in television documentaries about the October Revolution. Sometimes at the bottom of the screen will appear the word 'reconstruction'. This is very misleading, since there was never such an event to reconstruct. The truth is that there are no contemporary films of October 1917. What modern programme-makers invariably use are the powerful images from the feature film *October*, made in 1927 on the tenth anniversary by the celebrated Bolshevik film-maker Sergei Eisenstein (see page 250).

The Bolshevik forces did not need to storm the gates; there was nobody defending them. The Winter Palace was a vast building many times larger than London's Buckingham Palace. The Red

Key terms

Cossacks
The remnants of the elite cavalry regiment of the tsars.

Amazons
A special corps of female soldiers recruited by Kerensky.

Guards simply strolled in through the back doors. This was enough to make the defenders give up. The Cossacks walked off when confronted by the Red Guards. After that, it did not take much pressure to persuade the cadets and the Amazons that it was better for them to lay down their arms and go home rather than die in a futile struggle.

The sounding of its guns in a pre-arranged signal by the pro-Soviet crew of the cruiser *Aurora*, moored in the River Neva, convinced the remaining members of the government that their position was hopeless. As many as were able, escaped unnoticed out of the building. Kerensky, having earlier left the city in a vain effort to raise loyal troops, fled to the American embassy. He later slipped out of Petrograd disguised as a female nurse and made his way to the United States, where he eventually became a professor of history.

The Bolsheviks take power

The Bolsheviks did not seize power; it fell into their hands. The speed and ease with which it had happened surprised even Lenin. In the early hours of 27 October he said to Trotsky: 'From being on the run to supreme power makes one dizzy.' He then rolled himself up in a large fur coat, lay down on the floor and went to sleep.

On the following evening the All-Russian Congress of Soviets began its first session. The opening formalities had barely been completed when the chairman, who happened to be Lev Kamenev, the Bolshevik who had originally opposed the rising, informed the delegates that they were now the supreme authority in Russia; the Petrograd Soviet had seized power in their name and had formed a new government. Kamenev then read out to the bewildered delegates the list of 14 names of the new government they had supposedly just appointed. The 14 were all Bolsheviks or left SRs. At the head of the list of **commissars** who made up the new *Sovnarkom* was the name of the Chief Minister – Vladimir Ilyich Lenin.

The right-wing SRs and the Mensheviks walked out, protesting that it was not a taking of power by the Soviets but a Bolshevik coup. Trotsky jeered after them that they and their kind had 'consigned themselves to the garbage heap of history'. Lenin then announced to the Bolshevik and SR delegates who had remained that they would now proceed 'to construct the towering edifice of socialist society'.

Key dates

The Winter Palace seized by the Bolsheviks; Kerensky flees from Petrograd: 25–26 October 1917

First session of the All-Russian Congress of Soviets: 25 October 1917

Sovnarkom established: 26 October 1917

Lenin claims power in the name of the All-Russian Congress of Soviets: 27 October 1917

Key terms

Commissars
Russian for 'ministers'; Lenin chose the word because, he said, 'it reeks of blood'.

Sovnarkom
Russian for government or cabinet.

Отъ Военно - Революціоннаго Комитета при Петроградскомъ Совѣтѣ Рабочихъ и Солдатскихъ Депутатовъ.

Къ Гражданамъ Россіи.

Временное Правительство низложено. Государственная власть перешла въ руки органа Петроградскаго Совѣта Рабочихъ и Солдатскихъ Депутатовъ Военно-Революціоннаго Комитета, стоящаго во главѣ Петроградскаго пролетаріата и гарнизона.

Дѣло, за которое боролся народъ: немедленное предложеніе демократическаго мира, отмѣна помѣщичьей собственности на землю, рабочій контроль надъ производствомъ, созданіе Совѣтскаго Правительства — это дѣло обезпечено.

ДА ЗДРАВСТВУЕТЪ РЕВОЛЮЦІЯ РАБОЧИХЪ, СОЛДАТЪ И КРЕСТЬЯНЪ!

Военно-Революціонный Комитетъ
при Петроградскомъ Совѣтѣ
Рабочихъ и Солдатскихъ Депутатовъ.

25 октября 1917 г. 10 ч. утра.

To the People of Russia reads the headline of this poster, 25 October 1917, declaring that the Provisional Government has fallen. It goes on in the name of the Soviet to promise peace and land to the people.

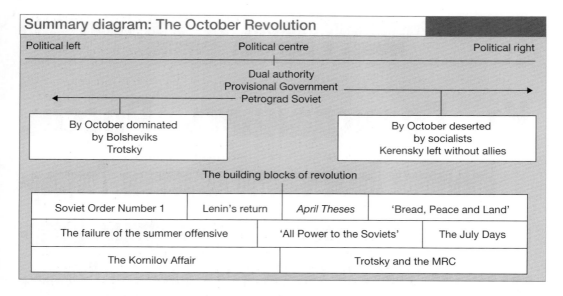

Summary diagram: The October Revolution

Political left	Political centre	Political right

Dual authority
Provisional Government
Petrograd Soviet

By October dominated by Bolsheviks Trotsky	By October deserted by socialists Kerensky left without allies

The building blocks of revolution

Soviet Order Number 1	Lenin's return	*April Theses*	'Bread, Peace and Land'
The failure of the summer offensive		'All Power to the Soviets'	The July Days
The Kornilov Affair		Trotsky and the MRC	

5 | Reasons for Bolshevik Success

Trotsky later said that the key factors in the Bolshevik success of October 1917 were:

- the failure of the Petrograd garrison to resist
- the existence of the Military Revolutionary Committee.

He claimed that the Soviet decision to create the Military Revolutionary Committee had sounded the death knell of the Provisional Government. The Bolsheviks' control of the MRC gave them 'three-quarters if not nine-tenths' of their victory in the October Revolution. Since Trotsky was a major player in the drama played out in October 1917, his views demand respect. But his analysis was largely concerned with the immediate events of October. The success of the coup had as much to do with government weakness as with Bolshevik strength, a weakness that was in-built into the Provisional Government from the start.

Provisional Government weakness

The collapse of tsardom had left a power vacuum. Although the Provisional Government held office between February and October 1917, it never held power. It lacked the ruthlessness that the desperate situation demanded. Furthermore, from the first, its authority was weakened by the existence of the Petrograd Soviet. Unable to fight the war successfully and unwilling to introduce the reforms that might have given it popular support, the Provisional Government tottered towards collapse. When it was challenged in October 1917 by the Bolsheviks, who themselves had been on the point of political extinction in July, it was friendless. It gave in with scarcely a show of resistance.

Key question
Why was there so little resistance to the Bolsheviks in October 1917?

The failure of the Provisional Government to rally effective military support in its hour of need followed from its political failure over the previous eight months. It was not that the Provisional Government was bitterly rejected by the Russian people. It was more a matter of its inability to arouse genuine enthusiasm. Kerensky's government had come nowhere near to solving Russia's problems. Its support had evaporated. Economically incompetent and militarily incapable, the Provisional Government was not considered worth struggling to save. In October 1917 the Bolsheviks were pushing against an already open door.

It should be emphasised that the Provisional Government had never been meant to last. As its very title suggested, it was intended to be an interim government. Along with its partner in the dual authority, the Petrograd Soviet, its role was to provide a caretaker administration until an All-Russian Constituent Assembly was formed after the autumn election. The assembly was the ultimate dream of all liberals and democrats; it would be the first fully elected, nationwide, democratic parliament in Russia's history. All parties, including the Bolsheviks, were committed to it.

As a consequence, the Provisional Government was always open to the charge that as an unelected, self-appointed body it had no right to exercise the authority that properly belonged to the Constituent Assembly alone. Such limited strength as the Provisional Government had came from its claim to be the representative of the February Revolution. Lenin had made it his task to undermine that claim.

Weakness of the non-Bolshevik parties

Key question
Why was it the Bolsheviks, and not any of the other parties, who took power in October 1917?

An obvious question is why none of the other parties was able to mount a serious challenge to the Bolsheviks for the leadership of the Revolution between February and October. One answer is that they had all accepted February as a genuine revolution. Consequently, it made sense for them to co-operate with the Provisional Government, which claimed to represent the progressive forces in Russia.

The result was that the supposedly revolutionary parties, such as the SRs, were prepared to enter into coalition with the Kadets, the dominant party in the government, and await the convening of the Constituent Assembly. This gave the Bolsheviks a powerful propaganda weapon, which Lenin exploited. He charged the socialists with having sold out to the bourgeoisie.

Another explanation is that the other parties were weakened by their support for the war. None of them opposed the continuation of the struggle against Germany with the consistency that Lenin's Bolsheviks did after April 1917. The non-Bolshevik parties regarded it as Russia's duty to defeat the enemy. The SRs, the Mensheviks and, indeed, some individual Bolsheviks believed wholeheartedly in a revolutionary war against bourgeois Germany. On the left of the Menshevik Party there was a vociferous wing of international revolutionaries who saw the war as the ideal opportunity for beginning the worldwide class struggle.

The Menshevik position

As committed Marxists, the Mensheviks had good reason for co-operating with the Provisional Government rather than opposing it. They saw the February Revolution as marking a critical stage in the class war, when the bourgeoisie had overthrown the old feudal forces represented by the tsar. This stage of the dialectic, Marx had argued, was the necessary prelude to the revolution of the proletariat.

However, the Mensheviks judged that since Russia did not yet possess a proletariat large enough to be a truly revolutionary force, it was their immediate task to align themselves with the other parties and work for the consolidation of the bourgeois revolution. When this had been achieved, the Mensheviks could then turn to the ultimate objective of a proletarian rising. One of the interesting paradoxes of the Russian Revolution is that, in strictly theoretical terms, the Mensheviks were always more consistent in their Marxism than were Lenin and his Bolsheviks.

Russia's lack of a party-political tradition

It is important to remember the absence of a tradition of legitimate party politics in tsarist Russia. With the fall of tsardom the various parties found themselves for a brief, heady period free to advance their views. But there were no accepted rules of political conduct that they could follow. The arts of negotiation and compromise, which had developed in more advanced political systems elsewhere, were unknown in Russia. In their absence, politics was reduced to a simple question of who could gain power and then assert it over others.

Lenin expressed it in the simple formulation 'who, whom?' What he was asking was who held power and over whom it was exercised. Democracy did not enter into it. Power would go to the most flexible and the most determined party. The Bolsheviks under Lenin perfectly fitted this requirement. They were prepared to adjust to circumstance if the occasion demanded. Their land policy was evidence of this (see page 99). But they never lost sight of their basic goal, the seizure of power.

Down to October 1917 the Bolshevik position was far from unassailable; the near-fiasco of the July Days had shown how narrow the gap between success and failure could be. Nor can it be said that the Bolshevik takeover in October was inevitable; that depended as much on the weakness and mistakes of their opponents as upon their own resolution. Yet what is clear is that none of the contending parties was as well equipped as the Bolsheviks to exploit the crises facing Russia in 1917.

Bolshevik ruthlessness

Tseretelli, a prominent Menshevik, admitted: 'Everything we did at that time was a vain effort to hold back a destructive elemental flood with a handful of insignificant chips.' Struve, a liberal *émigré*, observed: 'Only Bolshevism was logical about revolution and true to its essence, and therefore in the revolution it conquered.'

Iraklii Tseretelli (1882–1959)
A Georgian revolutionary and a leading member of the Petrograd Soviet before its domination by the Bolsheviks.

Key figure

Émigrés
Those who fled from Russia after the Revolution, either out of fear or from a desire to plan a counter-strike against the Bolsheviks.

Key term

Milyukov, the Kadet leader, shared Struve's view of the Bolsheviks: 'They knew where they were going, and they went in the direction that they had chosen once and for all towards a goal that came nearer with every new, unsuccessful, experiment of compromise.'

Lenin's Bolsheviks were a new breed of politician: utterly self-confident, scornful of all other parties and ideas, and totally loyal to their leader. Their drive and utter conviction came from a belief that they were an unstoppable force of history. As Trotsky put it: 'The party in the last analysis is always right, because the party is the only historical instrument given to the proletariat to resolve its fundamental tasks.' The ruthlessness of the Bolsheviks did not guarantee their success, but it did mean that no other party could hope to gain or hold power unless it was able to overcome the challenge of these dedicated revolutionaries. In the event, none of the other parties was ever in a position to do this.

The role of mutual misunderstanding

An irony of the pre-October situation was that both the Provisional Government and the Bolsheviks overestimated each other's power, each delaying their moves against the other for fear of overplaying their hand. Historians have often wondered why the Provisional Government did not make a more sustained effort to destroy the Bolsheviks politically. It is true that some arrests were made, but the government's efforts at suppression were half-hearted.

One reason, odd though it seems in retrospect, is that Kerensky's government was more frightened of an attack from the right than from the left. Kerensky himself once said: 'We have no enemies on the left.' Fear of a tsarist reaction against the revolution preoccupied the thoughts of many in the government. For much of 1917, Kornilov was regarded as a bigger threat than Lenin.

This was not entirely unrealistic. The Bolsheviks were not militarily strong. **Sukhanov**, a Menshevik eyewitness of the events of 1917, calculated that so limited was Bolshevik strength at the time of the October Rising that 'a good detachment of 500 men would have been enough to liquidate **Smolny** and everybody in it'. Trotsky agreed, but asked pointedly where the Provisional Government was to get 500 good men to fight for it.

For their part, the Bolsheviks similarly miscalculated the strength and determination of the Provisional Government. Lenin expected to be summarily shot if ever the government's agents found him. This was why he was either incognito or absent altogether from Petrograd for long periods during the critical time between the two revolutions of 1917.

Key question
In what ways did the Bolsheviks and the Provisional Government overestimate each other's strength?

Key figure

Nikolai Sukhanov (1882–1939)
A leading member of the SRs, who opposed Kerensky's war policies but was denounced by the Bolsheviks after the October Revolution.

Key term

Smolny
The Bolshevik headquarters in Petrograd, housed in what had been a young ladies' finishing school.

Lenin's role in 1917

It says much for Lenin's forcefulness as leader that despite his
frequent absences from Petrograd between February and October
he continued to dominate the actions of the Bolshevik Party.
Trotsky later made an interesting assessment of the part played by
Lenin in the October Revolution:

However, most historians are now careful not to overstate Lenin's
power to dictate events in 1917. In the standard Bolshevik version
of what happened, Lenin was portrayed as having fulfilled his
plans for revolution along the lines he had laid down in such
writings as his 1902 pamphlet *What Is to Be Done?* This had
visualised the development of a tightly knit, disciplined Bolshevik
Party that would seize power in the name of the masses at the
opportune moment (see page 23). Yet the structure and authority
of his party in 1917 were markedly different from Lenin's 1902
model. The evidence of the many disputes within the Bolshevik
ranks over policy between February and October 1917 and well
into 1918 suggests that they were by no means as disciplined or
centrally controlled as the Party later claimed to have been.

Part of the explanation for this is that the composition of the
Party had changed in ways that Lenin and the Central Committee
had not planned. After the February Revolution there had been a
large increase in membership, which the Central Committee had
not wanted but which, in the heady but politically confused
situation following the fall of tsardom, it seemed unable to prevent.
The following figures indicate the remarkable transformation
which the Bolshevik Party underwent in 1917.

Table 4.1: Membership of the Bolshevik Party in 1917

February	24,000
April	100,000
October	340,000 (60,000 in Petrograd)

Modern commentators view this influx of Party members as an
aspect of the general **radicalisation** of Russian politics that
occurred as the Provisional Government got into increasing
difficulties. What had helped to prepare the ground for the
successful Bolshevik coup in October was the growth in the
Petrograd factories of workers' committees which, while not
necessarily pro-Bolshevik, were certainly not pro-government. One
result of the anti-government agitation of these committees was
that when the open challenge to the Provisional Government
came in October, Kerensky's desperate appeal for support from
the people of Petrograd went unheeded.

Key question
How far was the
Bolshevik success
due to Lenin?

Radicalisation
A movement
towards more
sweeping or
revolutionary ideas.

Key term

Some key books in the debate:
Edward Acton, *Critical Companion to the Russian Revolution* (Edward Arnold, 1990)
Edward Acton, *Rethinking the Russian Revolution* (Edward Arnold, 1990)
Edward Acton and Tom Stableford, *The Soviet Union* (University of Exeter Press, 2005)
David Christian, *Imperial and Soviet Russia: Power, Privilege and the Challenge of Modernity* (Macmillan, 1997)
Isaac Deutscher, *Trotsky* (Oxford University Press, 1954–70)
Orlando Figes, *A People's Tragedy: The Russian Revolution 1891–1924* (Jonathan Cape, 1996)
Sheila Fitzpatrick, *The Russian Revolution 1917–1932* (Oxford University Press, 1994)
Richard Pipes, *The Russian Revolution 1899–1919* (Collins Harvill, 1990)
Richard Pipes, *Three Whys of the Russian Revolution* (Pimlico, 1998)
Richard Pipes (ed.), *The Unknown Lenin: From the Soviet Archives* (Yale University Press, 1996)
Richard Sakwa, *The Rise and Fall of the Soviet Union 1917–1991* (Routledge, 1999)
Robert Service, *Lenin: A Biography* (Macmillan, 2004)
Robert Service, *Stalin* (Macmillan, 2006)
Norman Stone, *The Eastern Front, 1914–1917* (Penguin, 1998)
R.G. Suny (ed.), *The Russian Revolution and Bolshevik Victory* (Heath, 1990)
Dmitri Volkogonov, *Lenin: Life and Legacy* (HarperCollins, 1994)
Dmitri Volkogonov, *Stalin: Triumph and Tragedy* (Weidenfeld and Nicolson, 1991)
Dmitri Volkogonov, *The Rise and Fall of the Soviet Empire: Political Leaders from Lenin to Gorbachev* (HarperCollins, 1998)
Dmitri Volkogonov, *Trotsky: the Eternal Revolutionary* (Free Press, 1996)

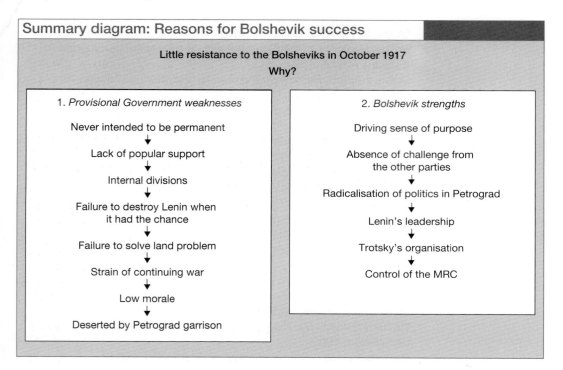

Summary diagram: Reasons for Bolshevik success

Little resistance to the Bolsheviks in October 1917
Why?

1. *Provisional Government weaknesses*

Never intended to be permanent
↓
Lack of popular support
↓
Internal divisions
↓
Failure to destroy Lenin when
it had the chance
↓
Failure to solve land problem
↓
Strain of continuing war
↓
Low morale
↓
Deserted by Petrograd garrison

2. *Bolshevik strengths*

Driving sense of purpose
↓
Absence of challenge from
the other parties
↓
Radicalisation of politics in Petrograd
↓
Lenin's leadership
↓
Trotsky's organisation
↓
Control of the MRC

Study Guide: AS Question

In the style of OCR
To what extent was the continuation of the First World War the main reason for the overthrow of the Provisional Government in the October Revolution?   (50 marks)

Exam tips
The cross-references are intended to take you straight to the material that will help you to answer the question.

The Provisional Government's decision to continue in the First World War was an important factor in its overthrow. Russia's repeated military defeats, the dislocation in transport, inflationary prices and food shortages saw mutinies, strikes and political unrest in 1917 that opposition groups exploited (pages 94–5). However, your answer needs to balance this factor against other reasons for the Revolution. You might consider, for example:

- the dual authority (pages 88–91) and 'provisional' nature of the government (pages 108–9)
- its failure to solve the land question (pages 99–100)
- its weakness in dealing with the July Days (pages 96–8)
- the threat posed by Kornilov (pages 100–1)
- the activities and growing popularity of the Bolsheviks (pages 91–4)
- its failure to counter the planned coup of October 1917 (pages 102–6).

Try to demonstrate in your essay how these factors were often interlinked and state clearly where you stand on the relative importance of the First World War as a factor.

5 The Bolsheviks in Power, 1917–20

POINTS TO CONSIDER
The successful Bolshevik rising of October 1917 marked the beginning rather than the end of the Russian Revolution. The big test was whether the Bolsheviks could retain their power and build upon it. Their efforts to do so are studied in this chapter under the following headings:

- the problems confronting the Bolsheviks
- the dissolution of the Constituent Assembly
- the Treaty of Brest-Litovsk, 1918
- the Russian Civil War, 1918–20
- the foreign interventions, 1918–20.

Key dates

1917	November	Bolsheviks issue the Decrees on Land and Workers' Control
		Elections for the Constituent Assembly
	December	Armistice signed at Brest-Litovsk
		Cheka created
1918–20		Russian Civil War and foreign interventions
1918–21		War communism
1918	January	Bolsheviks forcibly dissolve the Constituent Assembly
		Red Army established
	March	Treaty of Brest-Litovsk
	June	Decree on Nationalisation
	July	Forced grain requisitions begin
		Murder of the tsar and his family
	September	Red Terror officially introduced
1919	March	Comintern established
		Bolshevik Party renamed the Communist Party
1920	April	Invading Red Army driven from Poland

1 | The Problems Confronting the Bolsheviks

In power, the Bolsheviks under Lenin faced huge difficulties in trying to consolidate their hold over what had been the tsarist empire. These can be identified as four basic questions:

- Could the Bolsheviks survive at all?
- If so, could they extend their control over the whole of Russia?
- Could they negotiate a swift end to the war?
- Could they bring economic stability to Russia?

The traditional Soviet view was that after the Bolsheviks had taken power under Lenin they transformed old Russia into a socialist society by following a set of measured, planned reforms that had been previously prepared. Few historians now accept that as the truth of what happened. Lenin's policy is now seen as having been a **pragmatic** adjustment to the harsh realities of the situation.

From the beginning, the Bolshevik regime was engaged in a desperate struggle for survival. In their government of Russia, the Bolsheviks were working from hand to mouth. They had few plans to help them. This was because before 1917 they had spent their time in preparing for revolution. They had given little thought to the details of how affairs would be organised once this had been achieved. It had always been a Marxist belief that after the triumph of the proletariat the state would 'wither away'. Trotsky had expressed this simple faith at the time of his appointment in October 1917 as **Commissar for Foreign Affairs** when he said: 'All we need to do is issue a few decrees, then shut up shop and go home.' But circumstances were not to allow such a relaxed approach to government.

The distribution of power

Lenin claimed that the October Revolution had been a taking of power by the soviets. In fact, it had been a seizure of power by the Bolshevik Party. Nevertheless, Lenin persisted with the notion that *Sovnarkom* had been appointed to govern by the Congress of Soviets. According to this view, the distribution of power in revolutionary Russia took the form of a pyramid with *Sovnarkom* at the top, drawing its authority from the Russian people, who expressed their will through the soviets at the base (see Figure 5.1).

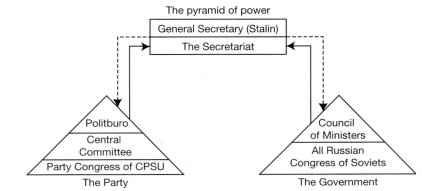

Figure 5.1: The distribution of power in revolutionary Russia.

The reality was altogether different. Traditional forms of government had broken down in 1917 with the fall of tsardom and the overthrow of the Provisional Government. This meant the Bolsheviks ruled *de facto*, not **de jure**. To put it another way, they were in a position to make up their own rules. And since not all the soviets were dominated by the Bolsheviks, who in any case were a minority party, Lenin had no intention of letting true democracy get in the way.

De jure
By legitimate legal right.

The notion that it was the soviets who had taken power and now ruled was simply a convenient cover. From the beginning, whatever the claims may have been about soviets being in authority, it was in fact the Bolsheviks who held power. The key body here was the Central Committee of the Bolshevik Party (later known as the Politburo). It was this organisation under Lenin's direction that provided the members of the government. In a sense, *Sovnarkom* was a wing of the Bolshevik Party.

In theory, the Central Committee derived its authority from the All-Russian Congress of the Bolshevik Party, whose locally elected representatives voted on policy. In practice, the Congress and the local parties did as they were told. This was in keeping with Lenin's insistence that the Bolshevik Party operate according to the principle of democratic centralism (see page 26), a formula which guaranteed that power was exercised from the top down, rather than the bottom up.

The government of Soviet Russia as it had developed by the time of Lenin's death in 1924 had two main features:

- Sovnarkom (the Council of People's Commissars) which was responsible for creating government policies
- the Secretariat (equivalent to a Civil Service) which was responsible for carrying out these policies.

Both these bodies were staffed and controlled by the Bolshevik party. It has to be stressed that the vital characteristic of this governmental system was that the party ruled. By 1922 all other political parties had been outlawed and Russia was a one-party state. Membership of that one party was essential for all who held government or administrative posts at whatever level. The Soviet government was thus the formal expression of the Party's control. As Figure 5.1 shows, the overlapping power of party and government can best understood as two parallel pyramids of power.

Whatever the theories about the power structure, the fact was that Lenin was the government. Like the tsars, Lenin ruled by decree; his signature on a document gave it the force of law. In Trotsky's words: 'From the moment the provisional government was declared deposed, Lenin acted in matters large and small as the government'.

The Bolsheviks' early measures

In Bolshevik theory the October Revolution had marked the victory of the proletariat over the bourgeoisie, of socialism over capitalism. But theory was of little immediate assistance in the circumstances of late 1917. A hard slog lay ahead if the Bolsheviks were truly to transform the Russian economy.

Before the October Revolution, Lenin had written powerfully against landlords and grasping capitalists, but he had produced little by way of a coherent plan for their replacement. It is understandable, therefore, that his policy after taking power in 1917 was a pragmatic one. He argued that the change from a bourgeois to a proletarian economy could not be achieved overnight. The Bolshevik government would continue to use the existing structures until the transition had been completed and a fully fledged socialist system could be adopted. This transitional stage was referred to as 'state capitalism'. Lenin explained it to his colleagues in the following terms:

> The majority of specialists are bourgeois. For the present we shall have to adopt the old bourgeois method and agree to pay higher salaries for the 'services' of the biggest bourgeois specialists. All who are familiar with the situation see the necessity of such a measure. Clearly it is a compromise measure.

Immediate problems

Lenin was aware that there were many Bolsheviks who wanted the immediate introduction of a sweeping revolutionary policy, but he pointed out that the new regime simply did not possess the power to impose this. Its authority did not run much beyond Petrograd and Moscow. Until the Bolsheviks could exercise a much wider political and military control, their policies would have to fit the prevailing circumstances. The war against Germany and Austria had brought Russia to the point of economic collapse:

- The shortage of raw materials and investment capital had reduced industrial production to two-thirds of its 1914 level.
- Inflation had rocketed.
- The transport system had been crippled.
- Hunger gripped large areas of Russia. Grain supplies were over 13 million tons short of the nation's needs.
- Within a few months of the October Revolution, the food crisis had been further deepened by the ceding to Germany of Ukraine, Russia's richest grain-producing region (see page 126).

All Lenin's economic policies from 1917 on can be seen as attempts to deal with these problems, the most pressing being whether Russia could produce enough to feed itself. Lenin was a realist on the peasant question. Although he considered that the future lay with the industrial workers, he was very conscious that the peasantry, who made up the mass of the population, were the food producers. The primary consideration, therefore, was how best the peasants could be persuaded or forced to provide adequate food supplies for the nation.

Immediately after coming to power, the new government introduced two measures that are usually regarded as having initiated Bolshevik economic policy. These were the 'Decree on Land' and the 'Decree on Workers' Control', both issued in November 1917. However, these were not so much new departures as formal recognitions of what had already taken place.

Key date

The Bolsheviks issue the Decrees on Land and Workers' Control: November 1917

The 'Decree on Land'

The key article of the 'Decree on Land' stated:

> Private ownership of land shall be abolished for ever. All land, whether
> state, crown, monastery, church, factory, private, public, peasant, etc.
> shall be confiscated without compensation and become the property
> of the whole people, and pass into the use of all those who cultivate it.

The decree gave Bolshevik approval to what had been happening
in the countryside since the February Revolution: in many areas
the peasants had overthrown their landlords and occupied their
property. Lenin had earlier accepted this when he had adopted
the slogan 'Land to the Peasants' (see page 99).

The 'Decree on Workers' Control

The 'Decree on Workers' Control' was also largely concerned with
authorising what had already occurred. During 1917 a large
number of factories had been taken over by the workers. However,
the workers' committees that were then formed seldom ran the
factories efficiently. The result was a serious fall in industrial
output. The decree accepted the workers' takeover, but at the
same time it instructed the workers' committees to maintain 'the
strictest order and discipline' in the workplace.

Passing decrees was one thing, enforcing them another. A
particular problem for the government was that not all the
workers' committees were dominated by Bolsheviks. Until the
Party gained greater control at shop floor level it would be difficult
for the central government to impose itself on the factories.
Nevertheless, the government pressed on with its plans for
establishing the framework of state direction of the economy, even
if effective central control was some way off. In December,
Vesenkha was set up 'to take charge of all existing institutions for
the regulation of economic life'.

Initially, *Vesenkha* was unable to exercise the full authority
granted to it. However, it did preside over a number of important
developments:

- The banks and the railways were nationalised.
- Foreign debts were cancelled (see page 138).
- The transport system was made less chaotic.

These were important practical achievements, which suggested
how effective centralised control might become should the
Bolshevik regime be able to gain real power.

Principal changes introduced by the Bolsheviks, October 1917–July 1918

- Decrees on Peace, Land and Workers' Control.
- The old class system declared to be abolished.
- Moscow brought under Red (Bolshevik) Control.
- All titles abolished – 'comrade' becomes the standard greeting.
- The old legal system replaced with 'people's courts'.
- Creation of the *Cheka*.

Key terms

Vesenkha
The Supreme
Council of the
National Economy.

Cheka
The letters of the
word stood for the
Russian words for
'the All-Russian
Extraordinary
Commission for
Fighting Counter-
revolution, Sabotage
and Speculation' –
the secret police.

- An armistice, followed by a peace treaty, with Germany.
- *Vesenkha* set up to plan the economy.
- The Red Army founded.
- Russia formally becomes the Russian Socialist Federal Soviet Republic (RSFSR).
- The Bolshevik Party retitled the Communist Party.
- The Russian calendar modernised in line with the system used in the advanced world (though old dating kept when referring to the 1917 Revolution).
- The Marriage Code gives husbands and wives equal rights.
- Schools brought under state control.

Key date

Creation of the *Cheka*: December 1917

Creation of the *Cheka*, 1917

While some Bolsheviks may have found the initial pace of revolutionary change too slow for their liking, there was no doubting that Lenin was determined to impose absolute Bolshevik rule by the suppressing of all political opposition. A development that gave the Bolsheviks muscle in dealing with their opponents was the creation of the *Cheka* in the weeks following the October coup.

Key term

Counter-revolution
A term used by the Bolsheviks to cover any action of which they disapproved by branding it as reactionary and opposed to progress.

In essentials, the *Cheka* was a better-organised and more efficient form of the *Okhrana*, the tsarist secret police, at whose hands nearly every Bolshevik activist had suffered. Its express purpose was to destroy '**counter-revolution** and sabotage', terms that were so elastic they could be stretched to cover anything of which the Bolsheviks disapproved.

The *Cheka*, which was to change its title several times over the years, but never its essential character, remains the outstanding expression of Bolshevik ruthlessness (see page 145).

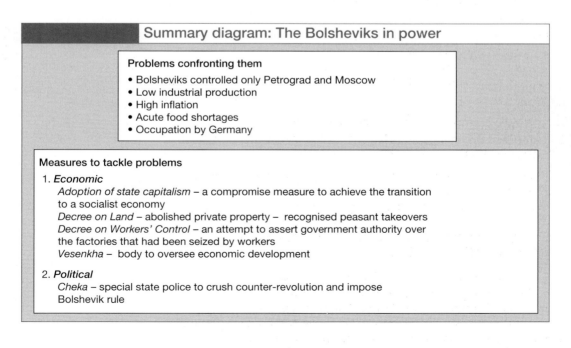

Summary diagram: The Bolsheviks in power

Problems confronting them
- Bolsheviks controlled only Petrograd and Moscow
- Low industrial production
- High inflation
- Acute food shortages
- Occupation by Germany

Measures to tackle problems

1. *Economic*
   Adoption of state capitalism – a compromise measure to achieve the transition to a socialist economy
   Decree on Land – abolished private property – recognised peasant takeovers
   Decree on Workers' Control – an attempt to assert government authority over the factories that had been seized by workers
   Vesenkha – body to oversee economic development

2. *Political*
   Cheka – special state police to crush counter-revolution and impose Bolshevik rule

2 | Dissolution of the Constituent Assembly, January 1918

Key question
What does the dissolution of the Constituent Assembly reveal about Lenin's attitude towards the exercise of power?

As a revolutionary, Lenin had never worried much about how many people supported the Bolsheviks. Mere numbers did not concern him. He had no faith in democratic elections, which he dismissed as tricks by which the bourgeoisie kept itself in power. His primary objective was not to win mass support, but to create a party capable of seizing power when the opportune moment came. This was why he had refused to join a broad-front opposition movement before 1917 and why he had consistently opposed any form of co-operation with the Provisional Government.

After the successful October coup in 1917, Lenin was even more determined not to allow elections to undermine the Bolsheviks' newly won power. However, there was an immediate problem. The October Revolution had come too late to prevent the elections to the All-Russian Constituent Assembly from going ahead in November as planned. When the results came through by the end of the year, they did not make pleasant reading for the Bolsheviks:

- They had been outvoted by nearly two to one by the Social Revolutionaries (SRs).
- They had won only 24 per cent of the total vote.
- They had gained barely a quarter of the seats in the Assembly (see Table 5.1).

Table 5.1: Results of the election for the Constituent Assembly, November 1917

	Votes	*Seats*
SRs	17,490,000	370
Bolsheviks	9,844,000	175
National minority groups	8,257,000	99
Left SRs (pro-Bolshevik)	2,861,000	40
Kadets	1,986,000	17
Mensheviks	1,248,000	16
Total	41,686,000	717

Key dates

Elections for the Constituent Assembly: November 1917

Bolsheviks forcibly dissolve the Constituent Assembly: January 1918

Lenin had originally supported the idea of a Constituent Assembly, not out of idealism but for purely expedient reasons: it offered a way of further weakening the authority of the Provisional Government. Now, however, with his party in power, he had no need of an Assembly. Furthermore, since it was overwhelmingly non-Bolshevik it would almost certainly make life difficult for his government.

One possibility was that he could have tried to work with the new Assembly. But that was not how Lenin operated. He was not a democrat; he did not deal in compromise. He was a revolutionary who believed that the only way to govern was not by compromise but by totally crushing all opposition.

Hence, his response to the Constituent Assembly, when it gathered in January 1918, was simple and ruthless. After only one day's session, it was dissolved at gunpoint by the Red Guards. A few members tried to protest, but, with rifles trained on their heads, their resistance soon evaporated. It was a bitter end to the dreams of liberals and reformers. There would not be another democratic body in Russia until after the collapse of Soviet communism over 70 years later.

Lenin's motives for dissolving the Assembly

Lenin's act of violence in January 1918 has to be viewed in context. The Bolsheviks' hold on power was precarious. Indeed, the prospects of Bolshevik survival at all seemed slim. There was strong and widespread opposition to them inside the country. Moreover, Russia was still at war with Germany, and the Allies – France and Britain – were all set to interfere should the new Russian government make a separate peace. In such an atmosphere, the Bolsheviks were not prepared to consider power sharing.

Lenin justified the Bolshevik action by arguing that the original reason for electing an Assembly, the establishing of an all-Russian representative body, had already been achieved by the creation of a Soviet government in October 1917. The people's will had expressed itself in the October Revolution. The Constituent Assembly was, therefore, superfluous. More than that, it was corrupt. The elections, he asserted, had been rigged by the SRs and the Kadets; consequently, the results did not truly reflect the wishes of the Russian people. In such circumstances, Lenin declared:

> To hand over power to the Constituent Assembly would again be to compromise with the malignant bourgeoisie. Nothing in the world will induce us to surrender the Soviet power. The Soviet Revolutionary Republic will triumph no matter what the cost.

Commenting on Lenin's attitude at this stage, Trotsky approvingly and revealingly noted that Lenin was always ready to back his theories with force by using 'sharpshooters'. He recorded a remark Lenin had made to him in private: 'The dissolution of the Constituent Assembly by the Soviet Government means a complete and frank liquidation of the idea of democracy by the idea of dictatorship.'

Reactions to the crushing of the Assembly

Lenin's ruthlessness caused unease among some of his own supporters. **Maxim Gorky**, one of the Bolshevik Party's leading intellectuals, wrote at the time:

> The best Russians have lived for almost 100 years with the idea of a Constituent Assembly as a political organ that could provide Russian democracy as a whole with the possibility of freely exercising its will. On the altar of this sacred idea rivers of blood have been spilled – and now the 'people's commissars' have ordered the shooting of this democracy.

Many foreign communists were appalled by Lenin's behaviour. **Rosa Luxemburg**, a Polish socialist, condemned 'the elimination

Key figures

Maxim Gorky (1868–1936)
Russian novelist and playwright – arguably, the most influential of all Soviet writers.

Rosa Luxemburg (1871–1919)
Revolutionary feminist and Marxist, she was killed in an unsuccessful Spartacist (Communist) rising in Germany in January 1919.

of democracy' in Russia. She complained bitterly that the 'remedy' provided by Lenin and Trotsky was 'worse than the disease it is supposed to cure'.

Such criticisms did not move Lenin. As he saw it, the desperately vulnerable position the Bolsheviks were in – attempting to impose themselves on Russia while surrounded by enemies on all sides – demanded the sternest of measures. Nor was he short of theory to justify his actions. The concept of democratic centralism, which required the absolute obedience of party members to the leaders (see page 26), perfectly fitted the situation in which the Bolsheviks found themselves.

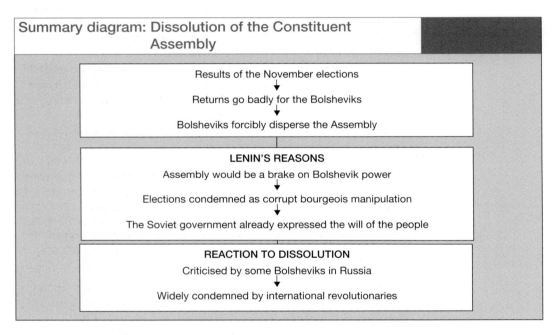

Summary diagram: Dissolution of the Constituent Assembly

Results of the November elections
↓
Returns go badly for the Bolsheviks
↓
Bolsheviks forcibly disperse the Assembly

LENIN'S REASONS
Assembly would be a brake on Bolshevik power
↓
Elections condemned as corrupt bourgeois manipulation
↓
The Soviet government already expressed the will of the people

REACTION TO DISSOLUTION
Criticised by some Bolsheviks in Russia
↓
Widely condemned by international revolutionaries

3 | The Treaty of Brest-Litovsk, 1918

Lenin and Trotsky were united in their suppression of the Constituent Assembly. However, there was a marked difference of attitude between them over the issue of the war with Germany. Both wanted it ended but they disagreed on how this could best be achieved. Lenin wanted an immediate peace; Trotsky wanted a delay.

Lenin had shifted his position. At the time of his return to Russia in April 1917 he had been calling for an anti-imperialist revolutionary war (see pages 92–4). But now his thinking ran along the following lines. Russia's military exhaustion made it impossible for it to fight on successfully. If Germany eventually won the war on both fronts, it would retain the Russian territory it now possessed. But if Germany lost the war against the Western Allies, Russia would regain its occupied lands. In the first eventuality, Russia would not be worse off; in the second it would actually gain. It was therefore pointless for Bolshevik Russia to continue to fight.

Key question
Why were the Bolsheviks willing to accept the humiliation of Russia in the Treaty of Brest-Litovsk?

Key date

Armistice signed at Brest-Litovsk: December 1917

An interesting aspect of Lenin's readiness to make peace with Germany was that it was not wholly ideological. Between 1914 and 1917 the German Foreign Office had given substantial amounts of money to Lenin and the Bolsheviks in the hope that if they succeeded in their revolution they would pull Russia out of the war (see page 92). Germany continued to finance Lenin even after the October Revolution and the armistice of December 1917. A settlement with Germany was therefore very much in Lenin's interests since it was the best guarantee against the drying up of this lucrative source of Bolshevik revenue.

Trotsky took a middle position between Lenin, who wanted a peace straight away, and those Bolsheviks and Left Revolutionaries who pressed for the continuation of the war as a revolutionary crusade against imperialist Germany. Trotsky shared Lenin's view that Bolshevik Russia had no realistic chance of successfully continuing the military struggle against Germany. However, in the hope that within a short time the German armies would collapse on the Western Front and revolution would follow in Germany, Trotsky was determined to make the peace talks a protracted affair. He wanted to buy time for Bolshevik agitators to exploit the mutinies in the Austro-German armies.

The Bolsheviks' tactics at Brest-Litovsk

This approach, for which Trotsky coined the slogan 'neither peace, nor war', was intended to confuse and infuriate the German delegation at Brest-Litovsk, the Polish town where the Germans and Russians gathered to discuss peace terms. Trotsky showed his contempt for what he called 'bourgeois propriety' by consistently flouting the traditional etiquette of European diplomacy. He would yawn loudly while German representatives were speaking and start private conversations with his Bolshevik colleagues rather than listen to what was being said. When he did join in the formal negotiations, he would ignore the point under discussion and launch into revolutionary speeches praising the October coup in Russia and calling on Germany to overthrow its corrupt bourgeois government.

Germany's chief negotiator, Field-Marshal **Hindenburg**, complained:

Key figure

Paul von Hindenburg (1847–1934)
Prussian aristocrat, soldier and statesman, President of Germany from 1925 to 1934.

> Trotsky degraded the conference-table to the level of a tub-thumper's street corner. Lenin and Trotsky behaved more like victors than vanquished, while trying to sow the seeds of political dissolution in the ranks of our army.

What Hindenburg had failed to grasp was that Trotsky and Lenin did indeed see themselves as victors – potential if not actual. They were not perturbed by the thought of national defeat. Their conviction was that time and history were on their side. They believed that a great international political victory was imminent. It is important to remember that Lenin and Trotsky were **international revolutionaries**. They had only a limited loyalty towards Russia as a nation. Their first concern was to spread the proletarian revolution worldwide.

Key term

International revolutionaries
Marxists who were willing to sacrifice national interests in the cause of a worldwide rising of the workers.

This readiness to subordinate Russian national interests explains why, to the dismay of most Russians and many Bolsheviks, the Soviet delegation at Brest-Litovsk was eventually willing to sign a devastating peace treaty as soon as it became clear that the exasperated Germans were seriously considering marching to Petrograd to overthrow Lenin's government.

Trotsky's outlook as an international revolutionary did not prevent him from scoring a sharp nationalist propaganda point. Before signing the treaty on 3 March 1918, Sokolnikov, the Soviet representative, declared, under instructions from Trotsky, that it was not a freely negotiated settlement but a German *diktat* imposed on a helpless Russia. Backing was given to this claim by the terms of the treaty, which could hardly have been more humiliating for Russia.

Treaty of Brest-Litovsk: March 1918

Key date

Terms of the treaty

- A huge slice of territory, amounting to a third of European Russia, stretching from the Baltic to the Black Sea and including Ukraine, Russia's major grain source, was ceded to Germany or its allies.
- The land lost by Russia – about a million square kilometres – contained a population of 45 million.
- Russia was required to pay 3 billion roubles in war **reparations**.

Lenin's reasons for accepting the treaty

Aware that the signing of the treaty would be resented by many Bolsheviks, who were still pressing for a revolutionary struggle against Germany, Lenin stressed that his policy was the only realistic one:

> Our impulse tells us to rebel, to refuse to sign this robber peace. Our reason will in our calmer moments tell us the plain naked truth – that Russia can offer no physical resistance because she is materially exhausted by three years of war.

He acknowledged that there were Russians willing to fight on in a great cause. But they were 'romanticists' who did not understand the situation. Wars were not won by idealism alone; resources and technical skills were needed. The plain truth was that Bolshevik Russia did not yet have these in sufficient quantity to match Germany. Therefore, 'the Russian Revolution must sign the peace to obtain a breathing space to recuperate for the struggle'.

Lenin added that he expected that, before long, Russia would be in a position to reclaim its lost territories, since in the aftermath of the war a violent conflict would soon develop among the capitalist powers. The main struggle would be between 'English and German **finance capital**.' His rallying cry was, therefore, 'Let the Revolution utilise this struggle for its own ends.'

Lenin's argument was a powerful one, yet he still experienced great difficulty in convincing his colleagues. The issue was debated bitterly in the Central Committee. In the end, Lenin gained his way only by a majority of one in a crucial Committee division.

Key terms

Diktat
A settlement imposed on a weaker nation by a stronger.

Reparations
Payment of war costs by the loser to the victor.

Finance capital
Lenin's term for the resource used by stronger countries to exploit weaker ones. By investing heavily in another country, a stronger power made that country dependent on it. It was a form of imperialism.

A profound issue lay at the base of Bolshevik disagreements. To understand this, it has to be re-emphasised that Lenin and Trotsky were primarily international revolutionaries. They expected workers' risings, based on the Russian model, to sweep across Europe. Purely national conflicts would soon be superseded by the international class struggle of the workers. Lenin and Trotsky regarded the crippling terms of the Treaty of Brest-Litovsk as of small account when set against the great sweep of world revolution.

The 'Left Communists'

Not all Bolsheviks shared this vision. A number, known as **'Left Communists'**, condemned the signing of the treaty at Brest-Litovsk. In the end, after days of wrangling, it was only Lenin's insistence on the absolute need for Party loyalty in a time of crisis that finally persuaded them reluctantly to accept the treaty. Even then, serious opposition to Lenin's leadership might well have persisted had not the turn of military events in western Europe saved the day.

What eventually destroyed the argument of the Left Communists and the Left SRs was the collapse of Germany's western front in August 1918, followed by the almost total withdrawal of German forces from Russia. Lenin's gamble that circumstances would soon make the Treaty of Brest-Litovsk meaningless had paid off. It strengthened his hold over the party and provided the opportunity to expel the Left SRs from the government and to outlaw them politically.

Key term

'Left Communists'
Bolsheviks who were convinced that their first task was to consolidate the October Revolution by driving the German imperialist armies from Russia. The term was later used to describe Party members who opposed the NEP (see page 161).

Summary diagram: The Treaty of Brest-Litovsk 1918

Divergent attitudes among the Bolsheviks towards the war
Some wanted the continuation of a revolutionary war against Germany
Others wanted an immediate peace to lessen strains on Russia

Lenin took a realistic stance:
– Russia could not win, so best make peace so as to fight another day

Trotsky took a compromise position:
– 'Neither peace, nor war'
– Russia could not win, but delay peace settlement as long as possible to encourage mutiny in Germany
– Used deliberately disruptive tactics at talks

The Treaty

Harsh terms imposed on Russia:
– Lost a third of its European lands
– Together with the 45 million people in them
– Russia was to pay 3 billion roubles in reparations

Consequence

– Further conflict between Lenin and Left SRs
– But defeat of Germany in November 1918 seemed to justify his policy

4 | The Russian Civil War, 1918–20

The crushing by the Bolsheviks of the Constituent Assembly in January 1918, followed by their outlawing of all other parties, showed that they were not prepared to share power. This bid for absolute authority made civil war highly likely, given that the Bolsheviks had only a limited grip on Russia in the early years after the October Revolution. They were bound to face military opposition from their wide range of opponents who were not prepared to accept subjection to the absolute rule of a minority party.

Modern research strongly suggests that Lenin truly wanted a destructive civil war. Although it involved obvious dangers to the Bolsheviks, Lenin was convinced that his forces could win and that in winning they would wipe out all their opponents, military and political. Better to have a short, brutal struggle than face many years of being harassed and challenged by the anti-Bolsheviks, who were a large majority in Russia, as the Constituent Assembly election results had shown all too clearly (see page 122).

Lenin knew that had the Bolsheviks chosen to co-operate in a coalition of all the revolutionary parties in 1918, two consequences would have followed:

- A successful counter-revolution would have been easier to mount since the socialist parties would have had a popular **mandate** to govern.
- The Bolsheviks would have been unable to dominate government since they were very much a minority compared with the Mensheviks and Social Revolutionaries.

It was the second consequence that Lenin refused to contemplate. As Dominic Lieven, an outstanding modern scholar, observes: 'Some Bolsheviks would have accepted a socialist coalition but Lenin was not one of them. The Bolshevik leader rejected this course and pursued policies, which, as he well knew, made civil war inevitable.'

Reds, Whites and Greens

The conflict that began in the summer of 1918 was not just a matter of the Bolsheviks (the **Reds**) facing their political enemies (the **Whites**) in a military struggle. From the start, the Civil War was a more complex affair. It involved yet another colour – the **Greens**.

A class war or a national struggle?

The Bolsheviks presented the struggle as a class war, but it was never simply that. The sheer size of Russia often meant that local or regional considerations predominated over larger issues. The prime concern of the Greens, such as the Ukrainians and the Georgians, in fighting was to establish their independence from Russia.

It was ironic that although most of the leading Bolsheviks were non-Russian, their rule was seen by many as yet another attempt to reassert Russian authority over the rest of the country – the very situation that had prevailed under the tsars. As in all civil wars, the

Key question
How far was Lenin personally responsible for the Civil War?

Key terms

Mandate
The authority to govern granted by a majority of the people through elections.

Reds
The Bolsheviks and their supporters.

Whites
The Bolsheviks' opponents, including monarchists, looking for a tsarist restoration, and those parties that had been outlawed or suppressed by the new regime.

Greens
Largely made up of groups from the national minorities; the best known of the Green leaders was **Nestor Makhno**.

Key question
Who were the opposing sides in the war?

Key figure

Nestor Makhno (1889–1935)
A one-time Bolshevik who organised a guerrilla resistance to the Reds in Ukraine.

disruption provided a cover for settling old scores and pursuing personal vendettas, and it was not uncommon for villages or even families to be divided against each other.

A war about food

On occasion the fighting was simply a desperate struggle for food. Famine provided the backdrop to the Civil War. The breakdown in food supplies that had occurred during the war against Germany persisted. Until this was remedied, whole areas of Russia remained hungry.

The failure of the new regime to end hunger was an important factor in creating the initial military opposition to the Bolsheviks in 1918. In addition to the problems of a fractured transport system, Lenin's government was faced with the loss to Germany of Ukraine, Russia's main wheat-supply area. In March 1918, the month in which the Brest-Litovsk Treaty was signed, the bread ration in Petrograd reached its lowest ever allocation of 50 grams per day. Hunger forced many workers out of the major industrial cities.

By June 1918 the workforce in Petrograd had shrunk by 60 per cent and the overall population had declined from 3 million to 2 million. A visitor to the city at this time spoke of 'entering a metropolis of cold, of hunger, of hatred, of endurance'. The Bolshevik boast that October 1917 had established worker control of Russian industry meant little now that starving workers were deserting the factories in droves.

Challenge from the SRs

The desperate conditions encouraged open challenges to the Bolsheviks from both left and right. The SRs, who had been driven out of the government for their refusal to accept the Brest-Litovsk settlement, organised an anti-Bolshevik coup in Moscow, which in 1918, for security reasons, replaced Petrograd as the capital of Soviet Russia. The civil war could therefore be said to have begun not as a counter-revolution but as an effort by one set of revolutionaries to take power from another. In that sense it was an attempted revenge by a majority party, the SRs, against a minority party, the Bolsheviks, for having usurped the authority that they claimed was properly theirs.

The SRs' military rising in Moscow failed, but their terrorism came closer to success. Lenin narrowly survived two attempts on his life, in July and August. The second attempt, by **Dora Kaplan**, an SR fanatic, left him with a bullet lodged in his neck, an injury which contributed to the strokes that brought about his death six years later. In their desperation at being denied any say in government, the SRs joined the Whites in their struggle against Lenin's Reds.

The Czech Legion

Armed resistance to the Bolsheviks had occurred sporadically in various parts of Russia since October 1917. What gave focus to this struggle was the behaviour in the summer of 1918 of one of the foreign armies still in Russia. Forty thousand Czechoslovak troops,

Key figure

Dora (Fanny) Kaplan (1890–1918) A Socialist Revolutionary who had been sentenced to death under the tasrist regime for bomb making, she resolved to kill Lenin in reprisal for his outlawing of the SRs.

who had volunteered to fight on the Russian side in the First World War as a means of gaining independence from Austria-Hungary, found themselves isolated after the Treaty of Brest-Litovsk. They formed themselves into the Czech Legion and decided to make the long journey eastwards to Vladivostok.

Their aim was eventually to rejoin the Allies on the western front in the hope of winning international support for the formation of an independent Czechoslovak state. The Bolsheviks resented the presence of this well-equipped foreign army making its way arrogantly across Russia. Local soviets began to challenge the Czech Legion, and fierce fighting accompanied its progress along the Trans-Siberian Railway.

Well armed and supplied, the troops of the Czech Legion aboard an armoured train in 1918. How does this picture help to explain why the presence of the Czech Legion in Russia was such a problem for the Bolsheviks?

Armed resistance spreads

All this encouraged the Whites, and all the revolutionary and liberal groups who had been outlawed by the Bolsheviks, to come out openly against Lenin's regime.

- The SRs organised a number of uprisings in central Russia and established an anti-Bolshevik Volga 'Republic' at Samara.
- A White 'Volunteer Army', led by General **Denikin**, had already been formed in the Caucasus region of southern Russia from tsarist loyalists and outlawed Kadets.
- In Siberia, the presence of the Czech Legion encouraged the formation of a White army under Admiral **Kolchak**, the self-proclaimed 'Supreme Ruler of Russia'.
- In Estonia, another ex-tsarist general, **Yudenich**, began to form a White army of resistance.

Anton Denikin (1872–1947) Supported Kornilov in 1917, and escaped from Petrograd after the October coup to form his own army in Novocherkassk in southern Russia.

Key figure

White units appeared in many other regions. The speed with which they arose indicated just how limited Bolshevik control was outside the cities of western Russia.

Bolshevik victory

The patchwork of political, regional and national loyalties inside Russia made the Civil War a confused affair. It is best understood as a story of the Bolsheviks' resisting attacks on four main fronts and then taking the initiative and driving back their attackers until they eventually withdrew or surrendered. Unlike the First World War, the Civil War was a war of movement, largely dictated by the layout of Russia's railway system. It was because the Bolsheviks were largely successful in their desperate fight to maintain control of the railways that they were able to keep themselves supplied, while denying the Whites the same benefit.

The reasons for the final victory of the Reds in the Civil War are not difficult to determine.

White weaknesses

- The various White armies fought as separate detachments.
- Apart from their obvious desire to overthrow the Bolsheviks, they were not bound together by a single aim.
- They were unwilling to sacrifice their individual interests in order to form a united anti-Bolshevik front. This allowed the Reds to pick off the White armies separately.
- In the rare cases in which the Whites did consider combining, they were too widely scattered geographically to be able to bring sufficient pressure to bear on the enemy.
- The Whites were too reliant on supplies from abroad, which seldom arrived in sufficient quantities, in the right places, at the right time.
- The Whites lacked leaders of the quality of Trotsky.

Red strengths

The Reds, in contrast, had a number of overwhelming advantages:

- They remained in control of a concentrated central area of western Russia, which they were able to defend by maintaining their inner communication and supply lines.
- The two major cities, Petrograd and Moscow, the administrative centres of Russia, remained in their hands throughout the war, as did most of the railway network.
- The Reds also possessed a key advantage in that the areas where they had their strongest hold were the industrial centres of Russia. This gave them access to munitions and resources denied to the Whites.
- The dependence of the Whites on supplies from abroad appeared to prove the Red accusation that they were in league with the foreign interventionists (see page 140). The Civil War had produced a paradoxical situation in which the Reds were able to stand as champions of the Russian nation as well as proletarian revolutionaries.
- The Red Army was brilliantly organised and led by Trotsky.

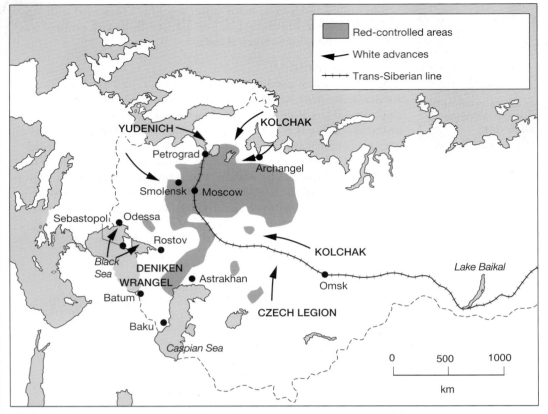

Figure 5.2: The Russian Civil War, 1918–20.

Trotsky's role

Trotsky's strategy as the Reds' Commissar for War was simple and direct:

Key question
What strategy did
Trotsky follow?

- to defend the Red Army's internal lines of communication
- to deny the Whites the opportunity to concentrate large forces in any one location
- to prevent the Whites from maintaining regular supplies.

The key to this strategy was control of Russia's railways. Trotsky viewed the role of the railways as equivalent to that of the cavalry in former times. They were the means of transporting troops swiftly and in large numbers to the critical areas of defence or attack. It was no accident that the decisive confrontations between Reds and Whites took place near rail junctions and depots.

Trotsky's broad strategy was successful. Once the Reds had established an effective defence of their main region around Petrograd and Moscow, they were able to exhaust the Whites as an attacking force and then drive them back on the major fronts until they scattered or surrendered.

Profile: Leon Trotsky (1879–1940)

1879	– Born into a Ukrainian Jewish family
1898	– Convicted of revolutionary activities and exiled to Siberia
1902	– Adopts the name Trotsky
	– Escapes from exile and joined Lenin in London
1903	– Sides with the Mensheviks in the SD split
1905	– Becomes chairman of St Petersburg Soviet
1906	– Exiled again to Siberia
1907	– Escapes again and flees abroad
1907–17	– Lives in various European countries and in the USA
1917	– Returns to Petrograd after the February Revolution
	– The principal organiser of the October coup
	– Appointed Foreign Affairs Commissar
1918	– Negotiates the Treaty of Brest-Litovsk
1918–20	– As War Commissar, creates the Red Army
1921	– Crushes the Kronstadt Rising
	– Destroys the trade unions in Russia
1924–27	– Outmanoeuvred in the power struggle with Stalin
1927	– Sentenced to internal exile at Alma Ata
1929	– Banished from the USSR
1929–40	– Lives in various countries
	– Writes prodigiously on revolutionary theory, in opposition to Stalin
1940	– Assassinated in Mexico on Stalin's orders

Trotsky's real name was Leon (Lev) Bronstein. He was born into a Jewish landowning family in Ukraine in 1879. Rebellious from an early age, he sided with the peasants on his family's estate. Yet, like Lenin, he rejected 'economism' (see page 23), the attempt to raise the standards of peasants and workers by improving their conditions. He wanted to intensify class warfare by exploiting grievances, not to lessen it by introducing reforms.

1905 Revolution
As a revolutionary, Trotsky's sympathies lay with the Mensheviks, and it was as a Menshevik that he became president of the St Petersburg Soviet during the 1905 Revolution. His activities led to his arrest and exile. Between 1906 and 1917 he lived in a variety of foreign countries, developing his theory of 'permanent revolution', the notion that revolution was not a single event but a continuous process of international class warfare.

Chairman of the Petrograd Soviet
Following the collapse of tsardom in the February Revolution, Trotsky returned to Petrograd and immediately joined the Bolshevik Party. He became chairman of the Petrograd Soviet, a position that he used to organise the Bolshevik rising that overthrew the Provisional Government in October 1917.

Commissar for Foreign Affairs

In the Bolshevik government that then took over, Trotsky became Commissar for Foreign Affairs. He was the chief negotiator in the Russo-German talks that resulted in Russia's withdrawal from the war in 1918 under the Treaty of Brest-Litovsk.

The Civil War

He then became Commissar for War and achieved what was arguably the greatest success of his career, the victory of the Red Army in the Civil War of 1918–20. As a hardliner, Trotsky fully supported Lenin's repressive policy of war communism. He plotted the destruction of the Russian trade unions, and in 1921 ordered the suppression of the rebellious Kronstadt workers.

Power struggle

In terms of ability, Trotsky ought to have been the main contender in the power struggle that followed Lenin's death. But he was never fully accepted by his fellow Bolsheviks, which enabled Stalin to isolate him. Trotsky's concept of permanent revolution was condemned as anti-Soviet, since it appeared to put international revolution before the establishment of 'socialism in one country', Stalin's term for the consolidation of Communist rule in the USSR.

Exile again

In 1929, Trotsky was exiled from the USSR. He spent his last 11 years in a variety of countries, attempting to develop an international following opposed to the Soviet regime. In 1939 he founded the Fourth International, a movement of anti-Stalin Marxists drawn from some 30 countries.

Death

Trotsky's end came in 1940 in Mexico City, when a Soviet agent acting on Stalin's direct orders killed him by driving an ice-pick into his head.

Red brutality

The Reds and Whites continually accused each other of committing atrocities. Both sides did undoubtedly use terror to crush opposition in the areas they seized. The actual fighting was not unduly bloody; it was in the aftermath, when the civilian population was cowed into submission, that the savagery usually occurred. The Reds gained recruits by offering defeated enemy troops and neutral civilians the stark choice of enlistment or execution.

Although the Reds imposed a reign of terror, the Whites' own record in ill-treating local populations was equally notorious. To the ordinary Russian there was little to choose between the warring sides in the matter of brutality. By the end of the Civil War, whatever initial peasant sympathy the Reds had gained had been lost by the severity of their grain-requisitioning methods.

Key question
Why did the peasantry support the Reds?

However, the Whites were unable to present themselves as a better alternative. All they could offer was a return to the pre-revolutionary past. This was particularly damaging to them in relation to the land question. The Reds continually pointed out that all the lands that the peasants had seized in the Revolutions of 1917 would be forfeited if ever the Whites were to win the war. It was this fear more than any other that stopped the peasants from giving their support to the Whites.

The importance of morale

Key question
In what way was morale a factor in the Reds' victory?

Waging war is not just a matter of resources and firepower. Morale and dedication play a vital role. Throughout the struggle the Reds were sustained by a driving sense of purpose. Trotsky, as the Bolshevik War Commissar, may have been extreme in his methods, but he created an army that proved capable of fighting with an unshakable belief in its own eventual victory (see page 149).

Set against this, the Whites were never more than an un-coordinated group of forces whose morale was seldom high. They were a collection of dispossessed socialists, liberals and moderates, whose political differences often led them into bitter disputes among themselves. Save for their hatred of Bolshevism, the Whites lacked a common purpose. Throughout the Civil War the White cause was deeply divided by the conflicting interests of those who were fighting for national or regional independence and those who wanted a return to strong central government. Furthermore, no White leader emerged of the stature of Trotsky or Lenin, around whom an effective anti-Bolshevik army could unite.

Effects of the Civil War on the Bolsheviks
Toughness

Key question
What effect did the Civil War have on the character of Bolshevism?

Key date
The Bolshevik Party renamed the Communist Party: March 1919

On the domestic front, the Civil War proved to be one of the great formative influences on the Bolshevik Party (renamed the Communist Party in 1919). Their attempts at government took place during a period of conflict in which their very survival was at stake. The development of the Party and the government has to be set against this background. The Revolution had been born in war, and the government had been formed in war. Of all the members of the Communist Party in 1927, a third had joined in the years 1917–20 and had fought in the Red Army. This had created a tradition of military obedience and loyalty. The Bolsheviks of this generation were hard men, forged in the fires of war.

Authoritarianism

A number of modern analysts have emphasised the central place that the Civil War had in shaping the character of Communist rule in Soviet Russia. Robert Tucker stresses that it was the military aspect of early Bolshevik government that left it with a 'readiness to resort to coercion, rule by administrative fiat [commands], centralised administration [and] summary justice'. No regime placed in the Bolshevik predicament between 1917 and 1921 could have survived without resort to authoritarian measures.

Centralisation

The move towards centralism in government increased as the Civil War dragged on. The emergencies of war required immediate day-to-day decisions to be made. This led to effective power moving away from the Central Committee of the Communist (Bolshevik) Party, which was too cumbersome, into the hands of the two key sub-committees set up in 1919, the **Politburo** and the **Orgburo**, which could act with the necessary speed. In practice, the authority of *Sovnarkom*, the official government of Soviet Russia, became indistinguishable from the rule of these party committees, which was served by the **Secretariat**.

Politburo
Short for Political Bureau, the inner cabinet of the ruling Central Committee of the CPSU.

Key term

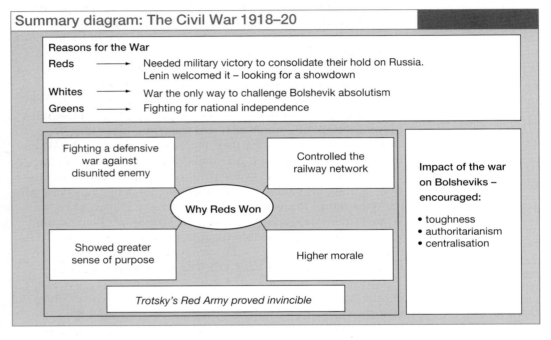

Summary diagram: The Civil War 1918–20

Reasons for the War

Reds ⟶ Needed military victory to consolidate their hold on Russia. Lenin welcomed it – looking for a showdown

Whites ⟶ War the only way to challenge Bolshevik absolutism

Greens ⟶ Fighting for national independence

Why Reds Won
- Fighting a defensive war against disunited enemy
- Controlled the railway network
- Showed greater sense of purpose
- Higher morale

Trotsky's Red Army proved invincible

Impact of the war on Bolsheviks – encouraged:
- toughness
- authoritarianism
- centralisation

5 | The Foreign Interventions, 1918–20

Allied attitudes towards the Revolution

When tsardom collapsed in 1917 the immediate worry for the western Allies was whether the new regime would keep Russia in the war. If revolutionary Russia made a separate peace, Germany would be free to divert huge military resources from the eastern to the western front. To prevent this, the Allies offered large amounts of capital and military supplies to Russia to keep it in the war. The new government eagerly accepted the offer; throughout its eight months in office from February to October 1917 the Provisional Government remained committed to the war against Germany in return for Allied war credits and supplies.

This produced an extraordinary balance. On one side stood Lenin and his anti-war Bolsheviks financed by Germany; on the other the pro-war Provisional Government funded by the Allies.

Key question
What led foreign powers to intervene in Russia?

Orgburo
Short for Organisation Bureau, responsible for developing the Communist Party's policies.

Secretariat
The civil service that put Communist Party policies into practice.

Key terms

However, the October Revolution destroyed the balance. The collapse of the Provisional Government and the seizure of power by the Bolsheviks had precisely the effect hoped for by Germany and feared by the Allies. Within weeks, an armistice had been agreed between Germany and the new government, and fighting on the eastern front stopped in December 1917.

The initial response of France and Britain was cautious. In the faint hope that the Bolsheviks might be persuaded to continue the fight against Germany, the same support was offered to them as to their predecessors. David Lloyd George, the British Prime Minister, declared that he was neither for nor against Bolshevism, but simply anti-German. He was willing to side with any group in Russia that would continue the war against Germany.

Allied attitudes harden

However, the Treaty of Brest-Litovsk in March 1918 ended all hope of Lenin's Russia renewing the war against Germany. From now on, any help given by Britain to anti-German Russians went necessarily to anti-Bolshevik forces. It appeared to the Bolsheviks that Britain and its allies were intent on destroying them. This was matched by the Allies' view that in making a separate peace with Germany the Bolsheviks had betrayed the Allied cause. The result was a fierce determination among the Allies to prevent their vital war supplies, previously loaned to Russia and still stockpiled there, from falling into German hands.

Soon after the signing of the Treaty of Brest-Litovsk, British, French and American troops occupied the ports of Murmansk in the Arctic and Archangel in the White Sea (see map page 139). This was the beginning of a two-year period during which armed forces from a large number of countries occupied key areas of European, central and Far Eastern Russia.

Once the First World War had ended in November 1918, the attention of the major powers turned to the possibility of a major offensive against the Bolsheviks. Among those most eager for an attack were Winston Churchill, then a British cabinet minister, and Marshal Foch, the French military leader. They were alarmed by the creation of the **Comintern** and by the spread of revolution in Germany and central Europe:

- In January 1918 the 'Spartacists', a German Communist movement (named after Spartacus, the leader of a slave rebellion in ancient Rome), tried unsuccessfully to mount a coup in Berlin.
- In 1918–19 a short-lived Communist republic was established in Bavaria.
- In March 1919 in Hungary a Marxist government was set up under Béla Kun, only to fall five months later.

Key term

Comintern
Short for the Communist International, a body set up in Moscow in March 1919 to organise worldwide revolution.

Key date

Comintern established: March 1919

THE PERIL WITHOUT.

'The Peril Without.' A British cartoon of April 1919, showing the Bolsheviks as ravenous wolves preparing to attack a peaceful Europe. Britain and France were among the leading western countries who feared that revolutionary Bolshevism would spread across Europe. What influence might such images as these have in shaping British attitudes towards Bolshevik Russia?

The interventions spread

There was also a key financial aspect to anti-Bolshevism in western Europe. One of the first acts of the Bolshevik regime was to declare that the new government had no intention of honouring the foreign debts of its predecessors. In addition, it nationalised a large number of foreign companies and froze all foreign assets in Russia. The bitter reaction to what was regarded as international theft was particularly strong in France, where many small- and middle-scale financiers had invested in tsarist Russia. It was the French who now took the lead in proposing an international campaign against the Reds, the main features of which were the following:

- In 1918, British land forces entered Transcaucasia in southern Russia and also occupied part of central Asia.
- British warships entered Russian Baltic waters and the Black Sea, where French naval vessels joined them.
- The French also established a major land base around the Black Sea port of Odessa.
- In April 1918, Japanese troops occupied Russia's far eastern port of Vladivostok.

- Four months later, units from France, Britain, the USA and Italy joined them.
- Czech, Finnish, Lithuanian, Polish and Romanian forces crossed into Russia.
- In 1919, Japanese and United States troops occupied parts of Siberia.

Principal armies attempting to destroy Bolshevism

— Under Bolshevik rule November 1918

- - - Maximum advance of the anti-Bolshevik forces 1918–19

▨ Remnant of anti-Bolshevik forces, defeated 1920–1

---- Established Russian frontiers, March 1921–October 1939

Figure 5.3: The foreign interventions, 1918–21.

An important point to stress is that these were not co-ordinated attacks; there was little co-operation between the occupiers. The declared motive of Britain, France, Germany, Italy, Japan and the USA was the legitimate protection of their individual interests. The objective of Czechoslovakia, Finland, Lithuania, Poland and Romania, all of which directly bordered western Russia, was to achieve their separatist aim, which went back to tsarist times, of gaining independence from Russia.

Failure of the interventions

Key question
Why did the foreign interventions not succeed?

Despite the preaching of an anti-Bolshevik crusade by influential voices in western Europe, no concerted attempt was ever made to unseat the Bolshevik regime. This was shown by the relative ease with which the interventions were resisted. The truth was that, after four long years of struggle against Germany, the interventionists had no stomach for a prolonged campaign. There were serious threats of mutiny in some British and French regiments ordered to embark for Russia. Moreover, trade unionists who were sympathetic towards the new 'workers' state' refused to transport military supplies bound for Russia.

After the separate national forces had arrived in Russia, there was seldom effective liaison between them. Furthermore, such efforts as the foreign forces made to co-operate with the White armies were half-hearted and came to little. The one major exception to this was in the Baltic States, where the national forces, backed by British warships and troops, crushed a Bolshevik invasion and obliged Lenin's government to recognise the independence of Estonia, Latvia and Lithuania, a freedom that they maintained until taken over by Stalin in 1940.

Such interventionist success was not repeated elsewhere. After a token display of aggression, the foreign troops began to withdraw. By the end of 1919 all French and American troops had been recalled, and by the end of 1920 all other western forces had left. It was only the Japanese who remained in Russia for the duration of the Civil War, not finally leaving until 1922.

Propaganda success for the Bolsheviks

In no real sense were these withdrawals a military victory for the Bolsheviks, but that was exactly how they were portrayed in Soviet propaganda. Lenin's government presented itself as the saviour of the nation from foreign conquest; all the interventions had been imperialist invasions of Russia intent on overthrowing the Revolution. This apparent success over Russia's enemies helped the Bolshevik regime recover the esteem it had lost over its 1918 capitulation to Germany. It helped to put resolve into the doubters in the party and it lent credibility to the Bolshevik depiction of the Whites as agents of foreign powers, intent on restoring reactionary tsardom.

Key date
Invading Red Army
driven from Poland:
April 1920

War against Poland

The failure of the foreign interventions encouraged the Bolsheviks
to undertake what proved to be a disastrous attempt to expand
their authority outside Russia. In 1920 the Red Army marched into
neighbouring Poland, expecting the Polish workers to rise in
rebellion against their own government. However, the Poles saw
the invasion as traditional Russian aggression and drove the Red
Army back across the border. Soviet morale was seriously damaged,
which forced Lenin and the Bolsheviks to rethink the whole
question of international revolution.

Key question
What was Lenin's
attitude towards
foreign affairs?

Lenin's approach to foreign affairs

Lenin adopted an essentially realistic approach. He judged that
the Polish reverse, the foreign interventions in Russia, and the
failure of the Communist revolutions in Germany and Hungary all
showed that the time was not ripe for world revolution. The
capitalist nations were still too strong. The Bolsheviks would,
therefore, without abandoning their long-term revolutionary
objectives, adjust their foreign policy to meet the new situation.
The Comintern would continue to call for world revolution, but
Soviet Russia would soften its international attitude.

   Lenin's concerns were very much in the tradition of Russian
foreign policy. Western encroachment into Russia had been a
constant fear of the tsars. That long-standing Russian worry had
been increased by the hostility of European governments to the
October Revolution and by their support of the Whites during the
Civil War. Lenin's reading of the international situation led him to
conclude that discretion was the better part of valour. Under him,
Soviet foreign policy was activated not by thoughts of expansion
but by the desire to avoid conflict.

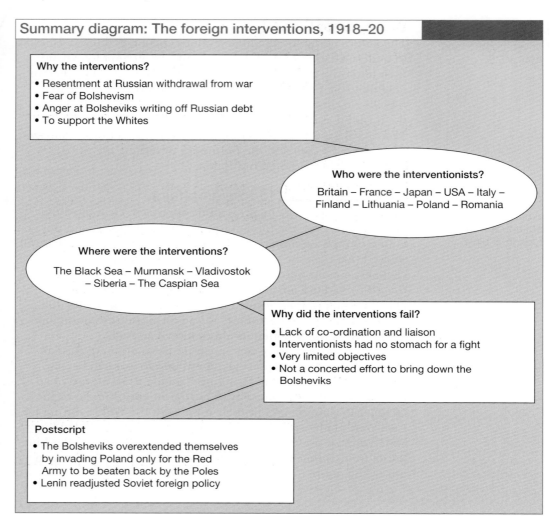

Summary diagram: The foreign interventions, 1918–20

Why the interventions?

- Resentment at Russian withdrawal from war
- Fear of Bolshevism
- Anger at Bolsheviks writing off Russian debt
- To support the Whites

Who were the interventionists?

Britain – France – Japan – USA – Italy – Finland – Lithuania – Poland – Romania

Where were the interventions?

The Black Sea – Murmansk – Vladivostok – Siberia – The Caspian Sea

Why did the interventions fail?

- Lack of co-ordination and liaison
- Interventionists had no stomach for a fight
- Very limited objectives
- Not a concerted effort to bring down the Bolsheviks

Postscript

- The Bolsheviks overextended themselves by invading Poland only for the Red Army to be beaten back by the Poles
- Lenin readjusted Soviet foreign policy

Study Guide: AS Question
In the style of OCR

To what extent was Lenin's victory in the Civil War due to the weakness of his opposition? (50 marks)

Exam tips

The cross-references are intended to take you straight to the material that will help you to answer the question.

Lenin owed his victory to a number of factors. Although you should devote a good portion of your answer to analysing the weaknesses of his opposition, these reasons should then be set against other factors before you arrive at a conclusion. Focus at the start on the weaknesses of the opposition. You might discuss some of the following:

- the divisive nature of the opposition (pages 128–131, 135)
- poor leadership (page 131)
- a heavy dependence on overseas supplies (page 131)
- the fact that the Whites failed to win peasant support (pages 134–5)
- the failure of international support (pages 136–40).
- the contribution of Trotsky and the Red Army (pages 132–4,149)
- the Reds' control of a central area of Russia (page 131).

Finally, ensure you reach a balanced judgement that relates back to the question.

6

Lenin's Revolution, 1917–24

POINTS TO CONSIDER
The development of the Soviet state under Lenin after 1917 remains a crucial and controversial aspect of the Russian Revolution. The issues it raises are considered in this chapter under the following themes:

- the Red Terror
- war communism
- the Kronstadt Rising, 1921
- the New Economic Policy (NEP)
- society under Lenin
- Lenin's role as a revolutionary
- interpretations of the Russian Revolution.

Key dates

1918–20	The Red Terror
1918 January	Red Army established
	Decree on Separation of Church and State
June	Decree on Nationalisation
July	Murder of the tsar and his family
	War communism
	Forced grain requisitions begin
1921 March	The Kronstadt Rising
	Introduction of the NEP
	The decree against factionalism
1922–3	Lenin suffers a number of strokes
1922 December	The Soviet state becomes the USSR (Union of Soviet Socialist Republics)
1923	The Scissors Crisis
1924 January	Death of Lenin

1 | The Red Terror

The repression that accompanied the spread of Bolshevik control over Russia between 1918 and 1921 was so severe that it became known as the Terror. Whether the severity was justified remains a matter of debate. One argument is that the extreme measures that Lenin's government adopted were the only response possible to the problems confronting the Bolsheviks after the October Revolution, in particular the need to win a desperate civil war.

An opposing view is that repression was not a reaction to circumstances but was a defining characteristic of **Marxism-Leninism**, a creed that regarded itself as uniquely superior to all other ideologies. An extension of this argument is that there was something essentially totalitarian about Lenin himself. He did not know how to act in any other way. He had always accepted the necessity of terror as an instrument of political control. Before 1917 he had often made it clear that a Marxist revolution could not survive if it were not prepared to smash its enemies: 'Coercion is necessary for the transition from capitalism to socialism. There is absolutely no contradiction between Soviet democracy and the exercise of dictatorial powers.'

The chief instruments by which the Bolsheviks exercised their policy of terror were the *Cheka* and the Red Army, both of which played a critical role during the Civil War.

The *Cheka*

This state police force, often likened historically to the **Gestapo**, had been created in December 1917 under the direction of the ruthless **Felix Dzerzhinsky**. Lenin found him the ideal choice to lead the fight against the enemies of the Revolution. Dzerzhinsky never allowed finer feelings or compassion to deter him from the task of destroying the enemies of Bolshevism. His remorseless attitude was shown in the various directives that issued from the *Cheka* headquarters in Moscow.

> Our Revolution is in danger. Do not concern yourselves with the forms of revolutionary justice. We have no need for justice now. Now we have need of a battle to the death! I propose, I demand the use of the revolutionary sword which will put an end to all counter-revolutionaries.

The *Cheka*, which was to change its title several times over the years, but never its essential character, remains the outstanding expression of Bolshevik ruthlessness. Operating as a law unto itself, and answerable only to Lenin, it was granted unlimited powers of arrest, detention and torture, which it used in the most arbitrary and brutal way. It was the main instrument by which Lenin and his successors terrorised the Russian people into subservience and conformity.

Key question
Were Lenin's terror tactics a temporary response to a desperate situation or an expression of Russian communism's true character?

Key date

Red Terror officially introduced: September 1918

Key terms

Marxism-Leninism
The notion that Marx's theory of class war as interpreted by Lenin was an unchallengeably accurate piece of scientific analysis.

Gestapo
The secret police in Nazi Germany.

Key figure

Felix Dzerzhinsky (1877–1926)
An intellectual of Polish aristocratic background who sought to atone for his privileged origins by absolute dedication to the Bolshevik cause.

Murder of the Romanovs, July 1918

In July 1918 a group of SRs assassinated the German ambassador as a protest against the Treaty of Brest-Litovsk. A month later an attempt was made on Lenin's life (see page 129), followed by the murder of the Petrograd chairman of the *Cheka*. These incidents were made the pretext for a Bolshevik reign of terror. It was in this atmosphere that a local *Cheka* detachment, on Lenin's personal order, executed the ex-tsar and his family in a basement room of a house in Yekaterinburg in the Urals on 17 July 1918. They were mown down in a hail of revolver shots fired by a ten-man execution squad.

After abdicating in February, Nicholas had hoped that he and his family would be granted haven in Britain, but, after making an initial offer of asylum, neither the British government nor the British monarch, George V, was willing to risk the diplomatic problems that they feared might follow if the Romanovs were allowed to settle in Britain.

Similarly, the German Kaiser, a cousin of the ex-tsar and godfather to his son, Alexei, had declined to offer the family sanctuary in Germany. His official reason was that such an offer might be read as implying support for the tsar's restoration, which would compromise German neutrality now that Russia and Germany were at peace following the signing of the Brest-Litovsk Treaty in March (see page 124). A more probable explanation is that the Kaiser was anxious not to upset the radical parties in Germany, which were already using Germany's increasingly desperate position in the war to threaten revolution.

The shooting of the Romanovs was the violent climax of eight months of indecision during which the Bolsheviks, having seized the royal family after the October Revolution, had hesitated over what to do with them. Nicholas, Alexandra and their five children had been moved together to a number of different locations to prevent tsarist supporters from attempting to rescue them.

The Bolsheviks had thought of putting Nicholas on public trial for his crimes against the Russian people during his reign. Trotsky was a strong proponent of the idea. Lenin, however, considered that the Bolsheviks' precarious hold on power made this too risky; he feared that as long as the Romanov family stayed alive, they would remain a potential centre for tsarist reaction. It was vital, he said, 'to remove the possibility of the monarchist banner reappearing on the scene'.

But the assassination was not simply a security move. There was a disturbing personal aspect to it. Lenin intended it as an act of revenge on the pre-1917 Russian world that he hated. Lenin's biographer Robert Service puts it in these chilling terms:

> [Lenin] exterminated the Romanovs because they had misruled Russia. But he also turned to such measures because he enjoyed – really enjoyed – letting himself loose against people in general from the *ancien régime*. He hated not only the Imperial family but also the middling people who had administered and controlled Russia before 1917.

Murder of the tsar and his family: July 1918

Key date

Key term

Canonisation
Formal bestowing
of sainthood.

In 1991, skeletal remains that had been discovered earlier in a grave outside Yekaterinburg were subjected to special forensic matching programmes and DNA testing. The results confirmed that these were the bodies of Nicholas, his wife and three of their children. In 1998 the remains were given honoured burial in the chapel of the St Peter and Paul Fortress in St Petersburg, the traditional resting place of the Russian tsars. In 2000, Nicholas and his family were **canonised** by the Russian Orthodox Church. Later tests confirmed in 2008 that further bones which had been discovered were the remains of the two children not accounted for up to then, Alexei and Maria.

The *Cheka* wages class war

The murder of the Romanovs without benefit of trial was typical of the manner in which the *Cheka* went about its business throughout Russia. In accordance with Dzerzhinsky's instructions, all pretence of legality was abandoned; the basic rules relating to evidence and proof of guilt no longer applied. Persecution was directed not simply against individuals, but against whole classes. This was class war of the most direct kind.

> Do not demand incriminating evidence to prove that the prisoner has opposed the Soviet government by force or words. Your first duty is to ask him to which class he belongs, what are his origins, his education, his occupation. These questions should decide the fate of the prisoner.

Some Bolsheviks were uneasy about the relentless savagery of the *Cheka*, but there were no attempts to restrict its powers. The majority of party members accepted that the hazardous situation they were in justified the severity of the repression. The foreign interventions and the Civil War, fought out against the background of famine and social disorder, threatened the existence of the Communist Party and the government. This had the effect of stifling criticism of the *Cheka*'s methods. Dzerzhinsky declared that the proletarian revolution could not be saved except by 'exterminating the enemies of the working class'. This was an echo of Lenin's demand that the new Russia should be 'cleansed of harmful insects, parasites and bandits'.

Key question
What role did Trotsky play in the Terror?

Trotsky's role

Trotsky, who became Commissar for War after the signing of the Treaty of Brest-Litovsk, complemented Dzerzhinsky's work. Trotsky used his powers to end the independence of the trade unions, which had first been legalised in 1905. Early in 1920 the workers were brought under military discipline on the same terms as soldiers. They were forbidden to question orders, could not negotiate their rates of pay or conditions, and could be severely punished for poor workmanship or not meeting production targets. Trotsky dismissed the unions as 'unnecessary chatterboxes' and told them: 'The working classes cannot be nomads. They must be commanded just like soldiers. Without this there can be no serious talk of industrialising on new foundations.'

A photo montage, showing the enormous efforts Trotsky put into his work as Commissar of War. One of the most remarkable features of Trotsky's activities was the use of his special train in which he travelled over 70,000 miles during the Civil War. It was not just a train. It was a town on wheels, serving as mobile command post, military headquarters, troop transporter, radio station, court martial, propaganda unit, publishing centre, arsenal and administrative office. In Trotsky's own words: 'The train linked the front with the base, solved urgent problems on the spot, educated, appealed, supplied, rewarded and punished.' How much did the victory of the Reds in the Civil War owe to Trotsky?

Red Army established:
January 1918

Political commissars
Party workers whose
function was to
accompany the
officers of the Red
Army permanently
and report on their
conduct. No military
order carried final
authority unless
a commissar
countersigned it.

The Red Army

Trotsky's outstanding achievement as Commissar for War was his
creation of the Red Army, which more than any other factor
explains the survival of the Bolshevik government. This has
obvious reference to the Reds' triumph in the Civil War, but the
Red Army also became the means by which the Bolsheviks
imposed their authority on the population at large.

Lenin showed his complete trust in Trotsky by giving him a
totally free hand in military matters. From his heavily armed
special train, which served as his military headquarters and
travelled vast distances, Trotsky supervised the development of a
new fighting force in Russia. He had inherited 'The Workers' and
Peasants' Red Army', formed early in 1918. Within two years he
had turned an unpromising collection of tired Red Guard veterans
and raw recruits into a formidable army of 3 million men.
Ignoring the objections of many fellow Bolsheviks, he enlisted
large numbers of ex-tsarist officers to train the rank and file into
efficient soldiers. As a precaution, Trotsky attached **political
commissars** to the army. These became an integral part of the Red
Army structure.

Lenin addressing a
crowd in Moscow in
May 1920. Trotsky
and Kamenev are on
the steps of the
podium. This photo
later became
notorious when in
Stalin's time it was
air-brushed to remove
Trotsky from it.
Despite such later
attempts to deny
Trotsky's role in the
Revolution he had
undoubtedly been
Lenin's right-hand
man.

Trotsky tolerated no opposition within the Red Army from officers or men. The death sentence was imposed for desertion or disloyalty. In the heady revolutionary days before Trotsky took over, the traditional forms of army discipline had been greatly relaxed. Graded ranks, special uniforms, saluting and deferential titles were dropped as belonging to the reactionary past. Trotsky, however, had no truck with such fanciful experiments. He insisted that the demands of war meant that discipline had to be tighter, not looser.

Although 'commander' replaced the term 'officer', in all other key respects the Red Army returned to the customary forms of rank and address, with the word 'Comrade' usually prefixing the standard terms, as in 'Comrade Captain'. The practice of electing officers, which had come into favour in the democratic atmosphere of the February Revolution, was abandoned, as were soldiers' committees.

Conscription

Trotsky responded to the Civil War's increasing demand for manpower by enforcing conscription in those areas under Bolshevik control. (The Whites did the same in their areas.) Under the slogan 'Everything for the Front', Trotsky justified the severity of the Red Army's methods by referring to the dangers that Russia faced on all sides. Those individuals whose social or political background made them suspect as fighting men were nevertheless conscripted, being formed into labour battalions for back-breaking service behind the lines, such as digging trenches, loading ammunition and pulling heavy guns.

Most of the peasants who were drafted into the Red Army proved reluctant warriors and were not regarded as reliable in a crisis. Desertions were commonplace, in spite of the heavy penalties. The Bolsheviks judged that the only dependable units were those drawn predominantly from among the workers. Such units became in practice the elite corps of the Red Army. Heroic stories of the workers as defenders of the Revolution quickly became legends.

Red idealism

Not everything was achieved by coercion; there were idealists among the troops who believed sincerely in the Communist mission to create a new proletarian world. Theirs was a vital contribution to the relatively high morale of the Reds. Although by the standards of the European armies of the time, the Red Army was short of equipment and expertise, within Russia it soon came to outstrip its White opponents in its efficiency and sense of purpose.

Despite Trotsky's military triumphs, his authority did not go unchallenged. He met opposition from local Red commanders and commissars over tactics. His most notable dispute was with Joseph Stalin, who acted as political commissar in the Caucasus. Their legendary personal hostility dates from the Civil War days. Nonetheless, whatever the disputes, there was no doubting that Trotsky's organisation and leadership of the Red Army was the major factor in the survival of Bolshevik Russia.

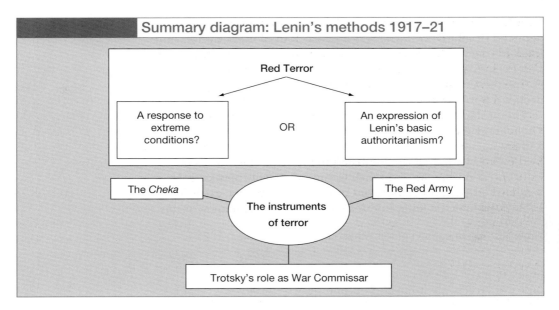

Summary diagram: Lenin's methods 1917–21

Red Terror

A response to extreme conditions?   OR   An expression of Lenin's basic authoritarianism?

The *Cheka*   The instruments of terror   The Red Army

Trotsky's role as War Commissar

2 | War Communism, 1918–21

Key question
Why was war communism introduced?

In the summer of 1918, Lenin began to introduce a series of harshly restrictive economic measures that were collectively known as 'war communism'. The chief reason for the move away from the system of state capitalism that had operated up to then was the desperate situation created by the Civil War. Lenin judged that the White menace could be met only by an intensification of authority in those regions which the Reds controlled (approximately 30 of the 50 provinces of European Russia). The change in economic strategy has to be seen, therefore, as part of the terror that the Bolsheviks operated in these years. Every aspect of life – social, political and economic – had to be subordinated to the task of winning the Civil War.

Effect on industry

The first step towards war communism as a formal policy was taken in June 1918. The existence of the *Cheka* and the Red Army enabled Lenin to embark on a policy of **centralisation**, knowing that he had the means of enforcing it. By that time also, there had been a considerable increase in Bolshevik influence in the factories. This was a result of the infiltration of the workers' committees by political commissars. This development helped prepare the way for the issuing of the Decree on Nationalisation in June 1918, which within two years brought practically all the major industrial enterprises in Russia under central government control.

However, nationalisation by itself did nothing to increase production. It was imposed at a time of severe industrial disruption, which had been caused initially by the strains of the war of 1914–17 but which worsened during the Civil War. Military needs were given priority, so that resources to those industries not considered essential were denied.

Key term

Centralisation
The concentration of political and economic power at the centre.

Key date

The Decree on Nationalisation, which laid down a programme for the takeover by the state of the larger industrial concerns: 28 June 1918

The situation was made more serious by the factories' being deprived of manpower. This was a result both of conscription into the Red Army and of the flight from the urban areas of large numbers of inhabitants, who left either in search of food or to escape the Civil War. The populations of Petrograd and Moscow dropped by a half between 1918 and 1921.

The problems for industry were deepened by hyperinflation. The scarcity of goods and the government's policy of continuing to print currency notes effectively destroyed the value of money. By the end of 1920 the rouble had fallen to 1 per cent of its worth in 1917. All this meant that while war communism tightened the Bolshevik grip on industry, it did not lead to economic growth. Table 6.1 shows the failure of war communism in economic terms.

Table 6.1: A comparison of industrial output in 1913 and in 1921

	1913	1921
Index of gross industrial output	100	31
Index of large-scale industrial output	100	21
Electricity (million kilowatt hours)	2039	520
Coal (million tons)	29	8.9
Oil (million tons)	9.2	3.8
Steel (million tons)	4.3	0.18
Imports (at 1913 rouble value (millions))	1374	208
Exports (at 1913 rouble value (millions))	1520	20

Effects on agriculture

For Lenin, the major purpose of war communism was to tighten government control over agriculture and force the peasants to provide more food. But the peasants proved difficult to bring into line. As a naturally conservative class, they were resistant to central government, whether tsarist or Bolshevik. The government blamed the resistance on the *kulaks*, who, it was claimed, were hoarding their grain stocks in order to keep prices artificially high. This was untrue. There was no hoarding. The plain truth was that the peasants saw no point in producing more food until the government, which had become the main grain purchaser, was willing to pay a fair price for it.

Grain requisitioning

However, exasperated by the peasants' refusal to conform, the government condemned them as counter-revolutionaries and resorted to coercion. *Cheka* requisition squads were sent into the countryside to take the grain by force. In August 1918 the People's Commissar for Food issued the following orders:

> The tasks of the requisition detachments are to: harvest winter grain in former landlord-owned estates; harvest grain on the land of notorious *kulaks*; every food requisition detachment is to consist of not less than 75 men and two or three machine guns. The political commissar's duties are to ensure that the detachment carries out its duties and is full of revolutionary enthusiasm and discipline.

Key question
What was the impact of war communism on agriculture?

Kulaks
Bolshevik term for the class of rich, exploiting peasants.

Key term

Forced grain requisitions begin: July 1918

Key date

Between 1918 and 1921 the requisition squads systematically terrorised the countryside. The *kulaks* were targeted for particularly brutal treatment. Lenin ordered that they were to be 'mercilessly suppressed'. In a letter of 1920 he gave instructions that one hundred *kulaks* were to be hanged in public in order to terrify the population 'for hundreds of miles around'.

Yet the result was largely the reverse of the one intended. Even less food became available. Knowing that any surplus would simply be confiscated, the peasants produced only the barest minimum to feed themselves and their family. Nevertheless, throughout the period of war communism, the Bolsheviks persisted in their belief that grain hoarding was the basic problem. Official reports continued to speak of 'concealment everywhere, in the hopes of selling grain to town speculators at fabulous prices'.

Famine

By 1921 the combination of requisitioning, drought and the general disruption of war had created a national famine. The grain harvests in 1920 and 1921 produced less than half the amount gathered in 1913. Even *Pravda*, the government's propaganda newssheet, admitted in 1921 that one in five of the population was starving. Matters became so desperate that the Bolsheviks, while careful to blame the *kulaks* and the Whites, were prepared to admit there was a famine and to accept foreign assistance. A number of countries supplied Russia with aid. The outstanding contribution came from the USA, which, through the **American Relief Association** (ARA), provided food for some 10 million Russians.

Despite such efforts, foreign help came too late to prevent mass starvation. Of the 10 million fatalities of the Civil War period, over half starved to death. Lenin resented having to accept aid from the ARA and ordered it to withdraw from Russia in 1923 after two years' work there, during which time it had spent over $60 million in relief work.

Key term

American Relief Association
A body formed by Herbert Hoover (a future President of the USA, 1929–33) to provide food and medical supplies to post-First World War Europe.

A pile of unburied bodies in a cemetery in Buzuluk, grim testimony to the famine that struck the region in 1921. Similar tragedies were common across Russia, reducing some areas to cannibalism. How does this picture help to explain why Lenin abandoned war communism in 1921 and introduced NEP?

Figure 6.1: Areas of Russia worst hit by famine.

The end of war communism

What is now known is that Lenin positively welcomed the famine as providing an opportunity to pursue his destruction of the Orthodox Church. In a letter of 1922 he ordered the Politburo to exploit the famine by shooting priests, 'the more, the better'. He went on:

> It is precisely now and only now when in the starving regions people are eating human flesh and thousands of corpses are littering the roads that we can (and therefore must) carry out the confiscation of the church valuables with the most savage and merciless energy.

By 1921 the grim economic situation had undermined the original justification for war communism. During its operation, industrial and agricultural production had fallen alarmingly. Yet this did not mean the policy necessarily became unpopular among the Bolsheviks themselves. Indeed, there were many in the Party who, far from regarding it as a temporary measure to meet an extreme situation, believed that it represented true

Key question
In what ways was war communism an extension of the Red Terror?

Nikolai Bukharin (1888–1938)
The leading political thinker in the party, he had helped organise the Bolshevik takeover in Moscow in 1917.

Yevgeny Preobrazhensky (1886–1937)
Regarded as a major economic expert by the Bolsheviks, he was noted for his revolutionary writings.

revolutionary communism. The Party's leading economists, **Nikolai Bukharin** and **Yevgeny Preobrazhensky**, urged that war communism should be retained as the permanent economic strategy of the Bolshevik government. They saw it as true socialism in action since it involved:

- the centralising of industry
- the ending of private ownership
- the squeezing of the peasants.

The policy of war communism was maintained even after the victory of the Red Army in the Civil War. The systematic use of terror by the *Cheka*, the spying on factory workers by political commissars, and the enforced requisitioning of peasant grain stocks all continued. As a short-term measure the policy had produced the results Lenin wanted, but its severity had increased Bolshevik unpopularity.

Lenin himself clung to war communism as long as he could. However, the failure of the economy to recover and the scale of the famine led him to consider possible alternative policies. He was finally convinced of the need for change by widespread anti-Bolshevik risings in 1920–1. These were a direct reaction against the brutality of requisitioning. One in particular was so disturbing that Lenin described it as a lightning flash that illuminated the true reality of things. He was referring to the Kronstadt Rising of 1921, the most serious challenge to Bolshevik control since the October Revolution.

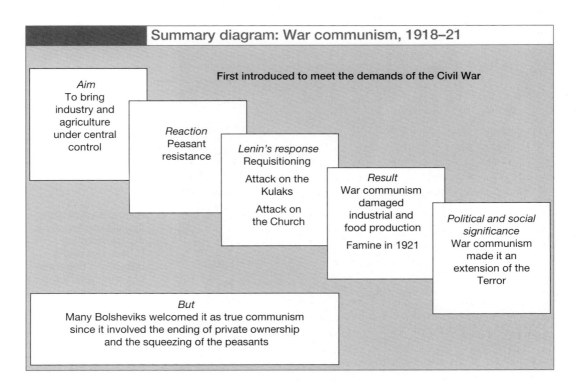

Summary diagram: War communism, 1918–21

First introduced to meet the demands of the Civil War

Aim
To bring industry and agriculture under central control

Reaction
Peasant resistance

Lenin's response
Requisitioning

Attack on the Kulaks

Attack on the Church

Result
War communism damaged industrial and food production

Famine in 1921

Political and social significance
War communism made it an extension of the Terror

But
Many Bolsheviks welcomed it as true communism since it involved the ending of private ownership and the squeezing of the peasants

3 | The Kronstadt Rising, 1921

As long as unrest had been confined to the peasants and to the Bolsheviks' political enemies, it had been a containable problem. What became deeply worrying to Lenin in 1921 was the development of opposition to war communism within the Party itself. Two prominent Bolsheviks, **Alexander Shlyapnikov** and **Alexandra Kollontai**, led a 'Workers' Opposition' movement against the excesses of war communism. Kollontai produced a pamphlet in which she accused the party leaders of losing touch with the proletariat:

> The workers ask – who are we? Are we really the prop of the class dictatorship, or just an obedient flock that serves as a support for those who, having severed all ties with the masses, carry out their own policy and build up industry without any regard to our opinions?

Key question
What led to the rising?

The Kronstadt Rising: March 1921

Key date

Alexander Shlyapnikov (1885–1937) Commissar (minister) of Labour.

Alexandra Kollontai (1872–1952) An ardent feminist and the outstanding woman in the Bolshevik Party (see page 169).

Key figures

Alexandra Kollontai – the leading female in the ranks of the Bolsheviks and a consistent supporter of Lenin from the time of his return to Petrograd in April 1917 until the Kronstadt Rising. Why did Alexandra Kollontai oppose Lenin over the Kronstadt affair?

Picking up the cue given by the 'Workers' Opposition', groups of workers in Petrograd went on strike early in 1921, justifying their actions in an angrily worded proclamation:

> A complete change is necessary in the policies of the Government. First of all, the workers and peasants need freedom. They don't want to live by the decrees of the Bolsheviks; they want to control their own destinies. Comrades, preserve revolutionary order! Determinedly and in an organised manner demand: liberation of all the arrested Socialists and **non-partisan** working-men; abolition of martial law; freedom of speech, press and assembly for all who labour.

Key term

Non-partisan
Politically neutral, belonging to no party.

By February 1921, thousands of Petrograd workers had crossed to the naval base on Kronstadt. There they linked up with the sailors and dockyard workers to demonstrate for greater freedom. They demanded that in a workers' state, which the Bolshevik government claimed Soviet Russia to be, the workers should be better, not worse, off than in tsarist times. In an attempt to pacify the strikers, Lenin sent a team of political commissars to Kronstadt. They were greeted with derision. Petrechenko, a spokesman for the demonstrators, rounded bitterly on the commissars at a public meeting:

> You are comfortable; you are warm; you commissars live in the palaces … Comrades, look around you and you will see that we have fallen into a terrible mire. We were pulled into this mire by a group of Communist bureaucrats who, under the mask of Communism, have feathered their nests in our republic. I myself was a Communist, and I call on you, Comrades, to drive out these false Communists who set worker against peasant and peasant against worker. Enough shooting of our brothers!

The Kronstadt manifesto

Key question
Why was the rising so disturbing for Lenin and the Bolsheviks?

Early in March the sailors and workers of Kronstadt elected Petrechenko as chairman of a fifteen-man Revolutionary Committee, responsible for representing their grievances to the government. This committee produced a manifesto which included the following demands:

1. New elections to the soviets, to be held by secret ballot.
2. Freedom of speech and of the press.
3. Freedom of assembly.
4. Rights for trade unions and the release of imprisoned trade unionists.
5. Ending of the right of Communists to be the only permitted socialist political party.
6. The release of Left-wing political prisoners.
7. The ending of special food rations for Communist Party members.
8. Freedom for individuals to bring food from the country into the towns without confiscation.
9. Withdrawal of political commissars from the factories.
10. Ending of the Communist Party's monopoly of the press.

It was not the demands themselves that frightened the Bolsheviks; it was the people who had drafted them – the workers and sailors of Kronstadt. They had been the great supporters of the Bolsheviks in 1917 (see page 96). Trotsky had referred to them as 'the heroes of the Revolution'. It was these same heroes who were now insisting that the Bolshevik government return to the promises that had inspired the October Revolution. For all the efforts of the Bolshevik press to brand the Kronstadt protesters as White agents, the truth was that they were genuine socialists who had previously been wholly loyal to Lenin's government but who had become appalled by the regime's betrayal of the workers' cause.

The rising crushed

Angered by the growing number of strikers and their increasing demands, Trotsky ordered the Red Army under General **Tukhachevsky** to prepare to cross the late winter ice linking Kronstadt to Petrograd and crush 'the tools of former tsarist generals and agents of the interventionists'. An ultimatum was issued to the demonstrators. When this was rejected, Tukhachevsky gave the signal for his force, made up of Red Army units and *Cheka* detachments, to attack. After an artillery bombardment, 60,000 Red troops stormed the Kronstadt base. The sailors and workers resisted fiercely. Savage fighting occurred before they were finally overcome. Tukhachevsky reported back to Trotsky:

> The sailors fought like wild beasts. I cannot understand where they found the might for such rage. Each house where they were located had to be taken by storm. An entire company fought for an hour to capture one house and when the house was captured it was found to contain two or three soldiers at a machine-gun. They seemed half-dead, but they snatched their revolvers and gasped, 'We didn't shoot enough at you bastards.'

Kronstadt was the clearest proof yet that the Bolsheviks, far from representing the nation's workers, were a minority elite who had imposed themselves by force on the people of Russia. The rising proved to be a pivotal moment in the history of Soviet and, indeed, world Communism. Those who were basically supportive of the Marxist principles on which Communism was based but who turned away from it because of its brutal authoritarianism are said to have experienced their 'Kronstadt moment'.

Aftermath of the rising

Immediately after the rising had been suppressed, the ringleaders who had survived were condemned as White reactionaries and shot. In the succeeding months the *Cheka* hunted down and executed those rebels who had escaped from Kronstadt. Lenin justified the severity on the grounds that the rising had been the work of the bourgeois enemies of the October Revolution: 'Both the Mensheviks and the Socialist Revolutionaries declared the Kronstadt movement to be their own.'

Key figure

Mikhail Tukhachevsky (1893–1937) A resourceful commander during the 1914–17 war against Germany, he joined the Bolsheviks in 1917 and played a major role in crushing White resistance during the Civil War. A founder of the Red Army.

However, as well as being a propagandist, Lenin was also a realist. He took the lesson of Kronstadt to heart. To avoid the scandal and embarrassment of another open challenge to his party and government, he decided it was time to soften the severity of war communism.

At the Tenth Conference of the Communist Party, which opened in March 1921, Lenin declared that the Kronstadt Rising had 'lit up reality like a lightning flash'. This was the prelude to his introduction of the New Economic Policy (NEP), a move intended to tackle the famine and, in doing so, to lessen the opposition to Bolshevism. However, this was to be a purely economic adjustment. Lenin was not prepared to make political concessions: Communist control was to be made even tighter.

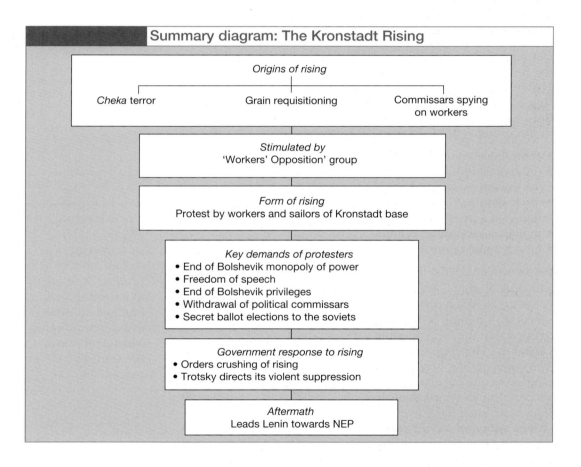

Summary diagram: The Kronstadt Rising

Origins of rising

Cheka terror — Grain requisitioning — Commissars spying on workers

Stimulated by
'Workers' Opposition' group

Form of rising
Protest by workers and sailors of Kronstadt base

Key demands of protesters
• End of Bolshevik monopoly of power
• Freedom of speech
• End of Bolshevik privileges
• Withdrawal of political commissars
• Secret ballot elections to the soviets

Government response to rising
• Orders crushing of rising
• Trotsky directs its violent suppression

Aftermath
Leads Lenin towards NEP

4 | The New Economic Policy (NEP)

As with the policy it replaced, the NEP was intended by Lenin primarily to meet Russia's urgent need for food. Whatever the purity of the revolutionary theory behind war communism, it had clearly failed to deliver the goods. State terror had not forced the peasants into producing larger grain stocks. Pragmatic as ever, Lenin judged that if the peasants could not be forced, they must be persuaded. The stick had not worked so now was the time to offer the carrot. He told the delegates at the 1921 Party Congress:

> We must try to satisfy the demands of the peasants who are dissatisfied, discontented, and cannot be otherwise. In essence the small farmer can be satisfied with two things. First of all, there must be a certain amount of freedom for the small private proprietor; and, secondly, commodities and products must be provided.

Despite the deep disagreements that were soon to emerge within the Bolshevik Party over the NEP, the famine and the grim economic situation in Russia led the delegates to give unanimous support to Lenin's proposals when they were first introduced. The decree making the NEP official government policy was published in the spring of 1921. Its essential features were:

- central economic control to be relaxed
- the requisitioning of grain to be abandoned and replaced by a **tax in kind**
- the peasants to be allowed to keep their food surpluses and sell them for a profit
- public markets to be restored
- money to be reintroduced as a means of trading.

Lenin was aware that the new policy marked a retreat from the principle of state control of the economy. It restored a mixed economy in which certain features of capitalism existed alongside socialism. Knowing how uneasy this made many Bolsheviks, Lenin stressed that the NEP was only a temporary concession to capitalism. He emphasised that the Party still retained control of 'the commanding heights of the economy', by which he meant large-scale industry, banking and foreign trade. He added: 'We are prepared to let the peasants have their little bit of capitalism as long as we keep the power.'

The adoption of NEP showed that the Bolshevik government since 1917 had been unable to create a successful economy along purely ideological lines. Lenin admitted as much. He told party members that it made no sense for Bolsheviks to pretend that they could pursue an economic policy that took no account of the circumstances.

Key question
What were Lenin's motives in introducing the NEP?

Key date
Introduction of the NEP: March 1921

Key term
Tax in kind
The peasants' surrendering a certain amount of produce, equivalent to a fixed sum of money – contrasted with requisitioning, which had meant the seizure of all the peasants' stocks.

Key question
How did Lenin
preserve party unity
over the NEP?

Bolshevik objections to the NEP

Lenin's realism demanded that political theory take second place to economic necessity. It was this that troubled the members of the party, such as Trotsky and Preobrazhensky, who had regarded the repressive measures of war communism as the proper revolutionary strategy for the Bolsheviks to follow. To their mind, bashing the peasants was exactly what the Bolsheviks should be doing, since it advanced the Revolution. It disturbed them that the peasants were being appeased and that capitalist ways were being tolerated. Trotsky described NEP as 'the first sign of the degeneration of Bolshevism'.

A main complaint of the objectors was that the reintroduction of money and private trading was creating a new class of profiteers whom they derisively dubbed '**Nepmen**'. It was the profiteering that Victor Serge, a representative of the Left Bolsheviks, had in mind when he described the immediate social effects of NEP: 'the cities we ruled over assumed a foreign aspect; we felt ourselves sinking into the mire. Money lubricated and befouled the entire machine just as under capitalism.'

NEP became such a contentious issue among the Bolsheviks that Lenin took firm steps to prevent the party being torn apart over it. At the Tenth Party Congress in 1921, at which the NEP had been formally announced, he introduced a resolution 'On Party Unity'. The key passage read:

> The Congress orders the immediate dissolution, without exception, of all groups that have been formed on the basis of some platform or other, and instructs all organisations to be very strict in ensuring that no manifestations of **factionalism** of any sort be tolerated. Failure to comply with this resolution of the Congress is to entail unconditional and immediate expulsion from the party.

The object of this proposal was to prevent 'factions' within the party from criticising government or Central Committee decisions. An accompanying resolution condemned the 'Workers' Opposition', the group that had opposed the brutalities of war communism and that had been involved in the Kronstadt Rising. The two resolutions on party loyalty provided a highly effective means of stifling criticism of the NEP.

At the same time as Lenin condemned factionalism, he also declared that all political parties other than the Bolsheviks were now outlawed in Soviet Russia. 'Marxism teaches that only the Communist Party is capable of training and organising a vanguard of the proletariat and the whole mass of the working people.' This was the logical climax of the policy, begun in 1918, of suppressing all opposition to Bolshevik rule. Lenin's announcements at this critical juncture made it extremely difficult for doubting members to come out and openly challenge NEP, since this would appear tantamount to challenging the party itself.

Key terms

'**Nepmen**'
Those who stood to gain from the free trading permitted under the New Economic Policy: the rich peasants, the retailers, the traders, and the small-scale manufacturers.

Factionalism
The forming within the Party of groups with a particular complaint or grievance. Lenin used the term to brand as disloyal those Bolsheviks who opposed his policies.

Key date
The decree against factionalism: March 1921

Bukharin's role

What also helped preserve Bolshevik unity was the decision by Bukharin, the outstanding Bolshevik economist, to abandon his opposition to the NEP and become its most enthusiastic supporter. His new approach was expressed in his appeal to the peasants: 'Enrich yourselves under the NEP.' Bukharin believed that the greater amount of money the peasants would have, as a result of selling their surplus grain, would stimulate industry, since their extra income would be spent on buying manufactured goods. It is significant that during the final two years of Lenin's life, when he became increasingly exhausted by a series of crippling strokes, it was Bukharin who was his closest colleague. The last two articles published under Lenin's name, 'On Co-operation' and 'Better Fewer, but Better', were justifications of the NEP. Both were the work of Bukharin.

The success of the NEP

In the end, the most powerful reason for the party to accept the NEP proved to be a statistical one. The production figures suggested that the policy worked. By the time of Lenin's death in 1924, the Soviet economy had begun to make a marked recovery. Table 6.2 indicates the scale of this.

Key question
How far did the NEP meet Russia's needs?

Table 6.2: Growth under the NEP

	1921	1922	1923	1924
Grain harvest (million tons)	37.6	50.3	56.6	51.4
Value of factory output (in millions of roubles)	2004	2619	4005	4660
Electricity (million kilowatt hours)	520	775	1146	1562
Average monthly wage of urban worker (in roubles)	10.2	12.2	15.9	20.8

Lenin's claim that under the NEP the Bolsheviks would still control 'the commanding heights of the economy' was shown to be substantially correct by the census of 1923. Figure 6.2 and Table 6.3 indicate that, in broad terms, the NEP had produced an economic balance: while agriculture and trade were largely in private hands, the state dominated Russian industry.

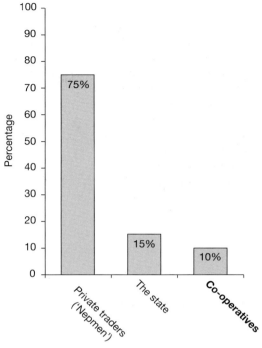

Figure 6.2: Bar chart showing share of trade in 1924.

Table 6.3: Balance between main types of enterprise

	Proportion of industrial workforce (%)	Average number of workers in each factory
Private enterprises	12	2
State enterprises	85	155
Co-operatives	3	15

The 'Scissors Crisis', 1923

The NEP was not a total success. Its opponents criticised it on the grounds that the balance it appeared to have achieved was notional rather than real. The fact was that industry failed to expand as fast as agriculture. The 'Nepmen' may have done well, but there was high unemployment in the urban areas. The disparity between agricultural and industrial growth rates had led by 1923 to a situation that became known as the 'Scissors Crisis'. This was the figurative way in which Trotsky, at the Twelfth Party Congress in that year, likened the problem created by the widening gap between industrial and agricultural prices to the open blades of a pair of scissors (see Figure 6.3).

Ironically, the crisis was caused in part by the revival of agriculture and the ending of the famine. In 1922 and 1923, kinder weather and an increase in the amount of land under cultivation produced greater harvests, which then led to a fall in the price of food.

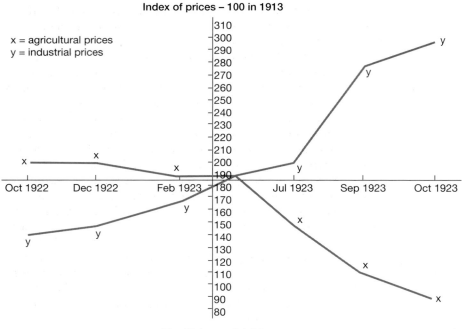

Index of prices – 100 in 1913

x = agricultural prices
y = industrial prices

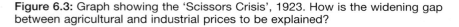

The 'Scissors Crisis'

Figure 6.3: Graph showing the 'Scissors Crisis', 1923. How is the widening gap between agricultural and industrial prices to be explained?

However, this was not matched by a comparable drop in the price of industrial goods. Factories took much longer than the land to recover from the chaos of the Civil War and were unable to meet the growing demand for manufactured goods. The scarcity of factory products drove up their price at the same time as the increased amount of food available was reducing the cost of agricultural products.

The net result was that the peasants found that they were having to sell their produce at too low a price for them to be able to afford the inflated cost of manufactured goods. This resurrected the very problem that had originally led Lenin to adopt the NEP: the danger that the peasants would lose their incentive to produce surplus food. Should this recur, the Russian economy overall would return to the depressed condition of the war communism period.

With Lenin's illness restricting him from playing an effective political role, divisions within the party re-emerged. Trotsky declined to serve on a special 'Scissors Committee' set up by the Central Committee at the height of the crisis in October 1923. Instead, he became the spokesman of 'the Platform of 46', a group of 46 party members who issued an open letter condemning the government's 'flagrant radical errors of economic policy', which had subordinated Soviet Russia's needs to the interests of the 'Nepmen'. Trotsky's arguments were strengthened by the undeniable failure of **Gosplan** to formulate a national economic strategy. *Gosplan* issued a number of impressive-sounding

Gosplan
From 1921 on, the new name for *Vesenkha*, the government's economic planning agency.

Key term

pronouncements, but it achieved little in the practical field. After three years, its chairman had to admit that Soviet Russia still lacked 'a single economic plan'.

A confrontation between supporters and critics of NEP was averted for the time being by an upturn in the economy. After October 1923 the retail price of industrial goods began to fall from the critically high level of that month. Industry continued to recover and an abundant harvest guaranteed the maintenance of food supplies. The blades of the scissors began to close. By 1924, industry had largely recovered from the depression into which it had sunk before the introduction of the NEP in 1921.

Yet these were only temporary gains; they were no guarantee of permanent economic or political stability. The question of how long the NEP would continue to operate and whether it genuinely represented the aspirations of the Soviet state remained unsettled at the time of Lenin's death in 1924. The period from 1917 to 1924 had shown the wide gap between revolutionary theory and economic reality. It could be argued that Bolshevik policy in these years, far from being a matter of structured economic planning, was never anything more than a set of fragmented responses to a series of desperate situations.

Key date

Death of Lenin:
January 1924

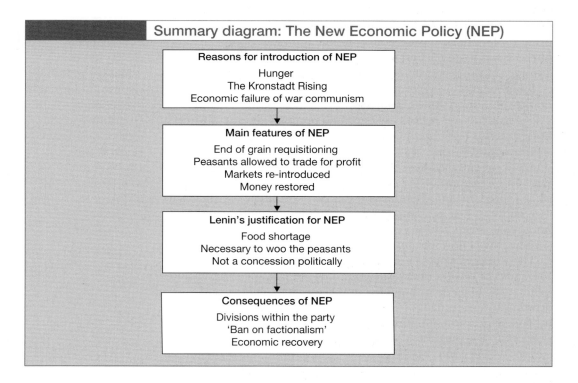

Summary diagram: The New Economic Policy (NEP)

Reasons for introduction of NEP

Hunger
The Kronstadt Rising
Economic failure of war communism

Main features of NEP

End of grain requisitioning
Peasants allowed to trade for profit
Markets re-introduced
Money restored

Lenin's justification for NEP

Food shortage
Necessary to woo the peasants
Not a concession politically

Consequences of NEP

Divisions within the party
'Ban on factionalism'
Economic recovery

5 | The Shaping of Soviet Society under Lenin

Culture and the arts

In Russia after the 1917 Revolution, the Bolsheviks claimed that their proletarian triumph had liberated the people from the weaknesses that had tainted all previous societies. The people were now ready to be transformed into a new species. Lenin was reported to have said: 'Man can be made whatever we want him to be.' Trotsky claimed that the aim of the Communist state was to produce *homo sovieticus*, 'an improved version of man'.

To achieve this, people could not be left to themselves; they would have to be moulded. Culture would have to be shaped by the power of the state. The result was that, following a brief period of apparent artistic freedom after the October Revolution, culture came under state control. The outstanding example of this was the *Proletkult* movement. In theory, this was the spontaneous creation by the workers of a new Russian culture. In practice, there was little real contribution from ordinary people. Cultural expression was the preserve of a small artistic establishment: writers, composers, artists and film-makers.

Proletkult pre-dated the Revolution. It had begun earlier in the century as a movement led by **Anatoli Lunarcharsky** with the aim and mission of educating the masses. Lenin saw in it a means of extending Bolshevik control. In 1917 he appointed Lunarcharsky as **Commissar of Enlightenment**. Lunarcharsky saw his role as using Proletkult as 'a source of agitation and propaganda'. The purpose was to attack and destroy the reactionary prejudices and attitudes of pre-revolutionary Russia.

It had been Lenin's original hope that after October 1917 the new revolutionary Russia would see a great expansion of culture. The word 'culture' is not easy to define precisely. In one obvious sense it refers to the refined aspects of life, such as music, art, sculpture and writing. But, in the sense that Marx and Lenin understood culture, these things did not exist separately. They were an expression of the class structure of society itself. That was what Trotsky meant when he said that 'every ruling class creates its own culture'. Just as a feudal society has a feudal culture and a bourgeois society a bourgeois culture, so, too, a proletarian society, such as Russia now was, must have a proletarian culture.

The works of writers and artists, therefore, would now express the values of revolutionary Russia. If they did not, then they would be unacceptable. As with politics and economics, culture and artistic expression had to serve the state. There was to be no place for free expression and individualism in Soviet culture. Lenin laid it down that 'the purpose of art and literature is to serve the people'.

There were some Bolsheviks who believed that a new people's culture would grow naturally out of the existing conditions. Lenin rejected this. He was not prepared to wait for such an evolution. The task was to eradicate the remnants of Russia's cultural past and construct a new, wholly socialist form. That is why he

◀ Key question
What place did culture have in Lenin's Russia?

Key terms

Homo sovieticus
A mock Latin term invented to describe the new 'Soviet man'.

Proletkult
Proletarian culture.

Commissar of Enlightenment
Equivalent to an arts minister.

Key figure

Anatoli Lunarcharsky (1875–1933)
A Marxist writer, critic and playwright passionately committed to the idea of raising the cultural and educational standards of ordinary Russians.

approved of Proletkult's willingness to see its role not as narrowly cultural but as covering all aspects of life, including politics and religion. By 1922 a range of Proletkult artistic and sporting organisations had been set up across Russia. These included:

- writers' circles
- amateur dramatic groups – including street theatre
- art studios
- poetry workshops
- musical appreciation societies.

Many of these were based in factories; there was even a 'Proletarian University' specially set up in Moscow for factory workers. On the surface, all this seemed to indicate a flowering of workers' culture, but the hard fact was that the art, music, architecture and literature that ordinary people were supposed to enjoy were dictated by the intelligentsia. It was they who decided what the workers' tastes should be and who enjoyed such artistic freedom as prevailed after 1917. And even here restrictions soon set in. By 1920, Lenin had become concerned by developments. The artistic control he had originally looked for seemed too loose. He did not want Proletkult to become an independent organisation within the state. He instructed that it be brought under much tighter supervision within Lunarcharsky's Commissariat of the Enlightenment. As a result, Proletkult by 1922 had been largely disbanded.

Proletkult's fate was part of the campaign that Lenin launched in 1922 against the intelligentsia, his last major initiative before he died. Angered by criticisms from writers and university academics about his policies of war communism and the NEP, he ordered the GPU (the new title of the *Cheka*) to impose strict censorship on the press and on academic publications. Branded variously as 'counter-revolutionaries, spies, and corrupters of student youth', hundreds of writers and university teachers were imprisoned or sent into exile.

It was not a totally dark picture. Literacy rose from 43 to 51 per cent. There was also the fact that some of the arts did reach a wider audience and that works of artistic merit were produced. Experiment with form was allowable; hence abstract art was permitted. But the content, the substance, had to be socialist. The meaning or a message of a work, whether a poem, play, novel, sculpture or opera, had to be pro-government. Anything critical of the Communist system, however well dressed up or packaged, was not tolerated.

This was typified in Lenin himself. As a younger man he had loved classical music, particularly Beethoven's late string quartets, which sent him into raptures. But his reaction made him feel ashamed; he was allowing himself to be seduced by a bourgeois notion of beauty. He resolved to give up Beethoven and dedicate himself single-mindedly to revolutionary study.

Religion

Karl Marx had described religion as 'the opium of the people'. He was not being simply dismissive; he was making a profound historical point. His argument was that religious belief and worship were what people turned to in order to deaden the pain of life. Since all periods of history were times of conflict, suffering was ever-present. Only with the victory of the proletariat would people understand there was no longer any need to believe in God and the afterlife. They would then realise that religion was a mere superstition used by class oppressors to keep the people down.

Having come to power, Lenin put this Marxist notion into action. Revolutionary Russia with the proletariat now in control was to be a secular state with no place for organised religion. This intention was immediately declared in the Decree on Separation of Church and State. The measure had two aims: to break the hold of the clergy, and to undermine the religious faith of the peasants, for whom the Bolsheviks had a particular distaste as representing the most backward features of old Russia. The main terms of the decree were as follows:

- Church properties were no longer to be owned by the clergy, but by the local soviets, from which churches would have to be rented for public worship.
- Clergy were no longer to be paid salaries or pensions by the state.
- The Church was no longer to have a central organisation with authority over local congregations.
- Religious teaching in schools was forbidden.

Over the next three years the Bolsheviks built on this decree to wage war against the Orthodox Church. Its leaders, such as Metropolitan (Archbishop) Benjamin, its chief spokesman in Moscow, who dared to speak out against the regime and its methods, were subjected to a show trial before being imprisoned. By the time of Lenin's death in 1924, over 300 bishops had been executed and some 10,000 priests imprisoned or exiled. The head of the Church, Patriarch Tikhon, at first resisted bravely, issuing powerful denunciations of the godless attacks upon the Church, but he then broke under the stress and became totally subservient to the regime, which used him thereafter as a puppet.

It soon became common practice for churches and monasteries to be looted and desecrated by the *Cheka*, acting under government direction. Such moves were backed by a widespread propaganda campaign to ridicule religion and the Church. The press poured out daily mockeries. Plays and street theatre presentations sometimes subtly, more often crudely, jeered at the absurdities of faith and worship. Judaism and Islam did not escape. Those faiths, too, were pilloried.

Religion was too deeply embedded in Russian tradition for it to be totally eradicated in this way, but it was driven underground. Peasants continued to pray and worship as their forebears had, but they could no longer risk doing so publicly.

Key question
Why were the Bolsheviks so determined to destroy religious faith?

Decree on Separation of Church and State: 20 January 1918

Key date

Women and the family

It was a firm Marxist belief that women were abused under **capitalism**. The principal instrument of their subjection was marriage. This one-sided social contract turned women into victims since it made them, in effect, the property of their husbands. It was the perfect example of the exploitative capitalist system. It was not surprising, therefore, that on taking power the Bolsheviks should have taken immediate steps to raise the status of women and undermine marriage as an institution. In the two years after 1917, decrees were introduced which included such innovations as:

Key question
How did the status of women change in Bolshevik Russia?

Key term

Capitalism
The predominant economic system in Europe and the USA, based on private ownership and the making of profits – condemned by Marxists as involving the exploitation of the poor by the rich.

- legal divorce if either partner requested it
- recognition of illegitimate children as full citizens
- the legalising of abortion
- the state to be responsible for the raising of children.

These changes derived from the notion that 'love' was a bourgeois concept based on a false view of the relations between the sexes and between parents and children. It was believed that once such romantic nonsense was recognised for what it was, a structured, ordered society would follow.

However, plans for setting up large boarding schools where children would be permanently removed from their parents and brought up in social equality were soon dropped. They were simply too costly. There were also growing doubts about whether the attack on the family was well advised.

It is always easier to be revolutionary in political matters than in social ones. The family was the traditional social unit in Russia, and it proved impossible to replace it simply on the basis of a theory. Where would the carers of the young come from? Were there not biological and emotional bonds between parents and children with which it would be dangerous to tamper? It was an area where Marxism-Leninism did not have any workable answers. It is significant that in a later period Stalin strongly disapproved of divorce and insisted on the social value of the family as the basic unit in Soviet society (see page 265).

Alexandra Kollontai

The outstanding woman in the party was Alexandra Kollontai (1872–1952). She was the voice of early Russian feminism and a pioneer among Bolshevik women (see page 156). In her writings she advanced the idea that women need to be liberated sexually, politically and psychologically. She argued that free love was the only relationship that guaranteed equality for women. For her, the family was a prison; children should be reared by society at large.

Kollontai was a fascinating woman and an important international feminist, but she was untypical as a Bolshevik. It might be thought that, given the views of Kollontai and the general desire of the Bolsheviks to eradicate old values, revolutionary Russia would become a hotbed of sexual licence. It did not quite work that way. The Bolsheviks were an odd mixture of permissiveness and puritanism. Lenin was unimpressed by Kollontai's feminism. He found her emphasis on free love and casual relationships unwelcome in a society which under his direction was aiming at socialist conformity.

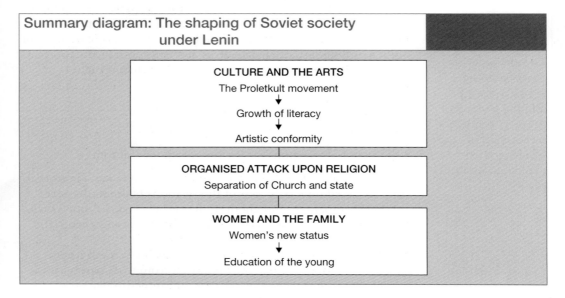

Summary diagram: The shaping of Soviet society under Lenin

CULTURE AND THE ARTS
The Proletkult movement
↓
Growth of literacy
↓
Artistic conformity

ORGANISED ATTACK UPON RELIGION
Separation of Church and state

WOMEN AND THE FAMILY
Women's new status
↓
Education of the young

6 | Lenin's Role as a Revolutionary

Key question
What principles guided Lenin as a revolutionary?

In name, it was the soviets that took power in October 1917, but in reality, it was the Bolsheviks, who proceeded to turn Russia into a one-party state. It took them years of bitter civil war to do it, but they alone of all the political parties in post-tsarist Russia had the necessary willingness to destroy whatever stood in their way.

Lenin as heir to Russian tradition

Although Lenin rejected the Russian past, he remained very much its inheritor. He had as little time for democracy as the tsars had. The rule of the Bolsheviks was a continuation of the absolutist tradition in Russia. The Civil War and the foreign interventions, by intensifying the threat to the Bolshevik government, provided it with the pretext for demanding total conformity from the masses and the Party members as the price of the Revolution's survival.

Yet it is doubtful whether, even without that threat, Bolshevism could have developed other than as an oppressive system. Its dogmatic Marxist creed made it as intolerant of other political ideas as tsardom had been. The forcible dissolution of the Constituent Assembly in 1918, the Terror and the crushing of the Kronstadt revolt in 1921 were clear proof of the absolutism of Bolshevik control. The Revolution of 1917 did not mark a complete break with the past. Rather, it was the replacement of one form of state authoritarianism with another.

Lenin's Marxism

Lenin's greatest single achievement as a revolutionary was to reshape Marxist theory to make it fit Russian conditions. The instrument that he chose for this was the Bolshevik Party. Although Lenin was careful always to describe his policies as democratic, for him the term had a particular meaning. Democracy was not to be reckoned as a matter of numbers but as a method of Party rule. Because the Party was the vehicle of historical change, its role was not to win large-scale backing but to direct the Revolution from above, regardless of the scale of popular support. 'No revolution', Lenin wrote, 'ever waits for formal majorities.'

It was because the power of the Party came before all other considerations that Lenin insisted that the country's legal system be subordinated to the Party's interests. The courts existed to enforce the Communist government's will not to operate some abstract concept of justice. As Lenin put it during the Civil War: 'The court is not to eliminate terror but to legitimise it.'

Lenin's view of the Russian proletariat

Lenin's political certainties followed logically from his view of the contemporary Russian working class. Its small size and limited political awareness meant that it could not achieve revolution unaided. It was, therefore, the historical mission of the enlightened Bolshevik Party to use its unique understanding of how human society worked to guide the proletariat towards its revolutionary destiny. Since authority flowed from the centre outwards, it was the role of the leaders to lead, the role of the Party members to follow. The special term describing this was 'democratic centralism'. Lenin defined it in these terms:

> Classes are led by parties, and parties are led by individuals who are called leaders. This is the ABC. The will of a class is sometimes fulfilled by a dictator. Soviet socialist democracy is not in the least incompatible with individual rule and dictatorship. What is necessary is individual rule, the recognition of the dictatorial powers of one man. All phrases about equal rights are nonsense.

With a small change in the political terminology, this could have served equally well as a justification for tsarist absolutism. Maxim Gorky, who had been one of Lenin's strongest supporters before the crushing of the Kronstadt Rising, came to be disillusioned with the coldness of his leader, remarking:

> Lenin is a gifted man who has all the qualities of a leader, including these essential ones: lack of morality and a merciless, lordly harshness towards the lives of the masses. As long as I can, I will repeat to the Russian proletariat, 'You are being led to destruction, you are being used as material in an inhuman experiment; to your leaders, you are not human.'

Bertrand Russell, who visited Soviet Russia in 1920 and met Lenin, was disturbed by the Soviet leader's evident cruelty. He noted that Lenin, far from being disturbed by the suffering caused by the Civil War, took a perverse delight in it. Russell recorded that 'his guffaw at the thought of those massacred made my blood run cold'. The attitude of mind that Russell observed was clearly expressed by Lenin at the time of the famine in 1921. Unhappy that revolutionary Russia had to accept aid from the ARA (see page 153), Lenin sneered: 'Talk of feeding the starving masses is nothing but the expression of saccharine-sweet sentimentality.'

Bertrand Russell (1872–1970) Celebrated British philosopher and socialist.

Key figure

Lenin's adaptability

A marked feature of Lenin as a revolutionary was his ability to adjust theory to fit circumstances. This pragmatic approach often led him to diverge from the strict pattern of the Marxist dialectic with its clear-cut stages of class revolution (see page 22), but it made him and his followers infinitely adaptable. In his writings and speeches he always insisted that his ideas were wholly in accordance with those of Marx. However, in practical terms, Lenin's role in Russia after April 1917 was that of a skilled opportunist who outmanoeuvred a collection of opponents who never matched him in sense of purpose and sheer determination.

A fascinating example of his adaptability is his approach to Party funding. For a brief period after 1917 the Bolsheviks attempted to do away with money on the grounds that it belonged to the capitalist age that the October Revolution had replaced with the rule of the proletariat. But this was an ideological gesture. Lenin knew that it was nonsense and that it was impossible for a modern state to function without using a basic currency. Very soon, money was in use again in Soviet Russia.

It is interesting to observe Lenin's methods of raising money both before and after taking power. Prior to the October Revolution, the Bolsheviks' main sources of income were:

• donations from supporters
• money paid by members to the Party when they married
• the proceeds from robbery and terrorism
• the diversion of workers' funds
• payments from the German government.

After taking power the Bolsheviks had the following at their disposal:

• the resources of the Russian state
• the property and possessions seized from 'enemies of the state'
• the foreign investments and loans, which the Bolsheviks made their own by refusing to honour all tsarist debts.

A noteworthy feature of Soviet expenditure after 1917 was that a larger proportion of it went on funding foreign policy than on investing in Russia's domestic economy. Most of the spending abroad went in payments to foreign Communist parties and supporters of the Comintern. In 1921, for example, the **CPGB**, whose own self-generated income for that year was only £100, received £21,000 from Lenin's government, a figure that matched the annual income of the British Labour Party in this period.

The 'telescoped revolution'

Lenin used his concept of the **'telescoped revolution'** as a very useful instrument that allowed the Bolsheviks to organise revolution against the Provisional Government without having to wait for the Russian proletariat to grow substantially in size. It was not necessary for the Russian workers to initiate the Revolution; it was enough that it was carried out in their name by the Bolsheviks, the special agents of historical change and the true voice of the proletariat.

This readiness to make Marxist theory conform to practical necessity was very evident in Lenin's economic policies. A basic belief in Marxism was that political systems were determined by the economic structure on which they rested. Lenin turned this idea upside down. His government after 1917 used its political power to determine the character of the economy. His flexible approach was then shown in 1921 when he introduced the NEP, a policy that entailed the abandonment of war communism and a reversion to capitalism.

Lenin was perfectly clear about what his ultimate objectives were, but he was wholly unprincipled in the methods he used to achieve them. The end justified the means. This approach was fully consistent with his interpretation of the scientific nature of Marxism. Once the concept of the historical inevitability of the proletarian revolution had been accepted, it followed that the binding duty of revolutionaries was to work for that end by whatever means necessary.

The Bolsheviks' belief that they were the special agents of historical change led logically to their destruction of all other political parties. Since history was on their side, the Bolsheviks had the right to absolute control.

Lenin the international revolutionary

A vital factor to stress when assessing Lenin's role is that he regarded himself primarily as an international revolutionary. Originally he expected that the successful Bolshevik seizure of power in October 1917 would be the first stage in a worldwide proletarian uprising. When this proved mistaken, he had to adapt to a situation in which Bolshevik Russia became an isolated revolutionary state, beset by internal and external enemies.

Lenin responded by making another major adjustment to Marxist theory. Marx had taught that proletarian revolution would be an international class movement. Yet the 1917 Revolution had been the work not of a class but of a party, and had been restricted to one nation. Lenin explained this in terms of a delayed revolution: the international rising would occur at some point in the future; in the interim, Soviet Russia must consolidate its own individual revolution.

This placed the Bolshevik government and its international agency, the Comintern, in an ambiguous position. What was their essential role to be? At Lenin's death in 1924, this question – whether Soviet Russia's primary aim was world revolution or national survival – was still unresolved.

Lenin's legacy

To help in estimating the impact Lenin had on Russia, it is worth listing the main features of his legacy. At his death in 1924 the Soviet Union exhibited the following characteristics:

Key question
What were the main features of Lenin's legacy?

- The one-party state – all parties other than the Bolsheviks had been outlawed.
- The bureaucratic state – despite the Bolsheviks' original belief in the withering away of the state, central power increased under Lenin and the number of government institutions and officials grew.
- The police state – the *Cheka* was the first of a series of secret police organisations in Soviet Russia whose task was to impose government control over the people.
- The ban on factionalism – prevented criticism of leadership within the party; in effect, a prohibition of free speech.
- The destruction of the trade unions – with Lenin's encouragement, Trotsky had destroyed the independence of the trade unions, with the result that the Russian workers were entirely at the mercy of the state.
- The politicising of the law – under Lenin, the law was operated not as a means of protecting society and the individual but as an extension of political control. He declared that the task of the courts was to apply revolutionary justice. 'The court is not to eliminate terror but to legitimise it.'
- The system of purges and show trials, which were to become a notorious feature of Stalinism (see page 225), had first been created under Lenin. Outstanding examples of these were the public trials of the Moscow clergy between April and July 1922 and of the SRs between June and August of the same year.
- Concentration camps – at the time of Lenin's death there were 315 such camps. Developed as part of the Red Terror, they held White prisoners of war, rebel peasants, *kulaks*, and political prisoners, such as SRs, who were considered a threat to Soviet authority.
- Prohibition of public worship – the Orthodox churches had been looted, then closed, their clergy arrested or dispersed, and atheism adopted as a replacement for religious belief.
- The USSR, the only communist state, had strained relations with the outside world.

Lenin's greatest legacy to Soviet Russia was authoritarianism. He returned Russia to the absolutism that it had known under the tsars. In that sense, Bolshevism was a continuation of, not a break with, Russia's past. The apparatus of the tyranny that Stalin was later to exercise over the Soviet people was already in place at the time of Lenin's death.

Summary diagram: Lenin as a revolutionary

Lenin as heir to Russian tradition
↓
Lenin's Marxism
↓
Lenin's view of the Russian proletariat
↓
Lenin's adaptability
↓
Lenin the international revolutionary

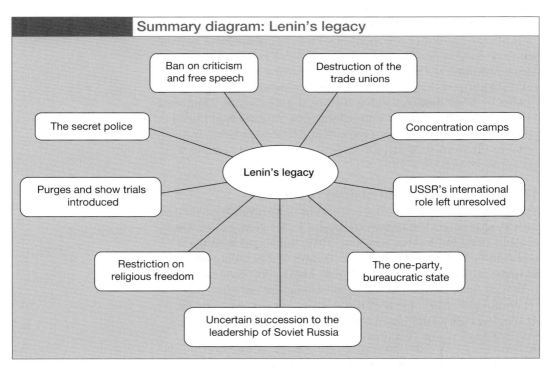

Summary diagram: Lenin's legacy

Ban on criticism and free speech

Destruction of the trade unions

The secret police

Concentration camps

Lenin's legacy

Purges and show trials introduced

USSR's international role left unresolved

Restriction on religious freedom

The one-party, bureaucratic state

Uncertain succession to the leadership of Soviet Russia

7 | Interpreting the Russian Revolution

Key question
What was the real
character of the
Russian Revolution of
1917?

The Revolution that Lenin created was an extraordinary
experiment that changed the political, social, cultural and
economic life of Russia and had a massive impact on the world at
large. The collapse of Communism in the USSR in the early 1990s
seemed to indicate that the experiment had failed. But that served
only to increase interest in the subject. The following paragraphs
list the major interpretations between 1917 and the present. There
have been so many important studies of the theme that the listing
has to be a very selective one. Nevertheless, although it does not
include all the theories that have been put forward, it does
indicate some of the principal approaches.

The traditional Soviet view

The official version put out and maintained by the **Communist
Party of the Soviet Union** (**CPSU**) claimed that in 1917 Lenin and
his Bolshevik Party had seized power in the name of the people
and had then gone on to create a workers' state. In doing this,
they were fulfilling the scientific principles first defined by Karl
Marx, who had spoken of the inevitable triumph of the proletariat
over the bourgeoisie. This view of what had happened was the only
one permitted in the USSR until the 1990s.

**Communist Party of
the Soviet Union
(CPSU)**
The new name
adopted by the
Bolshevik Party in
1919.

Key term

It is worth pointing out that Soviet historians were not neutral
scholars; they were state employees who were required to be
active promoters of the Revolution. A typical expression of their
official approach was given in 1960 by the Academy of Sciences,
the Soviet body that controlled historical publications: 'The study
of history has never been a mere curiosity, a withdrawal into the
past for the sake of the past. Historical science has been and
remains an arena of sharp ideological struggle and remains a
class, party history.'

The theory of 'the unfinished revolution'

The theory of 'the unfinished revolution' is associated particularly
with Trotsky and his followers. It argues that a genuine workers'
revolution had indeed occurred in 1917, but it had then been
betrayed by Lenin's successors. According to this school of
thought, which was powerfully represented in the West by such
writers as Isaac Deutscher and Adam Ulam, the initial
revolutionary achievement of the workers was perverted by the
deadening rule of the bureaucratic and repressive CPSU under
Stalin. That was why Lenin's revolution was unfinished.

The 'optimist' view

The 'optimist' view is an interpretation advanced by Russian
émigrés (those who fled abroad to escape the Revolution) and held
by such historians as George Katkov. The 'optimism' lay in their
claim that imperial Russia had been successfully transforming itself
into a modern, democratic, industrial society until weakened by
the 1914–17 war. However, at that point the Bolsheviks, who were

in the pay of the German government, had unscrupulously exploited the nation's difficulties to seize power in an illegal coup and then created a Communist tyranny that diverted Russia from the path of progress.

The 'pessimist' view

In the 1960s, Leopold Haimson, an American scholar, had a major impact on studies of the Revolution. He suggested that, far from moving towards modernisation, imperial Russia by 1914 was heading towards revolutionary turmoil. Hence the term 'pessimist'. He argued that the First World War made little difference. Russia was suffering an 'institutional crisis'. Haimson meant by this that an unbridgeable gap had developed between the reactionary tsarist establishment and the progressive professional classes and urban workers. So great was the divide that violent revolution was the unavoidable outcome.

The post-*glasnost* Soviet view

During the years of the Gorbachev reforms of the late 1980s in the USSR, a more open-minded approach became noticeable among Soviet historians. Many of them were now prepared to admit that mistakes had been made by the Bolsheviks. The leading exponent of this new honesty was Dmitri Volkogonov, who concluded that Stalin's tyranny was a logical continuation of the authoritarianism of Lenin and the Bolsheviks after 1917. Volkogonov paid tribute to the work of Leonard Schapiro and Robert Conquest, Western historians who had been initially sympathetic to Soviet Communism but whose subsequent researches led them to depict it as essentially oppressive.

Key term

Glasnost
Russian for 'openness', used as a description of the reforming policies adopted by the Soviet leader Mikhail Gorbachev in the late 1980s and early 1990s.

Post-Soviet revisionism

The collapse of the Communist Party and the disintegration of the USSR in the 1990s had a profound impact on historical thinking. Interpretation is rarely neutral. The way historians view the past is always influenced by their experiences of the present. The survival of Soviet Russia for nearly 75 years had helped to give strength to the Marxist analysis of history. The very existence of this Communist state was taken by its supporters to be proof that it had come into being in accordance with the scientific laws of the dialectic – the clash of class against class until the final victory of the workers.

However, once the Communist Party and the USSR had collapsed, this rigid view of history lost its appeal. After 1991, those writers on Russia who had never accepted the view that history was pre-shaped by unchangeable social laws regained their confidence. They reasserted the importance of what individuals and groups had actually done. The Russian Revolution had unfolded the way it had, not in accordance with the dialectic but because individuals and groups had chosen to behave in a particular way rather than in another.

Such views were given added credibility by the opening of the Russian archives after the fall of Communism in 1991. The new non-Communist government allowed access to the hundreds of thousands of documents that had lain unexamined in the Soviet state archives during the previous 75 years. Before he died in 1995, Volkogonov used these to write a revisionist trilogy of biographies on Lenin, Stalin and Trotsky in which he detailed their mistakes and failings. A number of Western scholars were also permitted to study the Russian documentary treasure trove. Robert Service's celebrated biography of Lenin drew on the previously unseen Lenin manuscripts.

No single identifiable viewpoint has yet emerged. Indeed, outstanding modern historians such as Orlando Figes, Richard Pipes and Robert Service differ on a whole range of issues. But what they share is a **non-determinist approach**. In Russia, nothing was pre-ordained, nothing absolutely had to happen the way it did. Politics was crucial. Things occurred the way they did because of the decisions made by the participants.

Non-determinist approach
Rejection of the idea that history follows a fixed, inevitable course.

Key term

The October Revolution as a cultural revolution

An interesting line of interpretation has developed among younger historians, involving less concentration on individuals and a greater emphasis on the broad social shifts occurring in late imperial Russia. The claim is not that Lenin and the Bolsheviks were unimportant but that they were representatives rather than initiators of the revolutionary movement we associate with them. In simplified form, the argument is that late-tsarist society was undergoing a profound cultural revolution brought about by modernisation. Although Russian conservatives tried to resist change, change was occurring nonetheless; industrialisation and contact with western countries fundamentally altered the character of society to the point where it fractured.

So, although Lenin and the Bolsheviks in political terms were a minority, fringe party working to take power, their real significance was that, without knowing it, they represented a deeper driving force for change within society. This view is effectively expressed by the American historian Robert C. Williams:

> Of all the political parties of imperial Russia, Bolshevism may have seemed the most unlikely to seize power in 1917. Yet a deeper and more extensive knowledge of Russian society and culture has made it possible for historians to discover roots of social support and cultural resonance in a movement previously associated with raw political power. We now know that Bolshevism was more supported from below by workers and peasants, and more embedded in the deep structure of Russian culture than we thought.

The view of the 'cultural revolutionists' has not won universal acceptance among historians, but it has added another dimension to the ongoing debate about one of modern history's most controversial issues.

Some key books in the debate:
Edward Acton, *Critical Companion to the Russian Revolution* (Edward Arnold, 1990)
Edward Acton, *Rethinking the Russian Revolution* (Edward Arnold, 1990)
Jane Burbank, *Intelligentsia and Revolution: Russian Views of Bolshevism* (Oxford University Press, 1992)
David Christian, *Imperial and Soviet Russia: Power, Privilege and the Challenge of Modernity* (Macmillan, 1997)
Isaac Deutscher, *Trotsky* (Oxford University Press, 1954–70)
Orlando Figes, *A People's Tragedy: The Russian Revolution 1891–1924* (Jonathan Cape, 1996)
Sheila Fitzpatrick, *The Russian Revolution, 1917–32* (Oxford University Press, 2001)
Anna Geifman (ed.), *Russia under the last Tsar: Opposition and Subversion 1894–1917* (Blackwell, 1999)
George Katkov and Harold Shukman, *Lenin's Path to Power* (Macdonald, 1971)
John Keep, *The Russian Revolution: A Study in Mass Mobilization* (New York, 1972)
Richard Pipes, *Russia under the Bolshevik Regime* (Collins Harvill, 1994)
Richard Pipes, *The Russian Revolution 1899–1919* (Collins Harvill, 1990)
Richard Pipes (ed.), *The Unknown Lenin: From the Soviet Archives* (Yale, 1996)
Richard Pipes, *Three Whys of the Russian Revolution* (Pimlico, 1998)
Hans Rogger, *Russia in the Age of Modernisation and Revolution* (Longman, 1983)
Robert Service, *Lenin: A Biography* (Macmillan, 2000)
Ian D. Thatcher (ed.), *Late Imperial Russia: Problems and Perspectives* (Manchester University Press, 2005)
Dmitri Volkogonov, *Lenin: Life and Legacy* (HarperCollins, 1994)
Dmitri Volkogonov, *Stalin: Triumph and Tragedy* (Weidenfeld and Nicolson, 1991)
Dmitri Volkogonov, *The Rise and Fall of the Soviet Empire: Political Leaders from Lenin to Gorbachev* (HarperCollins, 1997)
Dmitri Volkogonov, *Trotsky: The Eternal Revolutionary* (Free Press, 1996)

Study Guide: AS Question

In the style of OCR

To what extent did the New Economic Policy fulfil its aims by 1924?

(50 marks)

Exam tips

The cross-references are intended to take you straight to the material that will help you to answer the question.

The question asks 'To what extent', which means you must analyse and evaluate the aims of the NEP in the light of the situation in 1924. Examine the aims according to their importance. You might include some of the following points:

- to improve agricultural and industrial output after the failure of war communism (pages 151–5, 160)
- to win over opposition to the Bolsheviks after the Kronstadt mutiny (pages 156–9).

In assessing the outcome of NEP, you might refer to the following developments:

- trade, agricultural and industrial productivity (page 162)
- negative views of NEP – the Scissors Crisis of 1923 (pages 163–4)
- political consequences (pages 161, 164–5).

Balance your arguments for and against success/failure before reaching a conclusion.

7 Stalin's Rise to Power, 1924–9

POINTS TO CONSIDER

When Lenin, the Bolshevik leader, died, he left many problems but no obvious successor. Few Russian Communists gave thought to Stalin as a likely leader. Yet five years later, after a bitter power struggle, it was Stalin who had outmanoeuvred his rivals and established his authority over the Party and the nation. How he achieved this is the subject of this chapter, whose main themes are:

• Lenin and Stalin
• the roots of Stalin's power
• the power struggle after Lenin's death
• the defeat of Trotsky and the Left
• the defeat of the Right.

Key dates

1924		Death of Lenin
		The Politburo declares USSR to be ruled by a collective leadership
	May	Lenin's 'Testament' suppressed
1925		Trotsky loses his position as War Commissar
		Kamenev and Zinoviev head 'the United Opposition'
1926		Trotsky joins Kamenev and Zinoviev in the Left political bloc, which is defeated by Stalin's supporters
1927		Trotsky dismissed from the Central Committee
		Stalin persuades Congress to expel Trotsky from the CPSU
		Trotsky sent into exile
1928		Stalin attacks the Right over agricultural policy
1929		The leading figures on the Right finally defeated by Stalin and demoted in the CPSU
		Trotsky exiled from the USSR

1 | Lenin and Stalin

Key question
How significant was Stalin's career before 1924?

Most historians used to believe that Stalin's pre-1924 career was unimportant. They accepted the description of him by Nickolai Sukhanov, dating from 1922, as a 'dull, grey blank'. But researches in the Soviet archives over the past twenty years have indicated that the notion of Stalin as a nonentity is the opposite of the truth. A leading British authority, Robert Service, has shown that Stalin was very highly regarded by Lenin and played a central role in the Bolshevik Party.

Another British scholar, Simon Sebag Montefiore, in an exhaustive study of Stalin's early career, has stressed that far from being a grey blank, Stalin was an indispensable Bolshevik organiser before 1917. He was the brains behind many of the violent campaigns that raised money for the party.

Before 1917 the Bolshevik Party had been only a few thousand strong, and Lenin had known the great majority of members personally. He had been impressed by Stalin's organising ability, insensitivity to suffering, and willingness to obey orders. He once described him as 'that wonderful **Georgian**', a reference to his work as an agitator among the non-Russian peoples. With Lenin's backing, Stalin had risen by 1912 to become one of the six members of the Central Committee, the policy-making body of the Bolshevik Party. He had also helped to found the Party's newspaper, *Pravda*.

The October Revolution and Civil War

Having spent the war years, 1914–17, in exile in Siberia, Stalin returned to Petrograd in March 1917. His role in the October Revolution is difficult to disentangle. Official accounts written after he had taken power were a mixture of distortion and invention, with any unflattering episodes totally omitted. What is reasonably certain is that Stalin was loyal to Lenin after the latter's return to Petrograd in April 1917. Lenin instructed the Bolsheviks to abandon all co-operation with other parties and to devote themselves to preparing for a seizure of power. As a Leninist, Stalin was opposed to the **'October deserters'**, such as Kamenev and Zinoviev (see page 104).

During the period of crisis and civil war that accompanied the efforts of the Bolsheviks to consolidate their authority after 1917, Stalin's non-Russian background proved invaluable. His knowledge of the minority peoples of the old Russian Empire led to his being appointed **Commissar for Nationalities**. Lenin had believed that Stalin's toughness well qualified him for this role. As Commissar, Stalin became the ruthless Bolshevik organiser for the whole of the Caucasus region during the Civil War from 1918 to 1920. This led him into a number of disputes with Trotsky, the Bolshevik Commissar for War. Superficially the quarrels were about strategy and tactics, but at a deeper level they were a clash of wills. They proved to be the beginning of a deep personal rivalry between Stalin and Trotsky.

Key terms

Georgian
A member of the tough race of people who inhabit the rugged land of Georgia.

'October deserters'
Bolsheviks who in October 1917, believing that the Party was not yet strong enough, had advised against a Bolshevik rising.

Commissar for Nationalities
Minister responsible for liaising with the non-Russian national minorities.

Profile: Joseph Stalin (1879–1953)

1879	– Born in Georgia
1899	– His revolutionary activities lead to expulsion from Tiflis seminary
1905	– Meets Lenin for first time
1907	– Organises the Tiflis atrocity
1912	– Adopts the name Stalin
	– Becomes a member of the Central Committee of the Bolshevik Party
	– Helps to found *Pravda*, the Bolshevik newspaper
1914–17	– In exile in Siberia
1917	– Returns to Petrograd
	– People's Commissar for Nationalities
1919	– Liaison Officer between the Politburo and the Orgburo
	– Head of the Workers' and Peasants' Inspectorate
1922	– General Secretary of the Communist (Bolshevik) Party
1924	– Delivers the oration at Lenin's funeral

Stalin, meaning 'man of steel', was not his real name. It was simply the name he adopted in 1912, the last in a series of 40 aliases that Joseph Vissarionovich Djugashvili had used to avoid detection as a revolutionary.

Early life

He was born in Georgia, a rugged province in the south of the Russian Empire, renowned for the fierceness of its people. Blood feuds and family vendettas were common. Georgia had only recently been incorporated into the Russian Empire. Tsarist government officials often wrote in exasperation of the difficulties of trying to control a savage people who refused to accept their subordination to Russia.

This was the stock from which Stalin came. His drunken father eked out a miserable existence as a cobbler, and the family appears to have lived in constant poverty. There have been suggestions that both Stalin's admiration of all things Russian and his contempt for middle-class intellectuals derived from a sense of resentment over his humble non-Russian origins. Stalin's mother was a particularly devout woman, and it was largely through her influence that her son was enrolled as a student in a Georgian Orthodox seminary in Tiflis, the capital of Georgia. This did not show religious fervour on Stalin's part. The fact was that at this time in imperial Russia, attendance at a Church academy was the only way to obtain a Russian-style education, an essential requirement for anyone from the provinces who had ambition. Stalin seems to have been attracted less by theology than by the political ideas with which he came into contact.

Expulsion from the seminary

In the seminary records for 1899 there is an entry beside Stalin's name that reads 'expelled for not attending lessons – reasons unknown'. We now know the reasons: he had become involved in the Georgian resistance movement, agitating against tsarist control.

His anti-government activities drew him into the Social Democratic Workers' Party. From the time of his expulsion from the seminary to the Revolution of 1917, Stalin was a committed follower of Lenin. He threw himself into the task of raising funds for the Bolsheviks; his specialities were bank hold-ups and train robberies.

Stalin the bank robber

His most notorious success occurred in 1907 when he plotted the seizure of a wagon train delivering notes and bullion to the largest bank in Tiflis. In a scene reminiscent of the American Wild West, police and guards were mown down in a hail of rifle and pistol fire; bombs were then thrown under the wagons, blowing men and horses into bloody fragments and shattering the windows of the buildings that overlooked Yerevan Square, where the bank stood. Notes, bullion and bank boxes were grabbed and bundled into waiting horse carriages, which were then frantically driven off in great clouds of dust while onlookers cowered in fear of their lives. Fifty people died in the raid and as many were seriously injured. The Bolshevik raiders made off with the equivalent of £1.7 million.

By 1917, Stalin had been arrested eight times and had been sentenced to various periods of imprisonment and exile. Afterwards he tended to despise those revolutionaries who had escaped such experiences by fleeing to the relative comfort of self-imposed exile abroad.

Lenin's testament

Although Stalin had been totally loyal to Lenin, there were two particular occasions when he had aroused Lenin's anger. After the Civil War had ended, Stalin, despite being himself a Georgian, had been curt and off-hand in discussions with the representatives from Georgia. Lenin, anxious to gain the support of the national minorities for the Bolshevik regime, had to intervene personally to prevent the Georgians leaving in a huff. On another occasion, in a more directly personal matter, Lenin learned from his wife, Krupskaya, that in a row over the Georgian question Stalin had subjected her to 'a storm of the coarsest abuse', telling her to keep her nose out of state affairs and calling her a 'whore'. The very day that Lenin was informed of this, 22 December 1922, he dictated his testament as a direct response.

His main criticism read: 'Comrade Stalin, since becoming General Secretary of the Party in 1922, has concentrated enormous power in his hands; and I am not sure he always knows how to exercise that power with sufficient caution.' In a later postscript Lenin again stressed Stalin's rudeness, which was unacceptable in a General Secretary, who should be a person of tact capable of preventing divisions developing within the Party. Lenin went on to urge the comrades 'to think about ways of removing Comrade Stalin from that position'. But this was not done. Lenin was too ill during the last

Death of Lenin: 21 January 1924

Key date

year of his life to be politically active. At his death in January 1924, he had still not taken any formal steps to remove Stalin, and the 'Testament' had not been made public.

Stalin's position in 1924

In the uncertain atmosphere that followed Lenin's death, a number of pieces of luck helped Stalin promote his own claims. However, it would be wrong to ascribe his success wholly to good fortune. The luck had to be used. Stalin may have lacked brilliance, but he had great ability. His particular qualities of perseverance and willingness to undertake laborious administrative work were ideally suited to the times.

The government of Soviet Russia, as it had developed by 1924, had two main features: the **Council of People's Commissars**, and the Secretariat (see page 118). Both these bodies were staffed and controlled by the Bolshevik Party. It has to be stressed that the vital characteristic of this governmental system was that the party ruled. By 1922, Soviet Russia was a one-party state. Membership of that one party was essential for all who held government posts at whatever level.

As government grew in scope, certain posts that initially had not been considered especially significant began to provide their holders with the levers of power. This had not been the intention, but was the unforeseen result of the emerging pattern of Bolshevik rule. It was in this context that Stalin's previous appointments to key posts in both government and Party proved vital. These had been:

- People's Commissar for Nationalities (1917). In this post, Stalin was in charge of the officials in the many regions and republics that made up the USSR (the official title of the Soviet state after 1922).
- Liaison Officer between Politburo and Orgburo (1919). This post placed him in a unique position to monitor both the Party's policy and the Party's personnel.
- Head of the Workers' and Peasants' Inspectorate (1919). This position entitled him to oversee the work of all government departments.
- General Secretary of the Communist Party (1922). In this position he recorded and conveyed Party policy. This enabled him to build up personal files on all the members of the Party. Nothing of note happened that Stalin did not know about.

Stalin became the indispensable link in the chain of command in the Communist Party and the Soviet government. Above all, what these posts gave him was the power of **patronage**. He used this authority to place his own supporters in key positions. Since they then owed their place to him, Stalin could count on their support in the voting in the various committees that made up the organisation of the Party and the government.

Such were the levers in Stalin's possession during the Party in-fighting over the succession to Lenin. No other contender came anywhere near matching Stalin in his hold on the Party machine.

Key question
How had Stalin been able to rise up the Bolshevik ranks?

Key terms

The Council of People's Commissars
The cabinet of ministers responsible for creating government policies.

Patronage
The power to appoint individuals to official posts in the Party and the government.

Whatever the ability of the individuals or groups who opposed him, he could always outvote and outmanoeuvre them.

The Lenin enrolment

Stalin had also gained advantage from recent changes in the structure of the Communist Party. Between 1923 and 1925 the Party had set out to increase the number of true proletarians in its ranks. This was known as 'the Lenin enrolment'. It resulted in the membership of the CPSU rising from 340,000 in 1922 to 600,000 by 1925.

The new members were predominantly poorly educated and politically unsophisticated, but they were fully aware that the many privileges that came with Party membership depended on their being loyal to those who had first invited them into the Bolshevik ranks. The task of vetting 'the Lenin enrolment' had fallen largely to the officials in the Secretariat, who worked directly under Stalin as General Secretary. In this way, the expansion of the Party added to his growing power of patronage. It provided him with a reliable body of votes in the various Party committees at local and central level.

Key question
What was the significance for Stalin of 'the Lenin enrolment'?

The attack on factionalism

Another lasting feature of Lenin's period that proved of great value to Stalin was what had become known as the 'attack upon factionalism'. This referred to Lenin's condemnation in 1921 of divisions within the Party (see page 161). What this rejection of 'factionalism' effectively did was to frustrate any serious attempt to criticise Party decisions or policies. It became extremely difficult to mount any form of legitimate opposition within the CPSU. Stalin benefited directly from the ban on criticism of the Party line. The charge of 'factionalism' provided him with a ready weapon for resisting challenges to the authority he had begun to exercise.

Key question
How did Lenin's 'attack upon factionalism' help Stalin?

The Lenin legacy

There was an accompanying factor that legitimised Stalin's position. Stalin became heir to the 'Lenin legacy'. By this is meant the tradition of authority and leadership that Lenin had established during his lifetime, and the veneration in which he was held after his death. It is barely an exaggeration to say that in the eyes of the Communist Party, Lenin became a god. His actions and decisions became unchallengeable, and all arguments and disputes within the Party were settled by reference to his statements and writings. Lenin became the measure of the correctness of Soviet theory and practice. Soviet Communism became Leninism. After 1924, if a Party member could assume the mantle of Lenin and appear to carry on Lenin's work, he would establish a formidable claim to power. This is exactly what Stalin began to do.

Key question
How did the 'Lenin legacy' benefit Stalin?

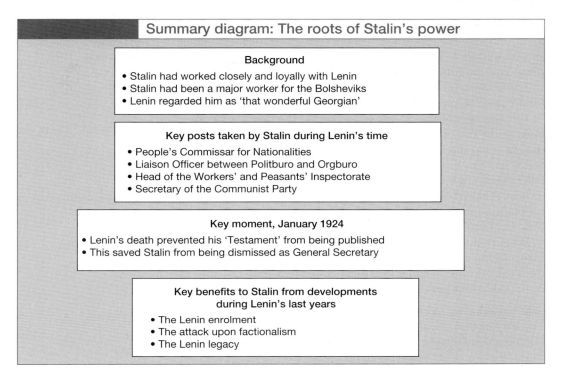

Summary diagram: The roots of Stalin's power

Background
- Stalin had worked closely and loyally with Lenin
- Stalin had been a major worker for the Bolsheviks
- Lenin regarded him as 'that wonderful Georgian'

Key posts taken by Stalin during Lenin's time
- People's Commissar for Nationalities
- Liaison Officer between Politburo and Orgburo
- Head of the Workers' and Peasants' Inspectorate
- Secretary of the Communist Party

Key moment, January 1924
- Lenin's death prevented his 'Testament' from being published
- This saved Stalin from being dismissed as General Secretary

Key benefits to Stalin from developments during Lenin's last years
- The Lenin enrolment
- The attack upon factionalism
- The Lenin legacy

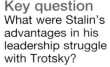

Key question
What were Stalin's advantages in his leadership struggle with Trotsky?

Key figures

Aleksei Rykov (1881–1938)
Chairman of the Central Committee of the CPSU.

Mikhail Tomsky (1880–1937)
The minister responsible for representing (in practice, controlling) the trade unions.

2 | The Power Struggle after Lenin's Death

Lenin's funeral

Immediately after Lenin's death, the Politburo, whose members were Stalin, Trotsky, **Rykov**, **Tomsky**, Kamenev and Zinoviev, publicly proclaimed their intention to continue as a collective leadership, but behind the scenes the competition for individual authority had already begun. In the manoeuvring, Stalin gained an advantage by being the one to deliver the oration at Lenin's funeral. The sight of Stalin as leading mourner suggested a continuity between him and Lenin, an impression heightened by the contents of his speech, in which, in the name of the Party, he humbly dedicated himself to follow in the tradition of the departed leader:

> In leaving us, Comrade Lenin commanded us to keep the unity of our Party. We swear to thee, Comrade Lenin, that we will honour thy command. In leaving us, Comrade Lenin ordered us to maintain and strengthen the dictatorship of the proletariat. We swear to thee, Comrade Lenin, that we will exert our full strength in honouring thy command.

Since Stalin's speech was the first crucial move to promote himself as Lenin's successor, it was to be expected that Trotsky, his chief rival, would try to counter it in some way. Yet Trotsky was not even present at the funeral. It was a very conspicuous absence, and it is still difficult to understand why Trotsky did not appreciate the importance of appearances following Lenin's death in January 1924.

Initially he, not Stalin, had been offered the opportunity of making the major speech at the funeral. But not only did he decline this, he also failed to attend the ceremony itself. His excuse was that Stalin had given him the wrong date, but this simply was not true. Documents show that he learned the real date early enough for him to have reached Moscow with time to spare. Instead he continued his planned journey and was on holiday on the day of the funeral. This was hardly the image of a dedicated Leninist.

What makes Trotsky's behaviour even stranger is he was well aware of the danger that Stalin represented. In 1924 he prophesied that Stalin would become 'the dictator of the USSR'. He also gave a remarkable analysis of the basis of Stalin's power in the Party:

> He is needed by all of them; by the tired radicals, by the bureaucrats, by the Nepmen, the upstarts, by all the worms that are crawling out of the upturned soil of the manured revolution. He knows how to meet them on their own ground, he speaks their language and he knows how to lead them. He has the deserved reputation of an old revolutionary. He has will and daring. Right now he is organising around himself the sneaks of the Party, the artful dodgers.

This was a bitter but strikingly accurate assessment of how Stalin had made a large part of the Party dependent on him. But logically such awareness on Trotsky's part should have made him eager to prevent Stalin from stealing an advantage. His reluctance to act is a fascinating feature of Trotsky's puzzling character.

Trotsky's character

Trotsky had a complex personality. He was one of those figures in history who may be described as having been their own worst enemy. Despite his many gifts and intellectual brilliance, he had serious weaknesses that undermined his chances of success. At times, he was unreasonably self-assured; at other critical times, he suffered from diffidence and lack of judgement. An example of this had occurred earlier, at the time of Stalin's mishandling of the Georgian question. Lenin's anger with Stalin had offered Trotsky a golden opportunity for undermining Stalin's position, but for some reason Trotsky had declined to attack.

A possible clue to his reluctance is that he felt inhibited by his Jewishness. Trotsky knew that in a nation such as Russia, with its deeply ingrained anti-Semitism, his race made him an outsider. A remarkable example of his awareness of this occurred in 1917, when Lenin offered him the post of Deputy Chairman of the Soviet government. Trotsky rejected it on the grounds that his appointment would be an embarrassment to Lenin and the

Key date
The Politburo declares a collective leadership: 1924

Key question
What were Trotsky's weaknesses?

government. 'It would', he said, 'give enemies grounds for claiming that the country was ruled by a Jew.' It may have been similar reasoning that allowed Stalin to gain an advantage over him at the time of Lenin's funeral.

Suppression of Lenin's 'Testament'

Key date

Lenin's 'Testament' suppressed: May 1924

A dangerous hurdle in Stalin's way was Lenin's 'Testament'. If it were to be published, Stalin would be gravely damaged by its contents. However, here, as so often during this period, fortune favoured him. Had the document been made public, not only would Lenin's criticisms of Stalin have been revealed, but so too would those concerning Trotsky, Zinoviev and Kamenev. Nearly all the members of the Politburo had reason for suppressing the 'Testament'.

When the Central Committee were presented with the document in May 1924, they realised that it was too damning broadly to be used exclusively against any one individual. They agreed to its being shelved indefinitely. Trotsky, for obvious personal reasons, went along with the decision, but in doing so he was declining yet another opportunity to challenge Stalin's right to power. In fact it was Trotsky, not Stalin, whom the Politburo regarded as the greater danger.

Attitudes towards Trotsky

Key term

Triumvirate
A ruling or influential bloc of three persons.

Kamenev and Zinoviev joined Stalin in an unofficial **triumvirate** within the Politburo. Their aim was to isolate Trotsky by exploiting his unpopularity with large sections of the Party. The 'Lenin enrolment' helped them in this. The new proletarian members were hardly the type of men to be impressed by the cultured Trotsky. The seemingly down-to-earth Stalin was much more to their liking.

The attitude of Party members towards Trotsky was an important factor in the weakening of his position. Colleagues tended to regard Trotsky as dangerously ambitious and his rival Stalin as reliably self-effacing. This was because Trotsky was flamboyant and brilliant, while his rival was unspectacular and methodical. Trotsky was the type of person who attracted either admiration or distaste, but seldom loyalty. That was why he lacked a genuine following. It is true that he was highly regarded by the Red Army, whose creator he had been, but this was never matched by any comparable political support. Trotsky failed to build a power base within the party. This invariably gave him the appearance of an outsider.

Adding to his difficulties in this regard was the doubt about his commitment to Bolshevism. Until 1917, as Lenin had noted in his 'Testament', Trotsky had belonged to the Mensheviks (see page 38). This led to the suspicion that his conversion had been a matter of expediency rather than conviction. Many of the old-guard Bolsheviks regarded Trotsky as a Menshevik turncoat who could not be trusted.

Bureaucratisation

Despite the attacks upon him, Trotsky attempted to fight back. The issue he chose was bureaucratisation. He defined this as the abandonment of genuine discussion within the Party and the growth in power of the Secretariat, which was able to make decisions and operate policies without reference to ordinary Party members.

Trotsky had good reason to think he had chosen a powerful cause. After all, Lenin himself in his last writings had warned the Party against the creeping dangers of bureaucracy. Accordingly, Trotsky pressed his views at the Party Congresses and in the meetings of the Central Committee and the Politburo. His condemnation of the growth of bureaucracy was coupled with an appeal for a return to **'Party democracy'**. He expanded his arguments in a series of essays, the most controversial of which was 'Lessons of October', in which he criticised Kamenev and Zinoviev for their past disagreements with Lenin. The assault was ill-judged, since it invited retaliation in kind. Trotsky's Menshevik past and his divergence from Leninism were highlighted in a number of books and pamphlets, most notably Kamenev's *Lenin or Trotsky?*

As a move in the power struggle, Trotsky's campaign for greater Party democracy was misjudged. Trotsky's censures on bureaucracy left Stalin largely unscathed. In trying to expose the growing bureaucracy in the Communist Party, Trotsky overlooked the essential fact that Bolshevik rule since 1917 had always been bureaucratic. Indeed, it was because the Soviet state functioned as a bureaucracy that Party members received privileges in political and public life. Trotsky's line was hardly likely to gain significant support from Party members who had a vested interest in maintaining the Party's bureaucratic ways.

Disputes over the New Economic Policy

Trotsky's reputation was further damaged by the issue of the New Economic Policy (NEP), which Lenin had introduced to meet the food supply crisis in 1921. From the first, Trotsky had been disturbed by the retreat from strict socialism that the NEP entailed (see page 161).

When introducing the NEP in 1921, Lenin had emphasised that it was a temporary, stopgap measure. However, at the time of his death in 1924 the question was already being asked as to how long in fact the NEP was meant to last. Was it not becoming a permanent policy? The Party members who were unhappy with it, among whom Trotsky was the most prominent, saw its continuation as a betrayal of revolutionary principle. They objected to a policy that, in effect, allowed the peasants to dictate the pace of Soviet Russia's advance towards full Communism. A serious division had developed between Left Communists and Right Communists.

Although fierce disputes were to arise over the issue, initially the disagreement was simply about timing: how long should the NEP be allowed to run? However, in the power struggle of the

Key question
What did Trotsky mean by 'bureaucratisation'?

Party democracy
Trotsky was not pressing for democracy in the full sense of all party members having a say. His aim was to condemn the centralising of power from which Stalin had gained such benefit.

Key term

Key question
How was Trotsky weakened by the NEP issue?

1920s these minor differences deepened into questions of political soundness and Party loyalty. A rival's attitude towards the NEP might be a weakness to be exploited; if it could be established that his views indicated deviant Marxist thinking, it became possible to destroy his position in the Party.

Stalin did precisely this. He used Trotsky's attitude towards the NEP as a way of undermining him. Trotsky had finally backed Lenin over the NEP in 1921, but there was little doubt as to how deeply he disapproved of the policy. This had been clearly evident in 1923 when Trotsky had led a group of Party members in openly criticising *Gosplan* for putting the interests of the Nepmen above those of the Revolution and the Russian people (see page 164). He urged a return to a much tighter state control of industry and warned that under the NEP the revolutionary gains made under war communism would be lost.

Stalin was quick to suggest to Party members who already looked on Trotsky as a disruptive force that he was indeed suspect. The interesting point here is that Stalin's own view of the NEP was far from clear at this stage. He had loyally supported Lenin's introduction of it in 1921, but had given little indication as to whether, or how long, it should be retained after Lenin's death. He preferred to keep his own views to himself and play on the differences between his colleagues.

Disputes over modernisation

Key question
Why was there a Left–Right division over the question of how the USSR should modernise?

The NEP debate was one aspect of a question that remained unanswered at Lenin's death: how should the Soviet Union plan for the future? This would have been a demanding issue regardless of whether there had been a power struggle. What the rivalry for leadership did was to intensify the argument. The USSR was a poor country. To modernise, and overcome its poverty, it would have to industrialise. Recent history had shown that a strong industrial base was an absolute essential for a modern state, and there was common agreement among Soviet Communists about that. The quarrel was not over whether the USSR should industrialise, but over how and at what speed.

History had further shown that the industrial expansion that had taken place in the previous century, in such countries as Germany and Britain, had relied on a ready supply of resources and the availability of capital for investment. Russia was rich in natural resources, but these had yet to be effectively exploited, and it certainly did not possess large amounts of capital. Nor could it easily borrow any; after 1917 the Bolsheviks had rejected **capitalist methods of finance**. Moreover, even if the Bolsheviks had been willing to borrow, there were few countries after 1917 willing to risk the dangers of investing in revolutionary Russia.

The only usable resource, therefore, was the Russian people themselves, 80 per cent of whom were peasants. To achieve industrialisation, it was necessary that the peasants be persuaded or forced into producing a food surplus, which could then be sold abroad to raise capital for industrial investment. Both Left and

Key term

Capitalist methods of finance
The system in which the owners of private capital (money) increase their wealth by making loans on which interest has to be paid later by the borrower.

Right agreed that this was the only solution, but whereas the Right were content to rely on persuasion, the Left demanded that the peasantry be forced into line.

It was Trotsky who most clearly represented the view of the Left on this. He wanted the peasants to be coerced into co-operating. However, for him the industrialisation debate was secondary to the far more demanding question of Soviet Russia's role as the organiser of international revolution. His views on this created a wide divergence between him and Stalin, expressed in terms of a clash between the opposed notions of 'permanent revolution' and 'socialism in one country'.

'Permanent revolution' versus 'socialism in one country'
'Permanent revolution'

Key question
What were the essential features of Trotsky's concept of 'permanent revolution'?

What inspired Trotsky's politics was his belief in 'permanent revolution', which was made up of a number of key ideas:

- Revolution was not a single event but a permanent (continuous) process in which risings took place from country to country.
- The events in Russia since 1917 were simply a first step towards a worldwide revolution of the proletariat.
- Individual nations did not matter, the interests of the international working class were paramount.
- True revolutionary socialism could be achieved in the USSR only if an international uprising took place.

Trotsky believed that the USSR could not survive alone in a hostile world. With its vast peasant population and undeveloped proletariat, Russia would prove 'incapable of holding her own against conservative Europe'. He contended that the immediate task of the USSR was 'to export revolution'. That was the only way to guarantee its survival.

It should be stressed that at no point did Trotsky call for the Soviet Union to be sacrificed to some theoretical notion of world revolution. His argument was an opposite one: unless there was international revolution, the Soviet Union would go under. Stalin, however, ignored the subtlety of his opponent's reasoning. He chose to portray Trotsky as someone intent on damaging the Soviet Union.

'Socialism in one country'

Key question
What were the essential features of Stalin's notion of 'socialism in one country'?

Stalin countered Trotsky's notion of 'permanent revolution' with his own concept of 'socialism in one country'. He meant by this that the nation's first task was to consolidate Lenin's Revolution and the rule of the CPSU by turning the USSR into a modern state capable of defending itself against its internal and external enemies. The Soviet Union, therefore, must work:

- to overcome its present agricultural and industrial problems by its own unaided efforts

- to go on to build a modern state, the equal of any nation in the world
- to make the survival of the Soviet Union an absolute priority, even if this meant suspending efforts to create international revolution.

Stalin used the contrast between this programme and Trotsky's to portray his rival as an enemy of the Soviet Union. Trotsky's ideas were condemned as an affront to Lenin and the Bolshevik Revolution. An image was created of Trotsky as an isolated figure, a posturing Jewish intellectual whose vague notions of international revolution threatened the security of the Soviet Union.

Trotsky's position was further weakened by the fact that throughout the 1920s the Soviet Union had a constant fear of invasion by the combined capitalist nations. Although this fear was ill-founded, the tense atmosphere it created made Trotsky's notion of the USSR's engaging in foreign revolutionary wars appear even more irresponsible. A number of historians, including E.H. Carr and Isaac Deutscher, have remarked on Stalin's ability to rally support and silence opponents at critical moments by assuming the role of the great Russian patriot concerned to save the nation from the grave dangers that threatened it.

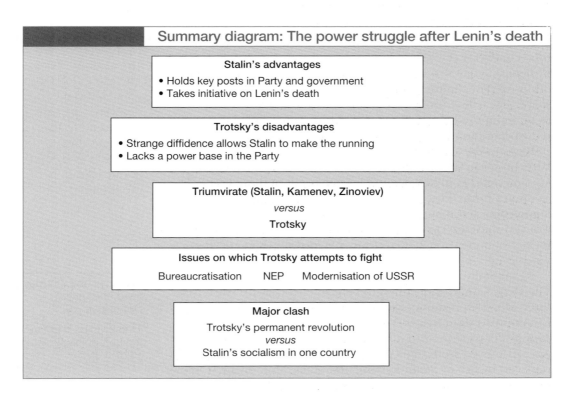

Summary diagram: The power struggle after Lenin's death

Stalin's advantages
- Holds key posts in Party and government
- Takes initiative on Lenin's death

Trotsky's disadvantages
- Strange diffidence allows Stalin to make the running
- Lacks a power base in the Party

Triumvirate (Stalin, Kamenev, Zinoviev)
versus
Trotsky

Issues on which Trotsky attempts to fight
Bureaucratisation   NEP   Modernisation of USSR

Major clash
Trotsky's permanent revolution
versus
Stalin's socialism in one country

3 | The Defeat of Trotsky and the Left

Trotsky's failure in the propaganda war of the 1920s meant that he was in no position to persuade either the Politburo or the Central Committee to vote for his proposals. Stalin's ability to **'deliver the votes'** in the crucial divisions was decisive. Following a vote against him in the 1925 Party Congress, Trotsky was relieved of his position as Commissar for War. Lev Kamenev and Grigory Zinoviev, the respective chairmen of the Moscow and **Leningrad** soviets, played a key part in this. They used their influence over the local Party organisations to ensure that it was a pro-Stalin, anti-Trotsky Congress that gathered.

Kamenev and Zinoviev

With Trotsky weakened, Stalin turned to the problem of how to deal with the two key other figures, Kamenev and Zinoviev, whom he now saw as potential rivals. Kamenev and Zinoviev had been motivated by a personal dislike of Trotsky, who at various times had tried to embarrass them by reminding the Party of their failure to support Lenin in October 1917. Now it was their turn to be ousted.

In the event, they created a trap for themselves. In 1925, Kamenev and Zinoviev, worried by the USSR's economic backwardness, publicly stated that it would require the victory of proletarian revolution in the capitalist nations in order for the Soviet Union to achieve socialism. Zinoviev wrote: 'When the time comes for the revolution in other countries and the proletariat comes to our aid, then we shall again go over to the offensive. For the time being we have only a little breathing space.' He called for the NEP to be abandoned, for restrictions to be reimposed on the peasants and for enforced industrialisation.

It was understandable that Kamenev and Zinoviev, respective Party bosses in the Soviet Union's only genuinely industrial areas, Moscow and Leningrad, should have thought in these terms. Their viewpoint formed the basis of what was termed the '**United Opposition**' but it appeared to be indistinguishable from old Trotskyism. It was no surprise, therefore, when Trotsky joined his former opponents in 1926 to form a 'Trotskyite–Kamenevite–Zinovievite' opposition bloc.

Again Stalin's control of the Party machine proved critical. The Party Congress declined to be influenced by pressure from the 'United Opposition'. Stalin's chief backers among the Right Communists were Rykov, Tomsky and Bukharin. They and their supporters combined to outvote the bloc. Kamenev and Zinoviev were dismissed from their posts as soviet chairmen, to be replaced by two of Stalin's staunchest allies, Molotov in Moscow and Kirov in Leningrad. It was little surprise that soon afterwards, Trotsky was expelled from both the Politburo and the Central Committee.

Key question
What were the basic weaknesses of the Left in their challenge to Stalin?

Key date

The CPSU Congress votes against Trotsky, so that he loses his position as War Commissar: 1925

Key terms

'Deliver the votes'
To use one's control of the party machine to gain majority support in key votes.

Leningrad
Petrograd was renamed in Lenin's honour after his death.

United Opposition
(or New Opposition)
The group led by Kamenev and Zinoviev, who called for an end to the NEP and the adoption of a rapid industrialisation programme.

Key dates

Kamenev and Zinoviev head 'the United Opposition: 1925

Trotsky joins them in the Left political bloc: 1926

Trotsky dismissed from the Central Committee: October 1927

Trotsky dismissed from the Communist Party: November 1927

Trotsky sent into internal exile: November 1927

Trotsky exiled from the Soviet Union: January 1929

Trotsky exiled

Trotsky still did not admit defeat. In 1927, on the tenth anniversary of the Bolshevik rising, he tried to rally support in a direct challenge to Stalin's authority. Even fewer members of Congress than before were prepared to side with him and he was again outvoted. His complete failure led to the Congress's accepting Stalin's proposal that Trotsky be expelled from the Party altogether. An internal exile order against him in 1927 was followed two years later by total exile from the USSR.

Stalin's victory over Trotsky was not primarily a matter of ability or principle. Stalin won because Trotsky lacked a power base. Trotsky's superiority as a speaker and writer, and his greater intellectual gifts, counted for little when set against Stalin's grip on the Party machine. It is difficult to see how, after 1924, Trotsky could ever have mounted a serious challenge to his rival. Even had his own particular failings not stopped him from acting at vital moments, Trotsky never had control of the political system as it operated in Soviet Russia. Politics is the art of the possible. After 1924 all the possibilities belonged to Stalin, and he used them.

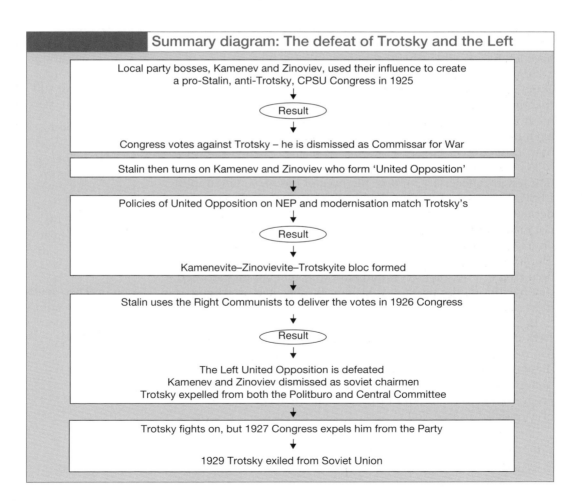

Summary diagram: The defeat of Trotsky and the Left

Local party bosses, Kamenev and Zinoviev, used their influence to create a pro-Stalin, anti-Trotsky, CPSU Congress in 1925
↓
Result
↓
Congress votes against Trotsky – he is dismissed as Commissar for War

Stalin then turns on Kamenev and Zinoviev who form 'United Opposition'
↓
Policies of United Opposition on NEP and modernisation match Trotsky's
↓
Result
↓
Kamenevite–Zinovievite–Trotskyite bloc formed
↓
Stalin uses the Right Communists to deliver the votes in 1926 Congress
↓
Result
↓
The Left United Opposition is defeated
Kamenev and Zinoviev dismissed as soviet chairmen
Trotsky expelled from both the Politburo and Central Committee
↓
Trotsky fights on, but 1927 Congress expels him from the Party
↓
1929 Trotsky exiled from Soviet Union

4 | The Defeat of the Right

Although Stalin's victory over the Right Opposition is best studied as a feature of his industrialisation programme (see page 210), it is important also to see it as the last stage in the consolidation of his authority over the Party and over the USSR. The defeat of the Right marks the end of any serious attempt to limit his power. From the late 1920s to his death in 1953 he would become increasingly dictatorial.

The major representatives of the Right were Rykov, Tomsky and Bukharin, the three who had loyally served Stalin in his outflanking of Trotsky and the Left. Politically, the Right were by no means as challenging to Stalin as the Trotskyite bloc had been. What made Stalin move against them was that they stood in the way of the industrial and agricultural schemes that he began to implement in 1928.

Collectivisation and industrialisation

Historians are uncertain as to when Stalin finally decided that the answer to the Soviet Union's growth problem was to impose **collectivisation** and **industrialisation**. It is unlikely to have been an early decision; the probability is that it was another piece of opportunism. Having defeated the Left politically, he may then have felt free to adopt their economic policies.

Some scholars have suggested that in 1928 Stalin became genuinely concerned about the serious grain shortage and decided that the only way to avoid a crisis was to resort to the drastic methods of collectivisation. It no longer mattered that this had been the very solution that the Left had advanced, since they were now scattered.

For some time it had been the view of Bukharin and the Right that it was unnecessary to force the pace of industrialisation in the USSR. They argued that it would be less disruptive to let industry develop its own momentum. The state should assist, but it should not direct. Similarly, the peasants should not be controlled and oppressed; this would make them resentful and less productive. The Right agreed that it was from the land that the means of financing industrialisation would have to come, but they stressed that by offering the peasants the chance to become prosperous, far more grain would be produced for sale abroad.

Bukharin argued in the Politburo and at the Party Congress in 1928 that Stalin's aggressive policy of state **grain procurements** was counter-productive. He declared that there were alternatives to these repressive policies. Bukharin was prepared to state openly what everybody knew but was afraid to admit: that Stalin's programme was no different from the one that Trotsky had previously advocated.

Key question
What was the attitude of the Right towards the NEP and industrialisation?

Key terms

Collectivisation
The abolition of private property and the forcing of the peasants to live and work in communes.

Industrialisation
Stalin's crash programme for revolutionising the USSR's productive economy by concentrating on the output of heavy goods such as iron and steel.

Grain procurements
Enforced collections of fixed quotas of grain from the peasants.

Weaknesses of the Right

The Right suffered from a number of weaknesses, which Stalin was able to exploit: these related to their ideas, their organisation, and their support.

Key question
Why were the Right unable to mount a successful challenge to Stalin?

Ideas
* Their economic arguments were not unsound, but in the taut atmosphere of the late 1920s, created by fear of invasion, they appeared timid and unrealistic.
* Their plea for a soft line with the peasants did not accord with the Party's needs. What the threatening times required was a dedicated resistance to the enemies of revolution both within the USSR and outside.
* Stalin was able to suggest that the Right were guilty of underestimating the crisis facing the Party and the Soviet Union. He declared that it was a time for closing the ranks in keeping with the tradition of 1917.

Key date

Stalin attacks the Right over agricultural policy: 1928

Stalin showed a shrewd understanding of the mentality of Party members. The majority were far more likely to respond to the call for a return to a hard-line policy, such as had helped them survive the desperate days of the Civil War, than they were to risk the Revolution itself by untimely concessions to a peasantry that had no real place in the proletarian future. The Party of Marx and Lenin would not be well served by the policies of the Right.

Organisation
* The difficulty experienced by the Right in advancing their views was the same as that which had confronted the Left. How could they impress their ideas upon the Party while Stalin remained master of the Party's organisation?
* Bukharin and his colleagues wanted to remain good Party men, and it was this sense of loyalty that weakened them in their attempts to oppose Stalin. Fearful of creating 'factionalism', they hoped that they could win the whole Party round to their way of thinking without causing deep divisions. On occasion they were sharply outspoken, Bukharin particularly so, but their basic approach was conciliatory.

All this played into Stalin's hands. Since it was largely his supporters who were responsible for drafting and distributing Party information, it was not difficult for Stalin to belittle the Right as a weak and irresponsible clique.

Key figures

Nikolai Uglanov (1886–1940)
An admirer and supporter of Bukharin.

Lazar Kaganovich (1893–1991)
A ruthless and ambitious young Politburo member from Ukraine.

Support
* The Right's only substantial support lay in the trade unions, whose Central Council was chaired by Tomsky, and in the CPSU's Moscow branch, where **Nikolai Uglanov** was the Party secretary.
* When Stalin realised that these might be a source of opposition, he acted quickly and decisively. He sent **Lazar Kaganovich** to undertake a purge of the suspect trade unionists.

- The Right proved totally incapable of organising resistance to this political blitz. **Vyacheslav Molotov**, Stalin's faithful henchman, was dispatched to Moscow, where he enlisted the support of the pro-Stalin members to achieve a similar purge of the local Party officials.

By early 1929 the Right had been trounced beyond recovery. Tomsky was no longer the national trade union leader; Uglanov had been replaced in the Moscow Party organisation; Rykov had been superseded as premier by Molotov, and Bukharin had been voted out as chairman of the Comintern and had lost his place in the Politburo. Tomsky, Rykov and Bukharin, the main trio of the 'Right Opportunists', as they were termed by the Stalinist press, were allowed to remain in the Party, but only after they had publicly admitted the error of their ways. Stalin's triumph over both Left and Right was complete. He was now in a position to exercise power as the new *vozhd*. The grey blank was about to become the Red tsar.

Key figure

Vyacheslav Molotov (1890–1986)
A prominent Bolshevik agitator in 1917, he became a lifelong and dedicated supporter of Stalin in home and foreign affairs. Winston Churchill, the British statesman, regarded him as an 'automaton'.

Key term

Vozhd
Russian for supreme leader, equivalent to *der Führer* in German.

Key date

The leading figures on the Right finally defeated by Stalin and demoted in the CPSU: 1929

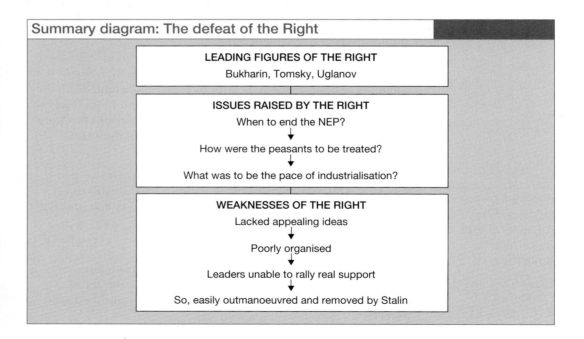

Summary diagram: The defeat of the Right

LEADING FIGURES OF THE RIGHT
Bukharin, Tomsky, Uglanov

ISSUES RAISED BY THE RIGHT
When to end the NEP?
↓
How were the peasants to be treated?
↓
What was to be the pace of industrialisation?

WEAKNESSES OF THE RIGHT
Lacked appealing ideas
↓
Poorly organised
↓
Leaders unable to rally real support
↓
So, easily outmanoeuvred and removed by Stalin

Study Guide: AS Question

In the style of OCR

Assess the reasons why Stalin was able to rise to power between 1924 and 1929. (50 marks)

Exam tips

The cross-references are intended to take you straight to the material that will help you to answer the question.

You are asked to 'assess' Stalin's rise to power. This means that you must explain, not list, the reasons, and, in doing so, indicate which reasons you consider to be the most important. Points should be analysed and supported with appropriate examples. Above all, try to avoid describing events or telling a story. You might analyse some of the following reasons:

- the skill with which Stalin outmanoeuvred his rivals, especially Trotsky, Bukharin, Zinoviev and Rykov (pages 187–94, 194–6, 196–8
- Stalin's power base as Commissar for Nationalities (page 182) and General Secretary of the Communist Party (page 185)
- Stalin's popular policy on agriculture (pages 190–6)
- Stalin's attractive political vision – 'socialism in one country' compared with Trotsky's goal of 'permanent revolution' (pages 192–3)
- Lenin's legacy: enrolment (page 186), anti-factionalism (page 186)
- Stalin's claim to be Lenin's heir (pages 186–7) and the fact that Lenin's 'Testament' was not publicly revealed (pages 187–8).

Stalin and the Soviet Economy

POINTS TO CONSIDER
A nation's economy is vital to its development. This is
particularly true of Stalin's Russia. Stalin decided that
the USSR could not survive unless it rapidly modernised
its economy. To that end, he set about completely
reshaping Soviet agriculture and industry. This had
immense economic, social and political consequences.
These are examined as three themes:

• Stalin's economic aims
• his collectivisation of the peasantry
• his massive industrialisation programme.

Key dates

1926	The critical resolution by the Party Congress on the future of the Soviet economy
1928	Collectivisation begins
	Start of the First Five-Year Plan (FYP)
1932–3	Widespread famine in the USSR
1933	Start of the Second FYP
1938	Start of the Third FYP
1941	German invasion and occupation of Russia

1 | Stalin's Economic Aims

In the late 1920s, Stalin decided to impose on the USSR a crash
programme of reform of the Soviet economy. Agriculture and
industry were to be revolutionised. The cue for the great change
had been provided in 1926 by a critical resolution of the Party
Congress 'to transform our country from an agrarian into an
industrial one, capable by its own efforts of producing the necessary
means'. Stalin planned to turn that resolution into reality.

Stalin's economic policy had one essential aim, the
modernisation of the Soviet economy, and two essential methods,
collectivisation and industrialisation. From 1928 onwards, with
the introduction of collectivisation and industrialisation, the
Soviet state took over the running of the nation's economy.

Key question
What were Stalin's
motives in
revolutionising the
Soviet economy?

The critical resolution
by the Party
Congress on the
future of the Soviet
economy: 1926

Key date

Key terms

Second revolution
Stalin's enforced modernisation of the Soviet economy.

Revolution from below
The CPSU claim that the 1917 Revolution had been a genuine rising of the people rather than a power grab by the Bolsheviks.

Political expediency
Refers to the pursuing of a course of action with the primary aim of gaining a political advantage.

Stalin called this momentous decision the '**second revolution**' to indicate that it was as important a stage in Soviet history as the original 1917 Revolution had been. The comparison was obviously intended to enhance his own status as a revolutionary leader following in the footsteps of Lenin. It is also frequently referred as a 'revolution from above'.

Revolution from above

In theory, 1917 had been a **revolution from below**. The Bolshevik-led proletariat had begun the construction of a state in which the workers ruled. Bukharin and the Right had used this notion to argue that since the USSR was now a proletarian society, the economy should be left to develop at its own pace, without interference from the government. But Stalin's economic programme ended such thinking. The state would now command and direct the economy from above.

A central planning agency known as *Gosplan* had been created earlier under Lenin (see page 164). However, what was different about Stalin's schemes was their scale and thoroughness. Under Stalin, state control was to be total. There was an important political aspect to this. He saw in a hard-line policy the best means of confirming his authority over Party and government.

Modernisation

Yet it would be wrong to regard Stalin's policy as wholly a matter of **political expediency**. To judge from his speeches and actions after 1928, he had become convinced that the needs of Soviet Russia could be met only by modernisation. By that, Stalin meant bringing his economically backward nation up to a level of industrial production that would enable it to catch up, and then overtake, the advanced economies of western Europe and the USA.

He believed that the survival of the Revolution and of Soviet Russia depended on the nation's ability to turn itself into a modern industrial society within the shortest possible time. That was the essence of his slogan 'socialism in one country' (see page 192). Stalin expressed himself with particular force in 1931:

> It is sometimes asked whether it is not possible to slow down the tempo somewhat, to put a check on the movement. No, comrades, it is not possible! The tempo must not be reduced! To slacken the tempo would mean falling behind. And those who fall behind get beaten. But we do not want to be beaten.
>
> No, we refuse to be beaten! One feature of old Russia was the continual beatings she suffered because of her backwardness. She was beaten by the Mongols. She was beaten by the Turks. She was beaten by the Polish and Lithuanian gentry. She was beaten by the British and French capitalists. She was beaten by the Japanese barons. All beat her – because of her backwardness: military

backwardness, cultural backwardness, political backwardness, industrial backwardness, agricultural backwardness. They beat her because to do so was profitable and could be done with impunity.

We are fifty or a hundred years behind the advanced countries. We must make good this distance in ten years. Either we do it, or we shall be crushed. This is what our obligations to the workers and peasants of the USSR dictate to us.

This passionate appeal to Russian history subordinated everything to the driving need for national survival. Stalin would later use this appeal as the pretext for the severity that accompanied the collectivisation of Russian agriculture.

Summary diagram: Stalin's economic aims

Aim
- A second revolution to modernise Russia

Motives
- To confirm his authority as leader
- To enable the Soviet Union to catch up with the economies of the Western world

Means
- Collectivisation
- Industrialisation

2 | Collectivisation

Stalin judged that the only way to raise the capital needed to develop Soviet industry was to use the land. The necessary first step towards this was the collectivisation of Russian agriculture. This involved taking the land from the peasants and giving it all to the state. The peasants would no longer farm the land for their own individual profit. Instead, they would pool their efforts and receive a wage. Stalin calculated that this change would allow the Soviet Union to use the collective profits from the land to finance a massive industrialisation programme. For him, the needs of the land were always subordinate to those of industry.

Two types of farm
Stalin defined collectivisation as 'the setting up of **collective farms** and **state farms** in order to squeeze out all capitalist elements from the land'. In practice, there was little difference between the two. Both types of farm were to be the means by which private peasant-ownership would be ended and agriculture made to serve the interests of the Soviet state. The plan was to group between 50 and 100 holdings into one unit. It was believed that large farms would be more efficient and would encourage the effective use of

Key question
How did Stalin plan to finance industrialisation?

Collective farms (*kolkhozy* in Russian) Co-operatives in which the peasants pooled their resources and shared the labour and the wages.

State farms (*sovkhozy* in Russian) Contained peasants who worked directly for the state for a wage.

Key terms

agricultural machinery. Indeed, the motorised tractor became the outstanding symbol of this mechanising of Soviet farming.

Efficient farming, so ran the argument, would have two vital results. It would create surplus food supplies that could be sold abroad to raise capital for Soviet industry and decrease the number of rural labourers needed and so release workers for the new factories.

The *kulaks*

Key question
What was Stalin's motivation in persecuting the *kulaks*?

Key date

Collectivisation begins: 1928

When introducing collectivisation in 1928, Stalin claimed that it was 'voluntary', the free and eager choice of the peasants. But in truth it was forced on a very reluctant peasantry. In a major propaganda offensive, he identified a class of '*kulaks*' who were holding back the workers' revolution by monopolising the best land and employing cheap peasant labour to farm it (see page 152). By hoarding their farm produce they kept food prices high, thus making themselves rich at the expense of the workers and poorer peasants. Unless they were broken as a class, they would prevent the modernisation of the USSR.

The concept of a *kulak* class has been shown by scholars to have been a Stalinist myth. The so-called *kulaks* were really only those hard-working peasants who had proved more efficient farmers than their neighbours. In no sense did they constitute the class of exploiting landowners described in Stalinist propaganda. Nonetheless, given the tradition of landlord oppression going back to tsarist times, the notion of a *kulak* class proved a very powerful one and provided the grounds for the coercion of the peasantry as a whole – middle and poor peasants, as well as *kulaks*.

Surplus peasants and grain

As a revolutionary, Stalin had little sympathy for the peasants. Communist theory taught that the days of the peasantry as a revolutionary social force had passed. The future belonged to the urban workers. October 1917 had been the first stage in the triumph of this proletarian class. Therefore, it was perfectly fitting that the peasantry should, in a time of national crisis, bow to the demands of industrialisation. Stalin used a simple formula. The USSR needed industrial investment and manpower. The land could provide both. Surplus grain would be sold abroad to raise investment funds for industry; surplus peasants would become factory workers.

One part of the formula was correct: for generations, the Russian countryside had been overpopulated, creating a chronic land shortage. The other part was a gross distortion. There was no grain surplus. Indeed, the opposite was the case. Even in the best years of the NEP, food production had seldom matched needs. Yet Stalin insisted that the problem was not the lack of food but its poor distribution; food shortages were the result of grain hoarding by the rich peasants. This argument was then used to explain the urgent need for collectivisation as a way of securing adequate food supplies. It also provided the moral grounds for the onslaught on the *kulaks*, who were condemned as enemies of the Soviet nation in its struggle to modernise itself in the face of international capitalist hostility.

Members of the communist youth league unearthing bags of grain hidden by peasants in a cemetery near Odessa. What opportunities did such searches give for oppressing the *kulaks*?

De-*kulak*isation

In some regions the poorer peasants undertook 'de-*kulak*isation' with enthusiasm, since it provided them with an excuse to settle old scores and to give vent to local jealousies. Land and property were seized from the minority of better-off peasants, and they and their families were physically attacked. Such treatment was often the prelude to arrest and deportation by **OGPU** anti-*kulak* squads, authorised by Stalin and modelled on the gangs that had persecuted the peasants during the state-organised terror of the Civil War period (1918–20).

The renewal of terror also served as warning to the mass of the peasantry of the likely consequences of resisting the state reorganisation of Soviet agriculture. The destruction of the *kulaks* was thus an integral part of the whole collectivisation process. As a Soviet official later admitted: 'Most Party officers thought that the whole point of de-*kulak*isation was its value as an administrative measure, speeding up tempos of collectivisation.'

OGPU
Succeeded the *Cheka* as the state security force. In turn it became the NKVD and then the KGB.

Key term

An anti-*kulak* demonstration on a collective farm in 1930. The banner reads: 'Liquidate the *kulaks* as a class'. Who was likely to have organised such a demonstration?

Key question
What were the effects of collectivisation on the peasantry?

Resistance to collectivisation

In the period between December 1929 and March 1930, nearly half the peasant farms in the USSR were collectivised. Yet peasants in their millions resisted. What amounted to civil war broke out in the countryside. The following details indicate the scale of the disturbances as recorded in official figures for the period 1929–30:

- Thirty thousand arson attacks occurred.
- The number of organised rural mass disturbances increased from 172 for the first half of 1929 to 229 for the second half.

A particularly striking feature of the disturbances was the prominent role women played in them. In Okhochaya, a village in Ukraine, the following riotous scene occurred. An eyewitness described how women broke into the barns where the requisition squads had dumped the grain that had been seized from the peasants:

> A crowd of women stormed the *kolkhoz* stables and barns. They cried, screamed and wailed, demanding their cows and seed back. The men stood a way off, in clusters, sullenly silent. Some of the lads had pitchforks, stakes, axes tucked in their sashes. The terrified granary man [guard] ran away; the women tore off the bolts and together with the men began dragging out the bags of seed.

The reason women had a leading role was that since it was they, as mothers and organisers of the household, who were invariably the first to suffer the harsh consequences of the new agricultural system, it was they who were often the first to take action. One peasant explained in illuminatingly simple terms why his spouse was so opposed to collectivisation: 'My wife does not want to socialise our cow.' There were cases of mothers with their children being in the front line of demonstrations and of women lying down in front of the tractors and trucks sent to break up the private farms and impose collectivisation on the localities. One peasant admitted:

> We [men] dared not speak at meetings. If we said anything that the organisers didn't like, they abused us, called us *kulaks*, and even threatened to put us in prison. We let the women do the talking. If the organiser tried to stop them, they made such a din that he had to call off the meeting.

The men also thought that the women would be less likely to suffer reprisals from the authorities, who certainly, to judge by court records, appeared reluctant initially to prosecute female demonstrators.

However, peasant resistance, no matter how valiant and desperate, stood no chance of stopping collectivisation. The officials and their requisition squads pressed on with their disruptive policies. Such was the turmoil in the countryside that Stalin called a halt, blaming the troubles on over-zealous officials who had become 'dizzy with success'. Many of the peasants were allowed to return to their original holdings. However, the delay was only temporary. Having cleared his name by blaming the difficulties on local officials, Stalin restarted collectivisation in a more determined, if somewhat slower, manner. By the end of the 1930s virtually the whole of the peasantry had been collectivised (see Figure 8.1).

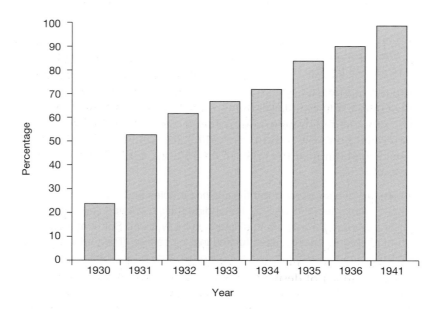

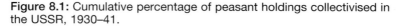

Figure 8.1: Cumulative percentage of peasant holdings collectivised in the USSR, 1930–41.

Upheaval and starvation

Behind these remarkable figures lay the story of a massive social upheaval. Bewildered and confused, the peasants either would not or could not co-operate in the deliberate destruction of their traditional way of life. The consequences were increasingly tragic. The majority of peasants ate their seed corn and slaughtered their livestock. There were no crops left to reap or animals to rear.

The Soviet authorities responded with still fiercer coercion, but this simply made matters worse: imprisonment, deportation and execution could not replenish the barns or restock the herds. Special contingents of Party workers were sent from the towns to restore food production levels by working on the land themselves. But their ignorance of farming only added to the disruption. By a bitter irony, even as starvation set in, the little grain that was available was being exported as 'surplus' to obtain the foreign capital that industry demanded. By 1932 the situation on the land was catastrophic.

Table 8.1: The fall in food consumption (in kilograms per head)

	Bread	Potatoes	Meat and lard	Butter
1928	250.4	141.1	24.8	1.35
1932	214.6	125.0	11.2	0.7

Table 8.2: The fall in livestock (in millions)

	Horses	Cattle	Pigs	Sheep and goats
1928	33	70	26	146
1932	15	34	9	42

The figures in Tables 8.1 and 8.2 refer to the USSR as a whole. In the urban areas there was more food available. Indeed, a major purpose of the grain requisition squads was to maintain adequate supplies to the industrial regions. This meant that the misery in the countryside was proportionally greater, with areas such as Ukraine and Kazakhstan suffering particularly severely. The devastation experienced by the Kazakhs can be gauged from the fact that in this period they lost nearly 90 per cent of their livestock.

National famine

Starvation, which in many parts of the Soviet Union persisted throughout the 1930s, was at its worst in the years 1932–3, when a national famine occurred. Collectivisation led to despair among the peasants. In many areas they simply stopped producing, either as an act of desperate resistance or through sheer inability to adapt to the violently enforced land system. Hungry and embittered, they made for the towns in huge numbers. It had, of course, been part of Stalin's collectivisation plan to move the

Key question
Why could the famine of the early 1930s not be dealt with effectively?

Key date

National famine: 1932–3

peasants into the industrial regions. However, so great was the migration that a system of internal passports had to be introduced in an effort to control the flow. Some idea of the horrors can be obtained from the following contemporary account:

> Trainloads of deported peasants left for the icy North, the forests, the steppes, the deserts. These were whole populations, denuded of everything; the old folk starved to death in mid-journey, newborn babes were buried on the banks of the roadside, and each wilderness had its little cross of boughs or white wood. Other populations, dragging all their mean possessions on wagons, rushed towards the frontiers of Poland, Rumania, and China and crossed them – by no means intact, to be sure – in spite of the machine guns … Agricultural technicians and experts were brave in denouncing the blunders and excesses; they were arrested in thousands and made to appear in huge sabotage trials so that responsibility might be unloaded on somebody.

Official silence

Despite overwhelming evidence of the tragedy that had overtaken the USSR, the official Stalinist line was that there was no famine. In the whole of the contemporary Soviet press there were only two oblique references to it. This conspiracy of silence was of more than political significance. As well as protecting the image of Stalin the great planner, it effectively prevented the introduction of measures to remedy the distress. Since the famine did not officially exist, Soviet Russia could not publicly take steps to relieve it. For the same reason, it could not appeal, as had been done during an earlier Russian famine in 1921, for aid from the outside world (see page 153).

Thus, what Isaac Deutscher, the historian and former Trotskyist, called 'the first purely man-made famine in history' went unacknowledged in order to avoid discrediting Stalin. Not for the last time, large numbers of the Soviet people were sacrificed on the altar of Stalin's reputation. There was a strong rumour that Stalin's second wife, **Nadezhda Alliluyeva**, had been driven to suicide by the knowledge that it was her husband's brutal policies that had caused the famine. Shortly before her death she had railed at Stalin: 'You are a tormentor, that's what you are. You torment your own son. You torment your wife. You torment the whole Russian people.'

The truth of Nadezhda Alliluyeva's charge has now been put beyond doubt by the findings of scholars who have examined the Soviet archives that were opened up after the fall of the USSR in the early 1990s. Lynne Viola in 2007 confirmed the horrific character of Stalin's treatment of the peasantry. In harrowing

Nadezhda Alliluyeva (1901–32) It has been suggested that Stalin's grief and desolation at his wife's suicide help to explain why he became increasingly embittered and unfeeling towards other people.

Key figure

detail, Viola described how, between 1930 and 1932, Stalin drove 2 million peasants into internal exile as slave labourers, a quarter of that number dying of hunger and exposure.

Her work, which built upon the pioneering studies of Robert Conquest, the first major western historian to chart Stalin's brutalities, serves as a belated and devastating corrective to the view advanced at the time by pro-Soviet sympathisers in the West that their hero Stalin was creating a paradise on earth. It is interesting that when **Nikita Khrushchev** launched his de-Stalinisation programme in the late 1950s (see page 271), he was careful to limit his censures to Stalin's crimes against the Communist Party. He avoided referring to his former leader's crimes against the Soviet people.

Key figure

Nikita Khrushchev (1894–1971)
Leader of the Soviet Union from 1956 to 1964.

Key question
How far did collectivisation satisfy the Soviet Union's economic needs?

Was collectivisation justifiable on economic grounds?

Even allowing for the occasional progressive aspect of collectivisation, such as the building and distributing of mechanised tractors, the overall picture remained bleak. The mass of the peasantry had been uprooted and left bewildered. Despite severe reprisals and coercion, the peasants were unable to produce the surplus food that Stalin demanded. By 1939, Soviet agricultural productivity had barely returned to the level recorded for tsarist Russia in 1913. But the most damning consideration still remains the man-made famine, which in the 1930s killed between 10 and 15 million peasants.

However, there is another consideration. The hard fact is that Stalin's policies did force a large number of peasants to leave the land. This was a process that Russia needed. Economic historians have often stressed that there was a land crisis in Russia that pre-dated Communism. Since the nineteenth century, land in Russia had been growing increasingly incapable of supporting the ever larger numbers of people who lived unproductively on it. Unless a major shift occurred in the imbalance between urban and rural dwellers, Russia would be in sustained difficulties. The nation needed to change from an agricultural and rural society to an urban and industrial one.

There is a case for arguing, therefore, that Stalin's collectivisation programme, brutally applied though it was, did answer one of the USSR's great needs. Leaving aside questions of human suffering, the enforced migration under Stalin made economic sense. It relieved the pressure on the land and provided the workforce that enabled the industrialisation programme to be started. Perhaps all this could be summed up by saying that Stalin's aims were understandable but his methods were unacceptable. He did the wrong thing for the right reason.

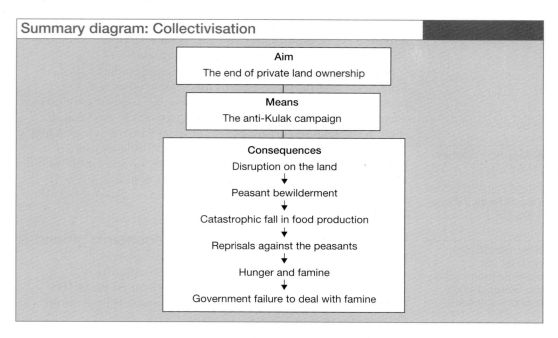

Summary diagram: Collectivisation

Aim
The end of private land ownership

Means
The anti-Kulak campaign

Consequences
Disruption on the land
↓
Peasant bewilderment
↓
Catastrophic fall in food production
↓
Reprisals against the peasants
↓
Hunger and famine
↓
Government failure to deal with famine

3 | Industrialisation

Key question
What were Stalin's aims for Soviet industry in the 1930s?

Stalin described his industrialisation plans for the USSR as an attempt to establish a war economy. He declared that he was making war on the failings of Russia's past and on the class enemies within the nation. He also claimed that he was preparing the USSR for war against its capitalist foes abroad. This was not simply martial imagery. Stalin regarded iron, steel and oil as the sinews of war. Their successful production would guarantee the strength and readiness of the nation to face its enemies.

For Stalin, therefore, industry meant heavy industry. He believed that the industrial revolutions that had made western Europe and North America so strong had been based on iron and steel production. It followed that the USSR must adopt a similar industrial pattern in its drive towards modernisation. The difference would be that whereas the West had taken the capitalist road, the USSR would follow the path of socialism.

Stalin had grounds for his optimism. It so happened that the Soviet industrialisation drive in the 1930s coincided with **the Depression** in the western world. Stalin claimed that the USSR was introducing into its own economy the technical successes of western industrialisation but was rejecting the destructive capitalist system that went with them. Socialist planning would enable the USSR to avoid the errors that had begun to undermine the western economies.

Soviet industrialisation under Stalin took the form of a series of Five-Year Plans (FYPs). *Gosplan* (see page 164) was required by Stalin to draw up a list of quotas of production ranging across the whole of Soviet industry. The process began in 1928 and, except for the war years 1941–5, lasted until Stalin's death in 1953. In all, there were five separate plans:

The Depression
A period of severe economic stagnation that began in the USA in 1929 and lasted throughout the 1930s. It affected the whole of the industrial world and was interpreted by Marxists as a sign of the final collapse of capitalism.

Key term

- First FYP   October 1928 to December 1932
- Second FYP   January 1933 to December 1937
- Third FYP   January 1938 to June 1941
- Fourth FYP   January 1946 to December 1950
- Fifth FYP   January 1951 to December 1955

The First Five-Year Plan, 1928–32

Key question
What was the purpose of the First Five Year Plan?

Key date

First Five-Year Plan: 1928–32

The term 'Plan' is misleading. The First FYP laid down what was to be achieved, but did not say how it was to be done. It simply assumed the quotas would be met. What the First FYP represented, therefore, was a set of targets rather than a plan.

As had happened with collectivisation, local officials and managers falsified their production figures to give the impression they had met their targets when in fact they had fallen short. For this reason, precise statistics for the First FYP are difficult to determine. A further complication is that three quite distinct versions of the First FYP eventually appeared.

Impressed by the apparent progress of the Plan in its early stages, Stalin encouraged the formulation of an 'optimal' plan that reassessed targets upwards. These new quotas were hopelessly unrealistic and stood no chance of being reached. Nonetheless, on the basis of the supposed achievements of this 'optimal' plan, the figures were revised, making them still higher. Western analysts suggest the figures in Table 8.3 as the closest approximation to the real figures.

Table 8.3: Industrial output

Product (in million tons)	1927–8 First plan	1932–3 'Optimal'	1932 Revised	1932 Actual
Coal	35.0	75.0	95–105	64.0
Oil	11.7	21.7	40–55	21.4
Iron ore	6.7	20.2	24–32	12.1
Pig iron	3.2	10.0	15–16	6.2

Propaganda and collective effort

Key question
How did the Soviet people respond to Stalin's call?

The importance of these figures should not be exaggerated. At the time it was the grand design, not the detail, that mattered. The Plan was a huge propaganda project that was aimed at convincing the Soviet people that they were personally engaged in a vast industrial enterprise. By their own efforts, they were changing the character of the society in which they lived and providing it with the means of achieving greatness.

Nor was it all a matter of state enforcement, fierce though that was. Among the young especially, there was an enthusiasm and a commitment that suggested that many Soviet citizens believed they were genuinely building a new and better world. The sense of the Soviet people as masters of their own fate was expressed in the slogan 'There is no fortress that we Bolsheviks cannot storm.'

John Scott, an American Communist and one of the many pro-Soviet western industrial advisers who came to the USSR at this time, was impressed by the mixture of idealism and coercion that characterised the early stages of Stalinist industrialisation. He described how the city of Magnitogorsk in the Urals was built from scratch:

> Within several years, half a billion cubic feet of excavation was done, forty-two million cubic feet of reinforced concrete poured, five million cubic feet of fire bricks laid, a quarter of a million tons of structured steel erected. This was done without sufficient labour, without necessary quantities of the most elementary materials. Brigades of young enthusiasts from every corner of the Soviet Union arrived in the summer of 1930 and did the groundwork of railroad and dam construction necessary. Later, groups of local peasants and herdsmen came to Magnitogorsk because of bad conditions in the villages, due to collectivisation. Many of the peasants were completely unfamiliar with industrial tools and processes. A colony of several hundred foreign engineers and specialists, some of whom made as high as one hundred dollars a day, arrived to advise and direct the work.

> From 1928 until 1932 nearly a quarter of a million people came to Magnitogorsk. About three-quarters of these new arrivals came of their own free will seeking work, bread-cards, better conditions. The rest came under compulsion.

'The Five-Year Plan' – a propaganda wall poster of the 1930s, depicting Stalin as the heroic creator of a powerful, industrialised, Soviet Union. He is overcoming the forces of religion, international capitalism, and Russian conservatism and backwardness. How does the poster attempt to achieve its effect of presenting Stalin as a hero?

Cultural revolution

The term 'cultural revolution' is an appropriate description of the significance of what was taking place under Stalin's leadership. Two renowned western analysts of Soviet affairs, Alec Nove and Sheila Fitzpatrick, have stressed this aspect. They see behind the economic changes of this period a real attempt being made to create a new type of individual, *homo sovieticus* (Soviet man), as if a new species had come into being. Stalin told a gathering of Soviet writers that they should regard themselves as 'engineers of the human soul' (see page 247).

Successes and achievements of the First FYP

Key question
How far did the First FYP achieve its objectives?

No matter how badly the figures may have been rigged at the time, the First FYP was an extraordinary achievement overall. Coal and iron production and the generation of electricity all increased in huge proportions. The production of steel and chemicals was less impressive, while the output of finished textiles actually declined.

A striking feature of the Plan was the low priority it gave to improving the material lives of the Soviet people. No effort was made to reward the workers by providing them with affordable consumer goods. Living conditions actually deteriorated in this period. Accommodation in the towns and cities remained substandard.

The Soviet authorities' neglect of basic social needs was not accidental. The Plan had never been intended to raise living standards. Its purpose was collective, not individual. It called for sacrifice on the part of the workers in the construction of a socialist state that would be able to sustain itself economically and militarily against the enmity of the outside world.

Resistance and sabotage

Key question
Why was there so little resistance to the FYP?

It was Stalin's presentation of the FYP as a defence of the USSR against international hostility that enabled him to brand resistance to the Plan as 'sabotage'. A series of public trials of industrial 'wreckers', including a number of foreign workers, were staged to impress the Party and the masses with the futility of protesting against the industrialisation programme. In 1928, in a prelude to the First FYP, Stalin claimed to have discovered an anti-Soviet conspiracy among the mining engineers of Shakhty in the Donbass region. Their subsequent public trial was intended to frighten the workers into line. It also showed that the privileged position of the skilled workers, the 'bourgeois experts', was to be tolerated no longer.

This attack upon the experts was part of a pattern in the First FYP that stressed quantity at the expense of quality. The push towards sheer volume of output was intended to prove the correctness of Stalin's grand economic schemes. Sheila Fitzpatrick has described this as being an aspect of Stalin's **gigantomania**, his love of mighty building projects such as canals, bridges and docks, which he regarded as proof that the USSR was advancing to greatness.

Key term

Gigantomania
The worship of size for its own sake.

Stalin's emphasis on gross output may also be interpreted as shrewd thinking on his part. He knew that the untrained peasants who now filled the factories would not turn immediately into skilled workers. It made sense, therefore, at least in the short term, to ignore the question of quality and to stress quantity. The result very often was that machines, factories and even whole enterprises were ruined because of the workers' lack of basic skills.

Stalin was seemingly untroubled by this. His notions of industrial 'saboteurs' and 'wreckers' allowed him to place the blame for poor quality and underproduction on managers and workers who were not prepared to play their proper part in rebuilding the nation. He used OGPU agents and Party **cadres** to terrorise the workforce. 'Sabotage' became a blanket term used to denounce anyone considered not to be pulling his weight. The simplest errors, such as being late for work or mislaying tools, could lead to such a charge.

Cadres
Party members who were sent into factories and to construction sites to spy and report back on managers and workers.

Key term

At a higher level, those factory managers or foremen who did not meet their production quotas might find themselves on public trial as enemies of the Soviet state. In such an atmosphere of fear and recrimination, doctoring official returns and inflating output figures became normal practice. Everybody at every level engaged in a huge game of pretence. This was why Soviet statistics for industrial growth were so unreliable and why it was possible for Stalin to claim in mid-course that since the First FYP had already met its initial targets, it would be shortened to a four-year plan. In Stalin's industrial revolution, appearances were everything. This was where the logic of 'gigantomania' had led.

Stalin: the masterplanner?

The industrial policies of this time had been described as 'the Stalinist blueprint' or 'Stalin's economic model'. Modern scholars are, however, wary of using such terms. Norman Stone, for example, interprets Stalin's policies not as far-sighted strategy but as 'simply putting one foot in front of the other as he went along'. Despite the growing tendency in all official Soviet documents of the 1930s to include a fulsome reference to Stalin the masterplanner, there was in fact very little planning from the top.

Key question
How far was the First FYP planned from the top?

It is true that Stalin's government exhorted, cajoled and bullied the workers into ever greater efforts towards ever greater production. But such planning as there was occurred not at national but at local level. It was the regional and site managers who, struggling desperately to make sense of the instructions they were given from on high, formulated the actual schemes for reaching their given production quotas. This was why it was so easy for Stalin and his Kremlin colleagues to accuse lesser officials of sabotage while themselves avoiding any taint of incompetence.

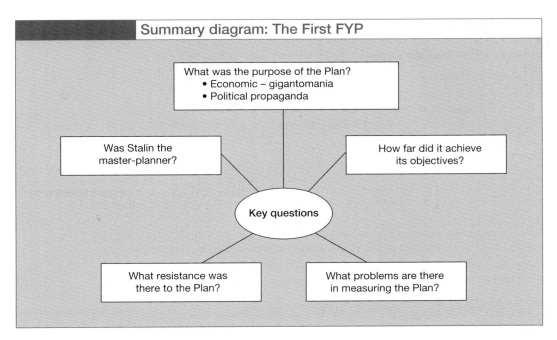

Summary diagram: The First FYP

What was the purpose of the Plan?
- Economic – gigantomania
- Political propaganda

Was Stalin the master-planner?

How far did it achieve its objectives?

Key questions

What resistance was there to the Plan?

What problems are there in measuring the Plan?

Key question
What were the main strengths and weaknesses of the Second and Third Five-Year Plans?

Key dates
Second Five-Year Plan: 1933–7

Third Five-Year Plan: 1938–41

The Second and Third Five-Year Plans

Although the Second and Third FYPs were modelled on the pattern of the First, the targets set for them were more realistic. Nevertheless, they still revealed the same lack of co-ordination as had characterised the First. Overproduction occurred in some parts of the economy, underproduction in others, which frequently led to whole branches of industry being held up for lack of vital supplies. For example, some projects had too little timber at times, while at other times they had enough timber but insufficient steel. Spare parts were hard to come by, which often meant broken machines standing unrepaired and idle for long periods.

The hardest struggle was to maintain a proper supply of materials; this often led to fierce competition between regions and sectors of industry, all of them anxious to escape the charge of failing to achieve their targets. As a result, there was hoarding of resources and a lack of co-operation between the various parts of the industrial system. Complaints about poor standards, carefully veiled so as not to appear critical of Stalin and the Plan, were frequent. What successes there were occurred again in heavy industry, where the Second FYP began to reap the benefit of the creation of large-scale plants under the First Plan.

Scapegoats

The reluctance to tell the full truth hindered genuine industrial growth. Since no one was willing to admit there was an error in the planning, faults went unchecked until serious breakdowns occurred. There then followed the familiar search for scapegoats. It was during the period of the Second and Third FYPs that Stalin's political purges were at their fiercest. In such an all-pervading atmosphere of terror the mere accusation of 'sabotage' was taken as a proof of guilt. Productivity suffered as a result. As Alec Nove observes in his *Economic History of the USSR* (see page 220):

Everywhere there were said to be spies, wreckers, diversionists. There was a grave shortage of qualified personnel, so the deportation of many thousands of engineers and technologists to distant concentration camps represented a severe loss.

Soviet workers and the Plans

Despite Stalin's claims to the contrary, the living standards of the workers failed to rise. This was due, in part, to the effects of the famine, but also to the continuing neglect in the Plans of consumer goods. Beyond the comfort to be gained from feeling that they were engaged in a great national enterprise, a theme constantly emphasised in the Soviet press, there were few material rewards to help the workers endure the severity of their conditions. Moreover, they had to accept their lot without complaint.

Key question
How were the workers affected by the FYPs?

The Stakhanovite movement, 1935

The Party's control of newspapers, cinema and radio meant that only a favourable view of the Plans was ever presented. The official line was that all was well and the workers were happy. Support for this claim was provided by the Stakhanovite movement, which was exploited by the authorities to inspire or shame workers into raising their production levels still higher. It was officially claimed in August 1935 that **Alexei Stakhanov**, a miner in the Donbass region, had single-handedly cut over 100 tons of coal in one five-hour shift, which was more than fourteen times his required quota.

His reported feat was seized on by the authorities as a glorious example of what was possible in a Soviet Union guided by the great and wise Joseph Stalin. Miners, indeed workers, everywhere were urged to match Stakhanov's dedication by similar **'storming'**. It all seemed very fine, but it proved more loss than gain. While some 'Stakhanovite' groups produced more output in factories and on farms, this was achieved only by their being given privileged access to tools and supplies and by the changing of work plans to accommodate them. The resulting disruption led to a loss of production overall in those areas where the Stakhanovite movement was at its most enthusiastic.

Alexei Stakhanov (1906–77)
As was later admitted by the Soviet authorities, though not until 1988, his achievement had been grossly exaggerated. He had not worked on his own but as part of a team, which had been supplied with the best coal-cutting machines available.

Key figure

'Storming'
An intensive period of work to meet a highly demanding set target.

Key term

Workers' rights

After 1917 the Russian trade unions had become powerless. In Bolshevik theory, in a truly socialist state, such as Russia now was, there was no distinction between the interests of government and those of the workers. Therefore, there was no longer any need for a separate trade union movement. In 1920, Trotsky had taken violent steps to destroy the independence of the unions and bring them directly under Bolshevik control. The result was that after 1920 the unions were simply the means by which the Bolshevik government enforced its requirements upon the workers.

Under Stalin's industrialisation programme any vestige of workers' rights disappeared. Strikes were prohibited and the traditional demands for better pay and conditions were regarded as selfishly inappropriate in a time of national crisis. A code of 'labour discipline' was drawn up, demanding maximum effort and output; failure to conform was punishable by a range of penalties from loss of wages to imprisonment in forced labour camps. On paper, wages improved during the Second FYP, but in real terms, since there was food rationing and high prices, living standards were lower in 1937 than they had been in 1928.

Living and working conditions

Throughout the period of the FYPs the Soviet government asserted that the nation was under siege. It claimed that unless priority was given to defence needs, the very existence of the USSR was at risk. Set against such a threat, workers' material interests were of little significance. For workers to demand improved conditions at a time when the Soviet Union was fighting for survival was unthinkable; they would be betraying the nation. It was small wonder, then, that food remained scarce and expensive, and severe overcrowding persisted.

Nearly all workers lived in overcrowded apartments. Public housing policy did produce a large number of tenement blocks in towns and cities. These were usually five-storey structures with no lifts. Quite apart from their architectural ugliness, they were a hazard to health. So great was the overcrowding that it was common for young families to live with their in-laws and equally common for four or five families to share a single lavatory and a single kitchen, which was often no more than an alcove with a gas ring. There were rotas for the use of these facilities. Queuing to relieve oneself or to cook was part of the daily routine.

There was money available, but the government spent it not on improving social conditions but on armaments. Between 1933 and 1937, defence expenditure rose from four to seventeen per cent of the overall industrial budget. By 1940, under the terms of the Third FYP, which renewed the commitment to heavy industrial development, a third of the USSR's government spending was on arms.

Key question
How successful had Stalin's economic reforms been by 1940?

Strengths of the reforms

In judging the scale of Stalin's achievement, it is helpful to cite such statistics relating to industrial output during the period of the first three FYPs as are reliable. The data in Table 8.4 are drawn from the work of the economic historian E. Zaleski, whose findings are based on careful analysis of Soviet and western sources.

The figures indicate a remarkable increase in production overall. In a little over twelve years, coal production had grown five times, steel six, and oil output had more than doubled. Perhaps the most impressive statistic is the one showing that electricity generation had quintupled. These four key products provided the basis for the war economy that enabled the USSR not only to survive four years of German occupation (1941–5) but eventually to win a great victory over Germany in May 1945.

Table 8.4: Industrial output during the first three FYPs

	1927	1930	1932	1935	1937	1940
Coal (million tons)	35	60	64	100	128	150
Steel (million tons)	3	5	6	13	18	18
Oil (million tons)	12	17	21	24	26	26
Electricity (million kWh)	18	22	20	45	80	90

Weaknesses

Stalin's economic reforms succeeded only in the traditional areas of heavy industry. In those sectors where unskilled and forced labour could be easily used, as in the building of large projects such as factories, bridges, refineries and canals, the results were impressive. However, the Soviet economy itself remained unbalanced. Stalin gave little thought to developing an overall economic strategy. Nor were modern industrial methods adopted. Old, wasteful techniques, such as using massed labour rather than efficient machines, continued to be used. Vital financial and material resources were squandered.

Stalin's love of what he called 'the Grand Projects of Communism' meant that no real attention was paid to producing quality goods that could then be profitably sold abroad to raise the money the USSR so badly needed. He loved to show off to foreign visitors the great projects that were either completed or under construction. Two enterprises of which he was especially proud were the city of Magnitogorsk (see page 212) and the **White Sea Canal**. Yet it was all vainglorious. Despite Stalin's boasts and the adulation with which he was regarded by foreign sympathisers, the simple fact remained that his policies had deprived the Soviet Union of any chance of genuinely competing with the modernising economies of Europe and the USA.

Moreover, his schemes failed to increase agricultural productivity or to raise the living standards of the Soviet workers. Stalin's neglect of agriculture, which continued to be deprived of funds since it was regarded as wholly secondary to the needs of industry, proved very damaging. The lack of agricultural growth resulted in constant food shortages that could be met only by buying foreign supplies. This drained the USSR's limited financial resources.

Despite the official veneration of Stalin for his great diplomatic triumph in achieving the Non-aggression Pact with Nazi Germany in August 1939, there was no relaxation within the Soviet Union of the war atmosphere. Indeed, the conditions of the ordinary people became even harsher. An official decree of 1940 empowered Stalin's government to encroach even further on workers' liberties. Direction of labour, enforced settlement of undeveloped areas, and severe penalties for slacking and absenteeism – these were some of the measures imposed under the decree.

In 1941, when the German invasion effectively destroyed the Third FYP, the conditions of the Soviet industrial workers were marginally worse than in 1928. Yet whatever the hardship of the workers, the fact was that in 1941 the USSR was economically

White Sea Canal
In fact, three canals linking Leningrad with the White Sea. Built predominantly by forced labourers, who died in their thousands, the canal proved practically worthless, since it was hardly used after construction.

Key term

German invasion and occupation of Russia: June 1941

Key date

strong enough to engage in an ultimately successful military struggle of unprecedented duration and intensity. In Soviet propaganda, this was what mattered, not minor questions of living standards. The USSR's triumph over Nazism would later be claimed as the ultimate proof of the wisdom of Stalin's enforced industrialisation programme.

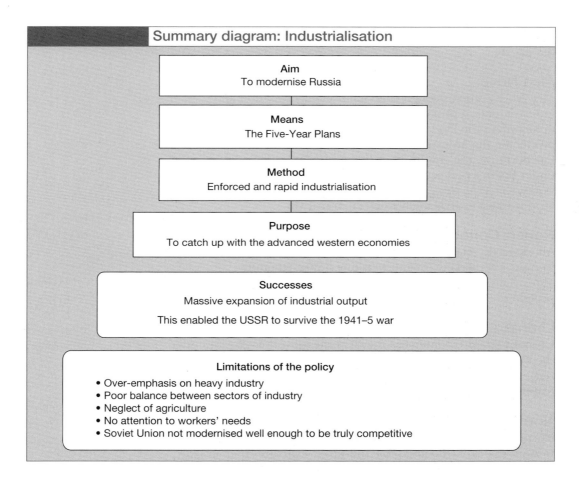

Summary diagram: Industrialisation

Aim
To modernise Russia

Means
The Five-Year Plans

Method
Enforced and rapid industrialisation

Purpose
To catch up with the advanced western economies

Successes
Massive expansion of industrial output
This enabled the USSR to survive the 1941–5 war

Limitations of the policy
- Over-emphasis on heavy industry
- Poor balance between sectors of industry
- Neglect of agriculture
- No attention to workers' needs
- Soviet Union not modernised well enough to be truly competitive

4 | The Key Debate

Many historians have contributed to the analysis of Stalin's economic policies, which remain a lively area of discussion. The central question that scholars address is:

> Did the policies benefit the Soviet Union and its people or were they introduced by Stalin primarily to consolidate his political hold on the USSR?

The following are the views of some of the main contributors to the debate.

Alec Nove

Alec Nove argued strongly that Stalin's collectivisation and industrialisation programmes were bad economics. They caused upheaval on the land and misery to the peasants without producing the industrial growth that the USSR needed. Furthermore, the condition of the industrial workers deteriorated under Stalin's policies. The living standards of Soviet factory workers in 1953 were barely higher than in 1928, while those of farm workers were actually lower than in 1913.

Robert Conquest

An especially sharp critic of Stalin's totalitarianism, Robert Conquest remarked: 'Stalinism is one way of attaining industrialisation, just as cannibalism is one way of attaining a high protein diet.'

Leonard Shapiro

Leonard Shapiro contended that had the industrial growth under the tsars continued uninterrupted beyond 1914 it would have reached no less a level of expansion by 1941 than that achieved by Stalin's terror strategy.

Norman Stone

Norman Stone has supported Shapiro's view by arguing that without the expertise and basic industrial structures that already existed in Russia before 1917, the Five-Year Plans would have been unable to reach the level of success that they did.

Sheila Fitzpatrick

Sheila Fitzpatrick broadly agreed with Nove's and Conquest's criticisms; she added that Stalin's 'gigantomania', his obsession with large-scale projects, distorted the economy at a critical time when it was calling out for proper investment and planning. She laid emphasis on Stalin's failure to improve Soviet living standards:

> Despite its promises of future abundance and the massive propaganda that surrounded its achievements, the Stalinist regime did little to improve the life of its people in the 1930s … .

Fitzpatrick also stressed, however, that Stalin's policies need to be seen in a broad social and political context. Harsh though Stalin was, he was trying to bring stability to a Soviet Russia that had known only turmoil and division since 1917.

Dmitri Volkogonov

Dmitri Volkogonov, who saw things at first hand as a soldier and administrator in 1930s Russia, suggested that the real purpose of Stalin's policies was only incidentally economic; the Soviet leader was aiming at removing all opposition to himself by making his economic policies a test of loyalty. To question his plans was to challenge his authority.

Peter Gattrell

An interesting viewpoint was offered by Peter Gattrell, who built on arguments first put forward by E.H. Carr. He acknowledged that Stalin was certainly severe and destructive in his treatment of people but pointed out that the outcome of collectivisation and industrialisation was an economy strong enough to sustain the USSR through four years of the most demanding of modern wars. Gattrell suggested that, hard though it is for the western liberal mind to accept, it may be that Russia could not have been modernised by any methods other than those used by Stalin.

David Hoffman

David Hoffman offers a strongly contrary argument by suggesting that Stalin's use of coercion in seeking economic and social change proved both inhumane and ineffective:

> Social change must be gradual and consensual if it is to succeed. Even if violence achieves superficial change, it does not permanently transform the way people think and act. Moreover in the Soviet case the means and ends were themselves in contradiction. State coercion by its very nature could not create social harmony. The arrest and execution of millions of people only sowed hatred, mistrust and disharmony in Soviet society.

Key terms

Neotraditionalism
A return to customary, established ways of doing things.

Blat
A system that operates through bribes, favours and connections.

Terry Martin

Terry Martin has also seen an essential contradiction in Stalin's economic policies. He has pointed out a basic paradox in Stalin's attempt to enforce modernisation on the Soviet Union. Martin notes that, contrary to what the Soviet leader intended, Stalin's methods did not take the USSR forward but returned it to **neotraditionalist** ways. In its attempt to get rid of market forces and competition, Stalin's programme of collectivisation and industrialisation, as actually practised, became as heavily dependent on *blat* as ever tsarist capitalism had been.

Robert Service

Stalin's outstanding biographer makes the following succinct assessment of the effects of his subject's collectivisation and industrialisation programme by 1940:

> Disruption was everywhere in the economy. Ukraine, south Russia, and Kazakhstan were starving. The *Gulag* [Russia's labour camp system] heaved with prisoners. Nevertheless the economic transformation was no fiction. The USSR under Stalin's rule had been pointed decisively in the direction of becoming an industrial, urban society. This had been his great objective. His gamble was paying off for him, albeit not for millions of victims. Magnitogorsk and the White Sea Canal were constructed at the expense of the lives of *Gulag* convicts, Ukrainian peasants and even undernourished, overworked factory labourers.

Some key books in the debate:
E. H. Carr, *A History of Soviet Russia* (Macmillan, 1979)
Robert Conquest, *Harvest of Sorrow* (Macmillan, 1988)
Robert Conquest, *The Great Terror: Stalin's Purge of the Thirties* (Penguin, 1971)
Sheila Fitzpatrick, *Everyday Stalinism: Ordinary Life in Extraordinary Times: Soviet Russia in the 1930s* (Oxford University Press, 1999)
Sheila Fitzpatrick (ed.), *Stalinism: New Directions* (Routledge, 2000)
Sheila Fitzpatrick, *The Cultural Front: Power and Culture in Revolutionary Russia* (Cornell University Press, 1992)
Peter Gattrell, *Under Command: The Soviet Economy 1924–53* (Routledge, 1992)
David L. Hoffman, *Stalinist Values: The Cultural Norms of Soviet Modernity* (Cornell University Press, 2003)
Alec Nove, *An Economic History of the USSR* (Penguin, 1972)
Alec Nove, *Stalinism and After* (Allen and Unwin, 1975)
Robert Service, *Stalin: A Biography* (Macmillan, 2004)
Norman Stone, *The Eastern Front* (1975)
Robert Tucker, *Stalinism: Essays in Historical Interpretation* (W. W. Norton, 1999)
Lynne Viola, *The Unknown Gulag: The Lost World of Stalin's Special Settlements* (Oxford University Press, 2007)
Dmitri Volkogonov, *Stalin: Triumph and Tragedy* (Weidenfeld and Nicolson, 1991)
Dmitri Volkogonov, *The Rise and Fall of the Soviet Empire* (HarperCollins, 1998)

Study Guide: AS Question
In the style of OCR
'The Five-Year Plans failed to achieve their aims during the 1930s.'
How far do you agree with this view? (50 marks)

Exam tips
The cross-references are intended to take you straight to the material that will help you to answer the question.

This question requires you to assess the achievements of the Five-Year Plans in the light of their aims, and then to reach an overall judgement. It would be wise to start with the aims, which may include the need to develop industry and agriculture for exports to raise capital; the need to catch up with the West (Stalin's avowed objective); to provide security and be prepared for war; and the desire to establish further control over Russian workers and peasants (pages 202–8, 210–19). In evaluating the achievements, you might link political, social and economic developments directly to their aims, or alternatively assess each of the Five-Year Plans in turn. Some of the following points might be discussed:

- industrial productivity in heavy industry, consumables and transport (pages 210–13)
- social and educational improvements (see Chapter 10, pages 257–60)
- working and living condition of peasants and urban workers (pages 216–17)
- impact on *kulaks* (pages 203–4)
- how far targets were actually met and the role of propaganda (pages 211–12)
- the position of Stalin (page 214)
- the extent to which the USSR was ready for war by 1939 (page 218–19).

Ensure that you supply a final assessment, perhaps indicating either the greatest failures or the greatest successes. Remember, you do not have to agree with the statement.

9 Stalin's Terror State

POINTS TO CONSIDER
With his defeat by 1929 of the Left and Right
Bolsheviks, Stalin had achieved personal power in the
Soviet Union. He went on to turn that power into
absolute control by a series of purges that continued
until his death in 1953. In this chapter these are
examined as:

- the early purges
- the post-Kirov Purges, 1934–6
- the Great Purge, 1936–9
- the purges as a study in Stalin's use of power.

Key dates

1932	Trial of the Ryutin group
1933	The purges begin under Yezhov's direction
1933–4	The legal system brought under Stalin's control
1934	Assassination of Kirov
	The purges as a terror system
	Intensification of the purges under Yagoda
1935	Yezhov, Vyshinsky and Beria take over the organising of the purges
1936–9	The 'Great Purge' of the Party, the army and the people
1937–8	The Yezhovschina persecutions in the localities
1941–5	Purges remove those accused of undermining the war effort
1945	Purging of Soviet people believed to have supported Germany
1949	The 'Leningrad Affair' leads to a further purge of the Party
1953	The 'Doctors' Plot', which began a purge of the medical profession; ended by the death of Stalin

1 | The Early Purges

Having become the *vozhd* of the Soviet Union by 1929, Stalin spent the rest of his life consolidating and extending his authority. The purges were his principal weapon for achieving this.

The Stalinist purges, which began in 1932, were not unprecedented. Under Lenin in the early 1920s, tens of thousands of 'anti-Bolsheviks' had been imprisoned in labour camps. Public trials, such as the Shakhty affair, had been held during the early stages of the First Five-Year Plan as a way of exposing industrial 'saboteurs' (see page 213).

However, even at this early stage, prosecutions had not been restricted to industrial enemies. In 1932 the trial of the **Ryutin group** had taken place. Ryutin and his supporters were publicly tried and expelled from the Party. This was the prelude to the first major purge of the CPSU by Stalin. Between 1933 and 1934 nearly 1 million members, over a third of the total membership, were excluded from the Party on the grounds that they were 'Ryutinites'. The purge was organised by **Nikolai Yezhov**, the chief of the Control Commission, the branch of the Central Committee responsible for Party discipline.

Nature of the early purges

At the beginning, Party purges were not as violent or as deadly as they later became. The usual procedure was to oblige members to hand in their **Party card** for checking, at which point any suspect individuals would not have their cards returned to them. This amounted to expulsion since, without cards, members were denied access to all Party activities. Furthermore, they and their families then lost their privileges in regard to employment, housing and food rations. The threat of expulsion was enough to force members to conform to official Party policy.

Under such a system it became progressively difficult to mount effective opposition. Despite this, attempts were made in the early 1930s to criticise Stalin, as the Ryutin affair illustrates. These efforts were ineffectual, but they led Stalin to believe that organised resistance to him was still possible.

The purges intensify

The year 1934 is an important date in Stalin's rise to absolute authority. It marks the point at which the purges developed into systematic terrorising not of obvious political opponents but of colleagues and Party members. It is difficult to explain precisely why Stalin initiated such a terror. Historians accept that they are dealing with behaviour that sometimes went beyond reason and logic. Stalin was deeply suspicious by nature and suffered from increasing **paranoia** as he grew older. Right up to his death in 1953 he continued to believe he was under threat from actual or potential enemies.

One historian, Alec Nove, offered this suggestion as to how Stalin's mind may have worked:

> The revolution from above caused great hardships, coercion left many wounds. Within and outside the Party, they might dream of revenge. Party leaders rendered politically impotent might seek to exploit the situation. So: liquidate them all in good time, destroy them and their reputations.

Robert Service writes that Stalin had 'a gross personality disorder' and adds:

> He had a Georgian sense of honour and revenge. Notions of getting even with adversaries never left him. He had a Bolshevik viewpoint on Revolution. Violence, dictatorship and terror were methods he and fellow party veterans took to be normal. The physical extermination of enemies was entirely acceptable to them.

Such thinking on Stalin's part meant that everyone was suspect and no one was safe. In Service's words, Stalin saw 'malevolent human agency in every personal or political problem he encountered'. Purges became not so much a series of episodes as a permanent condition of Soviet political life. Terror was all-pervading. Its intensity varied from time to time, but it was an ever-present reality throughout the remainder of Stalin's life.

Mechanisms of control

In the years 1933–4, Stalin centralised all the major law enforcement agencies:

- the civilian police
- the secret police
- labour camp commandants and guards
- border and security guards.

All these bodies were put under the authority of the **NKVD**, a body that was directly answerable to Stalin. To tighten control even further, legal proceedings were also made subject to central control. In addition, a special military court that stood outside the ordinary legal system was created to deal with 'serious crimes', a term that was elastic enough to cover any offences that Stalin and his ministers considered threatening to their authority. For example, 'counter-revolutionary activity' was designated a serious crime, but since the term was never precisely defined, it could be applied to any misdemeanour, no matter how trivial.

It was the existence of such a system that made the purges possible to operate on such a huge scale. The knowledge that anyone could be arrested at any time on the slightest of pretexts helped to maintain the atmosphere of terror and uncertainty that Stalin turned into a system of political and social control.

Key terms

Paranoia
A persecution complex that leaves sufferers with the conviction they are surrounded by enemies.

NKVD
The successor organisation to the *Cheka* and the OGPU.

Key date

The legal system brought under Stalin's control: 1933–4

2 | The Post-Kirov Purges, 1934–6

In Leningrad on 1 December 1934, a man named Leonid Nikolaev walked into the Communist Party headquarters and shot dead Sergei Kirov, the secretary of the Leningrad Soviet. The apparent motive was revenge; Kirov had been having an affair with the killer's wife. But dramatic though the incident was in itself, its significance went far beyond the tale of a jealous husband shooting his wife's lover. There is a strong probability that the murder of Kirov had been approved, if not planned, by Stalin himself. Nikita Khrushchev, in his secret speech of 1956 (see page 271), stated that Stalin was almost certainly behind the murder. However, a special study concluded in 1993 that, while Stalin may well have been guilty, the evidence against him consists of 'unverified facts, rumours and conjectures'.

Key date

Assassination of Kirov: 1 December 1934

Whatever the truth concerning Stalin's involvement, it was certainly the case that the murder worked directly to his advantage. Kirov had been a highly popular figure in the Party. A strikingly handsome Russian, he had made a strong impression at the Seventeeth Party Congress in 1934 and had been elected to the Politburo. He was known to be unhappy with the speed and scale of Stalin's industrialisation drive. He was also opposed to extreme measures being used as a means of disciplining Party members. If organised opposition to Stalin were to form within the Party, Kirov was the outstanding individual around whom dissatisfied members might rally. That danger to Stalin had now been removed.

Stalin was quick to exploit the situation. Within two hours of learning of Kirov's murder he had signed a '**Decree against Terrorist Acts**' (also known as the First of December Decree). Under the guise of hunting down those involved in Kirov's murder, a fresh purge of the Party was begun. Stalin claimed that the assassination had been organised by a wide circle of Trotskyites and Leftists, who must all be brought to account. There followed a large-scale round-up of suspected conspirators, who were then imprisoned or executed.

Key term

Decree against Terrorist Acts, 1934
Gave the NKVD limitless powers in pursuing the enemies of the state and the Party.

The atmosphere was caught in an account by Victor Serge, one of the suspects who managed to flee from the USSR at this time:

> The shot fired by Nikolaev ushered in an era of panic and savagery. The immediate response was the execution of 114 people, then the execution of Nikolaev and his friends; then the arrest and imprisonment of the whole of the former Zinoviev and Kamenev tendency, close on 3,000 persons; then the mass deportation of tens of thousands of Leningrad citizens, simultaneously with hundreds of arrests among those already deported and the opening of fresh secret trials in the prisons.

Party membership

It is an interesting coincidence that just as Stalin's path to power had been smoothed ten years earlier by 'the Lenin enrolment' (see page 186), so in 1934 his successful purge was made a great deal easier by a recent major shift in the make-up of the Party. During the previous three years, in 'the Stalin enrolment', the CPSU had recruited a higher proportion of skilled workers and industrial managers than at any time since 1917.

Stalin encouraged this as a means of tightening the links between the Party and those actually operating the First Five-Year Plan, but it also had the effect of bringing in a large number of members who joined the Party primarily to advance their careers. Acutely aware that they owed their privileged position directly to Stalin's patronage, the new members eagerly supported the elimination of the anti-Stalinist elements in the Party. After all, it improved their own chances of promotion. The competition for good jobs in Soviet Russia was invariably fierce. Purges always left positions to be filled. As the chief dispenser of positions, Stalin knew that the self-interest of these new Party members would keep them loyal to him. As Norman Stone, a western analyst of the Soviet Union, memorably put it:

> It was characteristic of Stalin to have his own allies 'marked' by their own subordinates: in Stalin's system identical thugs kept on replacing each other, like so many Russian dolls.

The full-scale purge that followed Kirov's murder in 1934 was the work of **Gengrikh Yagoda**, head of the NKVD. In 1935, Kirov's key post as Party boss in Leningrad was filled by **Andrei Zhdanov**. The equivalent position in Moscow was filled by another ardent Stalinist, Nikita Khrushchev. In recognition of his strident courtroom bullying of 'oppositionists' in the earlier purge trials, **Andrei Vyshinsky** was appointed State Prosecutor.

Stalin's fellow Georgian, **Lavrenti Beria**, was entrusted with overseeing state security in the national-minority areas of the USSR. With another of Stalin's protégés, **Alexander Poskrebyshev**, in charge of the Secretariat, there was no significant area of the Soviet bureaucracy that Stalin did not control. Public or Party opinion meant nothing when set against Stalin's grip on the key personnel and functions in Party and government. There had been rumours around the time of the Second FYP (see page 215) of a possible move to oust him from the position of Secretary-General. These were silenced in the aftermath of the Kirov affair.

The outstanding feature of the post-Kirov purge was the status of many of its victims. Prominent among those arrested were Kamenev and Zinoviev, who, along with Stalin, had formed the triumvirate after Lenin's death in 1924 and who had been the leading Left Bolsheviks in the power struggle of the 1920s. At the time of their arrest in 1935 they were not accused of involvement in Kirov's assassination, only of having engaged in 'opposition', a

Key question
What was the relationship between the growth in Party membership and the purges?

Key date

Intensification of the purges under Yagoda: 1934

Key figures

Gengrikh Yagoda (1891–1938)
Sadistic head of the NKVD, 1934–6; Stalin had him shot in 1938.

Andrei Zhdanov (1896–1948)
A dedicated follower of Stalin, he was described by one contemporary Communist, who managed to escape the purges, as 'a toady without an idea in his head'.

Andrei Vyshinsky (1883–1954)
A reformed Menshevik who became notorious for his brutal language and manner; he later served as Stalin's Foreign Secretary.

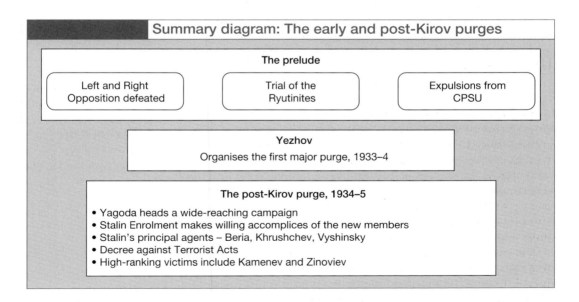

Key figures

**Lavrenti Beria
(1899–1953)**
A repellent mixture
of cruelty and
cowardice, a rapist
and child molester,
he rose to become
Stalin's chief
representative. He
lost influence after
Stalin's death;
despite begging on
his knees for his life,
he was shot in 1956.

**Alexander
Poskrebyshev
(1861–1965)**
Personal secretary to
Stalin for many
years after 1929, he
remained totally
loyal to his master
even though his wife
was tortured and
shot on Stalin's
orders.

charge that had no precise meaning, and therefore could not be answered. However, the significance of their arrest and imprisonment was plain to all: no Party members, whatever their rank or revolutionary pedigree, were safe.

Arbitrary arrest and summary execution became the norm. In the post-Stalin years it was admitted by Khrushchev that the Decree against Terrorist Acts had become the justification for 'broad acts that contravened socialist justice', a euphemism for mass murder. An impression of this can be gained from glancing at the fate of the representatives at the Party Congress of 1934:

- Of the 1996 delegates who attended, 1108 were executed during the next three years.
- In addition, out of the 139 Central Committee members elected at that gathering, all but 41 of them were put to death during the purges.

Leonard Shapiro, in his study of the CPSU, described these events as 'Stalin's victory over the Party'. From this point on, the Soviet Communist Party was entirely under his control. It ceased, in effect, to have a separate existence. Stalin had become the Party.

Summary diagram: The early and post-Kirov purges

The prelude

| Left and Right Opposition defeated | Trial of the Ryutinites | Expulsions from CPSU |

Yezhov
Organises the first major purge, 1933–4

The post-Kirov purge, 1934–5
- Yagoda heads a wide-reaching campaign
- Stalin Enrolment makes willing accomplices of the new members
- Stalin's principal agents – Beria, Khrushchev, Vyshinsky
- Decree against Terrorist Acts
- High-ranking victims include Kamenev and Zinoviev

3 | The Great Purge, 1936–9

It might be expected that once Stalin's absolute supremacy over the Party had been established, the purges would stop. But they did not; they increased in intensity. Stalin declared that the Soviet Union was in 'a state of siege' and called for still greater vigilance in unmasking the enemies within. In 1936 a progressive terrorising of the Soviet Union began which affected the entire population, but took its most dramatic form in the public show trials of Stalin's former Bolshevik colleagues. The one-time heroes of the 1917 Revolution and the Civil War were arrested, tried and imprisoned or executed as enemies of the state.

Remarkably, the great majority went to their death after confessing their guilt and accepting the truth of the charges levelled against them. Such was the scale of the persecution at this time, and so high-ranking were the victims, that it has gone down in history as 'the Great Purge' or 'the Great Terror'.

The descriptions applied to the accused during the purges bore little relation to political reality. 'Right', 'Left' and 'Centre' opposition blocs were identified and the groupings invariably had the catch-all term 'Trotskyite' tagged on to them, but such words were convenient prosecution labels rather than definitions of a genuine political opposition. They were intended to isolate those in the Communist Party and the Soviet state whom Stalin wished to destroy.

Stalin's terror programme breaks down conveniently into three sections:

- the purge of the Party
- the purge of the armed services
- the purge of the people.

The purge of the Party
The purging of the Left
The prelude to the Great Purge of 1936 was a secret letter sent from CPSU headquarters warning all the local Party branches of a terrorist conspiracy by 'the Trotskyite-Kamenevite-Zinovievite-Leftist Counter-Revolutionary Bloc' and instructing Party officials to begin rooting out suspected agents and sympathisers. Once this campaign of denunciation and expulsion had been set in motion in the country at large, Kamenev and Zinoviev were put on public trial in Moscow, charged with involvement in Kirov's murder and with plotting to overthrow the Soviet state. Both men pleaded guilty and read out abject confessions in court.

The obvious question is: 'Why did they confess?' After all, these men were tough Bolsheviks. No doubt, as was later revealed during de-Stalinisation, physical and mental torture were used. Possibly more important was their sense of demoralisation at having been accused and disgraced by the Party to which they had dedicated their lives and which could do no wrong. In a curious sense, their admission of guilt was a last act of loyalty to the Party.

Key question
Was there any logic to the Great Purge?

Key date
The 'Great Purge' of the Party, the army and the people: 1936–9

Key question
Why was there so little resistance from the Party members who were purged?

Whatever their reasons, the fact that they did confess made it extremely difficult for other victims to plead their own innocence. If the great ones of state and Party were prepared to accept their fate, on what grounds could lesser men resist? The psychological impact of the public confessions of such figures as Kamenev and Zinoviev was profound. It helped to create an atmosphere in which innocent victims submitted in open court to false charges and went to their death begging the Party's forgiveness.

It also shows Stalin's astuteness in insisting on a policy of public trials. There is little doubt that he had the power to conduct the purges without using legal proceedings. He could simply have had the victims bumped off. However, by making the victims deliver humiliating confessions in open court, Stalin was able to reveal the scale of the conspiracy against him and to prove the need for the purging to continue.

The purging of the Right

Key date

Yezhov, Vyshinsky and Beria take over the organising of the purges: 1935

This soon became evident after Kamenev and Zinoviev, along with fourteen other Bolsheviks, had been duly executed in keeping with Vyshinsky's notorious demand as prosecutor that they be shot 'like the mad dogs they are'. The details the condemned had revealed in their confessions were used to prepare the next major strike, the attack upon 'the Right deviationists'. Bukharin, Rykov and Tomsky were put under investigation but not yet formally charged. The delay was caused by the reluctance of some of the older Bolsheviks in the Politburo to denounce their comrades. Stalin intervened personally to speed up the process. Yagoda, who was considered to have been too lenient in his recent handling of the 'Trotskyite-Zinovievite bloc', was replaced as head of the NKVD by the less scrupulous Yezhov, whose name, like Vyshinsky's, was to become a byword for terror.

The 'Anti-Soviet Trotskyist Centre'

Key figures

Karl Radek (1885–1939)
A leading Bolshevik propagandist since 1905, he had been head of the Comintern in the early 1920s.

Georgy Pyatakov (1890–1937)
An economist who held a number of important government posts in the 1920s and 1930s.

Grigory Sokolnikov (1888–1939)
A finance minister under both Lenin and Stalin.

Meanwhile, the case for proceeding against Bukharin and the Right was strengthened by the revelations at a further show trial in 1937 at which seventeen Communists, denounced collectively as the 'Anti-Soviet Trotskyist Centre', were charged with spying for Nazi Germany. The accused included **Karl Radek** and **Georgy Pyatakov**, the former favourites of Lenin, and **Grigory Sokolnikov**, Stalin's Commissar for Finance during the First FYP. Radek's grovelling confession, in which he incriminated his close colleagues, including his friend Bukharin, saved him from the death sentence imposed on all but three of the other defendants. He died two years later, however, in an Arctic labour camp.

Yezhov and Vyshinsky now had the evidence they needed. In 1938, in the third of the major show trials, Bukharin and Rykov (Tomsky had taken his own life in the meantime) and eighteen other 'Trotskyite-Rightists' were publicly arraigned on a variety of counts, including sabotage, spying and conspiracy to murder Stalin. The fact that Yagoda was one of the accused was a sign of the speed with which the terror was starting to consume its own kind. **Fitzroy MacLean**, a British diplomat, was one of the foreign observers permitted to attend the trial. His description conveys the character of the proceedings:

> The prisoners were charged, collectively and individually, with every conceivable crime: high treason, murder, and sabotage. They had plotted to wreck industry and agriculture, to assassinate Stalin, to dismember the Soviet Union for the benefit of their capitalist allies. They were shown for the most part to have been traitors to the Soviet cause ever since the Revolution. One after another, using the same words, they admitted their guilt: Bukharin, Rykov, Yagoda. Each prisoner incriminated his fellows and was in turn incriminated by them.

Fitzroy MacLean (1911–96)
A young British diplomat and adventurer who took a keen personal interest in the purges.

Key figure

At one point in the trial Bukharin embarrassed the court by attempting to defend himself, but he was eventually silenced by Vyshinsky's bullying and was sentenced to be shot along with the rest of the defendants. In his final speech in court, Bukharin showed the extraordinary character of the Bolshevik mentality. Despite the injustice of the proceedings to which he had been subjected, he accepted the infallibility of the Party and of Stalin:

> When you ask yourself: 'If you must die, what are you dying for?' – an absolutely black vacuity suddenly rises before you. There was nothing to die for, if one wanted to die unrepented. And, on the contrary, everything positive that glistens in the Soviet Union acquires new dimensions in a man's mind. This in the end disarmed me completely and led me to bend my knees before the Party and the country … For in reality the whole country stands behind Stalin; he is the hope of the world.

The Stalin Constitution, 1936

A particular irony attached to Bukharin's execution. Only two years previously he had been the principal draftsman of the new constitution of the USSR. This 1936 Constitution, which Stalin described as 'the most democratic in the world', was intended to impress western Communists and Soviet sympathisers. This was the period in Soviet foreign policy when, in an effort to offset the Nazi menace to the USSR, Stalin was urging the formation of 'popular fronts' between the Communist parties and the various Left-wing groups in Europe. Among the things claimed in the Constitution were that:

- Socialism having been established, there were no longer any 'classes' in Soviet society.
- The basic civil rights of freedom of expression, assembly, and worship were guaranteed.

However, the true character of Stalin's Constitution lay not in what it said but in what it omitted. Hardly anywhere was the role of the Party mentioned; its powers were not defined and, therefore, were not restricted. It would remain the instrument through which Stalin would exercise his total control of the USSR. The contrast between the Constitution's democratic claims and the reality of the situation in the Soviet Union could not have been greater.

Lenin's General Staff of ⟨...⟩

STALIN, THE EXECUTIONER, ALONE REMAINS

RYKOV Shot	BUKHARIN Shot	SVERDLOV Dead	STALIN Survivor	ZINOVIEV Shot	KAMENEV Shot	TROTSKY In Exile	LENIN Dead
KOLLONTAI Missing?	URITSKY Dead	KRESTINSKY Shot	SMILGA Shot	NOGIN Dead	DZERZHINSKY Dead	BUBNOV Disappeared	SOKOLNIKOV In Prison
LOMOV ?	SHOMYAN Dead	BERZIN ?	MURANOV Disappeared	ARTEM Dead	STASSOVA Disappeared	MILIUTIN Missing	JOFFE Suicide

The Central Committee of The Bolshevik Party in 1917

This montage, composed by Trotsky's supporters, points to the remarkable fact that of the original 1917 Central Committee of the Bolshevik Party only Stalin was still alive in 1938. The majority of the other 23 members had, of course, been destroyed in the purges.

Key question
Why did Stalin regard the leaders of the Soviet armed forces as a threat to his power?

The purge of the armed forces

A significant development in the purges occurred in 1937 when the Soviet military came under threat. Stalin's control of the Soviet Union would not have been complete if the armed services had continued as an independent force. It was essential that they be kept subservient. Knowing that military loyalties might make a purge of the army difficult to achieve, Stalin took the preliminary step of organising a large number of transfers within the higher ranks in order to lessen the possibility of centres of resistance being formed when the attack came.

With this accomplished, Vyshinksy announced, in May 1937, that 'a gigantic conspiracy' had been uncovered in the Red Army. Marshal Mikhail Tukhachevsky (see page 158), the popular and talented Chief of General Staff, was arrested along with seven other generals, all of whom had been 'heroes of the Civil War'. On the grounds that speed was essential to prevent a military coup, the trial was held immediately, this time in secret. The charge was treason; Tukhachevsky was accused of having spied for Germany and Japan. Documentary evidence, some of it supplied by German intelligence at the request of the NKVD, was produced in proof.

The outcome was predetermined and inevitable. In June 1937, after their ritual confession and condemnation, Tukhachevsky and his fellow generals were shot. There appears to have been a particularly personal element in all this. The president of the secret court that delivered the death sentences was **Marshal Klimenty Voroshilov**, a devoted Stalinist, who had long been jealous of Tukhachevsky's talent and popularity.

Tukhachevsky's execution was the signal for an even greater bloodletting. To prevent any chance of a military reaction, a wholesale destruction of the Red Army establishment was undertaken. In the following eighteen months:

- All eleven War Commissars were removed from office.
- Three of the five Marshals of the Soviet Union were dismissed.
- Ninety-one members of the 101-man Supreme Military Council were arrested, of whom 80 were executed.
- Fourteen of the sixteen army commanders and nearly two-thirds of the 280 divisional commanders were removed.
- Half of the commissioned officer corps, 35,000 in total, were either imprisoned or shot.

At the height of the purge, extraordinary scenes were witnessed in some army camps where whole lorryloads of officers were taken away for execution. The Soviet navy did not escape the purges; between 1937 and 1939 all the serving admirals of the fleet were shot and thousands of naval officers were sent to labour camps. The Soviet air force was similarly decimated during that period, only one of its senior commanders surviving the purge.

The devastation of the Soviet armed forces, wholly unrelated to any conceivable military purpose, was complete by 1939. It left all three services seriously undermanned and staffed by inexperienced or incompetent replacements. Given the defence needs of the USSR, a theme constantly stressed by Stalin himself, the deliberate crippling of the Soviet military is the aspect of the purges that most defies logic. It suggests that Stalin had lost touch with reality.

The purge of the people

Stalin's achievement of total dominance over Party, government and military did not mean the end of the purges. The apparatus of terror was retained and the search for enemies continued. Purges were used to achieve the goals of the FYPs; charges of industrial sabotage were made against managers and workers in the factories. The purge was also a way of forcing the regions and nationalities into total subordination to Stalin.

The show trials that had taken place in Moscow and Leningrad, with their catalogue of accusations, confessions and death sentences, were repeated in all the republics of the USSR. The terror they created was no less intense for being localised. For example, between 1937 and 1939 in Stalin's home state of Georgia:

- two state prime ministers were removed
- four-fifths of the regional Party secretaries were removed
- thousands of lesser officials lost their posts.

Key figure

Marshal Klimenty Voroshilov (1881–1969) One of the founding members of the Bolshevik Party, he became a devoted Stalinist.

Key question Why did the purges continue?

Key figure

Béla Kun (1886–1939?)
Had been the leader of the short-lived communist government in Hungary in 1919.

These events were accompanied by a wide-ranging purge of the legal and academic professions. Foreign Communists living in the Soviet Union were not immune. Polish and German revolutionary exiles were rounded up by the score, many of them being subsequently imprisoned or executed. The outstanding foreign victim was **Béla Kun,** who was condemned and shot some time in either 1938 or 1939. The exact date of the execution is uncertain.

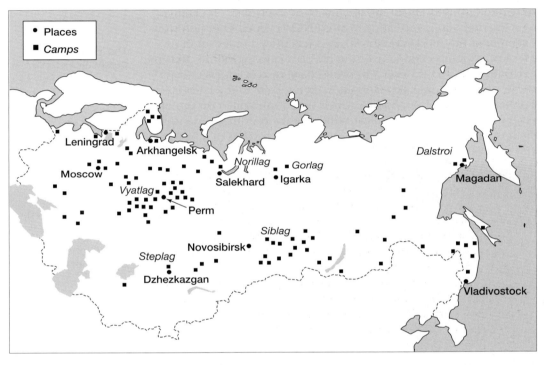

Figure 9.1: The Soviet Labour camps, 1937–57. By 1941, as a result of the purges, there were an estimated eight million prisoners in the *gulag*. The average sentence was ten years, which, given the terrible conditions in the camps, was equivalent to a death sentence. As an example of state-organised terror, Stalin's *gulag* stands alongside Hitler's concentration camps and Mao Zedong's *laogai* (Chinese prison camp system) in its attempt to suppress the human spirit.

Key term

Gulag
The vast system of prisons and labour camps that spread across the USSR during the purges.

Mass repression

Understandably, historians have tended to concentrate on the central and dramatic features of the purges, such as the show trials and the attack upon the Party and the Red Army. Yet no area of Soviet life entirely escaped the purges. Under Stalin, terror was elevated into a method of government. The constant fear that this created conditioned the way the Soviet people lived their lives. European scholars who have been working since the early 1990s in the newly opened archives in the former Soviet Union have discovered that in terms of numbers, the greatest impact of the purges was on the middle and lower ranks of Soviet society.

- One person in every eight of the population was arrested during Stalin's purges.
- Almost every family in the USSR suffered the loss of at least one of its members as a victim of the terror.

This was not an accidental outcome of the purges. The evidence now shows that in the years 1937–8, Yezhov deliberately followed a policy of mass repression. This **'Yezhovschina'** involved NKVD squads going into a range of selected localities, then arresting and dragging off hundreds of inhabitants to be executed. The killings were carried out in specially prepared NKVD zones. One notorious example of this was Butovo, a village some fifteen miles south of Moscow, which became one of the NKVD's killing grounds. Recent excavations by the Russian authorities have revealed mass graves there containing over 20,000 bodies, dating back to the late 1930s. Forensic analysis of the bodies, which were found piled on top of each other in neat rows, indicates that nightly over many months victims had been taken to Butovo and shot in batches of a hundred.

Yezhovschina

The period of widespread terror directed at ordinary Soviet citizens in the late 1930s and presided over by Yezhov, the head of the NKVD.

Key term

The Yezhovschina persecutions: 1937–8

Key date

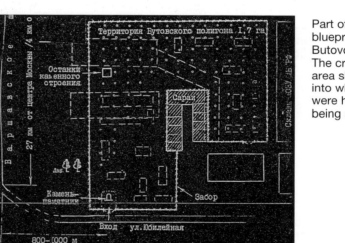

Part of an NKVD blueprint of the Butovo killing fields. The cross-hatched area shows the pit into which the victims were heaped after being shot.

The quota system

The number of victims to be arrested was laid down in set quotas as if they were industrial production targets. People were no longer regarded as individuals. It was the numbers, not the names, that mattered. There was no appeal against sentence, and the death warrant invariably required that the execution 'be carried out immediately'.

One incident illustrates the mechanical, dehumanised process. A woman whose neighbour had been arrested called at a police station to ask permission to look after the child the neighbour had had to leave behind. After leaving her waiting for two hours, the police then decided that since they were one short of their daily quota of people to be arrested, the caller would make up the number. She was grabbed and thrown into a cell.

Insofar as the terrorising of ordinary people had a specific purpose, it was to frighten the USSR's national minorities into abandoning any lingering thoughts of challenging Moscow's control and to force waverers into a full acceptance of Stalin's enforced industrialisation programme.

Stalin signing an order for the execution of 6600 condemned prisoners. An interesting point of comparison is that this number exceeded that of all those executed for political offences in tsarist Russia in the 100 years up to 1917.

The purges go full circle

In the headlong rush to uncover further conspiracies, interrogators themselves became victims and joined those they had condemned in execution cells and labour camps. Concepts such as innocence and guilt lost all meaning during the purges. The mass of the population were frightened and bewildered. Fear had the effect of destroying moral values and traditional loyalties. The one aim became survival, even at the cost of betrayal. In a 1988 edition devoted to the Stalinist purges, the Moscow *Literary Gazette* referred to 'the special sadism whereby the nearest relatives were forced to incriminate each other – brother to slander brother, husband to blacken wife'.

The chillingly systematic character of the purges was described in the minutes of a plenary session of the Central Committee, held in June 1957 during the **de-Stalinisation** period:

Key term

De-Stalinisation
The movement, begun by Khrushchev in 1956, to expose Stalin's crimes and mistakes against the Party.

Between 27 February 1937 and 12 November 1938 the NKVD received approval from Stalin, Molotov and Kaganovich for the Supreme Court to sentence to death by shooting 38,697. On one day, 12 November 1938, Stalin and Molotov sanctioned the execution of 3,167 people. On 21 November the NKVD received approval from Stalin and Molotov to shoot 229 people, including twenty-three members and candidate members of the Central Committee, twenty-two members of the Party Control Commission, twelve regional Party secretaries, twenty-one People's Commissars, 136 commissariat officials and fifteen military personnel.

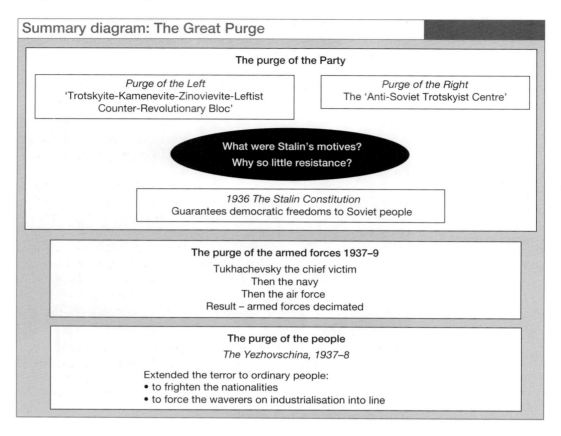

Summary diagram: The Great Purge

The purge of the Party

| *Purge of the Left*
'Trotskyite-Kamenevite-Zinovievite-Leftist
Counter-Revolutionary Bloc' | *Purge of the Right*
The 'Anti-Soviet Trotskyist Centre' |

What were Stalin's motives?
Why so little resistance?

1936 The Stalin Constitution
Guarantees democratic freedoms to Soviet people

The purge of the armed forces 1937–9

Tukhachevsky the chief victim
Then the navy
Then the air force
Result – armed forces decimated

The purge of the people

The Yezhovschina, 1937–8

Extended the terror to ordinary people:
• to frighten the nationalities
• to force the waverers on industrialisation into line

4 | The Purges as a Study in Stalin's Use of Power

Key question
Why did Stalin introduce and maintain such a destructive policy?

Stalin's use of terror as a political and social weapon is a grim but fascinating theme. It is still not possible for historians to give a precise figure of those destroyed during the purges. However, in the 1990s access to the files of the KGB was granted to scholars. Major studies, such as Anne Applebaum's *The Gulag* (2003), which complements the earlier pioneering study by Robert Conquest, *The Great Terror* (see page 222), enable us to quote the following figures as the most reliable now available:

• In 1934, 1 million were arrested and executed in the first major purge, mainly in Moscow and Leningrad.
• By 1937, 17 to 18 million had been transported to labour camps; 10 million of these died.
• By 1939, another 5 to 7 million had been 'repressed', 1 million of these being shot, another 1 to 2 million dying in the camps.

- In 1940 the occupation of the Baltic states (Lithuania, Estonia and Latvia), Bukovina and Bessarabia resulted in 2 million being deported, most of whom died.
- In 1941 the deportation to Siberia of various national groups, including Germans, Kalmyks, Ukrainians, Chechens and Crimean Tatars, led to the deaths of one-third of the 4 million involved.

It is disturbing to reflect that in the sheer scale of its misery and death, the Stalinist repression of the Soviet peoples far exceeded even the Nazi **Holocaust**.

Only a partial answer can be offered as to why Stalin engaged for so long in such a brutal exercise. One motive was obviously the desire to impose his absolute authority by bringing all the organs of Party and state under his control. Yet even after that aim had been achieved, the terror continued. The purges were so excessive and gratuitously vicious that they make logical analysis difficult. Stalin destroyed people not for what they had done but for what they might do. His suspicions and fears revealed a deeply distorted mind. That, indeed, was how Stalin's daughter, Svetlana Alliluyeva, explained his irrationality:

> As he'd got older my father had begun feeling lonely. He was so isolated from everyone that he seemed to be living in a vacuum. He hadn't a soul he could talk to. It was the system of which he himself was the prisoner and in which he was stifling from emptiness and lack of human companionship.

The key debate

> How far beyond Stalin did the responsibility for the purges and the terror spread?

Robert Service, one of the most celebrated biographers of Stalin, says of him: 'Nowadays, virtually all writers accept that he initiated the Great Terror.' Yet Service, along with all the leading experts in the field, is careful to acknowledge that, while Stalin was undoubtedly the architect of the terror, the responsibility for implementing it goes beyond Stalin. Historians, prompted by their reading of Russian archival material that has become available, suggest that Stalinism was not as monolithic a system of government as has been traditionally assumed. Attention has shifted to the disorganised state of much of Soviet bureaucracy, particularly at local level.

Key term

Holocaust
The genocide of 6 million Jews in occupied Europe between 1939 and 1945.

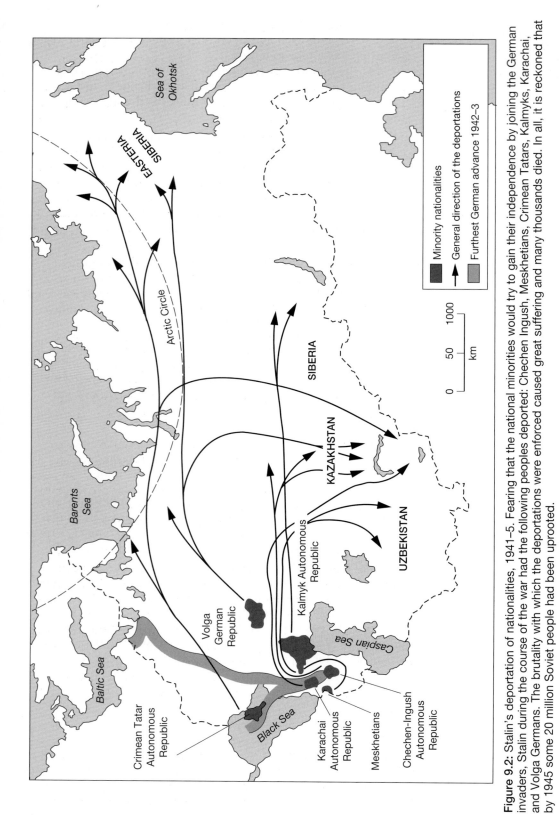

Figure 9.2: Stalin's deportation of nationalities, 1941–5. Fearing that the national minorities would try to gain their independence by joining the German invaders, Stalin during the course of the war had the following peoples deported: Chechen Ingush, Meskhetians, Crimean Tatars, Kalmyks, Karachai, and Volga Germans. The brutality with which the deportations were enforced caused great suffering and many thousands died. In all, it is reckoned that by 1945 some 20 million Soviet people had been uprooted.

Key question
Was Soviet
Communism
intrinsically violent?

The character of Soviet politics and society

The purges were clearly initiated by Stalin himself, but he, after·all, was only one man, no matter how powerful or feared. How the purges were actually carried out largely depended on the local Party organisation. Many welcomed the purges as an opportunity to settle old scores as well as a way of advancing themselves by filling the jobs vacated by the victims. It has to be acknowledged that the purges were popular with some Russians, those who believed their country could be prevented from slipping back into its historic weakness and backwardness only by being powerfully and ruthlessly led. To such people, Stalin was a genuine saviour whose unrelenting methods were precisely what the nation needed.

It is also arguable that the disruption of Soviet society caused by the massive upheavals of collectivisation and industrialisation destroyed any semblance of social cohesion and so encouraged Party and government officials to resort to the most extreme measures. Civil society as it existed in Russia was not strong or advanced enough to offer an alternative to what was being done in the name of the Communist revolution.

Richard Overy, a distinguished expert on modern European history, draws attention to the violence that he regards as having been intrinsic in Soviet Communism. He quotes Stalin's assertion that 'the law of violent proletarian revolution is an inevitable law of the revolutionary movement' and links it directly with Lenin's declaration that the task of Bolshevism was 'the ruthless destruction of the enemy'. The Stalinist purges, therefore, were a logical historical progression.

In this connection, other scholars have laid weight on how undeveloped the concepts of individual or civil rights were in Russia. Tsardom had been an autocracy in which the first duty of the people had been to obey. Lenin and the Bolsheviks had not changed that. Indeed, they had re-emphasised the necessity of obedience to central authority. The purges were a deadly but logical extension of that principle.

An interesting interpretation relating to the idea that violence was an irremovable feature of Russian Communism has been advanced by a number of modern scholars, among whom J. Arch Getty is the most prominent. Their suggestion is that the purges came from below as much as from above. They mean by this that the purges begun by Stalin were sustained in their ferocity by the lower ranking officials in government and Party who wanted to replace their superiors, whom they regarded as a conservative elite. This elite would never give up its power willingly, so it had to be smashed. Russian political tradition did not allow any alternative.

The *Nomenklatura*

It was certainly true that Stalin had no difficulty in finding eager subordinates to organise the purges. The common characteristic of those who led Stalin's campaigns was their unswerving personal loyalty to him, a loyalty that overcame any doubts they might have had regarding the nature of their work. They formed what became known as the **nomenklatura**, the new class of officials whom Stalin created to replace the thousands of Old Bolsheviks whom he eliminated in the purges.

One prominent historian, M. Agursky, has stressed this development as a major explanation of why terror became so embedded in the Stalinist system. The *nomenklatura* had no loyalty to the old Bolshevik tradition. They were all totally Stalin's men:

> To replace the old elite there came a new stratum which had no continuity with its predecessors for the purges took place in different phases and in the end liquidated the entire body of activists who had taken part in the Revolution and the Civil War.

Dedicated to Stalin, on whom their positions depended, the *nomenklatura* enjoyed rights and privileges denied to the rest of the population. Including their families, they numbered by the late 1930s an exclusive group of only 600,000 out of a population of 150 million. It was what came with the job that mattered: members had plentiful food rations, luxury accommodation, motor cars, specially reserved Party lanes for them to drive on, and top-quality education for their children (see page 259). Once in post, persons with such privileges were unlikely to risk them by questioning Stalin's orders. The more potential rivals they exterminated, the safer their jobs were.

Geoffrey Hosking, a major analyst of Russian history, has also described how the purges provided opportunities for the new type of Communist Party official: 'Local party bosses, naturally enough, exploited the purge to bolster their own patronage, advance their own clients, and get rid of their opponents.' Hosking makes the additional point that Stalin's realisation of how self-centred Party officials were intensified his determination not to lose control over them. That was the reason for both his maintenance of the terror and the willingness of his underlings to be the eager practitioners of it.

The role of ideology and idealism

In a major study, *Stalin: The Court of the Red Tsar* (2003), Simon Sebag Montefiore has illustrated the eagerness with which Stalin's top ministers carried out his campaigns of terror and persecution. Though they were terrified of him, they did not obey him simply out of fear. People like Yezhov, Beria and Molotov derived the same vindictive satisfaction from their work as their master. Like him, they appeared to have no moral scruples. Sebag Montefiore describes the extraordinary mixture of fear and callousness that made up the lives of the people he surrounded himself with in the **Kremlin** under his tsar-like rule:

Key terms

Nomenklatura
The Soviet 'establishment' – a privileged elite of officials who ran the Party machine.

Kremlin
The former tsarist fortress in Moscow that became the centre of Soviet government.

Key terms

Quasi-religious faith
A conviction so powerful that it has the intensity of religious belief.

Utopian
A belief in the attainability of a perfect society.

Chimera
A powerful but ultimately meaningless myth.

Stalin was utterly unique but many of his views and features such as dependence on death as a political tool, and his paranoia, were shared by his comrades. They lived on ice, killing others to stay alive, sleeping with pistols under their pillows, their wives murdered on Stalin's whim, their children living by a code of lies. Yet they kept their **quasi-religious faith** in the Bolshevism that justified so much death.

In reviewing Sebag Montefiore's book, David Satter, himself an authority on Stalin's Russia, adds the following insight into how and why the purges operated as they did:

> The Stalinist enterprise consisted of the effort to remake the social system of a vast country on the basis of a **utopian** ideology. In carrying out this task, Stalin and his henchmen in many ways resembled powerful bureaucrats anywhere, but these were bureaucrats freed of all moral restraints. Their duties as functionaries explained why the members of Stalin's court not only enthusiastically fulfilled execution quotas but insisted on over-fulfilling them.

A further insight into the Soviet mindset that permitted all this to happen is offered by the Russian historian Dimitri Volkogonov, a biographer of Stalin:

> People like Stalin regard conscience as a **chimera**. One cannot speak of the conscience of a dictator; he simply did not have one. The people who did his dirty deeds for him, however, knew full well what they were doing. In such people conscience had 'gone cold'. In consequence, the people allowed their own consciences to be driven into a reservation, thus giving the grand inquisitor the authority to carry on with his dark deeds.

Yet when seeking to explain the motives of those who implemented the vast terror that overtook the Soviet Union, one should not leave out the role of idealism. It may now be judged a perverted idealism, but it was compelling enough to those who shared it to convince them that the arrests, the shootings, the *gulag* were all justified since they were leading ultimately to the triumph of the Revolution and the creation of a Communist paradise on earth.

Some key books in the debate:
Svetlana Alliluyeva, *Twenty Letters to a Friend* (Penguin, 1968)
Anne Applebaum, *Gulag: A History of the Soviet Camps* (Penguin, 2003)
Robert Conquest, *The Great Terror: Stalin's Purge of the Thirties* (Penguin, 1971)
J. Arch Getty and R. T. Manning, *Stalinist Terror: New Perspectives* (Cambridge, 1993)
Geoffrey Hosking, *Russia and the Russians* (Allen Lane, 2001)
Alec Nove, *Stalinism and After* (Unwin Hyman, 1975)
Richard Overy, *The Dictators: Hitler's Germany and Stalin's Russia* (Allen Lane, 2004)
Donald Rayfield, *Stalin and His Hangmen: The Tyrant and Those Who Killed for Him* (Random House, 2003)
Simon Sebag Montefiore, *Stalin: The Court of the Red Tsar* (Knopf, 2004)
Robert Service, *Stalin: A Biography* (Macmillan, 2004)
Robert C. Tucker, *Stalinism – Essays in Historical Interpretation* (Transaction Publishers, 1999)
Lynne Viola, *The Unknown Gulag: The Lost World of Stalin's Special Settlements* (Oxford University Press, 2007)
Dmitri Volkogonov, *Stalin: Triumph and Tragedy* (Weidenfeld & Nicolson, 1991)

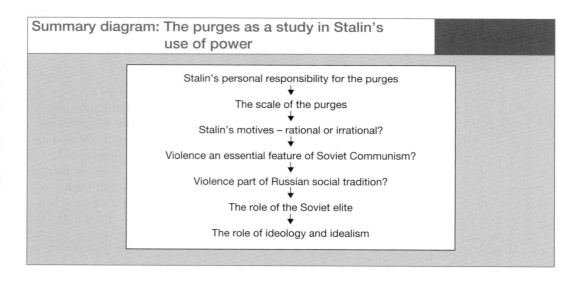

Summary diagram: The purges as a study in Stalin's use of power

Stalin's personal responsibility for the purges
↓
The scale of the purges
↓
Stalin's motives – rational or irrational?
↓
Violence an essential feature of Soviet Communism?
↓
Violence part of Russian social tradition?
↓
The role of the Soviet elite
↓
The role of ideology and idealism

Study Guide: AS Question

In the style of OCR

To what extent was fear and terror the main reason for Stalin's hold on power between 1929 and 1941? (50 marks)

Exam tips

The cross-references are intended to take you straight to the material that will help you to answer the question.

Several factors help to explain how Stalin's power was based on fear and terror. You might be tempted to describe the features of the police state that evolved in the 1930s or to focus on the purges and show trials, both of which are relevant issues. However, given that a number of factors need to be considered, it is important that a balanced argument is maintained, supported by carefully selected examples. Some of the following reasons could be analysed:

- the development of the secret police (pages 226–9)
- state control of the judiciary and show trials (pages 230–3)
- the purging of Party supporters, opponents and the army (pages 230–4)
- the establishment of labour camps (pages 234–7)
- the role of willing subordinates (pages 242–3)
- the 1936 Constitution (page 232).

10 Stalin and Stalinism, 1924–41

Key dates

1926	*Komsomol* created
1928	New religious persecution campaign
1932	Stalin calls for 'the engineering of the human soul'
1934	Death of Maxim Gorky
	Imprisonment of Osip Mandelstam
1935	Stakhanovite movement begins
	Soviet Academy of Sciences becomes controlling body over all scholars
1936–8	Repression of Soviet creative artists
1936	Ban on works of Dmitri Shostakovich
	New Soviet Constitution introduced
	Family laws restricting abortion, divorce and homosexuality
	'Housewives' Movement' created under Stalin's patronage
1938	Imprisonment of Vsevolod Meyerhold
1939	Eighteenth Congress of the CPSU carries Stalin worship to new level
1940	Literacy rate reaches 88 per cent
	500 churches are open for worship, compared with 50,000 in 1917
1941	USSR invaded by Germany

1 | Soviet Culture

Key question
What was the place of culture in the USSR under Stalin?

Lenin had declared that 'the purpose of art and literature is to serve the people'. Stalin was equally determined that culture should perform a social and political role in the Russia that he was building; the arts had to have the same driving purpose that his economic policies had. Culture was not simply a matter of refined tastes. It was an expression of society's values and had to be shaped and directed in the same way that agriculture and industry had. In creating the first truly socialist state there had to be a cultural revolution to accompany the political and economic one. It followed that the test to be applied to any aspect of culture was whether it promoted socialist values.

Key date
Stalin calls for 'the engineering of the human soul': 1932

In practice, what this came to mean was that, given the despotic power that Stalin wielded, cultural works in all their various forms from buildings to paintings, to novels, to operas had to conform to the standards set by Joseph Stalin. He became the great cultural judge and arbiter. Stalinist terror pervaded the realm of the arts, just as it did the political and industrial worlds. Artists who did not conform were as likely to be purged as politicians who were deemed to be a danger to Stalin, or industrial managers who did not meet their quotas.

Socialist realism

Key terms
Soviet Union of Writers
The body having authority over all published writers. Under Stalin's direction it had the right to ban or censor any work of which it disapproved.

Socialist realism
A form of representational art that the people can understand and relate to their own lives.

In 1932 Stalin famously declared to a gathering of Soviet writers that they were 'engineers of the human soul'. This was a highly revealing remark. What he was telling his audience was that their task was essentially a social, not an artistic, one. They were to regard themselves not as individuals concerned with self-expression, but as contributors to the great collective effort of reshaping the thinking and behaviour of the Soviet people.

This was a radical departure from the European tradition, which had always valued the right of the artist to express himself as he wished; that was the way genuine art was created. Stalin rejected such notions. Artists were to be treated as if they were part of the industrial system; their task was to create a useful product. Self-expression had to be subordinated to the political and social needs of the new nation. It was not the individual but the people who mattered. The artist's first task was to make his work appropriate and relevant to the society he was serving. If he failed to do this, he was engaging in bourgeois self-indulgence, making himself more important than the people he was meant to serve.

Writers

Key question
How did 'socialist realism' influence the work and lives of writers and artists?

It is not surprising, therefore, that when the **Soviet Union of Writers** was formed in 1934, it should have declared that its first objective was to convince all writers that they must struggle for '**socialist realism**' in their works. This could be best achieved by conforming to a set of guidelines. Writers were to make sure that their work:

- was acceptable to the party in theme and presentation
- was written in a style and vocabulary that would be immediately understandable to the workers who would read it
- contained characters whom the readers could either identify with as socialist role models or directly recognise as examples of class enemies
- was optimistic and uplifting in its message and thus advanced the cause of socialism.

These rules applied to creative writing in all its forms: novels, plays, poems and film scripts. It was not easy for genuine writers to continue working within these restrictions, but conformity was the price of acceptance, even of survival. Before his death in 1934, Maxim Gorky (see page 123) was the leading voice among Russian writers. He used his undoubted skills to praise Stalin's First Five-Year Plan not merely as a great industrial achievement but as something of 'the highest spiritual value'. Other writers found it less easy to sell their soul. One author, **Boris Pasternak**, later celebrated in the West for his *Dr Zhivago*, a novel that was forbidden in the USSR during his lifetime, found some way out of his dilemma by restricting himself to translating historical works into Russian.

Many others who were not prepared to compromise their artistic integrity lost their position, their liberty, and sometimes their lives. Surveillance, scrutiny and denunciations intensified throughout the 1930s. The author **Alexander Solzhenitsyn** spent many years in the *gulag* for falling foul of Stalin's censors. His documentary novels, such as *One Day in the Life of Ivan Denisovich* and *The Gulag Archipelago*, which was published after Stalin's death, describe the horrific conditions in the labour camps.

In such an intimidating atmosphere, suicides became common. Robert Service notes in his biography of Stalin that 'More great intellectuals perished in the 1930s than survived.' In 1934, **Osip Mandelstam**, a leading literary figure, was informed on following a private gathering of writers at which he had recited a mocking poem about Stalin, containing the lines 'Around him, fawning half-men for him to play with, as he prates and points a finger.' Mandelstam died four years later in the *gulag*. He once remarked: 'Only in Russia is poetry taken seriously, so seriously men are killed for it.'

Stalin took a close personal interest in new works. One word of criticism from him was enough for a writer to be thrown out of the Union, often followed by arrest and imprisonment. Part of the tragedy was the readiness of so many second- and third-rate writers to expose and bring down their betters as a means of advancing their own careers. This was a common characteristic of totalitarian regimes in the twentieth century. The atmosphere of repression and the demand for conformity elevated the mediocre to a position of influence and power. Fortunately, the coming of the war in 1941 brought some respite to the beleaguered writers, since they were now able to throw themselves wholeheartedly into the task of writing heroic tales of

Key dates

Death of Maxim Gorky: 1934

Imprisonment of Osip Mandelstam: 1934

Severe repression of Soviet creative artists: 1936–8

Key figures

Boris Pasternak (1890–1960)
A poet, essayist and novelist. His works were regarded by the authorities as implicitly critical of the Soviet system and therefore unacceptable.

Alexander Solzhenitsyn (b. 1918)
A deeply spiritual man and writer, he was regarded by the authorities as subversive. After his expulsion from the USSR in 1974 he became as critical of western materialism as he had been of Soviet communism.

Osip Mandelstam (1891–1938)
A poet and novelist, he strugggled in his writings after 1917 to uphold human dignity in the face of Soviet oppression.

the Russian people working for glorious victory under their beloved Stalin.

Historians have on occasion queried whether the term 'totalitarian' should be used to describe Stalinism, their argument being that the limited technology of the time simply did not allow total control to be imposed (see page 270). Yet after allowing for that point, the fact remains that Stalin's aim in culture, as in politics and economics, was total conformity. And it was the aim that created the atmosphere and conditioned the way in which artists worked.

Other art forms

The Union of Writers set the tone for all other organisations in the arts. Painting and sculpture, film-making, opera and ballet all had to respond to the Stalinist demand for socialist realism. Abstract and experimental forms were frowned upon because they broke the rules that works should be immediately accessible and meaningful to the public. Jazz was condemned as decadent.

Theatre and film

An idea of the repression that operated can be gained from the following figures:

- In 1936–7, 68 films had to be withdrawn in mid-production and another 30 taken out of circulation.
- In the same period, ten out of nineteen plays and ballets were ordered to be withdrawn.
- In the 1937–8 theatre season, 60 plays were banned from performance, ten theatres closed in Moscow and another ten in Leningrad.

A prominent victim was the director **Vsevolod Meyerhold** whose concept of **'total theatre'** had a major influence on European theatre. It might be thought that Meyerhold's techniques for bringing theatre closer to the people would have perfectly fitted the notion of socialist realism. But his appeal for artistic liberty, 'The theatre is a living creative thing. We must have freedom – yes, freedom', led to a campaign being mounted against him by the toadies who served Stalin. He was arrested in 1938. After a two-year imprisonment during which he was regularly flogged with rubber straps until he fainted, he was shot. His name was one on a list of 346 death sentences that Stalin signed on 16 January 1940.

Even the internationally acclaimed director **Sergei Eisenstein**, whose films *Battleship Potemkin* and *October*, celebrating the revolutionary Russian proletariat, had done so much to advance the Communist cause, was heavily censured. This was because a later work of his, *Ivan the Terrible*, was judged to be an unflattering portrait of a great Russian leader and therefore, by implication, disrespectful of Stalin.

Key questions
Was Stalinism a totalitarian system?

What was the impact of Stalinism on other art forms?

Key date
Imprisonment of Vsevolod Meyerhold: 1938

Key figure

Vsevolod Meyerhold (1874–1940)
Despite the international reputation he achieved, his innovatory theatrical methods meant he was never trusted by Lenin or Stalin.

Key term

'Total theatre'
The attempt to break down the barriers between actors and audience by revolutionary use of lighting, sound and stage settings.

Painting and sculpture

Painters and sculptors were left in no doubt as to what was required of them. Their duty to conform to socialist realism in their style and at the same time honour their mighty leader was captured in an article in the art magazine *Iskusstvo* commenting on a painting that had won a Stalin Prize in 1948:

> On a bright morning Comrade Stalin is seen walking in the vast collective farm fields with high-voltage power transmission lines in the distance. His exalted face and his whole figure are lit with the golden rays of springtime sun. The image of Comrade Stalin is the triumphant march of communism, the symbol of courage, the symbol of the Soviet people's glory, calling for new heroic exploits for the benefit of our great motherland.

Music

Since music is an essentially abstract form of art, it was more difficult for the Soviet censors to make composers respond to Stalin's notions of social realism. Nevertheless, it was the art form that most interested Stalin, who regarded himself as something of an expert in the field. He claimed to be able to recognise socialist music when he heard it and to know what type of song would inspire the people. He had many a battle with the Soviet Union's leading composer, **Dmitri Shostakovich**, who had a chequered career under Stalinism. In 1936, Shostakovich's opera *Lady Macbeth of Mtsensk* was banned on the grounds that it was 'bourgeois and formalistic'. In the same year, his fourth symphony was withdrawn from the repertoire for similar reasons.

However, as with a number of writers, the war gave Shostakovich the opportunity to express his deep patriotism. His powerful orchestral works, particularly the seventh symphony, composed during the siege of Leningrad in 1941, was a highly dramatic and stirring piece depicting in sound the courageous struggle and final victory of the people of the city. At the end of the war, in return for being reinstated he promised to bring his music closer to 'the folk art of the people'. This left him artistically freer than he had been before, though Stalin was still apt to criticise some of his new works. Shostakovich's growing international reputation helped protect him.

Key figures

Sergei Eisenstein (1898–1948)
An outstanding figure in world cinema; his use of light and shade in the creation of atmosphere and spectacle left a permanent mark on film as a popular art form.

Dmitri Shostakovich (1906–75)
Spent his creative life trying to keep one step ahead of the censors by exploiting their musical ignorance. He managed to survive Stalin and became recognised as one of the twentieth century's great composers.

Key date

Works of Dmitri Shostakovich banned: 1936

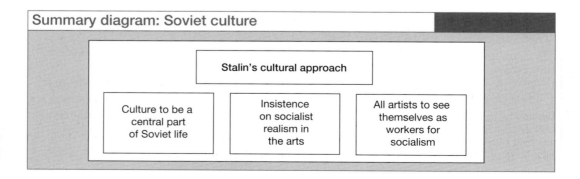

Summary diagram: Soviet culture

Stalin's cultural approach

- Culture to be a central part of Soviet life
- Insistence on socialist realism in the arts
- All artists to see themselves as workers for socialism

Key question
How did Stalin
establish a cult of
personality?

2 | Stalin's Cult of Personality

Adolf Hitler once wrote that 'the personality cult is the best form of government'. It is not certain whether Stalin ever read this, but it would be a fitting commentary on his leadership of the Soviet Union. One of the strongest charges made by Nikita Khrushchev in his attack on Stalin's record was that he had indulged in the cult of personality (see page 271). He was referring to the way Stalin dominated every aspect of Soviet life, so that he became not simply a leader but the embodiment of the nation itself. Similarly, the Communist Party became indistinguishable from Stalin himself as a person. Communism was no longer a set of theories; it was no longer Leninism. It was whatever Stalin said and did. Soviet Communism was Stalinism.

From the 1930s on, Stalin's picture began to appear everywhere. Every newspaper, book and film, no matter what its theme, carried a reference to Stalin's greatness. Every achievement of the USSR was credited to Stalin. Such was his all-pervasive presence that Soviet Communism became personalised around him. On occasion in private, Stalin protested that he did not seek the glorification he received, but, significantly, he made no effort to prevent it.

Ironically, in view of his later denunciation of Stalin, it was Nikita Khrushchev who did as much as anyone to promote the image of Stalin as a glorious hero. At the trial of Zinoviev and Kamenev in August 1936, Khrushchev cursed the defendants as 'Miserable pygmies!' and went on:

> They lifted their hands against the greatest of all men, our wise *vozhd*, Comrade Stalin. Thou, Comrade Stalin, hast raised the great banner of Marxism-Leninism high over the entire world and carried it forward. We assure thee, Comrade Stalin, that the Moscow Bolshevik organisation will increase Stalinist vigilance still more, will extirpate the Trotskyite-Zinovievite and close the ranks of the party around the great Stalin.

Khrushchev was the first to coin the term 'Stalinism', in 1936 at the introduction of the new Soviet Constitution in 1936: 'Our constitution is the Marxism-Leninism-Stalinism that has conquered one-sixth of the globe.' At the trial of Pyatakov and others, before an audience calculated by *Pravda* as being 200,000 in number, Khrushchev declared:

> By lifting their hands against comrade Stalin they lifted them against all the best that humanity possesses. For Stalin is hope, Stalin is expectation; he is the beacon that guides all progressive mankind. Stalin is our banner! Stalin is our will! Stalin is our victory!

Key dates
New Soviet
Constitution
introduced: 1936

Eighteenth Congress
of the CPSU carries
worship of Stalin to
new heights: 1939

At the Eighteenth Congress of the CPSU in March 1939, Khrushchev lauded the Soviet leader as 'our great inspiration, our beloved Stalin', extolling him as 'the greatest genius of humanity, teacher and *vozhd* who leads us towards Communism'.

ПОД ВОДИТЕЛЬСТВОМ ВЕЛИКОГО СТАЛИНА—ВПЕРЕД К КОММУНИЗМУ!

'Under the leadership of the great Stalin, forward to Communism!'

СПАСИБО РОДНОМУ СТАЛИНУ,

ЗА СЧАСТЛИВОЕ ДЕТСТВО!

'Thank you, dear Stalin, for our happy childhood!'

Posters from the 1930s, typical of the propaganda of the time, showing Stalin as the leader of his adoring people. Poster art was a very effective way for the Stalinist authorities to put their message across. In what ways do the posters illustrate the artistic notion of socialist realism?

It is one of the many paradoxes of Soviet history that the Communist movement, which in theory drew its authority from the will of the masses, became so dependent on the idea of the great leader. Such was Stalin's standing and authority that he transcended politics. Since he represented not simply the Party but the nation itself, he became the personification of all that was best in Russia. This was an extraordinary achievement for a Georgian, and it produced a further remarkable development. It became common to assert that many of the great achievements in world history were the work of Russians.

The claims reached ridiculous proportions: that Shakespeare was really a Russian, that Russian navigators had been the first Europeans to discover America and that Russian mathematicians had discovered the secrets of the atom long before western scientists had. Eventually Stalin overreached himself. He ordered his scientists to produce a popular soft drink equal in quality to the American capitalist Coca-Cola. They tried but finally had to admit that while Soviet science could achieve marvels, miracles were beyond it.

Propaganda

Key question
How was state propaganda used to promote Stalin's image?

The cult of personality was not a spontaneous response of the people. It did not come from below; it was imposed from above. The image of Stalin as hero and saviour of the Soviet people was manufactured. It was a product of the Communist Party machine, which controlled all the main forms of information: newspapers, cinema and radio. Roy Medvedev, a Soviet historian who lived through Stalinism, later explained:

> Stalin did not rely on terror alone, but also on the support of the majority of the people; effectively deceived by cunning propaganda, they gave Stalin credit for the successes of others and even in fact for 'achievements' that were in fact totally fictitious.

A fascinating example of building on the fictitious was the Stakhanovite movement (see page 216). It is now generally accepted that the official claim made in August 1935 that the miner Alexei Stakhanov had individually hewn fourteen times his required quota of coal in one shift was a fabrication. Nevertheless, so well was the story presented and developed by the authorities at the time that his achievement became a contemporary legend illustrating the heights of endeavour that could be reached by selfless workers responding to the appeals and the example of their great leader.

Worship of Stalin

Despite the Soviet attack on the Church, the powerful religious sense of the Russian people remained, and it was cleverly exploited by the authorities. Traditional worship with its veneration of the saints, its **icons**, prayers and incantations translated easily into the new regime. Stalin became an icon. This was literally true. His picture was carried on giant flags in processions. A French visitor watching at one of the **May Day** celebrations in Moscow's Red Square was staggered by the sight of a fly-past of planes all trailing huge portraits of Stalin. 'My God!' he exclaimed. 'Exactly, Monsieur,' said his Russian guide.

Key terms

Icons
Two-dimensional representations of Jesus Christ and the saints. The power and beauty of its icons is one of the great glories of the Orthodox Church.

May Day
or 'Labour Day' – usually reckoned as 1 May, traditionally regarded as a special day for honouring the workers and the achievements of socialism.

However, even May Day came to take second place to the celebration of Stalin's birthday each December. Beginning in 1929 on his fiftieth birthday, the occasion was turned each year into the greatest celebration in the Soviet calendar. Day-long parades in Red Square of marching troops, rolling tanks, dancing children and applauding workers, all presided over by an occasionally smiling Stalin high on a rostrum overlooking Lenin's tomb, became the high moment of the year. It was a new form of tsar-worship.

Stalin's wisdom and brilliance were extolled daily in *Pravda* and *Izvestiya*, the official Soviet newspapers. Hardly an article appeared in any journal that did not include the obligatory reference to his greatness. Children learned from their earliest moments to venerate Stalin as the provider of all good things. At school they were taught continually and in all subjects that Stalin was their guide and protector. It was an interesting aspect of the prescribed school curriculum (see page 258) that history was to be taught not as 'an abstract sociological scheme' but as a chronological story full of stirring tales of the great Russian heroes of the past such as **Ivan the Terrible** and **Peter the Great**, leading up to the triumph of Lenin and the Bolsheviks in 1917.

The climax of this story was Stalin, who, building on the work of Lenin, was securing and extending the Soviet Union. This adulation of Stalin was not confined to history books. There were no textbooks in any subject that did not extol the virtues of Stalin the master builder of the Soviet nation, inspiration to his people and glorious model for struggling peoples everywhere.

Eulogies of Stalin poured off the press, each trying to outbid the others in its veneration of the leader. Typical of the tone and contents was an official biography published by a group of Soviet writers in 1947:

> Stalin guides the destinies of a multinational Socialist state. His advice is taken as a guide to action in all fields of Socialist construction. His work is extraordinary for its variety; his energy truly amazing. The range of questions which engage his attention is immense. Stalin is wise and deliberate in solving complex political questions where a thorough weighing of pros and cons is required. At the same time, he is a supreme master of bold revolutionary decisions and of swift adaptations to changed conditions. Stalin is the Lenin of today.

Komsomol

A particularly useful instrument for the spread of Stalinist propaganda was ***Komsomol***, a youth movement that had begun in Lenin's time but was created as a formal body in 1926 under the direct control of the CPSU. Among its main features were the following:

- It was open to those aged between fourteen and 28 (a Young Pioneer movement existed for those under fourteen).

Key figures

Ivan the Terrible (reigned 1547–84) A powerful tsar who considerably extended Russian territory through conquest.

Peter the Great (reigned 1689–1725) A reforming tsar who attempted to modernise his nation by incorporating western European ways.

Key term

Komsomol The Communist Union of Youth.

Key date

Creation of *Komsomol*: 1926

- It pledged itself totally to Stalin and the Party (in this regard it paralleled the Hitler Youth movement in Nazi Germany).
- Membership was not compulsory but its attraction to young people was that it offered them the chance of eventual full membership of the CPSU, with all the privileges that went with it.
- It grew from 2 million members in 1927 to 10 million in 1940.

The idealism of the young was very effectively exploited by Stalin's regime. Komsomol members were among the most enthusiastic supporters of the Five-Year Plans, as they proved by going off in their thousands to help build the new industrial cities such as Magnitogorsk (see page 212). It was Komsomol that provided the flag wavers and the cheerleaders and that organised the huge gymnastic displays that were the centrepieces of the massive parades on May Day and Stalin's birthday.

Every political gathering was a study in the advancement of the Stalin cult. The exaggeration and the sycophantic character of it all are clear in the following extract from speech given by a delegate to the Seventh Congress of Soviets in 1935:

> Thank you, Stalin. Thank you because I am joyful. Thank you because I am well. Centuries will pass, and the generations still to come will regard us as the happiest of mortals, because we lived in the century of centuries, because we were privileged to see Stalin, our inspired leader. Yes, and we regard ourselves as the happiest of mortals because we are the contemporaries of a man who never had an equal in world history.
>
> The men of all ages will call on thy name, which is strong, beautiful, wise and marvellous. Thy name is engraven on every factory, every machine, every place on the earth and in the hearts of all men.

Stalin's popularity

Key question
How popular was Stalin in the Soviet Union?

It is difficult to judge how popular Stalin was in real terms. The applause that greeted his every appearance in public or in cinema newsreels is more likely to have been a matter of prudence than of real affection. The same is true of the tears shed by thousands at his passing in 1953. There was no way in which criticism or opposition could be voiced. The *gulag* was full of comrades who had spoken out of turn.

The intense **political correctness** of the day required that Stalin be publicly referred to as the faultless leader and inspirer of the nation. He made occasional broadcasts, but he was no orator. He could never match Hitler's gift for rousing an audience or Churchill's for inspiring one. In wartime it was the gravity of the situation that gave Stalin's broadcasts their power. Perhaps it was Stalin's own recognition of his limitations in this regard that explains why after 1945 he made only three public speeches, and these were only a few minutes long. Yet in an odd way Stalin's remoteness helped promote his image. Seen as a distant figure on a high rostrum or in the selected views of him in the official newsreels, he retained a powerful mystique.

Key term

Political correctness
The requirement that people conform to a prescribed set of opinions when expressing themselves to show that they have accepted the ideology of the leaders of society.

A fascinating insight into Stalin's standing with his own people was
provided in 1937 by **Leon Feuchtwanger**, a German visitor to the
Soviet Union in the 1930s, who was over-impressed by Stalin's
apparent economic successes but who remained a shrewd observer
of Soviet attitudes. He explained the particular character of
Stalin's popularity in these terms:

> The people were grateful to Stalin for their bread and meat, for the
> order in their lives, for their education and for creating their army
> which secured this new well-being. The people have to have
> someone to whom to express their gratitude, and for this purpose
> they do not select an abstract concept, such as 'communism', but a
> real man, Stalin. Their unbounded reverence is consequently not for
> Stalin, but for him as a symbol of the patently successful economic
> reconstruction.

Researchers from a later generation, such as Sheila Fitzpatrick,
aware of how little Stalin had done to improve the conditions of
the Soviet people, offer a different slant:

> Judging by the NKVD's soundings of public opinion, the Stalinist
> regime was relatively, though not desperately, unpopular in Russian
> towns. (In Russian villages, especially in the first half of the 1930s, its
> unpopularity was much greater.) Overall, as the NKVD regularly
> reported, the ordinary 'little man' in Soviet towns, who thought only
> of his own and his family's welfare, was 'dissatisfied with Soviet
> power', though in a somewhat fatalistic and passive manner. The
> post-NEP situation was compared unfavourably with NEP, and Stalin
> – despite the officially fostered Stalin cult – was compared
> unfavourably with Lenin, sometimes because he was more repressive
> but often because he let people go hungry.

The USSR's triumph in the Great Fatherland War of 1941–5 did
much to perpetuate the image of Stalin as national hero. Doubts
that might have been whispered about Stalin before the war
became scarcely possible to consider, let alone utter, after 1945.
The Soviet Union's triumph over Germany in 1945 was a
supreme moment in Russian history. Under Stalin the nation
had survived perhaps the most savage conflict in European
history. This gave him a prestige as the nation's saviour that
mattered far more than whether he was simply liked. The
important point was that the Soviet people held him in even
greater awe and fear than before. And, as the tsars had always
known, it does not matter whether a regime is loved as long as it
is feared.

**Leon Feuchtwanger
(1884–1958)**
Jewish novelist and
literary critic who
was exiled from
Nazi Germany in
the 1930s.

Key figure

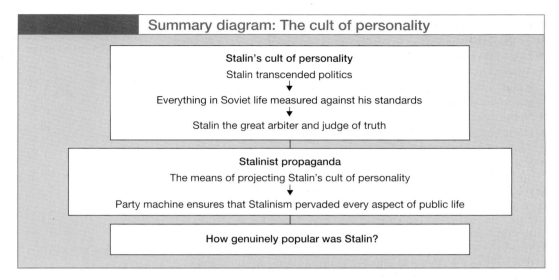

Summary diagram: The cult of personality

Stalin's cult of personality

Stalin transcended politics

↓

Everything in Soviet life measured against his standards

↓

Stalin the great arbiter and judge of truth

Stalinist propaganda

The means of projecting Stalin's cult of personality

↓

Party machine ensures that Stalinism pervaded every aspect of public life

How genuinely popular was Stalin?

Key question
Why was Stalin so determined to reform the Soviet education system?

3 | Education

The initial attitudes of Lenin and the Bolsheviks when they came to power were shaped by their general desire to reject bourgeois standards. In the field of education this led to an attack on book learning and traditional academic subjects. For a brief period, textbooks were thrown away, exams abolished, and schools either shut or opened only for a limited number of days. Young people were encouraged to learn trades and engage in activities that were of practical value.

But by the time Stalin came to power it was generally accepted that the dismissal of the old ways had gone too far. As in so many areas of Russian life, Stalin reversed the trends initiated by the Bolsheviks after 1917. His driving aim was to modernise the Soviet Union and he believed that to achieve this, the population, especially the young, must be made literate. He was aware of the complaints of parents and employers that young people were entering the workplace without having mastered the basic skills in reading and writing. To meet this crippling problem, formal education was made a priority. The need for discipline and order was stressed. It made little sense to insist on strict rules of conduct for workers in the factories if schools allowed pupils to behave in a free and easy manner. The education system must develop the same serious, committed attitude that prevailed in the workplace.

Key features of the education system developed under Stalin
- Ten years of compulsory schooling for all children.
- A core curriculum laid down: reading, writing, mathematics, science, history, geography, Russian (and for the national minorities their native language), Marxist theory.
- State-prescribed text books to be used.
- Homework to be a regular requirement.
- State-organised tests and examinations.
- School uniforms made compulsory (girls were obliged to have their hair in pigtails).
- Fees to be charged for the last three years (fifteen to eighteen) of non-compulsory secondary schooling.

The emphasis on regulation was not accidental. The intention behind these requirements, which were introduced during the 1930s, was to create a disciplined, trained generation of young people fully ready to join the workforce which was engaged through the Five-Year Plans in constructing the new Communist society.

Results of the reforms
The results of these education policies were impressive:

- Between 1929 and 1940 the number of children attending school rose from 12 million to 35 million.
- By 1939, schooling for eight- to fourteen-year-olds had become universal in the urban areas.
- Between 1926 and 1939 the literacy rate for the population over the age of nine increased from 51 to 88 per cent.

An egalitarian system?
The bulleted point above regarding the payment of fees may appear to challenge the notion of an egalitarian education system. But the official justification for it was that all societies, including socialist ones, need a trained section of the community to serve the people in expert ways. Doctors, managers, scientists, administrators and the like clearly required particular training in order to be able to fill that social role. Those who stayed on at school after fifteen were obviously young people of marked ability who would eventually go on to university to become the specialists of the future. This was undeniably a selection process, but the argument was that it was selection by ability, not, as in the corrupt tsarist days or in the decadent capitalist world, by class. Moreover, the requirement to pay fees would not prove an obstacle since there were many grants and scholarships in the gift of the government, the Party and the trade unions.

The role of the elite
That was the official line. But behind the undoubted rise in educational standards and the marked increase in literacy rates, the system was creating a privileged elite. This was one of the

Key question
Was the educational system genuinely egalitarian?

Literacy rate reaches 88 per cent: 1940

Key date

paradoxes of revolutionary Russia. Before 1917 the Bolsheviks had poured scorn on the bourgeois governing elites that monopolised power in all capitalist societies. But the equivalent very quickly developed in Soviet Russia. The intelligentsia that formed the *nomenklatura* appreciated that education was the key to opportunity; that is why they took great pains to ensure that their children received the best form of it. Private tuition and private education became normal for the elite of Soviet society.

The unfair and unsocialist nature of all this was covered up by claims that the schools were 'specialist' institutions for children with particular aptitudes, rather than a matter of privilege. The Party had the right to nominate those who were to receive the higher-grade training that would give them access to university. As university education expanded, it was Party members or their children who had the first claim on the best places. In the period 1928–32, for example, a third of all undergraduates were Party nominees. As graduates, they were then invited to enter one or other of the three key areas of Soviet administration: industry, the civil service or the armed services.

This educational and promotional process had an important political aspect. It enhanced Stalin's power by creating a class of privileged administrators who had every motive for supporting him since they were his creatures. Osip Mandelstam, the disgraced poet (see page 248), described this precisely:

> At the end of the twenties and in the thirties our authorities, making no concession to 'egalitarianism', started to raise the living standards of those who had proved their usefulness. Everybody was concerned to keep the material benefits he had worked so hard to earn. A thin layer of privileged people gradually came into being with **'packets'**, country villas and cars. Those who had been granted a share of the cake eagerly did everything asked of them.

Key term

'Packets'
Privileges and special benefits.

Key question
How did Soviet scholars respond to the demands of Stalinism?

Key date

The Soviet Academy of Sciences becomes the controlling body over all scholars: 1935

Universities

In intellectual terms, the Soviet Union's most prestigious institution was the Academy of Sciences. Based on the famed tsarist Imperial Academy, it became in the new Russia an umbrella body incorporating all the major research organisations, some 250 in number with over 50,000 individual members. The term 'sciences' translates broadly to cover all the main intellectual and scientific streams: the arts, agriculture, medicine, management. All the major scholars in their fields were academicians. In 1935 the Academy was brought under direct government control. In return for increased academic and social privileges, it pledged itself totally to Stalin in his building of the new Communist society. What this meant in practice was that all the academicians would henceforth produce work wholly in keeping with Stalinist values. They would become politically correct.

One particularly distressing aspect of this was that Soviet historians no longer engaged in genuine historical research and analysis. Their reputation and acceptance as scholars depended on their presenting history shaped and interpreted as Stalin wanted. They ceased to be historians in any meaningful sense and became intellectual lackeys of the regime.

The Lysenko affair

Where such academic subservience could lead was evident in an infamous case that damaged Soviet science and agriculture for decades. In the 1930s, **Trofim Lysenko**, a quack geneticist, claimed to have discovered ways of developing 'super-crops' that would grow in any season and produce a yield anything up to sixteen times greater than the harvests produced by traditional methods. Stalin, who had convinced himself that there was such a thing as 'socialist science', which was superior to that practised in the bourgeois West, was excited by Lysenko's claims and gave him his full support. This meant that, although the claims were in fact wholly false, based on rigged experiments and doctored figures, Lysenko was unchallengeable by his colleagues. Those who dared protest that his methods were faulty were removed from their posts and dumped in the *gulag*.

It was not until 1965, many years after Stalin's death in 1953, that Lysenko's ideas were finally exposed in the Soviet Union for the nonsense they were. The tragedy was that by then they had played a part in creating the famines that so frequently ravaged Stalin's Soviet Union.

Key question
What was the importance of the Lysenko affair?

Trofim Lysenko (1898–1976)
Appointed head of the Soviet Academy of Agricultural Sciences, he hounded those biologists who dared point out the absurdity of his theories.

Key figure

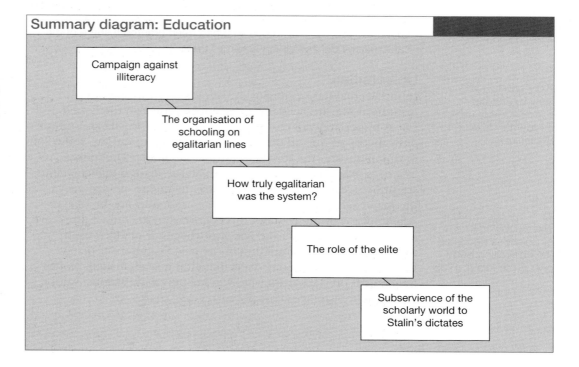

Summary diagram: Education

Campaign against illiteracy

The organisation of schooling on egalitarian lines

How truly egalitarian was the system?

The role of the elite

Subservience of the scholarly world to Stalin's dictates

4 | Health

Key questions
How effectively did
the Soviet Union
develop a public
health service?

What impact did the
war have on health
standards?

Key terms

Infant mortality
The number of
children who die per
100 or per 1000 of
all those in a
particular age group.

Tuberculosis
A wasting disease,
often affecting the
lungs, that was
especially prevalent
in imperial Russia.

In 1918, Lenin's Bolshevik government had set up the People's
Commissariat of Health. Its aim was nothing less than to provide a
free health service for all the people. The commissariat continued
to operate in Stalin's time with the same objective. But from the
beginning, the sad fact was that Soviet Russia never had the
resources to match its intentions. The disruptions of the Civil War
period made it impossible to develop a structured health service
on the lines originally envisaged. Things picked up in the better
economic conditions produced by the NEP. **Infant mortality**
dropped and the spread of contagious diseases was checked. But
famine remained a constant threat.

In the 1930s the collectivisation policy enforced by Stalin created
the largest famine in Russian history. This made the worst-hit areas –
Ukraine and Kazakhstan – places of death and disease. Such was the
scale of the horror that the existing health services in those regions
simply could not cope. Although some parts of the USSR were
relatively unscathed, it proved impossible to transfer medical
supplies from these areas on a big enough scale to provide real help
to the stricken regions. There was also the chilling fact that since
Stalin refused to acknowledge that there was a famine, no real effort
was made by the central government to deal with its consequences.

It is true that in the unaffected areas in the 1930s there was a
genuine advance in health standards. The number of qualified
doctors and nurses increased, and while the benefits of this may not
have reached the majority of the population, there were spectacular
successes that were made much of in Stalinist propaganda. Sanatoria
for the treatment of **tuberculosis**, and rest and retirement homes for
the workers, were created. There were even holiday centres, in such
places as Yalta on the Black Sea, where selected workers were sent as
a reward for their efforts. However, the number who enjoyed such
treatment was a tiny fraction of the workforce. The main
beneficiaries of improved medical care were not ordinary Russians
but Party members and the *nomenklatura*. It was one of the privileges
of belonging to the political establishment.

The idea of health for all was never abandoned, but it proved
difficult to maintain it as a priority during the headlong push for
industrial growth in the 1930s. It is true that factories and plants
were urged to provide crèches so that more mothers with young
children could be employed, but this was done primarily to meet
the needs of industry, not those of the mother. Childcare at the
factories was regimented by such measures as the requirement that
breastfeeding took place at a given time so as not to interfere with
production. One positive result of Stalin's insistence that Soviet
women see their primary role as mothers producing babies for the
nation was the setting up of clinics and a general improvement in
the standards of midwifery and gynaecology.

The war of 1941–5 intensified Soviet health problems. The
already meagre diet was further restricted by the rationing that had
to be imposed. The experience for the people in German-occupied

areas or in the regions under siege was unremittingly grim. The German seizure of the USSR's most productive regions denied vital food supplies to the Soviet people. Over 6 million civilian deaths were the result of starvation. In such circumstances it became meaningless to talk of public health.

There was no great improvement after the war. Stalin's concerns were industrial recovery and national defence. The annual budgets down to his death in 1953 showed a decline in the amount dedicated to improving health standards. Rationing was formally ended in 1947, but this did not mean that shortages had been genuinely overcome. Without the existence of a widespread black market, which was officially condemned by the authorities but in practice tolerated and, indeed encouraged by them, the workers would not have been able to supplement their meagre food and fuel supplies. Accommodation was scarcer and conditions in the factories were grimmer than they had been in wartime. Real wages were not permitted to rise above **subsistence level** and the rigours of the 'Labour Code' were not relaxed. When Stalin died in 1953, the lot of the Russian worker was harsher than at any time since 1917.

How healthy the Soviet people were under Stalin is not easy to measure precisely. The famines of the 1920s and 1930s were so frequent and severe and the horrors of the war period so grim that the question is largely irrelevant. The USSR under Stalin never formally abandoned its dream of creating a health service to outmatch that of the capitalist West. There were certainly organised attempts to train doctors, build hospitals and improve the health and hygiene of the workers. It should also be added that in some particular areas of medical research, eye surgery for example, the USSR led the world. But circumstances never allowed Stalin to pay more than lip-service to the notion of a fully-funded, comprehensive system of medical provision for the people. The simple fact was that as long as the Soviet Union could not feed its people adequately – and this was the case throughout the whole period of Stalinism – the idea of an effective health service remained an aspiration but was never a reality.

This survey should not close without reference to the millions of innocent Soviet citizens starved and worked to death in Stalin's *gulag*. To them, talk of a health policy under Stalin would have been a black and bitter joke.

Key term

Subsistence level
The bare minimum required to sustain life.

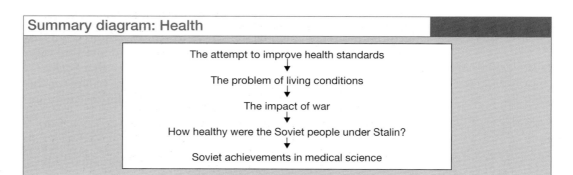

Summary diagram: Health

The attempt to improve health standards
↓
The problem of living conditions
↓
The impact of war
↓
How healthy were the Soviet people under Stalin?
↓
Soviet achievements in medical science

5 | Religion

Key question
What was the role of religion and the Orthodox Church in Stalin's Russia?

Key date

New campaign of persecution of religion: 1928

An organised attack on religion had been launched in Lenin's time (see page 168). This was renewed under Stalin, who, despite his own training as a priest and his mother's profound religious devotion, shared his predecessor's view that religion had no place in a socialist society.

Coinciding with the beginning of the First Five-Year Plan in 1928, a new campaign against the churches began. The Orthodox Church was again the main target, but all religions and denominations were at risk. Along with the prohibition on Orthodox churches and monasteries went the closure of synagogues and mosques. Clerics who refused to co-operate were arrested; thousands in Moscow and Leningrad were sent into exile. The timing was not accidental. Stalin's drive for industrialisation was on such an epic scale that it required the whole nation to be committed to it. That was why the purges became an accompaniment of it (see page 234). Conformity was essential and had to be imposed. Religion, with its other-worldly values, was seen as an affront to the collective needs of the nation.

A grandmother tries to drag her grand-daughter away from school to church. The wording reads: 'Religion is poison. Protect your children.' Why should the authorities have chosen to present the struggle between religion and education as a generational conflict?

The suppression of religion in the urban areas proved a fairly straightforward affair, but it was a different story in the countryside. The destruction of the rural churches and the confiscation of the relics and icons that most peasants had in their homes led to revolts in many areas. What particularly angered local people was the carrying away of the church bells. The authorities had failed to understand that what to their secular mind were merely superstitious practices were to the peasants a precious part of the traditions that shaped their daily lives. The result was widespread resistance across the rural provinces of the USSR. The authorities responded by declaring that those who opposed the restrictions on religion were really doing so in order to resist collectivisation. This allowed the requisition squads to brand the religious protesters as *kulaks* and to seize their property. Priests were publicly humiliated by being forced to perform demeaning tasks in public, such as clearing out pigsties and latrines.

Such was the misery the suppression created that Stalin instructed his officials to call a halt. This was not through compassion. The severity of the anti-religious programme had attracted worldwide attention. In March 1930, in protest against the persecutions, Pope Pius XI announced a special day of prayer throughout the Catholic Church. For diplomatic reasons, Stalin judged it prudent to take a softer line. But this was only temporary. In the late 1930s, as part of the Great Terror, the assault on religion was renewed. Some 800 higher clergy and 4000 ordinary priests were imprisoned, along with many thousands of the **laity**. By 1940 only 500 churches were open for worship in the Soviet Union – one per cent of the figure for 1917.

The war that for the USSR began in June 1941 brought a respite in the persecution of the churches. Stalin was aware of how deep the religious instinct was in the great majority of Russians. While official policy was to denigrate and ridicule religion at every opportunity, and the leading Communists were always anxious to display their distaste for it, there were occasions when it proved highly useful to the authorities. Wartime provided such an occasion. Stalin was shrewd enough to enlist religion in fighting the Great Patriotic War. The churches were reopened, the clergy released and the people encouraged to celebrate the great church ceremonies.

The majestic grandeur of the Orthodox liturgy provided a huge emotional and spiritual uplift. There are few things more nerve-tinglingly exciting than a Russian church congregation in full voice. Those besieged in Leningrad recorded that while worship did not lessen their hunger or soften the German bombardment, it lifted their morale and strengthened their resolve to endure the unendurable.

What is particularly fascinating and revealing is that for the period of the war the Soviet authorities under Stalin played down politics and emphasised nationalism. Talk of the proletarian struggle gave way to an appeal to defend holy Russia against the godless invaders. However, this did not represent any real freedom for the Orthodox Church. The price for being allowed to exist openly was its total subservience to the regime. In 1946, Stalin required that all the Christian denominations in the Soviet Union come under the authority of the Orthodox Church, which was made responsible for ensuring that organised religion did not become a source of political opposition.

Key term

Laity
The congregation who attend church services.

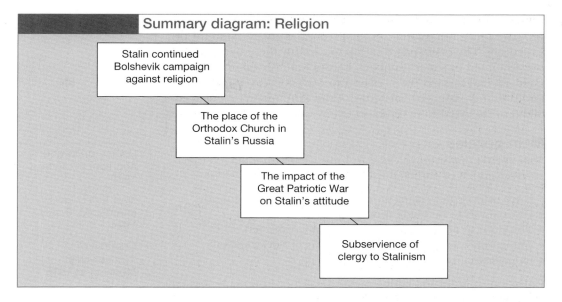

Summary diagram: Religion

Stalin continued Bolshevik campaign against religion

The place of the Orthodox Church in Stalin's Russia

The impact of the Great Patriotic War on Stalin's attitude

Subservience of clergy to Stalinism

6 | Women and the Family

Key question
Why did Stalin reverse the earlier Bolshevik policies regarding women and the family?

In keeping with their Marxist rejection of marriage as a bourgeois institution, Lenin's Bolsheviks had made divorce easier and had attempted to liberate women from the bondage of children and family. However, after only a brief experiment along these lines, Lenin's government had to come to doubt its earlier enthusiasm for sweeping change in this area (see page 169). Stalin shared its doubts. Indeed, by the time he was fully installed in power in the 1930s, he was convinced that the earlier Bolshevik social experiment had failed.

By the end of the 1930s the Soviet divorce rate was the highest in Europe, one divorce for every two marriages. This led Stalin to embark on what Sheila Fitzpatrick has called 'the great retreat'. He began to stress the value of the family as a stabilising influence in society. He let it be known that he did not approve of the sexual freedoms that had followed the 1917 Revolution, claiming, with some justification, that Lenin himself had not approved of the free love movement that had developed around such figures as Alexandra Kollontai (see page 169). Stalin argued that a good Communist was a socially responsible one, who took the duties of parenthood and family life seriously: 'a poor husband and father, a poor wife and mother, cannot be good citizens'.

It was as if Stalin, aware of the social upheavals his modernisation programme was causing, was trying to create some form of balance by emphasising the traditional social values attaching to the role of women as homemakers and child raisers. He was also greatly exercised by the number of orphaned children living on the streets of the urban areas. They were the victims of the disruption caused by the Civil War, collectivisation, and the growth in illegitimacy that resulted from the greater amount of casual sex. The orphanages set up to care for them had been overwhelmed by sheer numbers. Left to fend for themselves, the children had formed themselves into gangs of scavengers attacking and robbing passers-by. Disorder of this kind further convinced Stalin of the need to re-establish family values.

Main policies

Stalin's first major move came in June 1936 with a decree that reversed much of earlier Bolshevik social policy:

- Unregistered marriages were no longer to be recognised.
- Divorce was to be made more difficult.
- The right to abortion was to be severely restricted.
- The family was declared to be the basis of Soviet society.
- Homosexuality was outlawed.

Key dates

Decree outlawing abortion: 27 June 1936

New family laws introduced: 9 July 1944

Creation of 'Housewives' Movement: 1936

Conscious both of the falling birthrate and of how many Russians were dying in the Great Patriotic War, the authorities introduced measures in July 1944 reaffirming the importance of the family in communist Russia and giving incentives to women to have large numbers of children:

- Restrictions on divorce were tightened still further.
- Abortion was totally outlawed.
- Mothers with more than two children were to be made 'heroines of the Soviet Union'.
- Taxes were increased on parents with fewer than two children.
- The right to inherit family property was re-established.

The status of Soviet women

One group that certainly felt they had lost out were the female members of the Party and the intelligentsia, who, like Kollontai, had welcomed the Revolution as the beginning of female liberation. However, the strictures on sexual freedom under Stalin, and the emphasis on family and motherhood, allowed little room for the notion of the independent, self-sufficient female. Such gains as the feminists had made were undermined by Stalin's appeal for the nation to act selflessly in its hour of need.

Key question
Did women become more emancipated under Stalinism?

It is true that Soviet propaganda spoke of the true equality of women, but there was a patronising air about much that went on. *Zhenotdel*, set up under Lenin as an organisation to represent the views of the Party's female members, was allowed to lapse in 1930 on the grounds that its work was done. A 'Housewives' Movement' was created in 1936 under Stalin's patronage. Composed largely of the wives of high-ranking industrialists and managers, it set itself the task of 'civilising' the tastes and improving the conditions of the workers.

Key term

Zhenotdel
The Women's Bureau of the Communist Party.

In a less disturbed situation this might have made some impact, but, as with all the movements of Stalin's time, it has to be set against the desperate struggle in which the USSR was engaged.

Stalin continually spoke of the nation being under siege and of the need to build a war economy. This made any movement not directly concerned with industrial production or defence seem largely irrelevant. Most of the women's organisations fell into this category.

Female exploitation

There were individual cases of women gaining in status and income in Stalin's time. But these were very much a minority and were invariably unmarried women or those without children. Married women with children carried a double burden. The great demand for labour that followed from Stalin's massive industrialisation drive required that women became essential members of the workforce. So, despite the theory about women being granted equality under Communism, in practice their burdens increased. They now had to fulfil two roles: as mothers raising the young to take their place in the new society and as workers contributing to the modernisation of the Soviet Union. This imposed great strains upon them. This was especially the case in the war of 1941–5. The terrible death toll of men at the front and the desperate need to keep the armaments factories running meant that women became indispensable (see Figure 10.1).

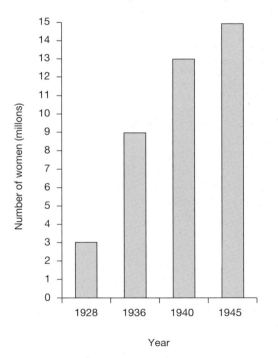

Figure 10.1: Number of women in the Soviet industrial workforce.

An equally striking statistic is that during the war, over half a million women fought in the Soviet armed forces. However, rather than improving the status of women, this left them more vulnerable to mistreatment. It has come to light from recently opened Soviet records and the confessions of Red Army veterans that female soldiers were routinely sexually abused, especially by the senior officers.

The clear conclusion is that for all the Soviet talk of the liberation of women under Stalinism, the evidence suggests that that they were increasingly exploited. They made a huge contribution to the Five-Year Plans and to wartime production. Without them the war effort could not have been sustained; by 1945, half of all Soviet workers were female. Yet they received no comparable reward. In fact, between 1930 and 1945 women's pay rates in real terms actually dropped. It is hard to dispute the conclusion of Geoffrey Hosking that 'the fruits of female emancipation became building blocks of the Stalinist **neopatriarchal** social system.'

Neopatriarchal
A new form of male domination.

Key term

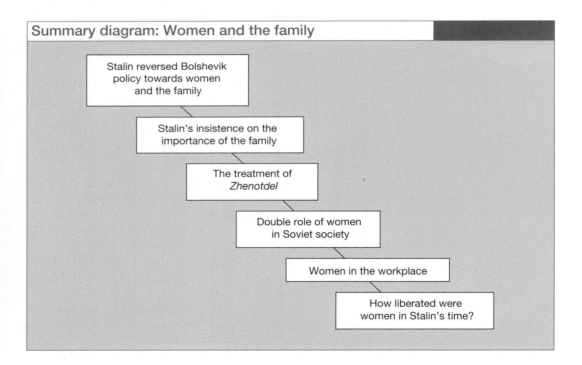

Summary diagram: Women and the family

Stalin reversed Bolshevik policy towards women and the family

Stalin's insistence on the importance of the family

The treatment of *Zhenotdel*

Double role of women in Soviet society

Women in the workplace

How liberated were women in Stalin's time?

Key questions
How did Stalin's reputation stand in 1941?

What was Stalin's record as national and Party leader?

Key term

Operation Barbarossa German codename for the invasion of the Soviet Union, launched without formal warning by Hitler on 22 June 1941.

7 | Stalin's Record

Stalin's record as Soviet leader

On the eve of the launching of **Operation Barbarossa** in June 1941, Stalin's reputation in the Soviet Union could hardly have been higher. He was officially lauded as the great leader who had:

- made himself an outstanding world statesman
- fulfilled the socialist revolution begun by Lenin
- purged the USSR of its internal traitors and enemies
- turned the USSR into a great modern economy through collectivisation and industrialisation.

These, of course, were achievements that Stalin claimed for himself through his propaganda machine. A more sober and more neutral estimate would have to include the negative side of Stalin's exercise of power since the late 1920s. His record judged in this way might include the following:

- Terror as a state policy.
- Authoritarian one-party rule by the CPSU.
- A single 'correct' ideology of Communism as dictated by Stalin.
- A misguided belief in the supremacy of Communist economic planning. Stalin's policy of collectivisation was so disruptive that it permanently crippled Soviet agriculture and left the USSR incapable of feeding itself.
- His policy of enforced industrialisation achieved a remarkable short-term success but prevented the USSR from ever developing a truly modern economy.
- The abuse and deportations suffered by the ethnic peoples of the Soviet empire left them with a burning hatred that would eventually help to bring down the USSR.

It was the memory of Lenin's dominance of the Bolshevik Party that endured as the most powerful legacy of the 1917 Revolution. After 1917, reverence for the achievements of Lenin became a vital part of Communist tradition. It was Stalin's ability to suggest that he was continuing the work of Lenin that eased his own path to supremacy after 1924. Circumstances had made loyalty to the Party and loyalty to Lenin inseparable. Similarly, by the late 1920s Stalin had succeeded in identifying his own authority with that of the rule of the Party. This made it extremely difficult for his fellow Communists to oppose him. To criticise Stalin was equivalent to doubting Lenin, the Party and the Revolution.

Stalin's intimate knowledge of the workings of the Secretariat aided him in his rise to power. By 1924 he had come to hold a number of important administrative positions, chief of which was the office of General Secretary of the CPSU. This left him ideally placed to control the appointment of members to the various posts within the Party's gift. Stalin became the indispensable linkman in the expanding system of Soviet government. Large numbers of Communist officials, the *nomenklatura* (see page 241), owed their positions to Stalin's influence. They could not afford to be disloyal to him. This gave him a power base that his rivals could not match. In the 1920s he was able to defeat all other contenders in the power struggle that followed Lenin's death.

The clear proof of how powerful Stalin had become was evident in the 1930s when he launched a series of purges of his real or imagined enemies in the government, the armed services and the Party. From then until his death in 1953 he exercised absolute authority over the Soviet Union.

Stalin's Russia

From time to time, analysts have suggested that Stalin was not all-powerful – no one individual in a nation can be – and that his power depended on the willingness of thousands of underlings to carry out his orders and policies. In one obvious sense this must be true; no one person can do it all. It is for this reason that many historians are reluctant to use the word **totalitarian** to describe his domination of the USSR.

What also worries them is that the term 'totalitarianism' is too often used to describe the dominant European regimes of the 1920 and 1930s, Hitler's Nazi Germany and Stalin's Communist Russia, as if the **authoritarian characteristics** they shared made them part of a common phenomenon. Their concern is that if these regimes are lumped together in this way, it blurs the real differences between them and diminishes the importance of the particular role of Stalin and the particular nature of the Soviet Union in the development of Stalinism.

However, there are other historians who, while not disputing the huge impact that Stalin had upon his country, point to other areas of significant development that occurred that did not depend on Stalin. This school of thought is sometimes referred to as the **bottom-up approach**. Writers in this school concentrate not so much on what Stalin did during the era he dominated the USSR, but rather on the reactions and attitudes of ordinary Soviet citizens. Sheila Fitzpatrick describes these historians as a 'new cohort' of post-Cold War scholars who 'approach Stalinism like **anthropologists**, analysing practices, **discourses**, and rituals'. They were greatly helped in this by the opening of the former Soviet archives in the 1990s, which allowed them to examine evidence previously closed to both Soviet and western scholars.

Yet exciting though these new developments among the younger generation of historians are, the hard fact remains that whatever were the attitudes of, and lives led by, ordinary Russians, it was Stalin who gave the USSR its essential shape. Whatever the motives of those who carried out Stalin's policies, he was the great motivator. Little of importance took place in the USSR of which he did not approve. That is why some prominent historians, such as Robert Tucker, still speak of Stalinism as 'revolution from above', meaning that the changes that occurred under Stalin were directed by him from the top down.

Key question
Was Stalin's Russia a totalitarian system?

Key terms

Totalitarianism
Absolute state control.

Authoritarian characteristics
A dominant ideology that justifies a system of state terror being imposed.

Bottom-up approach
Historical analysis of what was happening at the grass-roots level of society.

Anthropologists
Those who study the patterns of life of particular peoples and social groupings.

Discourse
A Marxist term relating to the prevailing ideas and culture within a society.

De-Stalinisation

It is significant that the first sustained attack upon Stalinism as a personal form of autocratic rule came from within the Soviet Union itself. In February 1956, Nikita Khrushchev, the Soviet leader, delivered a dramatic **'secret report'** to the Twentieth Congress of the CPSU. In a speech of remarkable range and venom, Khrushchev surveyed Stalin's career since the 1930s, exposing in detail the errors and crimes that Stalin had committed against the Party. Stalin had been guilty of 'flagrant abuses of power'. He had been personally responsible for the purges, 'those mass arrests that brought tremendous harm to our country and to the cause of socialist progress'.

Khrushchev quoted a host of names of innocent Party members who had suffered at Stalin's hands. Individual cases of gross injustice were cited and examples given of the brutality and torture used to extract confessions. Khrushchev's address was frequently interrupted by outbursts of amazement and disbelief from the assembled members as he gave the details of the Stalinist terror.

The special term that Khrushchev used to describe the Stalinism that he was condemning was 'the cult of personality'. He explained that he meant by this that all the mistakes perpetrated in the Soviet Union since the 1930s had been a consequence of Stalin's lust for personal power, his 'mania for greatness'. With hindsight, it can be seen that Khrushchev's speech set in motion a debate about the character of Stalin and Stalinism that still continues.

The key debate

For decades, scholars have been divided over the following issue:

> Was Stalin's despotism a logical progression from the authoritarianism of Lenin?

The reason why this is such a basic and important issue is that it goes to the heart of the question as to whether Marxist Communism was the perfect social and political system that its adherents claimed it to be. In Communist belief, the justification for the 1917 Revolution led by Lenin was that it had been the first stage in a process that would culminate in the creation of the perfect society. If that process came to be corrupted, there would have to be an explanation. How could a perfect system become imperfect? To answer this, committed Communists set out to prove that Stalin had diverted Lenin's revolution away from its true Marxist course. They claimed that the mistakes and terrors of the Stalin years were an aberration caused by Stalin's pursuit of his own personal power. Stalin's methods were not, therefore, a continuation of Lenin's policies but a departure from them; Stalinism was not a logical stage in the development of the Communist revolution but a betrayal of it.

Alexander Solzhenitsyn, the leading dissident in Stalin's Russia, who underwent long years of imprisonment in the *gulag*, condemned the attempts to explain Stalinism in those terms. In 1974 he wrote that the concept of Stalinism as a distinct and unusual period of Soviet history was vital for Soviet Communists because:

Key term

'Secret report' Krushchev's astounding revelations concerning Stalin's crimes against the Party. Although they were officially described as secret, details were soon known worldwide.

[T]hey shift onto it the whole bloody burden of the past to make their present position easier. It is no less necessary to those broad **Left-liberal circles** in the West which in Stalin's lifetime applauded highly coloured pictures of Soviet life.

But close study of our [Soviet] modern history shows there never was any such thing as Stalinism … Stalin was a very consistent and faithful – if also very untalented – heir to the spirit of Lenin's teaching.

Left-liberal circles
Westerners who were generally sympathetic towards Stalin and the USSR.

Key term

Interestingly, Stalin refused to allow the term 'Stalinism' to be used as if it represented something separate from traditional Communism. He always insisted that his task was to carry Lenin's ideas to fruition. The principal aspects of his government of Soviet Russia – collectivisation, industrialisation, 'socialism in one country', cultural conformity – were officially described as 'Marxism-Leninism in action'.

From exile, Trotsky challenged this: he claimed that Stalin had laid his dead bureaucratic hand on Russia, thus destroying the dynamic revolution that Lenin had created. Isaac Deutscher and Roy Medvedev, both of whom suffered personally under Stalin, followed Trotsky in suggesting that Stalin had perverted the basically democratic nature of Leninism into a personal dictatorship.

However, Solzhenitsyn regarded Stalin as a 'blind, mechanical executor of Lenin's will' and stressed that the apparatus of the police state was already in place when Stalin took over. One-party rule, the secret police, the use of terror tactics, show trials – these were already in existence by 1924. Solzhenitsyn's analysis was backed by western commentators such as Edward Crankshaw and Robert Conquest, who described Stalin's tyranny as simply a fully developed form of Lenin's essentially repressive creed of revolution.

Dmitri Volkogonov, the Russian biographer of the great trio who made the Russian revolution, Lenin, Stalin and Trotsky, went further. He suggested that not only was there a direct line of continuity between Lenin and Stalin but that the methods they used to impose Communism on Russia meant that the Soviet Union could never become a truly modern state:

The one-dimensional approach laid down by Lenin doomed Stalinism historically. By welding the Party organisation to that of the state, Stalinism gradually reshaped the legions of 'revolutionaries' into an army of bureaucrats. By adopting revolutionary methods to speed up the natural course of events, Stalinism ultimately brought the country to real backwardness.

Volkogonov also made the memorable suggestion that Stalinism, just like Leninism, had answered a need in Russian society for faith in a great overarching idea. For him, Stalinism was one more example of the persistent feature that shaped Russian history:

Stalinism, as the materialisation of Lenin's ideas, arose not only from the peculiarities of Russian history. Russia has always been a country of faith, the USSR no less, if only of the faith of anti-Christianity. Stalin was the embodiment of the system's drive for ideological faith.

Such interpretations were given powerful support by the opening up of the Soviet state archives in the 1990s following the fall of Communism and the break-up of the USSR. Robert Service, in his authoritative biography of Lenin, published in 2004, pointed to an essential link between Lenin and Stalin. Building on the work of such analysts as Robert Tucker, Richard Pipes and Walter Laqueur, Service produced compelling evidence to establish his claim that Stalin, far from corrupting Lenin's policies, had fulfilled them. He confirmed that all the main features of the tyranny that Stalin exerted over the Soviet state had been inherited directly from Lenin.

Key question
What was Stalinism?

Defining Stalinism

As the foregoing section indicates, there will probably never be total agreement as to what Stalinism actually was, but the following list suggests some of the principal features of the system that operated during the quarter of a century in which Stalin had mastery over the USSR, and which need to be considered when working towards a definition.

- Stalin ran the USSR by a *bureaucratic system of government*.
- Stalin fulfilled the work begun by Lenin of turning revolutionary Russia into a *one-party state* in which all parties, other than the CPSU, were outlawed.
- Political and social control was maintained by a *terror system* whose main instruments were regular purges and show trials directed against the Party, the armed services and the people.
- A *climate of fear* was deliberately created so that no one could relax or challenge Stalin's policies.
- Stalin created a *command economy*, with agriculture and industry centrally directed and no allowance made for local knowledge or initiative.
- Believing that Communism was based on scientific principles, Stalin insisted that the Soviet Union pursue the path of *socialist science*.
- Stalin's highly individual rule developed into a '*cult of personality*' that led to his becoming absolute in authority since he regarded himself as an embodiment of the Communist Party and the nation.
- Stalin encouraged the development of an *elite nomenklatura*, officials who were loyal to Stalin because their privileges depended on his favour. This stifled all criticism and made every official complicit in Stalin's crimes.
- Stalin created a *siege mentality* in the USSR. Even in peacetime, Stalin insisted that the Soviet people had to be on permanent guard from enemies within and hostile nations outside.
- Stalin was as intense a *nationalist* as ever the tsars had been. Notwithstanding its claim to be leading an international revolution, the Soviet Union under Stalin abandoned the active pursuit of revolution, making its priority instead the strengthening of the USSR as a nation.

- The Comintern, officially pledged to foment international revolution, spent its time defending the *interests of the USSR*.
- As the only Communist state in existence, the USSR was *internationally isolated* in a largely capitalist, hostile world.
- Stalin imposed his concept of '*revolution in one country*', a policy that subordinated everything to the interests of the Soviet Union as a nation. This involved the rejection of the Trotskyist alternative of '*permanent revolution*', which would have engaged the USSR in leading the movement for international revolution.
- Stalin's rule meant the suppression of any form of genuine democracy, since he operated on the principle, laid down by Lenin, of *democratic centralism*, which obliged members of the CPSU to accept uncritically and obey all orders and instructions handed down by the Party leaders.
- Under Stalin it was claimed the Soviet Union was a single class nation. Recognition was given only to the proletariat, in whose name and by whose authority Stalin held power. It was the role of the *proletariat* to destroy the remnants of all other classes.
- The USSR recognised only one correct and acceptable ideology, *Marxism-Leninism-Stalinism*. All other political, philosophical or religious belief systems were rejected.
- With the aim of creating a new type of human being, '*homo sovieticus*', the Soviet Union under Stalin demanded cultural conformity in accordance with the notion of socialist realism.
- The enforcement of cultural conformity was achieved by the maintenance of strict forms of *censorship*.

Such features have been succinctly summarised by Robert Tucker in this definition:

> Stalinism – born as the product of an unfinished proletarian revolution amidst a backward society encircled by a hostile capitalist environment – degenerated into a totally oppressive, dehumanizing ideology, expressing the interests of a gigantic bureaucratic elite.

One can predict with confidence that despite all the subtle changes of approach that will undoubtedly come as historians continue to bring fresh insights to the study of Stalinism, that definition will continue to stand.

Some key books in the debate on Stalin and Stalinism:
Robert Conquest, *Harvest of Sorrow* (Macmillan, 1988)
Robert Conquest, *The Great Terror: Stalin's Purge of the Thirties* (Penguin, 1971)
Barbara Engel and Anastasia Posadskaya-Vanderbeck (eds) *A Revolution of Their Own: Voices of Women in Soviet History* (Westview, 1997)
Sheila Fitzpatrick, *Everyday Stalinism: Ordinary Life in Extraordinary Times: Soviet Russia in the 1930s* (Oxford University Press, 1999)
Sheila Fitzpatrick, *Stalinism: New Directions* (Routledge, 2000)
David L. Hoffman, *Stalinist Values: The Cultural Norms of Soviet Modernity* (Cornell University Press, 2003)
Walter Laqueur, *Stalin: The Glasnost Revelations* (Macmillan, 1990)
Roy Medvedev, *Let History Judge: The Origins and Consequences of Stalinism* (Oxford University Press, 1989)
Richard Pipes (ed.), *The Unknown Lenin: From the Soviet Archives* (Yale University Press, 1996)
Simon Sebag Montefiore, *Stalin: The Court of the Red Tsar* (Knopf, 2004)
Robert Service, *Lenin: A Biography* (Macmillan, 2000)
Robert Service, *Stalin: A Biography* (Macmillan, 2004)
Alexander Solzhenitsyn, *The Gulag Archipelago* (Collins, 1974–8)
Robert C. Tucker, *Stalinism: Essays in Historical Interpretation* (Transaction Publishers, 1999)
Dmitri Volkogonov, *Lenin: Life and Legacy* (HarperCollins, 1994)
Dmitri Volkogonov, *Stalin: Triumph and Tragedy* (Weidenfeld & Nicolson, 1991)

Summary diagram: Stalin and Stalinism, 1924–41

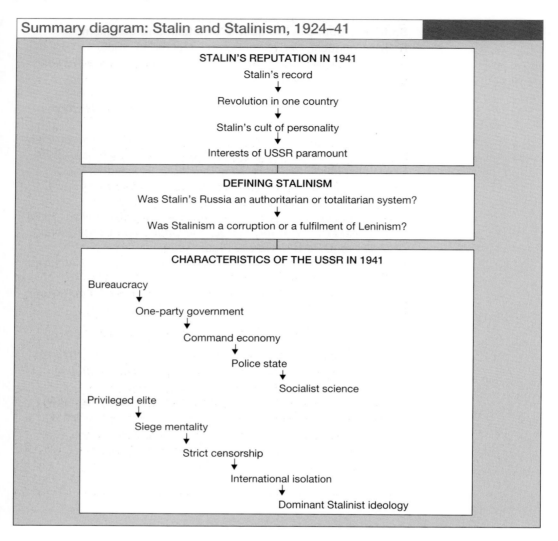

STALIN'S REPUTATION IN 1941

Stalin's record
↓
Revolution in one country
↓
Stalin's cult of personality
↓
Interests of USSR paramount

DEFINING STALINISM

Was Stalin's Russia an authoritarian or totalitarian system?
↓
Was Stalinism a corruption or a fulfilment of Leninism?

CHARACTERISTICS OF THE USSR IN 1941

Bureaucracy
↓
One-party government
↓
Command economy
↓
Police state
↓
Socialist science

Privileged elite
↓
Siege mentality
↓
Strict censorship
↓
International isolation
↓
Dominant Stalinist ideology

Study Guide: AS Question

In the style of OCR

Assess the importance of propaganda in the development of Stalin's cult of personality.   (50 marks)

Exam tips

The cross-references are intended to take you straight to the material that will help you to answer the question.

You might start by explaining what is meant by 'Stalin's cult of personality' (pages 251–7) before assessing the role that propaganda played in its development. You are likely to consider:

- education and the rewriting of history books (pages 257–260)
- the role of the Komsomol (pages 254–5)
- the role of the media i.e. literature, cinema, radio (pages 247–250)
- Stalinist iconography, May Day and birthday celebrations (page 253–4).

A counter-view, however, is that other factors were also important; for example:

- Many Russians benefited from Stalin's educational, health, social and economic achievements and praised him accordingly.
- Stalin did establish a strong and united army capable of standing up to and eventually defeating Hitler.
- The NKVD, purges, show trials and threat of labour camps silenced many of Stalin's critics, so that most Russians knew only of Stalin's achievements (see Chapter 9).

Glossary

Accommodationism   The idea that the Bolsheviks should accept the situation that followed the February Revolution in 1917 and co-operate with the Provisional Government.

Agents provocateurs   Agents who infiltrate opposition movements with the deliberate aim of stirring up trouble so as to expose the ringleaders.

Agrarian economy   The system in which food is produced on the land by arable and dairy farming and then traded.

All-Russian Congress of Soviets   A gathering of representatives from all the soviets formed in Russia between February and October 1917.

Amazons   A special corps of female soldiers recruited by Kerensky.

American Relief Association (ARA)   A body formed by Herbert Hoover (a future President of the USA, 1929–33) to provide food and medical supplies to post-First World War Europe.

Anarchy   Absence of government or authority, leading to disorder.

Anthropologists   Those who study the patterns of life of particular peoples and social groupings.

Authoritarian characteristics   A dominant ideology that justifies a system of state terror being imposed.

Autonomy   National self-government.

Balkans   The area of south-eastern Europe (fringed by Austria-Hungary to the north, the Black Sea to the east, Turkey to the south and the Adriatic Sea to the west) that had largely been under Turkish control.

Bi-cameral   A parliament made up of two chambers or houses, an upper and a lower.

Blat   A system that operates through bribes, favours and connections.

Bolsheviks   From *bolshinstvo*, Russian for majority.

Borsch   A thin soup made from mouldy beetroots.

Bosphorus   The narrow waterway linking the Black Sea with the Dardanelles.

Bottom-up approach   Historical analysis of what was happening at the grass-roots level of society.

Bourgeoisie   The owners of capital, the boss class, who exploited the workers but who would be overthrown by them in the revolution to come.

Buffer state   An area that lies between two states and so provides a form of protection for each against the other.

Cadres   Party members who were sent into factories and to construction sites to spy and report back on managers and workers.

Canonisation   Formal bestowing of sainthood.

Capital   The essential financial resource that provides the means for investment and expansion. No economy can grow without it.

Capitalism   The predominant economic system in Europe and the USA, based on private ownership and the making of profits – condemned by Marxists as involving the exploitation of the poor by the rich.

Capitalist methods of finance   The system in which the owners of private capital (money) increase their wealth by making loans on which interest has to be paid later by the borrower.

Capitalists   Russia's financiers and industrialists.

Catechism   The primer used for instructing the people in the essential points of the Christian faith.

Central Committee   The decision-making body of the Bolshevik Party.

Central Powers   Germany, Austria-Hungary, Turkey.

Centralisation   The concentration of political and economic power at the centre.

Cheka   The letters of the word stood for the Russian words for 'the All-Russian Extraordinary Commission for Fighting Counter-revolution, Sabotage and Speculation' – the secret police.

Chimera   A powerful but ultimately meaningless myth.

Collective farms (*kolkhozy* in Russian) Co-operatives in which the peasants pooled their resources and shared the labour and the wages.

Collectivisation   The abolition of private property and the forcing of the peasants to live and work in communes.

Comintern   Short for the Communist International, a body set up in Moscow in March 1919 to organise worldwide revolution.

Commissars   Russian for 'ministers'; Lenin chose the word because, he said, 'it reeks of blood'.

Commissar for Foreign Affairs   Equivalent to the Foreign Secretary in Britain.

Commissar for Nationalities   Minister responsible for liaising with the non-Russian national minorities.

Commissar of Enlightenment   Equivalent to an arts minister.

Commission   The awarding of officer rank.

Committee system   A process in which the deputies of the third duma formed various committees to discuss and advise on particular issues.

Communist Party of the Soviet Union (CPSU) The new name adopted by the Bolshevik Party in 1919.

Confidant   A person to whom one confides intimate secrets and a special trust.

Conscription   The forcing of large numbers of peasants into the army or navy.

Conservatism   Suspicion of change, and, therefore, resistance to it.

Co-operative   Group of workers or farmers working together on their own enterprise.

Cossacks   The elite cavalry regiment of the tsars.

Council of People's Commissars   The cabinet of ministers responsible for creating government policies.

CPGB   The Communist Party of Great Britain, formed in 1920, disbanded in 1991.

Counter-revolution   A term used by the Bolsheviks to cover any action of which they disapproved by branding it as reactionary and opposed to progress.

'Dark masses'   The term used in court and government circles to signify the fear and contempt they felt towards the peasants who made up four-fifths of the population.

De facto   A term used to denote the real situation, as compared to what it should or might be in theory or in law.

De jure   By legitimate legal right.

Decree against Terrorist Acts, 1934   Gave the NKVD limitless powers in pursuing the enemies of the state and the Party.

'Deliver the votes'   To use one's control of the party machine to gain majority support in key votes.

Depression, the   A period of severe economic stagnation that began in the USA in 1929 and lasted throughout the 1930s. It affected the whole of the industrial world and was interpreted by Marxists as a sign of the final collapse of capitalism.

De-Stalinisation   The movement, begun by Khrushchev in 1956, to expose Stalin's crimes and mistakes against the Party.

Dialectic   The shaping force of history that, according to Marx, leads in every historical period to a violent struggle between the exploiting and the exploited classes of the day.

Dictatorship of the proletariat   The last but one stage of history, in which the victorious workers would hunt down and destroy all the surviving reactionaries.

Diktat   A settlement imposed on a weaker nation by a stronger.

Discourse   A Marxist term relating to the prevailing ideas and culture within a society.

Double-agent   A government spy who pretends to be spying for the opposition against the authorities but who reports plans and secrets back to the authorities.

'Dual authority'   Lenin coined this term to describe the uneasy alliance and balance of power between the Provisional Government and the Petrograd Soviet.

Duma   The Russian parliament, which existed from 1906 to 1917.

Economism   Putting the improvement of the workers' conditions before the need for revolution.

Emancipation Decree of 1861   The reform that abolished serfdom – a Russian form of slavery in which the landowner had total control over the peasants who lived or worked on his land.

Emigrant internationalists   Russian revolutionaries living in exile.

Émigrés   Those who fled from Russia after the Revolution, either out of fear or from a desire to plan a counter-strike against the Bolsheviks.

Entrepreneurialism   The dynamic, expansionist attitude associated with western commercial and industrial activity.

Factionalism   The forming within the Party of groups with a particular grievance. Lenin used the term to brand as disloyal those Bolsheviks who opposed his policies.

Fait accompli   An established situation that cannot be changed.

Finance capital   Lenin's term for the resource used by stronger countries to exploit weaker ones. By investing heavily in another country, a stronger power made that country dependent on it. It was a form of imperialism.

Georgian   A member of the tough race of people who inhabit the rugged land of Georgia.

'German woman'   The term used by anti-tsarists to suggest that Alexandra was spying for Germany.

Gestapo   The secret police in Nazi Germany.

Ghettos   Particular areas where Jews were concentrated and to which they were restricted.

Gigantomania   The worship of size for its own sake.

Glasnost   Russian for 'openness', used as a description of the reforming policies adopted by the Soviet leader Mikhail Gorbachev in the late 1980s and 1990s.

God's anointed   At their coronation, tsars were anointed with holy oil to symbolise that they governed by divine will.

Gold standard   The system in which the rouble, Russia's basic unit of currency, had a fixed gold content, thus giving it strength when exchanged with other currencies.

Gosplan   From 1921 on, the new name for *Vesenkha*, the government's economic planning agency.

Grain procurements   Enforced collections of fixed quotas of grain from the peasants.

Great spurt   The spread of industry and the increase in production that occurred in Russia in the 1890s.

Greens   Largely made up of groups from the national minorities; the best known of the Green leaders was Nestor Makhno.

Gulag   The vast system of prisons and labour camps that spread across the USSR during the purges.

Haemophilia   A condition in which the blood does not clot, leaving the sufferer with heavy, painful bruising and internal bleeding, which can be life-threatening.

Holocaust   The genocide of 6 million Jews in occupied Europe between 1939 and 1945.

Homo sovieticus   A mock Latin term invented to describe the new 'Soviet man'.

Icons   Two-dimensional representations of Jesus Christ and the saints. The power and beauty of its icons is one of the great glories of the Orthodox Church.

Indemnities   Payment of war costs demanded by the victors from the defeated.

Industrialisation   Stalin's crash programme for revolutionising the USSR's productive economy by concentrating on the output of heavy goods such as iron and steel.

Infant mortality   The number of children who die per 100 or per 1000 of all those in a particular age group.

Institutions   The formal structures on which a society depends, such as the government, the administrative system, the law, education, the economy.

Intelligentsia   The group in society distinguished by their intellectual or creative abilities, e.g. writers, artists, composers, teachers. In tsarist times, a cross-section of the educated and more enlightened members of Russian society who wanted to see their nation adopt progressive changes along western lines.

Interior Minister   Equivalent to Britain's Home Secretary.

International revolutionaries   Marxists who were willing to sacrifice national interests in the cause of a worldwide rising of the workers.

International Women's Day   A demonstration organised by socialist groups to demand female equality: 23 February 1917.

Izvestiya   'The Times', one of the USSR's official government newspapers.

Komsomol   The Communist Union of Youth.

Kremlin   The former tsarist fortress in Moscow that became the centre of Soviet government.

Kulaks   Bolshevik term for the class of rich, exploiting peasants. The notion was largely a myth. Rather than being a class of exploiters, the kulaks were simply the more efficient farmers, who were marginally more prosperous.

Labourists   Name adopted by the SRs, who as a party officially boycotted the elections to the first duma.

Laity   The congregation who attend church services.

'Left Communists'   Bolsheviks who were convinced that their first task was to consolidate the October Revolution by driving the German imperialist armies from Russia. The term was later used to describe Party members who opposed the NEP.

Left-liberal circles   Westerners who were generally sympathetic towards Stalin and the USSR.

Left Social Revolutionaries   The faction of the SRs that wanted to continue the policy of terrorism inherited from 'the People's Will'.

Legislative duma   A parliament with law-making powers.

Leningrad   Petrograd was renamed in Lenin's honour after his death.

Liberal ideas   Notions that called for limitations on the power of rulers and greater freedom for the people.

Mandate   The authority to govern granted by a majority of the people through elections.

Martial law   The placing of the whole population under direct military authority.

Marxism-Leninism   The notion that Marx's theory of class war as interpreted by Lenin was an unchallengeably accurate piece of scientific analysis.

May Day ('Labour Day')   Usually reckoned as 1 May, traditionally regarded as a special day for honouring the workers and the achievements of socialism.

Mensheviks   From *menshinstvo*, Russian for minority.

Militia   Local citizens called together and granted arms to deal with a crisis requiring force.

Mir   The traditional village community.

Modern industrial state   A nation whose economic development enables it to compete on equal terms with other advanced economies. This invariably means having a strong industrial base and sufficient capital to undertake progressive social reforms.

Monarchists   Those who wanted a restoration of tsardom.

National insurance   A system of providing workers with state benefits, such as unemployment pay and medical treatment, in return for regular contributions to a central fund.

National minority governments   A number of Russia's ethnic peoples exploited the Provisional Government's difficulties by setting up their own governments and claiming independence of central control.

Neopatriarchal   A new form of male domination.

Neotraditionalism   A return to customary, established ways of doing things.

Nepmen   Those who stood to gain from the free trading permitted under the New Economic Policy: the rich peasants, the retailers, the traders, and the small-scale manufacturers.

Nepotism   A system in which positions are gained through family connections rather than on merit.

NKVD   The successor organisation to the *Cheka* and the OGPU.

Nomenklatura   The Soviet 'establishment' – a privileged elite of officials who ran the Party machine.

Non-determinist approach   Rejection of the idea that history follows a fixed, inevitable course.

Non-partisan   Politically neutral, belonging to no party.

October deserters   Bolsheviks who in October 1917, believing that the Party was not yet strong enough, had advised against a Bolshevik rising.

OGPU   Succeeded the *Cheka* as the state security force. In turn it became the NKVD and then the KGB.

Okhrana   The tsarist secret police, whose special task was to hunt down subversives who challenged the tsarist regime.

Operation Barbarossa   German codename for the invasion of the Soviet Union, launched without formal warning by Hitler on 22 June 1941.

Orgburo   Short for Organisation Bureau, responsible for putting the Communist Party's policies into practice.

Packets   Privileges and special benefits.

Paranoia   A persecution complex that leaves sufferers with the conviction they are surrounded by enemies.

Parliamentary-bourgeois republic   Lenin's contemptuous term for the Provisional Government, which he dismissed as an unrepresentative mockery that had simply replaced the feudal control of the tsar with the bourgeois control of the old duma.

Party card   The official CPSU document granting membership and guaranteeing privileges to the holder. It was a prized possession in Soviet Russia.

Party democracy Trotsky was not pressing for democracy in the full sense of all party members having a say. His aim was to condemn the centralising of power from which Stalin had gained such benefit.

Passive disobedience A tactic in which opponents of a government challenge it not by violence but by refusing to obey particular laws.

Patronage The power to appoint individuals to official posts in the Party and the government.

'The people' The section of the population who truly represent the character and will of the Russian nation.

People's militia Volunteer law-enforcement officers drawn from ordinary people.

People's Will This group of SRs represented the most extreme element in pre-revolutionary Russia.

Petrograd For patriotic reasons, the German name for the capital, St Petersburg, was changed to the Russian form Petrograd in 1914.

Pogroms Fierce persecutions of the Jews, which often involved wounding or killing them and destroying their property.

Politburo Short for Political Bureau, the inner cabinet of the ruling Central Committee of the CPSU.

Political activists Those who believed necessary change could be achieved only through direct action.

Political commissars Party workers whose function was to accompany the officers of the Red Army permanently and report on their conduct. No military order carried final authority unless a commissar countersigned it.

Political correctness The requirement that people conform to a prescribed set of opinions when expressing themselves to show that they have accepted the ideology of the leaders of society.

Political expediency Refers to the pursuing of a course of action with the primary aim of gaining a political advantage.

Political subversives The SDs and SRs, as described by their opponents.

Populists (*Narodniks*) From the Russian word for 'the people'.

Pragmatic An approach in which policies are modified according to circumstance rather than in keeping with a fixed theory.

Pravda Russian for 'truth', the title of one of the USSR's official government newspapers.

Pre-Parliament A body drawn from a variety of parties, to fill the interim before the Constituent Assembly came into being.

Private enterprise Economic activity organised by individuals or companies, not the government.

Progressists A party of businessmen who favoured moderate reform.

Progressives
Those who believed in parliamentary governement for Russia.

Proletariat The exploited industrial workers, who, according to Marx, would triumph in the last great class struggle.

Proletkult Proletarian culture.

Quasi-religious faith A conviction so powerful that it has the intensity of religious belief.

Radicalisation A movement towards more sweeping or revolutionary ideas.

Reactionary Resistant to any form of progressive change.

Red Guards Despite the Bolshevik legend that these were the crack forces of the Revolution, the Red Guards, some 10,000 in number, were largely made up of elderly men recruited from the workers in the factories.

Reds The Bolsheviks and their supporters.

Reparations Payment of war costs by the loser to the victor.

Representative government   A form of rule in which ordinary people choose their government and have the power to replace it if it does not serve their interests.

Requisitioning   State-authorised takeover of property or resources.

Revolution from below   The CPSU claim that the 1917 Revolution had been a genuine rising of the people rather than a power grab by the Bolsheviks.

Revolutionary socialism   The takeover of the state by the peasants and workers.

Right Communists   Party members who wanted the NEP to continue.

Right Social Revolutionaries   The more moderate members, who believed in revolution as the ultimate goal but were prepared to work with other parties to improve the conditions of the workers and peasants.

Rightists   Not a single party; they represented a range of conservative views from right of centre to extreme reaction.

Romanov dynasty   The royal house that ruled Russia from 1613 to 1917.

Rural crisis   The problem of land shortage and overpopulation in the countryside produced by the huge increase in the number of people living in Russia in the late nineteenth century.

Ryutin group   The followers of M. N. Ryutin, a Right Communist who had published an attack on Stalin, describing him as 'the evil genius who has brought the Revolution to the verge of destruction'.

Schlieffen Plan   Dating from 1905, the plan was aimed at eliminating the danger to Germany of a two-front war against France and Russia by a lightning knock-out blow against France first.

Second revolution   Stalin's enforced modernisation of the Soviet economy.

'Secret report'   Krushchev's astounding revelations concerning Stalin's crimes against the Party. Although they were officially described as secret, details were soon known worldwide.

Secretariat   The civil service that put Communist Party policies into practice.

Serbian nationalists   Activists struggling for Serbia's independence from Austria-Hungary.

'Slavophiles'   Russians who urged that the nation should preserve itself as 'holy Russia', glorying in its Slavonic culture and traditions.

Smolny   The Bolshevik headquarters in Petrograd, housed in what had been a young ladies' finishing school.

Socialist realism   A form of representational art that the people can understand and relate to their own lives.

Soviet   A council made up of elected representatives.

Soviet Union of Writers   The body having authority over all published Soviet writers. Under Stalin's direction it had the right to ban or censor any work of which it disapproved.

Sovnarkom   Russian for government or cabinet.

Starets   Russian for holy man, the nickname Rasputin was given by the impressionable peasants, who believed he had superhuman powers.

State capitalism   The direction and control of the economy by the government, using its central power and authority.

State farms (*sovkhozy* in Russian)   Contained peasants who worked directly for the state for a wage.

Stavka   The high command of the Russian army.

Storming   An intensive period of work to meet a highly demanding set target.

Subsistence level   The bare minimum required to sustain life.

System of dating Until February 1918, Russia used the Julian calendar, which was 13 days behind the Gregorian calendar, the one in general use in most western countries by this time.

Tariffs Duties imposed on foreign goods to keep their prices high and therefore discourage importers from bringing them into the country.

Tax in kind The peasants' surrendering a certain amount of produce, equivalent to a fixed sum of money – contrasted with requisitioning, which had meant the seizure of all the peasants' stocks.

Telescoped revolution The notion that the final two stages of revolution, bourgeois and proletarian, could be compressed into one.

Total theatre The attempt to break down the barriers between actors and audience by revolutionary use of lighting, sound and stage settings.

Total war A struggle in which a whole nation, its people, resources and institutions, is involved.

Totalitarianism Absolute state control.

Trade recession A marked fall in the demand for goods, resulting in a cutback in production and the laying off of workers.

Triple Entente, 1907 Not a formal alliance, but a declared willingness by France, Britain and Russia to co-operate with each other.

Triumvirate A ruling or influential bloc of three persons.

Troika A three-man team.

Tuberculosis A wasting disease often affecting the lungs, that was especially prevalent in imperial Russia.

Ukraine The region in southern Russia containing the largest number of non-Russian people (23 million) in the empire. It was also the nation's largest food-producing region, hence its great importance.

Union of Municipal Councils A set of patriotic urban local councils.

Union of *Zemstva* A set of patriotic rural local councils.

United Opposition (or New Opposition) The group led by Kamenev and Zinoviev, who called for an end to the NEP and the adoption of a rapid industrialisation programme.

Universal suffrage An electoral system in which all adults have the right to vote.

Utopian A belief in the attainability of a perfect society.

Vesenkha The Supreme Council of the National Economy.

Verst Approximately two-thirds of a mile, or just over a kilomtre.

Vozhd Russian for supreme leader, equivalent to *der Führer* in German.

War credits Money loaned on easy repayment terms to Russia to finance its war effort.

'Westerners' Russians who believed that their nation had to model itself on the advanced countries of western Europe.

White Sea Canal In fact, three canals linking Leningrad with the White Sea. Built predominantly by forced labourers, who died in their thousands, the canal proved practically worthless, since it was hardly used after construction.

Whites The Bolsheviks' opponents, including monarchists looking for a tsarist restoration, and those parties that had been outlawed or suppressed by the new regime.

Yezhovschina The period of widespread terror directed at ordinary Soviet citizens in the late 1930s and presided over by Yezhov, the head of the NKVD.

Zemgor The joint body that devoted itself to helping Russia's war wounded, 1914–17.

Zemstvo (plural *zemstva*) Elected local councils.

Zhenotdel The Women's Bureau of the Communist Party.

Index